A Textbook of

Java Programming

A Textbook of
Java Programming

Surbhi Kakar

Assistant Professor
Institute of Innovation in Technology and Management
Guru Gobind Singh Indraprastha University
New Delhi

I.K. International Publishing House Pvt. Ltd.

NEW DELHI

Published by

I.K. International Publishing House Pvt. Ltd.
4435-36/7, Ansari Road, Daryaganj
New Delhi–110 002 (India)
E-mail: info@ikinternational.com
Website: www.ikbooks.com

ISBN: 978-93-85909-66-5

Published by Krishan Makhijani for I.K. International Publishing House Pvt. Ltd., 4435-36/7, Ansari Road, Daryaganj, New Delhi–110 002 and Printed by Rekha Printers Pvt. Ltd., Okhla Industrial Area, Phase II, New Delhi–110 020.

Dedicated to

God and my parents who taught me the meaning of life and what it means to be human.

Preface

The knowledge base in java programming is increasing widely due to contributions of researchers around the world. The gap seen in the academic publications is in their inability to address the requirements of first time learners to the subject in a lucid language. There lies the significance of this book, in making java, a simple, enjoyable and readable subject.

The book seeks to give a fillip to the existing body of knowledge in the subject. It intends to fill the gap between the prevailing theoretical knowledge and practical applicability of java programming. The book proposes to be a ready reference to researchers pursuing courses in information technology and industrial experts working in the domain of software development.

This book comprises fourteen chapters. The first four chapters explains the basic concepts such as data types, variables, arrays, operators and control structures. The next six chapters focuses upon the practical application of topics such as polymorphism, inheritance, exception handling and multithreading. The chapters towards the end teaches Graphical User Interface programming and networking using various java libraries.

Surbhi Kakar

Acknowledgements

Any academic work is the result of collective effort of many individuals. There are number of people who have contributed in having this book published. I would like to acknowledge my parents, parent's in-laws and my husband for providing an unrelenting support, time and space in completing this book. I would also acknowledge my well-wishers and colleagues who constantly provided me their valuable feedback to improve my writing.

Lastly, I would acknowledge, Dr. Sarmishtha Sarma, Associate Professor, Department of Management, Institute of Innovation in Technology and Management, who inspired me to become an author.

Surbhi Kakar

Contents

1

CHAPTER

Introduction

This chapter will enable you to learn the following:

- Features of java along with a contrast between procedure oriented and object oriented languages.
- A clear understanding of object oriented concepts.
- Writing the first java program using different styles of comments.
- Following naming conventions to write a simple java program.

1.1 HISTORY

Java is an object-oriented programming language which helps us solve complex problems through the use of object oriented concepts like inheritance, polymorphism and encapsulation. Java has reduced typical programming errors that were encountered in earlier languages like C/C++. Java was founded by Sun Micro Systems and is currently owned by Oracle. It was designed to facilitate communications over network.

In the year 1991, a group of engineers from Sun Microsystems called the "Green" James Gosling started working on the union of digital consumer devices and computers. The team worked hard and created the programming language that has reformed our world today– Java.

The Green Team started demonstration of their new language with an interactive, hand-held home entertainment controller, originally targeted at the digital cable television industry. Unfortunately, the concept being too advanced for them could not take off at that time. In 1995, with the advent of the Internet, the team announced that the Netscape Navigator Internet browser would incorporate Java technology.

Today, Java has not only pervaded the Internet, but it also serves as an invisible force behind many of the applications and devices that drive our day-to-day lives. Its applications range from mobile phones to handheld devices, games, navigation systems to e-commerce solutions.

1.2 PROCEDURE ORIENTED AND OBJECT ORIENTED PROGRAMMING

Table 1.1 Procedure oriented and object oriented programming

	Procedure Oriented Programming (POP)	Object Oriented Programming (OOP)
Division	Program is divided into small units called functions.	Program is divided into what is known as objects.
Emphasis	Emphasis is laid on functions (how it is to be done) rather than data.	Emphasis is laid upon data (what is to be done) rather than functions.
Approach	POP follows a top down approach.	OOP follows a bottom up approach.
Access Specifiers	No access specifiers available in POP.	We have access specifiers like private, public, etc., available here.
Data Movement	In POP, data can move between functions freely.	Here, objects communicate with each other via member functions.
Security	No provision of data hiding here so it is less secure.	OOP is supposed to be more secure since it delivers the feature of data hiding.
Data Access	POP uses mostly global data for sharing, thereby limiting the control over data access.	OOP provides a greater control over data access by making the data private or public as and when required.
Overloading	Overloading is not possible in POP.	Overloading can be done in various forms like constructor overloading, function overloading, etc.
Polymorphism	No concept of polymorphism is available here.	Polymorphism can be done in various forms like compile time polymorphism, runtime polymorphism.
Examples	C, Visual Basic, Fortran etc.	C++, Java, VB.NET, etc.

1.3 FEATURES OF JAVA

The source code in java is compiled using a java compiler. The source code is not directly converted into executable code, rather it is converted into an intermediate code representation known as *bytecode*. This bytecode is then executed by JVM, the Java Virtual Machine.

JVM is an abstract entity which provides a runtime environment for the java programs to run. Since it is an abstract entity, its implementation is given by JRE (Java Runtime Environment). This is the reason why we call java a *PLATFORM INDEPENDENT* language because the bytecode generated can be run on any hardware/software platform. Only the corresponding

JVM/JRE needs to be implemented for that machine. JIT, the Just in time Compiler is a part of JVM. It converts the repeatedly used instructions into native code which can be directly run on the CPU. JDK stands for Java Development Kit. It contains everything needed for the development of java programs like the JRE, the java compiler, the java interpreter, etc.

Following are some of the features of java that differentiate it from other programming languages:

- *Simple*: Java is syntactically similar to programming languages like C/C++ so it is easier to learn. In addition to it, a lot of complex features of C/C++ are either left out or they are implemented in a more sophisticated and simpler way.
- *Object Oriented:* Java is purely object oriented since everything is written inside a class. Even the main method is inside a class.
- *Robust*: Java is said to be a strictly typed language. This means that java source code is checked at compile time as well as on runtime (in case of exception handling). This feature makes java a robust language.
- *Multithreaded*: Java is designed in a way that multithreaded applications can be made out of it. A multithreaded application is one in which several parts of the same application can run concurrently. For example, a web application wherein you can download some music at a time and also search the songs on the list at the same time. Multithreading will be discussed later in detail in Chapter 10.
- *Architecture neutral (platform independent)*: There is no guarantee that a program written on windows machine will run tomorrow on a MAC machine. Java creates a version of code that is platform independent or architecture neutral known as the bytecode. This bytecode is capable of running on any hardware or software platform provided you have a Java Virtual Machine installed on your computer. This feature was not available in C/C++.
- *Interpreted and High Performance:*C and C++ are known to be low-level compiled languages. Since they are directly compiled into machine language, they offer higher performance but at the expense of portability and reliability. Earlier versions of java, were around 20 times slower than these traditional languages. But the speed they offer is just the right speed to run network based, interactive applications. As discussed above, java enables us to write platform independent code by compiling the source code into the bytecode. This bytecode can be easily converted directly into native code using a JUST IN TIME COMPILER which produces high performance execution of the code.
- *Distributed:* Java is also called a distributed language. It means it can access distributed resources on the web and then using its dynamic nature, loads classes at runtime according to the needs of the user. Java provides high level and low level support for networking. Taking an example of the URL class, one can easily access a remote file or resource. Also using the Remote Method Invocation (RMI) API (released in Java 1.1 version), one can invoke methods of remote objects as if they are local objects. Java also provides low level support for networking via sockets which will be discussed in detail in Chapter 14.

- *Dynamic*: Java is said to be a dynamic language. It is said so because we can load java classes and libraries at runtime in the java interpreter. These classes can be dynamically instantiated. Information regarding the classes used can also be retrieved at runtime. In addition to it, java lets us resolve accesses to objects at runtime by using runtime polymorphism which will be discussed in chapters 6 and 7.
- *Automatic Garbage Collection:* The most common and painful problem encountered in C, C++ languages was that of *memory leaks.* A memory leak is a problem wherein a piece of memory that is no longer being used, fails to be freed. This was due to garbage collection being done manually. But java supports automatic garbage collection. It keeps a check over such memory locations and frees them periodically. Garbage collection is a very vital part in any programming language as it enhances the performance of your system.

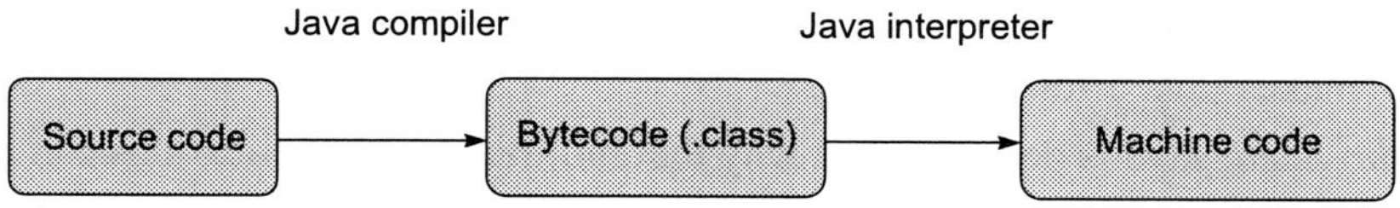

Fig 1.1 Flow of java program

1.4 OBJECT ORIENTED FEATURES

Java incorporates all the object oriented features that other object oriented languages like C++ possess. Some of the features are discussed below.

- *Abstraction*

  Abstraction is a concept wherein we tend to focus upon only the essential parts of the program leaving behind their implementation details which refers to how a program works. The interface of a program gives an indication to how a program looks like to the end user interacting with it. Does this mean that the implementation details are not important? No. They are equally significant just that they will be added as and when required. For instance, take an example of your smartphones, you are able to make calls, send messages, play games without even bothering how you are able to do it. In addition to it, how these features are implemented might be different for different mobile phones. We used to dial calls using a physical keypad earlier in our mobile phones but now its implementation has been changed to touch screen keyboards. Still, we are unaware about the details and we are happy with the transition. So for now just perceive this as, abstraction helps the user interact with an interface without even knowing how that interface is implemented. Further, this implementation can be different for different products.

  Benefits of abstraction:

  - Abstraction aids in software reuse. Since the same interface can be used repeatedly with different implementations.

- ❖ Consequently, it reduces the bugs in the system because the reused components are already successfully tested.
- ❖ Also, it decreases the development time significantly because the software is being reused.

▪ *Encapsulation and Information hiding*

Encapsulation is the process wherein we bind the data and the code together in a single unit known as *class*. The detailed description of a class will be discussed later. But for now, just understand the essentials behind it.

A class is a unit wherein we can bundle up data (instance variables) and code (methods) together. An object refers to an instance of a class. Therefore, an object has a state which defines the attributes possessed by it and a behaviour which depicts what operations it will perform (defined by its methods).

One of the examples of a class can be an animal with its attributes being its colour, breed etc. The operations it can perform can be eat, sleep, etc. These can be defined as the methods of the class.

Encapsulation is a way to attain *information hiding.* The purpose of encapsulation is to hide the data and code from the external world. To achieve data hiding/information hiding, the rule of thumb should be: *Make your data and code as inaccessible as you can. This separates the interface from its implementation.* Following are some of the benefits of information hiding that can be observed:

- ❖ Information hiding reduces the degree of coupling between the modules, which provides an ease in developing, testing or modifying modules in isolation.
- ❖ This decreases the development time of the system as the modules can be implemented in parallel.
- ❖ It allows us to write maintainable code because the modules can be enhanced without affecting the other modules in the system.
- ❖ As the modules have a lower degree of coupling between them it is easier to pick individual successful modules in isolation for reuse.

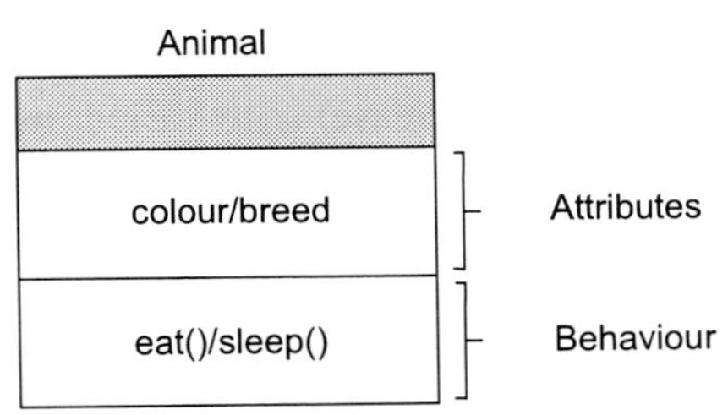

Fig. 1.2 Class: An example of encapsulation

- *Inheritance*

  Inheritance can be viewed as a 'IS A' relationship between two entities or classes. Have a look at the diagram below:

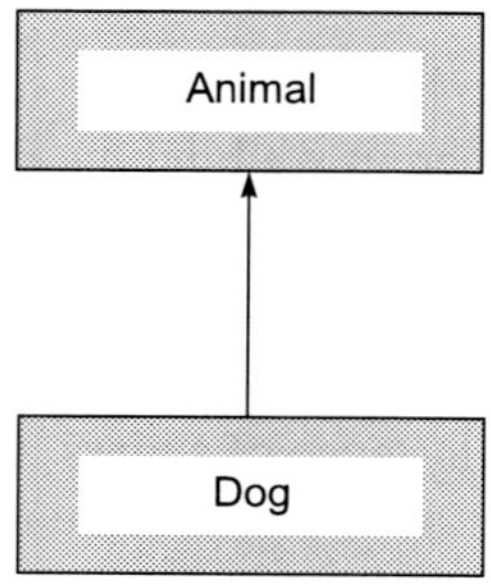

Fig. 1.3 An example of inheritance

Dog 'IS A' type of Animal. Therefore, dog can have its own attributes and behaviour in addition to the general attributes and behaviour of an Animal. For instance, all animals can eat or sleep but only a specific type of animal "dog" can bark. In object oriented languages like java, inheritance is the property by which one object can inherit/acquire the properties and behaviour of another object.

But why do we need it? The answer is *code reusability*. In our example above, *dog* can inherit the behaviour of *animal* (eat and sleep) and include its own behaviour as well (bark).

Benefits of Inheritance

- The most important advantage of inheritance is that it increases reusability of code.
- As a consequence, reusability decreases development time and makes our job easier.
- Further, reusing already tested code lessens the amount of bugs to be fixed.

- *Polymorphism*

  Polymorphism is the ability by which one interface can have multiple implementations. Confused?? Consider an example of a shape. A shape in itself is abstract (not defined) and can acquire multiple forms. It can be a rectangle, a square or even a hexagon! But each time the definitions for finding area of the figure would be different. This capability of having the same interface (area in our case) with varied implementations is supported by polymorphism. Another instance from the real world would be a car gearing system. We know that all the cars need a gearing system to regulate our drive smoothly. Now, a Fiat car gearing system implementation might be different from a Ford car gearing system. Notice, the interface of having a gearing system remains the same everywhere, just that how it is implemented for different models changes.

  Java supports polymorphism both at compile time as well as at runtime. This will be discussed in profundity in the later chapters.

Benefits of polymorphism

- Polymorphism helps us reuse the same interface for different situations and change the implementations as per our need.
- Reusing the code again decreases the development time and the number of bugs to be fixed.

1.5 CHARACTERISTICS OF JAVA

- Java is a completely object oriented language.
- Java has automatic garbage collection facility.
- Java breeds a bytecode version of the source code which makes the language platform independent.
- Java does not support structures and union.
- One cannot overload operators in java as in C++.
- It is not possible to declare unsigned integer in java.
- Java does not allow the usage of goto, sizeof and typedef.
- Pointers do not exist in java instead references do.
- Java objects are passed by reference only.
- Java does not allow passing of default arguments.
- Java does not have pre-processor statements.
- There are no header files and delete operator in java.
- Java does not support multiple inheritance but it can be provided through interfaces here.

1.6 PREREQUISITES FOR RUNNING JAVA PROGRAMS

Following are the prerequisites for running a java program on your machine.

- Install the latest version of jdk on your machine. Since java is a open source, it can be freely downloaded from the link http://www.oracle.com/technetwork/java/javase/downloads/jdk8-downloads-2133151.html.
- Identify your machine configuration and download the corresponding jdk version. If you have a windows 32-bit machine, look for jdk consistent to windowsx86.
- After downloading jdk, set the environment for your machine so that you can compile and run your java programs.

  Setting up environment for Windows 8

  - Right click on My Computer and go to the properties section.
  - Now click Advanced System settings and go to the Advanced tab.
  - Under this tab, click Environment variables.

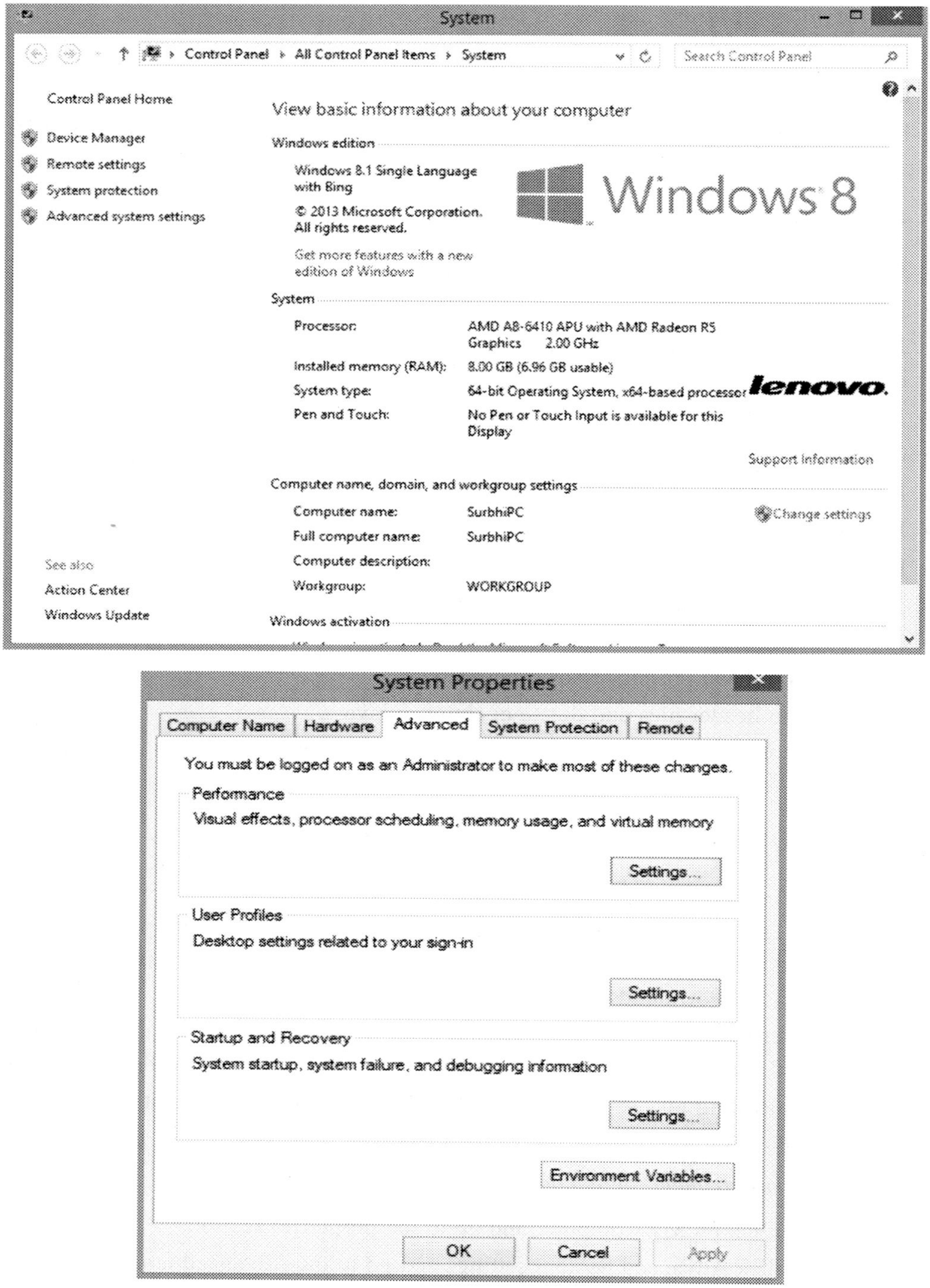
System
Control Panel > All Control Panel Items > System
Search Control Panel
Control Panel Home
Device Manager
Remote settings
System protection
Advanced system settings
View basic information about your computer
Windows edition
Windows 8.1 Single Language with Bing
© 2013 Microsoft Corporation. All rights reserved.
Get more features with a new edition of Windows
Windows 8
System
Processor: AMD A8-6410 APU with AMD Radeon R5 Graphics 2.00 GHz
Installed memory (RAM): 8.00 GB (6.96 GB usable)
System type: 64-bit Operating System, x64-based processor
Pen and Touch: No Pen or Touch Input is available for this Display
lenovo.
Support Information
Computer name, domain, and workgroup settings
Computer name: SurbhiPC
Full computer name: SurbhiPC
Computer description:
Workgroup: WORKGROUP
Change settings
See also
Action Center
Windows Update
Windows activation
System Properties
Computer Name
Hardware
Advanced
System Protection
Remote
You must be logged on as an Administrator to make most of these changes.
Performance
Visual effects, processor scheduling, memory usage, and virtual memory
Settings...
User Profiles
Desktop settings related to your sign-in
Settings...
Startup and Recovery
System startup, system failure, and debugging information
Settings...
Environment Variables...
OK
Cancel
Apply

Fig. 1.4

- Edit the already present path system variable and set its value to complete path where java executables are located and click Ok on all windows. Eg: C:\Program Files\Java\jdk1.7.0_75\bin;

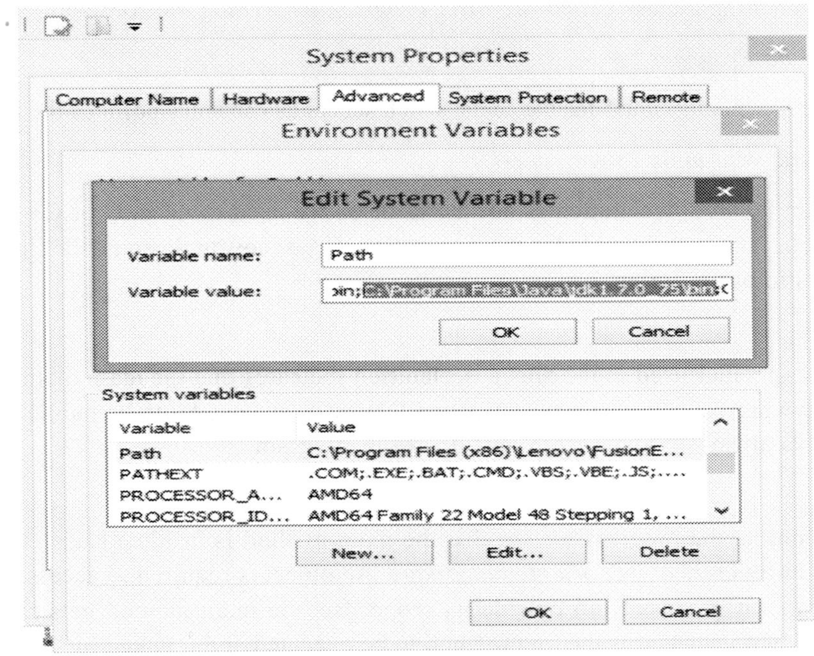

Fig 1.5

Setting up environment for Linux(Ubuntu)

The following commands will do the job for you. Type these commands on your terminal:

- sudo apt-get install python-software-properties
- sudo add-apt-repository ppa:webupd8team/java
- sudo apt-get update
- sudo apt-get install oracle-java7-set-default

1.7 FIRST JAVA PROGRAM

```
class MyFirstProgram
{
public static void main(String args[])
     {
     System.out.println("My First Java Program");
      }
}
```

Explanation

To create a java program you can either write the program in a text editor like Notepad or use an Integrated Development Environment (IDE) like NetBeans or Eclipse.

Now, we start creating a class called *My First Program* by writing the following statement:

class MyFirstProgram

Next, we write the main method for the class which serves as the entry point of the program..

public static void main (String args[])

Notice the main method declaration is not the same as we used to do in C or C++. Special specifiers like public, static are included in the declaration. Let us now understand the significance of these specifiers in our program.

public

The public access specifier used in the above declaration indicates that the main method can be accessed from anywhere outside the program as well. Why do we need it to be public? Because the main method is always invoked from outside of our program.

static

Having a closer look at the program we see that the main method is inside a class! This is the why we call java as a *purely object oriented language*. An object is required to access a specific method or a member of a class from outside its scope. But the main method gets called here without the use of an object as it is the first method to be executed and invoked by the operating system. Methods called without the use of an object are marked as static methods. The static keyword will be discussed in detail in upcoming chapters.

void

Every method declaration starts with a return type followed by a method name and its parameters. Here the return type for the main method is void which means it does not return any value.

main

The name of the method used above is main.

String args[]

String is a predefined class in java and not a data type. *args* is an array of instances of class String which is capable of holding only array of characters. This array is used to store command line arguments. The program above does not use any command line arguments, a closer look will be taken at the topic later.

Entering the main method we have the following statement:

System.out.println("My First Program");

System, here is a predefined class. *out* is an object of *PrintStream* class defined inside the System class which is connected to the standard output device, console. *println* is a method of the class *PrintStream* which is used to print the value passed as an argument in the method. In this case, it prints the statement "*My First Program*" onto the console and then prints a newline.

Saving the program

As the class name is *MyFirstProgram* so the file must also be saved with the name *MyFirstProgram.java*. All java programs are saved with the extension *.java.*

Compiling the program

If you have used a text editor to write the program then use command prompt to compile and run your program. For compiling the program write:

javac MyFirstProgram

on the command prompt. Before issuing the above command, make sure you are on the correct path where you have saved the file *MyFirstProgram.java. javac* used here refers to the java compiler. After you compile your program, a .class file (the bytecode) will be created for all the classes in your program. In our case, we will have *MyFirstProgram.class* file generated after the compilation process.

Executing the program

After the compilation phase, now the java interpreter comes into picture. The java interpreter executes the bytecode for us. To execute our program issue the following command on the command prompt:

java MyFirstProgram

This will execute our program and generate the output as "*MyFirstProgram*" on the console.

> Supposing we have the following classes in a file:
>
> *class Alpha*
>
> *class Beta*
>
> *class Gamma*
>
> Say, class Alpha has the main method and we save the file with any name which is not Alpha. java, for now let us consider it to be *AnyName.java*[1]. In this case, when we compile our file *AnyName.java*, we will issue the following command on the command prompt:
>
> *javac AnyName.java*

[1] AnyName.java will work if there is no public class in the file. There can be only one public class in a java file which should contain the main method (along with it, you can have multiple non-public classes) and the file name has to match with the public class name.

As a result, three bytecode files will be generated as *Alpha.class*, *Beta.class*, *Gamma.class*. To execute our file we will issue the command below:

java AnyName

After this command, the java interpreter will try to execute the above file. But it will result in an error stating "*Could not find or load main class AnyName*". This is because the compiler could not find the main method in a class called *AnyName*. Consequently, could not initiate execution. On the contrary, if we would have issued the following command:

java Alpha

our program would have successfully executed as this time, the compiler could find the main method in class Alpha.

1.8 STYLES OF COMMENTS

Comments in a programming language play an imperative role. They are not interpreted by the java interpreter. Instead, it helps the user reading the source code, gain understanding of what the code is all about. So make sure you incorporate comments in your code to make it understandable to any other user too. Because you never know who might be using the source code written by you! Comments can be categorized into two categories as discussed below:

Single-line comments

These are used to comment only a single line and denoted by a double slash://

Example:

```
class MyFirstProgram {
        public static void main(String args[]) //main function in the class
        {
        System.out.println("My First Java Program");
        }
}
```

In the code above, the commented statement will not be interpreted by the java interpreter, instead will be treated as a single line comment.

Multi-line Comments

These are used to comment multiple lines together. Again, they will not be interpreted by the interpreter and are denoted by /* */. Use this style when you want to comment a larger piece of code.

Example:

```
/*
 * This file is called MyFirstProgram.java
 */
```

```
class MyFirstProgram {
        public static void main(String args[]) //main function in the class
        {
        System.out.println("My First Java Program");
        }
}
```

1.9 NAMING CONVENTIONS

Naming conventions refer to the agreements established by java regarding how we name a set of variables, methods and classes. The book will also be majorly following naming conventions throughout.

Naming Conventions for Variables

Variables are identifiers in java used to hold a value which keeps on changing. This will be discussed at length in the coming chapters. The name of a variable can start from a letter and can be a combination of letters and digits. It can also include an underscore character. However, white spaces in a variable name are not permitted. Variable name if comprising of one word, will be in all lower case letters else the first letter of the subsequent words will be a capital letter.

isReady

Naming Conventions for Methods

Every method name starts with a lower case letter. For example, *main.* If the method name consists of more than one word, then the first letter of the word would be a lower case letter but the consequent first letters for every word will be a capital letters.

nextInt()

Naming Conventions for Classes

Every class name in java starts with a capital letter. For example, *Scanner*, a predefined class, starts with a capital *'S'*. If your class name has more than one word, then the first letter of every word in the class will be a capital letter.

MyFirstProgram

SUMMARY

Let's quickly brush up what we have learnt in this chapter:

- Java is a purely object oriented programming language.
- Its source code is not directly compiled into machine language rather converted into an intermediate representation called bytecode.
- Bytecode can be executed on any machine platform provided you have a java virtual machine installed. This is the reason why java is said to be architecture neutral/platform independent.

- Just in time compiler is used to convert repeatedly used instructions directly into native code (machine code).
- JDK is a development kit that contains all the tools required for java development such as java compiler, interpreter, etc.
- Main method is declared as public and static for the reason that it is called from outside our program as the java interpreter calls it and that too before any objects of the class are made.
- *System* and *String* are classes in java. *out* is stream object connected to console whereas *println* method is used to print on the console.
- Java follows all object oriented concepts of *encapsulation, abstraction, inheritance* and *polymorphism.*

COMMON ERRORS

- In case you get an error stating "could not find or load main class", check whether you are executing the correct .class file or not. This error generally comes across when we try to run a bytecode file which does not encompass the main method.
- Double-check while using some of the predefined classes and methods of java. They should follow the appropriate naming conventions as conferred above.
- When you use any of the predefined classes or methods in java, check whether you have imported its desired package or not. Packages will be described in detail in the forthcoming chapters. For now, just understand packages are a collection of java classes.
- If you are working with command prompt, and you make some amendments to your java code then always memorize to compile it again (even if you have done it once) so that the .class file is modified incorporating the changes done. If you forget to compile your code the next time, then you might not see the changes you made, in your output as the bytecode was never modified!

SELF-TEST

1. Discuss the features of java in detail.
2. Discuss the characteristics of java.
3. What are the different types of comments that can be made in java?
4. Why is main method termed public and static?
5. What does System.out.println statement infer?

PRACTICAL QUESTION

1. Write a program to print "Hello World".

2

CHAPTER

Data Types, Variables and Arrays

This chapter will enable you to learn the following:

- The various data types available in java.
- Declaring and initializing a variable. Learning about the scope and lifetime of the variables.
- Converting and promoting one type to other.
- Implementing one-dimensional, two-dimensional and three-dimensional arrays.

2.1 DATA TYPES

A *variable* in java is a named memory location which holds some value. This value can be of any type. It can be an integer value, a decimal value, a character or even an address! The types of these variables are determined by their *data types*. So, every variable has a data type which decides what *type* of value the variable will hold.

Data types are majorly classified into two types:

1. *Primitive data types*: ones which are predefined and known to the compiler. Example: int, short, etc.
2. *User defined data types:* ones which are defined by the user. Example: arrays, classes, interfaces. They are also called *reference types*.

Every data type can be characterized by the following three parameters:

- *Memory size:* As discussed above, every variable has a data type. The size of the data type for a variable is equal to the number of bits allocated for that variable.
- *Range:* Every data type has a minimum and a maximum value that it can hold. These values govern the range of a data type.
- *Default values:* Data types have a predefined default value which can be used in case a value is not explicitly initialized to a variable.

Java supports eight primitive types of data as follows:

- byte
- short
- int
- long
- float
- double
- char
- boolean

These types can be further clustered into four categories:

2.1.1 Integers

This group is used to represent whole numbers which can be signed, positive, or negative numbers. For instance, 123, -98, etc. What about the unsigned integer values?? Does java do not include them? Yes, you are correct. Java does not support unsigned positive values.

Integers comprise the succeeding data types:

- *byte:* is the smallest type among all the integer types.
    - *Memory size:* The size of a byte data type is 8 bits or 1 byte.
    - *Range:* The range of values it can hold vary from -128 to 127.

      The range for a type is easy to calculate. It can be calculated by the formula $-(2^{n-1})$ to $(2^{n-1})-1$ where n is the size of the data type. So for a byte variable the range can be calculated as:

      $$= -(2^{8-1}) \text{ to } (2^{8-1})-1$$
      $$= -(2^{7}) \text{ to } (2^{7})-1$$
      $$= -128 \text{ to } 127$$

    - *Default value:* The default value for a byte variable is 0.

  An example of how a byte variable can be declared is as follows:

  byte byteVariable;

  where *byteVariable* is a variable of byte data type.

- *short:* The specifications for a short variable are given below:
    - *Memory size:* The size for a short variable is 16 bits.
    - *Range:* The range of values a short variable can support are from -32768 to 32767.
    - *Default value:* for a short is 0.

  An example of how a short variable can be declared is:

  short shortVariable;

  where *shortVariable* is a short variable.

- *int:* The next in league is the int data type:
    - *Memory size:* for an int type is 32 bits.

- *Range:* The range of values supported by an int vary from 2,147,483,648 to 2,147,483,647.
- *Default value:* for an int is 0.

The declaration for an int data type can be done as:

int intVariable ;

where *intVariable* is a variable of int data type.

- *long:* Following are the requirements for a variable to be of long data type:
  - *Memory size:* The size for a long is 64 bits.
  - *Range:* The values for a long data type range from 9,223,372,036,854,775,808 to 9,223,372,036,854,775,807.
  - *Default value:* for a long variable is 0.

  A long variable can be declared as

  long longVariable;

  where *longVariable* is a variable of long data type.

//A simple program to illustrate use of long data type

```
public class DataTypeDemo {
    public static void main(String[] args) {
          long mSalary = 150000; // salary for a month
          long ySalary;
          ySalary = mSalary * 12;
          System.out.print("The yearly salary is " + ySalary);
    }
}
```

Output:

```
The yearly salary is 1800000
```

2.1.2 Floating Point Types (Rational Numbers)

This group encompasses data types which characterize numbers with a fractional part, i.e., decimal numbers. For example, 32.5, 52.345 etc. This collection further consists of the subsequent types:

- *float:* signifies values with a single precision. They are mainly used to represent numbers which have a fractional part.
  - *Memory size:* float occupies 32 bits in memory.
  - *Range:* float values can range from 1.4e–045 to 3.4e+038.
  - *Default value:* for a float variable is 0.0f.

Here is an example how a float variable can be declared:[1]

float floatVariable=6.7f;

- *double:* is said to represent rational values with double the precision of that of the float. It takes more space in memory as compared to that of the float but is faster and more accurate in performing calculations.

  The characteristics of a double variable are:

  - *Memory size:*for a double type is 64 bits.
  - *Range:* The range of values it can hold diverges from 4.9e–324 to 1.8e+308.
  - *Default value:* for a double is 0.0.

This is how a double variable can be declared:

double doubleVariable;

where *doubleVariable* is of double type

Here is a sample program depicting the usage of double data type

```
public class DataTypeDemo {
    public static void main(String[] args) {
            float radius = 2.3f;
            double pie = 3.14;
            double area = pie * radius * radius;
            System.out.println("The area of the circle is " + area);
    }
}
```

Output:

```
The area of the circle is 16.610599311256415
```

> **Note**
>
> *The 'f' appended at the time of initialization of a float variable indicates 32 bits of storage in memory for the variable radius. If you declare radius to be of type float and do not append 'f' with the value, compiler will generate an error since you are trying to put a double value into a variable of float type.*
>
> *By default, any floating point literal is of type double.*

2.1.3 Character

This category comprises the *char* data type that can hold single character values such as 'A', 'c' etc. The values are to be enclosed in single quotes. The char data type in java supports Unicode

[1] *Use float where you don't require a higher degree of precision. For instance while representing currency. While initializing a float variable, always append 'f' or 'F' with the value. This is a way to indicate to the compiler that only 32 bits must be reserved for the variable in the memory..*

characters provide provision for multiple languages like English, Hindi, French etc. This is the reason char data type in java is different from other programming languages.

- *Memory size:* char takes up a memory space of 16 bits.
- *Range:* The values stored differ from 0 to 65536.
- *Default value:* Its default value is a blank space, i.e., 'u0000' in memory where 'u' indicates the presence of a unicode character.

Program demonstrating usage of char data type

```
public class CharDataType {
    public static void main(String[] args) {
        char var1 = 'A';
        char var2 = 'B';
        System.out.println(var1 + var2);

    }
}
```

The above program will not concatenate the two characters A and B. Rather it will print the sum of ascii values of A and B, i.e., 131.

2.1.4 Boolean

Boolean is used to hold boolean values. Boolean values can be either *true* or *false*. They can be expedient to check whether two variables are equal or not. Generally, they are used in conditional expressions to return true or false.

- *Memory size:* Size of a boolean type is dependent upon the java virtual machine. Therefore, it fluctuates on different platforms.
- *Default value:* The default value for a boolean is false.

Program to signify the usage of boolean data type

```
public class BooleanDataType {
    public static void main(String[] args) {
        boolean var1 = false;
        int var2 = 5, var3 = 5;
        if (var1) // checks if the value of a evaluates to true
            System.out.println("Boolean value is true");
        else
            System.out.println("Boolean value returned is false");
        if (var2 == var3)
            System.out.println("The values of two variables are
            equal");
```

```
            else
                  System.out.println("The values of two variables are not
                  equal");
      }
}
```

Output:

```
Boolean value returned is false
The values of two variables are equal
```

2.2 VARIABLES

As mentioned earlier, a variable is a named memory location used to store values of different types. These types can be anything from an integer to a boolean.

Types of variables

- *Value Variables:* Variables which hold a primitive type as a value are called value variables.
- *Reference Variables:* Variables which hold an address of a type are called reference variables.
- *Instance Variables:* Variables which are directly defined inside the class are referred to as instance variables.
- *Parameter Variables:* Variables which are passed as parameters to a method or a constructor are called parameter variables.
- *Local Variables:* Variables which are defined inside a method, constructor, or any block for that matter, are known as local variables.

All these variables will be talked about in detail in different sections of the book. But for now keep these terms alive somewhere in your mind. Also, methods, constructors will also be conferred in the later chapters.

2.2.1 Variable Declaration and Initialization

The syntax for declaring a variable is given below:

Datatype variablename =value;

Where *Datatype* can be anything from a primitive data type to user defined data type. *variablename* is the name attached to the variable being declared. *value* is the value being devoted to the variable. Assigning a value to the variable is an optional part in the declaration process. Consider the example given below of declaring a variable of int type:

int a=5;

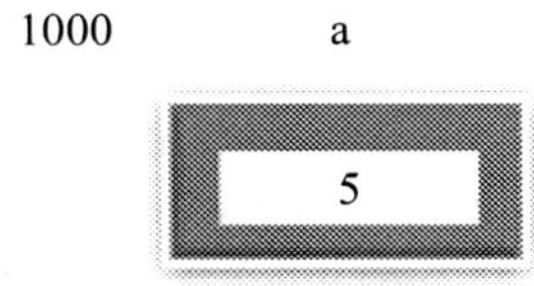

Fig. 2.1 Memory picture for a variable

The diagram explains what happens on giving the above declaration. Since 'a' is of int type, 32 bits of memory are reserved for this variable at a memory location determined by the operating system. The example address taken here is 1000. A name is attached to the memory location ('a' in our case). It is through this name that we will now reference this location. A value of 5 is initialized to this location. Following such type of diagrammatical representation helps one to clearly understand and comprehend a java program. But the question which remains is why do we at all declare variables? We will shortly see its solution by an example program.

Here is sample code to declare and initialize variables.

Note: The following code will generate a compile time error

```
public class VariableDemo {
    public static void main(String[] args) {
        int a, b; // declaring variables
        a = 5; // initializing variable
        System.out.println("The value of a " + a);
        System.out.println("The value of b " + b); // error
        System.out.println("The value of c " + c); // error
    }
}
```

In the above program, we have declared two variables 'a' and 'b'. But initialization is done only for the variable 'a'. This is the reason while printing the value of variable 'b', compiler generates an error since there is no value initialized to it. In addition to it, a compile time error is produced when an attempt to print the value of 'c' is made. Since 'c' has not been declared, the compiler does not know how many bits to allocate to the variable or is it really a variable or something else!

The memory picture for the above variables[2]:

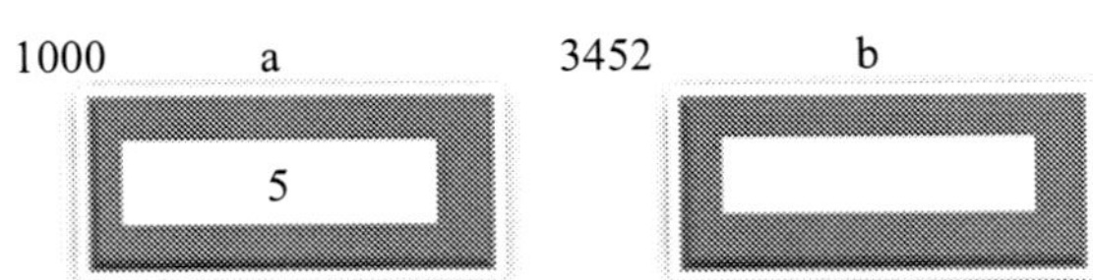

Fig. 2.2

[2] *The address for the memory locations are hypothetical and are used to make learning easier.*

2.2.1.1 Dynamic Initialization of a Variable

Dynamic initialization of a variable means initializing the value to a variable at runtime (dynamically). The example above initializes the value to a variable at compile time. Let's see how dynamic initialization can be done through an example program.

//Sample program for dynamic initialization

```
public class DVar {
    public static void main(String[] args) {
          double a = -3.2;
          double abs = Math.abs(a);
          System.out.println("The absolute value is:" + abs);

    }
}
```

Output:

```
The absolute value is:3.2
```

The program above uses two variables namely 'a' and 'abs' of double type. The value of 'a' is initialized with a constant value of -3.2. But the value of 'abs' is calculated at runtime when the abs method is called from predefined *Math* class. How methods are called from a class will be talked in the later chapters.

2.2.2 Scope and Lifetime of Variables

A block of codes defines a scope. But then *what is a scope?*In simple words, a new scope is created with a beginning of curly brace. All the variables declared within that curly brace belong to that scope. Once you encounter a closing curly brace, all these variables cease to exist outside. Consider the code fragment below as an example.

```
public class ScopeDemo { // outer scope
    public static void main(String[] args) {
          boolean a = false; // declaring and initializing local variable a
          if (a) // checking if the value of a evaluates to true
          { // starting an inner scope
                System.out.println("The value of a is " + a);
                boolean b = false;
          }

          a = true; // perfectly fine
          b = true; // error! b not accessible here
    }
}
```

In the program above, we start a class scope when a curly brace starts after '*ScopeDemo*'. The main method declares a new nested scope inside the class scope and declares a local boolean variable 'a'. Another nested scope initiates while we are checking for the value of 'a' to be true which declares one more variable 'b'. Now here's something you need to remember always! *Variables declared inside a nested scope are only visible/accessible in that scope. However, variables declared in the outer scope are accessible in its inner scope.* This is the reason variable 'a' is visible inside the nested scope of '*if block*' but variable 'b' is not accessible in the outer scope.

Lifetime of Variables

The lifetime of the variable is the time duration till which the variable is alive. The lifetime of the variables declared inside an inner scope will expire, the moment you come out of the scope. At this point, the variables are eligible for getting their memories released.

Ponder upon the below code, depicting the lifetime of the variables

```
public class LifeTimeDemo {
    public static void main(String[] args) {
            int var;
            for (var = 0; var<= 4; var++) {
                  int x = 0;
                  System.out.println("var=" + var);
                  x++;
                  System.out.println("x=" + x); // lifetime of x ends
            }
        } // lifetime of var ends
}
```

Output:

```
var=0
x=1
var=1
x=1
var=2
x=1
var=3
x=1
var=4
x=1
```

The above program declares two variables, namely, '*var*' and '*x*'. '*var*' is declared in the main method so its scope is localized to *main* only. Whereas '*x*' is declared in an inner scope defined by the '*for*' statement. The value of '*x*' is initialized to '0' every time we enter the block of '*for*'. The lifetime of '*x*' ends with ending of '*for*' statement. Consequently, the value of *x* remains the same throughout the '*for*' loop and the value of '*var*' gets updated.

2.2.3 Type Conversion and Casting

As we all know, every variable has a type, but not all types are compatible with each other. What is this *type compatibility* now? It is very common to assign the value of one variable to another while you are playing with variables in your java application. Java compiler checks whether or not it can perform such assignment by doing a compatibility test on these types. This compatibility test checks for two conditions:

1. *The size of the destination type to which the value is assigned should be greater than equal to the source type.*

   Example:

   ```
   public class TypeCompatibility {
           public static void main(String[] args) {
                   byte b = 4;
                   int i;
                   i = b;
           }
   }
   ```

   In the assignment above, variable '*b*' is said to be of the source type and variable '*i*' of the destination type. Thus, the variable whose value is initialized depicts the source type whereas the variable, into which the value is being initialized is called the destination type. Here, the size of the destination type '*int*' is 32 bits whereas that of the byte is 8 bits. Therefore, such type of assignment is possible in java and will not generate any error.

2. *The assignment being done should not result in loss of data.*

   ```
   public class TypeCompatiblity {
           public static void main(String[] args) {
                   int i = 5;
                   float f = 3.2f;
                   f = i; // possible
                   i = f; // error! Type mismatch
           }
   }
   ```

   In the above example, when you attempt to put the value of an *int* variable into a *float* variable, the compiler *does not* generate an error. On the other hand, when you perform the reverse operation, the compiler yields an error since assigning a *float* value to an *int* value results in loss of data.

   Such conversions where you don't have to explicitly convert one data type to other are known as *automatic type conversion* or *a widening operation.*

Type Casting

There are times when you have to work with different types and the compiler does not do the implicit conversion for you. It is then, you have to perform the conversions from one type to another explicitly.

```
public class TypeCastingDemo {
        public static void main(String[] args) {
                int i = 5;
                float f = 3.2f;
                i = (int) f; // explicit type casting
                System.out.print("The casted value is " +i);
        }
}
```

Output:

```
The casted value is 3
```

Here, while assigning the value of a float variable to an *int* variable, the operation violates condition 2 specified above. Therefore, the compiler fails to do the conversions implicitly instead the user has to explicitly cast the *float* value to an *int* value as done in the above program. This process is also called *narrowing operation.*

2.2.4 Type Promotion

So, we just differentiated between type conversion and type casting. Conversions take place implicitly and are performed by the compiler whereas, if the two conditions stated above do not satisfy an assignment operation, then one has to implement type casting. Now, imagine you are operating upon two variables, a *long* and a *double* and you attempt to multiply the two variables. What do you think, the type of the result will be? Let's see via an example program.

```
public class TypePromotionDemo {
    public static void main(String[] args) {
            long lVar = 23;
            double dVar = 32.5;
            long result = lVar * dVar; // Error! Type Mismatch
            double res = lVar * dVar; // promoted to double
            System.out.println("The promoted value is " + res);
    }
}
```

The above program explains the concept of type promotion.

While attempting an arithmetic operation between a *long* and a *double*, the type of the result will be automatically promoted to a larger type, *double* in our case. By the same token, if you have an operation between a *short* and a *byte*, the result will be promoted to *short* type.

2.3 ARRAYS

An array is a data structure used to hold elements of the same type. An integer array will store only integer values whereas a character array will store characters only.

Arrays in java are a *reference type and not a value type*. A *reference* variable is a variable which holds an address rather than a value.

All primitive types which you have studied earlier (*int, float*, etc), have predefined memory allocation for them. An *int* type has allocation for 32 bits, a *double* has it for 64 bits so on so forth. But, when we talk about reference types like arrays, their size can vary at runtime and so the memory allocated to them. This is the reason, why java handles arrays by references and not by value. Whereas, all primitive types in java are passed by value and are called value types.

2.3.1 One-dimensional Arrays

One-dimensional arrays are organized as a linear list in memory. Their indexes run from *0 to size-1* where *size* is size of the array in bytes.

Declaration Syntax for 1D array:

type array_name[]=new type[size];

or — *Both declarations are correct*

type []array_name=new type[size];

Here, the *type* refers to the type of array you want to declare. If the type is *int*, then the array is capable of storing only integer values. The *array_name* is the name of the reference through which you will manipulate or access the elements of the array. In other words, you can say it is the name of the array.

The *new* operator allocates memory to the array of *size* bytes. Notice the square brackets with the array name. They are used to portray that the following declaration is that of an array.

Example:

int iArray[]=new int[5]; (1)

Since the above statement is an assignment operation, it is executed from right to left.
After the new operator executes, the following happens in memory:

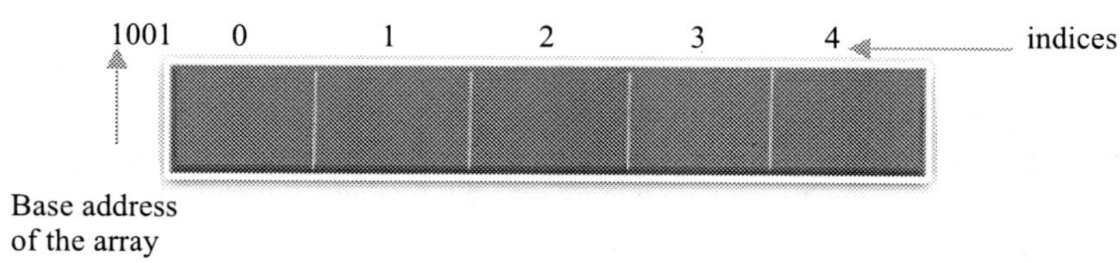

As per the figure above, the new operator allocates contiguous chunks of memory with indexes running from 0 to 4 on memory location 1001.

On implementing the left hand side of the expression (1), the memory picture changes to the following:

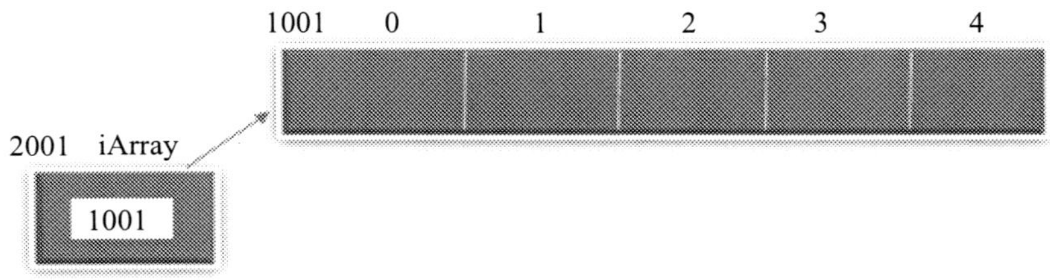

Fig. 2.3 Memory representation of 1D array

In the above figure, *iArray* is a reference which has its own address in memory(2001, in our case). It holds an address of the memory location allocated with the new operator (1001). So, we say, *iArray* points to the memory allocated by the new operator as depicted by the figure. This *iArray* will now be used to access or manipulate individual elements of the array. This is how we can access the elements of the array:

reference_name[index_to_be_accessed]

Therefore, *iArray[0]* will be used to access 0th element of the array, *iArray[1]* will be used to access 1st element of the array and so on. Remember, *the type of the reference should be same as the type of the memory location it is pointing to*. Notice the type of reference *iArray* and the type of memory allocated by the new operator is same, i.e., *int*.

Alternate declaration for a 1D array

type reference_name[]={*comma separated values*};

where *type* is the type of the values the array will hold (data type), *reference_name* is the name of the array and *values* are some of the fixed comma separated values being initialized to the array.

The following code snippet shows the declaration and usage of 1D array:

```
public class IDArrayDemo {
    public static void main(String[] args) {
        int iArray[] = new int[5];
        iArray[0] = 32;
        iArray[1] = 22;
        iArray[2] = 45;
        iArray[3] = 65;
        System.out.println("The fifth element of the array is:" +
        iArray[4]);
        System.out.println("The sixth element of the array is:" +
        iAsrray[5]); // oops!There is no sixth element in the array
}
  }
```

Output:

```
The fifth element of the array is:0
Exception in thread "main" java.lang.ArrayIndexOutOfBoundsException:5
at pkg1.SelfTest.main(SelfTest.java:11)
```

Notice the code minutely. In the program above, we have declared a 1D array accessible through *iArray*. Next, we assigned the elements to the array. Since, the size of the array is 5, it is capable of holding 5 elements from indexes 0 to 4. When we give a call to the *println* method and try to print *iArray[4]*, it does not result in an error even if we have not initialized the *iArray[4]* to any value. This is because by default, the elements of the array will be set to their default values. And the default value for an *int* is 0. Hence, the output for *iArray[4]* is zero.

But in case we wish to print the *iArray[5]*, it results in an exception called *java.lang.ArrayIndexOutOfBoundsException*. Exceptions and their handling will be conferred later but for now just remember that *you can only access elements of an array till size-1 index where size is the capacity of the array to hold elements. Any attempt to access an index of an array which does not exist will result into an exceptional error condition.*

//Sorting an array in ascending order

```
public class SortArray {
    public static void main(String[] args) {
        int number[] = { 34, 45, 460, 10, 72 };
        int len;
        len = number.length; // used to calculate length of an array
        System.out.println("Unsorted list");
        for (int i = 0; i<len; i++)
            System.out.println(" " + number[i]);
        for (int i = 0; i<len - 1; i++) {
            for (int j = i + 1; j<len; j++) {
                if (number[i] >number[j]) {
                    int temp = number[i];
                    number[i] = number[j];
                    number[j] = temp;
                }
            }
        }
        System.out.println("\nAscending order");
        for (int i = 0; i<len; i++)
            System.out.println(" " + number[i]);
        System.out.println("Descending order");
        for (int i = len - 1; i>= 0; i--)
            System.out.println(" " + number[i]);
    }
}
```

Output:

```
Unsorted list
 34
 45
 460
 10
 72

Ascending order
 10
 34
 45
 72
 460

Descending order
 460
 72
 45
 34
 10
```

2.3.2 Two-dimensional Arrays

Two-dimensional arrays are analogous to a 2D matrix organized as rows and columns. Each element in the array has row and a column index.

Syntax of a 2D array
int iArray=new int[3][3];

The above declaration is for a two-dimensional array where the first dimension represents the number of rows and the latter depicts the number of columns present in the array. In the example above we have three rows and three columns.

The following picture portrays how the elements in this array will be stored.

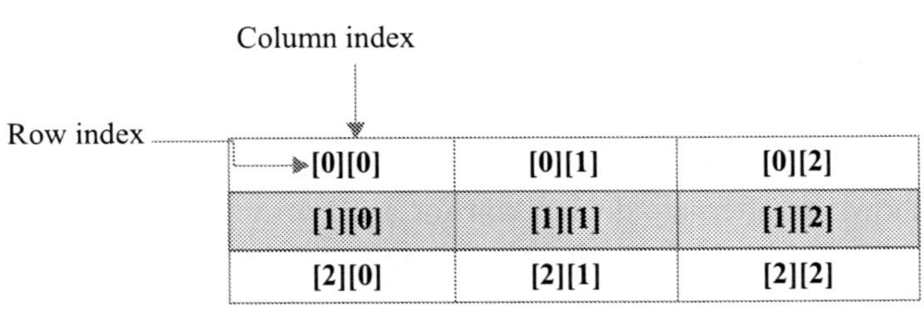

Fig. 2.4 Memory arrangement for a 2D array

//Sample program showing a 2D array

```
public class 2DArray {
public static void main(String[] args) {
          int[][] mat = new int[2][2];
          mat[0][0] = 1;
          mat[0][1] = 2;
          mat[1][0] = 3;
          mat[1][1] = 4;
          for (int i = 0; i< 2; i++) {
                for (int j = 0; j< 2; j++) {
                      System.out.print("mat[" + i + "]" + "[" + j +
                      "]:" + mat[i][j] + "\t"); //separating elements
                      //by a tab
                }
                System.out.println();       //printing a new line
          }
     }
}
```

Output:

```
mat[0][0]:1        mat[0][1]:2
mat[1][0]:3        mat[1][1]:4
```

Specifying the second dimension for a 2D array is optional. Have a look at the code below to gain a clear understanding about it.

```
public class 2DArray {
    public static void main(String[] args) {
          int[][] mat = new int[2][];
          mat[0] = new int[2]; // allocating memory of two columns
                               //for the first row
          mat[1] = new int[2]; // allocating memory of two columns
                               // for the second row
          mat[0][0] = 1;
          mat[0][1] = 2;
          mat[1][0] = 3;
          mat[1][1] = 4;
     }
}
```

The example shows an alternate declaration for a 2D array where the second dimension of the array is optional.[3] So, in the first place the compiler only allocates memory for two rows. Thereafter, for each row, memory allocation for two columns is done.

---

[3] *The second dimension of the array can be of different sized memory allocations. This means each row can correspond to varying number of columns.*

2.3.3 Multidimensional Arrays

Arrays can be extended to any dimension. An example of a three-dimensional array is discussed below:

```
public class 3DArray {
      public static void main(String[] args) {
            int[][][] mat = new int[2][2][2];
            for (int i = 0; i< 2; i++) {
                  for (int j = 0; j< 2; j++) {
                        for (int k = 0; k< 2; k++) {
                              mat[i][j][k] = i + j + k;
                              System.out.print(mat[i][j][k] + "\t");
                        }
                        System.out.println();
                  }
                  System.out.println();
            }
      }
}
```

Ouput:

```
0   1
1   2

1   2
2   3
```

In the array, *mat[2][2][2]*, declared above, the first dimension specifies the number of *segments*, second specifies the *number of rows* and the third dimension specifies the *number of columns*.

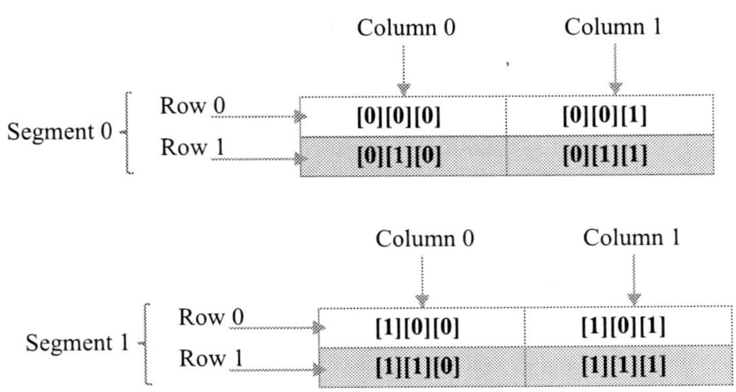

Fig. 2.5 Memory arrangement for a 3D array

2.3.4 Assigning a Reference to Another Array

References can be assigned to already existing arrays. Look at the code below:

```
public class ArrayDemo {
    public static void main(String[] args) {

            int[] arr = { 1, 2, 3, 4 };
            int[] arr1;
            arr1 = arr;
            System.out.println(arr1[3]);
        }
}
```

Output:

```
4
```

The above program can be explained in the following steps:

1. The first statement allocates memory of integer type putting some elements into it and then assigns a reference named *arr* to this location.

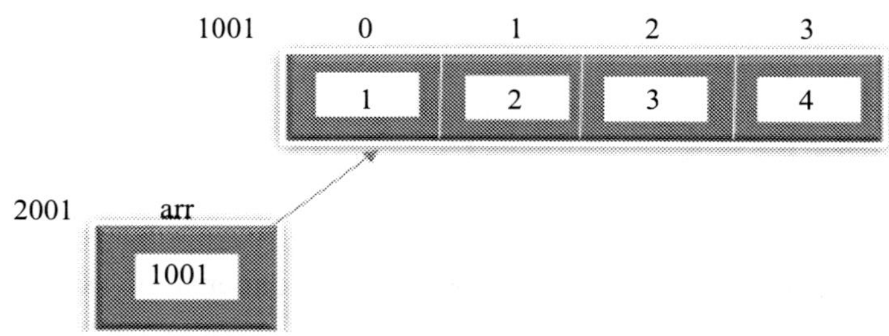

Fig. 2.6

2. The next statement creates another reference named *arr1* but this reference currently points nowhere.

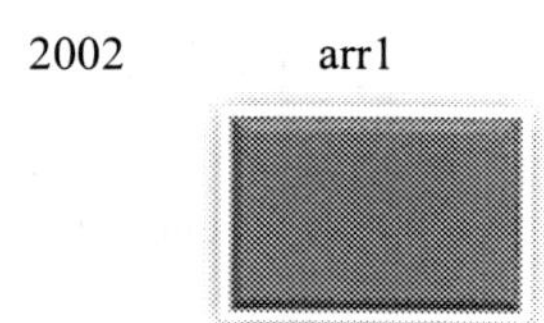

Fig 2.7

3. Next, since assignment operation operates from right to left, the contents of *arr* are assigned to *arr1*. But what are the contents of *arr*? *arr* is nothing but a reference which holds the address of a memory location, allocated in the first step. Therefore, this address is copied to *arr1* resulting in the below memory picture.

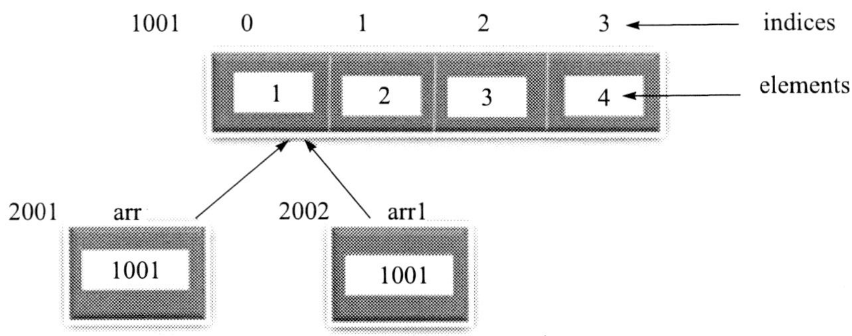

Fig. 2.8

4. Note, both references now hold the same address so we say they *point* to the same location. This is why printing *arr1[3]* prints the value 4. Thus, any changes made by any of the two references here will affect the same memory location.

2.3.5 Copying Arrays

In java, it is possible to copy the contents of one array to another. In fact, subsequence of one array can also be copied to another. To facilitate this, we have the following method defined in the *System* class:

```
public static void arrayCopy(Object src, int srcPos,
        Object dest, int destPos, int length);
```

where

src is the source array to copy from
dest is the destination array where the copying is to be done.
srcPos is the source array position from where the copying will start
destPos is the starting destination array position where the copying will be done
length is the number of array elements to be copied

The method is a public static method and returns no value. Because of its *public* nature it is accessible from everywhere. The *static* keyword will be discussed later but for now remember the following about the static methods:

Static methods belong to a class and they are invoked using a class name.

```
// Code depicting copying of arrays
public class CopyArray {
    public static void main(String[] args) {
        char arrFrom[] = { 'a', 'b', 'c', 'd', 'e' };
        char[] arrTo = new char[10];
        System.arraycopy(arrFrom, 2, arrTo, 3, 3);
```

```
                for (int i = 0; i<arrTo.length; i++) {
                        System.out.println("arr[" + i + "]:" + arrTo[i]);
                }
        }
}
```

Output:

```
arr[0]: □
arr[1]: □
arr[2]: □
arr[3]: c
arr[4]: d
arr[5]: e
arr[6]: □
arr[7]: □
arr[8]: □
arr[9]: □
```

The example above explains how the *arrayCopy* method can be used to copy one array to another. Notice the output carefully. Since copying was done in destination array starting from the third index till the fifth index, all the other indices are filled up with character default values where □ symbol is just denoting a character default value u0000.

SUMMARY

Coming to the end of the chapter, let us now put up a reverse gear and revise what all milestones we have achieved.

- Java supports eight primitive data types which can be summarized as follows:

Table 2.1

Data Types	Memory Size (bits)	Range	Default Value
byte	8	-128 to 127	0
short	16	-32768 to 32767	0
int	32	2,147,483,648 to 2,147,483,647	0
long	64	9,223,372,036,854,775,808 to 9,223,372,036,854,775,807	0
float	32	1.4e–045 to 3.4e+038	0.0f
double	64	4.9e–324 to 1.8e+308	0.0
char	16	0 to 65536	u0000
boolean	Dependent upon JVM	0 to 1	false

- A variable is memory location with a name which is used to hold a value.
- The scope of a variable is valid within the blocks in which it is declared whereas the lifetime of the variable is the time duration for which the variable is alive and can be accessed.
- Type casting has to be done explicitly and is required while we are dealing with incompatible types.
- Type promotion is promoting the type of the expression to a larger data type implicitly done by the compiler.
- Arrays are a continuous stream of memory locations holding elements of similar type and can be multidimensional.
- Arrays are reference types in java as they need a reference to access its elements.
- Memory is allocated for an array using the new operator.
- Copying of arrays can be done using the *arrayCopy* method defined in the *System* class.

COMMON ERRORS

Some of the common errors you will make while working with the above concepts are:

- Attempting to use a variable not defined.

```
int a=5;
b=7;
```

  Assigning 'b' a value will result into a compile time error *b cannot be resolved to a variable.*

- Using a variable without initializing value to it.

```
int a=5;
byte b;
a=b;                //local variable b might not have been initialized
```

- Accessing a variable outside its scope.

```
int a=7;
        if(a==7)
        {
                int b=7;
        }
b=6;                //compile time error! b cannot be resolved to an error
```

- Operating upon incompatible types and forgetting the cast.

```
int a=5;
byte b;
b=a;                //type mismatch
```

- Declaring a reference and not allocating memory to it.

  int []arr;

  arr[0]=5;

  The above statements will result in a compile time error as you are attempting to use a reference currently pointing nowhere.

SELF-TEST

1. Discuss the data types in java with an example of each.
2. How do you declare and initialize a variable in java?
3. What do you mean by scope and lifetime of a variable. Depict using an example.
4. What is typecasting in java? Why is it required?
5. Explain how arrays are handled in java with suitable examples.

PRACTICAL QUESTIONS

1. Write a program to check whether a string is palindrome or not.
2. Write a program to find the most frequently occurring integer in an array of integers.
3. Examine the code below and point out the errors:

```
public class SelfTest {

        public static void main(String[] args) {
                float f = 1.01;
                double d = 9.0;
                f = d;
                d = f;

        }

}
```

3
CHAPTER
Operators

This chapter will enable you to learn the following:

- Definition of an operator, operation and an operand.
- Types of operators available in java.
- Implementing the operators using simple java programs.

Operators define the task (operations) to be performed. These operations can vary from mathematical operations to logical operations. The entities on which the operation is performed by the operators are called *operands*. An *n-ary operator* works upon *n* operands. For instance, a unary operator works upon one operand whereas a binary operator operates upon two operands. In the expression below:

x+2;

x and 2 are the *operands* and + is the *operator*.

Java supports a wide range of operators that are discoursed below.

3.1 ASSIGNMENT OPERATOR

Assignment operator is a binary operator. It basically assigns the value of the right operand to the left operand. The following example would suffice it:

```
public class Assign {

    public static void main(String[] args) {
        double x = 4.3;
        double y;
        x = y; // error! The value of y does not exists
        y = x;

    }
}
```

In the example above, the assignment operation x=y, yields an error because we are attempting to assign the value of y to x and right now y does not hold any value. But, the expression, y=x works perfectly fine as this time we are initializing the value of x to y and x has a double value 4.3.

3.2 ARITHMETIC OPERATORS

These operators perform the basic mathematical operations like addition, subtraction, division, increment, decrement, etc. Described below is the list of all the arithmetic operators java supports.

Table 3.1 Arithmetic operators

Operator	Operator Name	Operator type	Operation performed	Example
+	Addition	Binary	Adds the operand at the left side of the operator with the right side. The reverse will also yield the same result in this case.	a+b
+	Unary Plus	Unary	Indicates the number is positive. Operands without a sign before them also indicate positivity of operands.	+a
–	Subtraction	Binary	Subtracts the operand at the right side of the operator from the left side. The reverse will not yield the same result in this case.	a–b
–	Unary minus	Unary	Indicates that the operand is negative.	–a
*	Multiplication	Binary	Multiplication of two operands from either side yields the same result.	a*b
/	Division	Binary	Dividing the operand at the left side of an operator by the operand at the right side.	a/b
%	Modulus	Binary	Returns the remainder on dividing the two operands.	a%b
++	Increment	Unary	Increments the value of the operand.	++a
––	Decrement	Unary	Decrements the value of the operand.	––a
+=	Addition Assignment	Binary	Shorthand notation for addition of two operands.	a+=b
–=	Subtraction Assignment	Binary	Shorthand notation for subtraction of two operands.	a–=b

*=	Multiplication Assignment	Binary	Shorthand notation for multiplication of two operands.	a*=b
/=	Division Assignment	Binary	Shorthand notation for division of two operands.	a/=b
%=	Modulus Assignment	Binary	Shorthand notation for modulo of two operands.	a%=b

3.2.1 Elementary Arithmetic Operators

The elementary arithmetic operators include *addition, subtraction, multiplication* and *division.* The subsequent code snippet uses the basic arithmetic operators:

```
public class ArithmeticDemo {

    public static void main(String[] args) {
            int a,b,c;
            a=5;
            b=6;
            c=a+b;
            System.out.println("The addition of two operands a and b is:"+
            c);
System.out.println("The addition of two operands is:" + a + b);   //oops!
//Doesn't  add the two operands rather concatenates them
            c=a-b;
            System.out.println("The subtraction of two operands a and b
            is:"+ c);
            c=a*b;
            System.out.println("The multiplication of two operands a and
            b is:"+ c);
            c=a/b;
            System.out.println("The division of two operands a and b is:"+
            c);
            }
    }
```

Ouput:

```
The addition of two operands a and b is:11
The addition of two operands is:56
The subtraction of two operands a and b is:-1
The multiplication of two operands a and b is:30
The division of two operands a and b is:0
```

Notice the output above carefully. Printing *a+b* does not print the addition of two operands rather it concatenates the value of operands without a space[1]. Hence, the output, 56. Also, while

[1] + operator, apart from performing the addition operation is also used to concatenate strings.

dividing the two operands, it results into a value of 0. Though, 5 divided by 6 is 0.83333. But as we are dealing with integer arithmetic and not floating point arithmetic, the output comes out to be a zero.

3.2.2 Modulus Operator

Alright, so now what's modulus operator? Aren't the division operator and modulus operator same? *No. The division operator returns you the quotient whereas the modulus operator returns you the remainder.* For example, if you attempt to divide 10 by 5, then division operator will give you 2 as the answer whereas the modulus will give you 0 as the remainder. Let us have a look at it through an example:

```
public class ModOperator {

    public static void main(String[] args) {
            long num=340;
            long divisor=2;
            long quotient=num/divisor;
            long rem=num%divisor;
            long origNum=quotient*divisor;
            System.out.println("The quotient is:"+quotient);
            System.out.println("The remainder is:"+rem);
            System.out.println("The original number before division
            is:"+origNum);

    }
}
```

Output:

```
The quotient is:170
The remainder is:0
The original number before division is:340
```

3.2.3 Increment and Decrement Operators

The increment and decrement operators are *unary* operators. They work upon one operand only. The increment operator increases the value of the operand by one whereas the decrement operator decreases the value of its operand by one.

Further, these can be divided into two types:

- *Pre-Increment and Pre-Decrement*
- *Post-Increment and Post-Decrement*

A Pre-increment/Pre-Decrement operator is the one which first increments or decrements the value of the operand and then uses that value in the expression. Whereas, on the other hand, a post-increment/post-decrement operator, uses the value of the operand in the expression first and then increments or decrements it respectively. Confused?? Alright, let us see by an example where the value of *a=1*.

x=a++; (1)

*x=a+*2; (2)

After the statement (1) is executed, the value of x outputs to 1. But then what did the increment operator do? It should have incremented the value of *a* here since it is the operand on which the increment operation is applied. Now, here's the catch. The above expression, since it is using a *post-increment operator* will first use the value of *a* as 1 in the expression and initialize it to *x*. And the next time when we use the value of *a*, we will be using the incremented value of *a*. Therefore, after we execute the statement (2), it results in an output of 4.

However, if the above two statements are replaced by a pre-increment operator, our expressions would somewhat look like this:

x=++a;

*x=a+*2;

The value of *x* after the first statement would be 2 and the next time would be 4 since now the value is being incremented first and then being used in the expression.

Same goes for pre-decrement and post-decrement operators just that they will decrement the values of their operands by one.

Have a look at the complete example demonstrating the use of increment and decrement operators:

```
public class IncDecOperator {

    public static void main(String[] args) {
        int x, a, b, c;
        a = 1;
        b = 3;
        x = ++a;
        System.out.println("x=" + x);
        System.out.println("a=" + a);
        c = --x;
        System.out.println("x=" + x);
        System.out.println("c=" + c);
        a = c++;
        System.out.println("a=" + a);
        System.out.println("c=" + c);
        b = x--;
```

```
                System.out.println("x=" + x);
                System.out.println("b=" + b);
                a++;
                System.out.println("a=" + a);
        }
}
```

Output:

```
x=2
a=2
x=1
c=1
a=1
c=2
x=0
b=1
a=2
```

Note
x++ is same as x=x+1 but it becomes a post-increment operation when used in an assignment operation.

3.2.4 Shorthand Operators

Shorthand operators are binary operators normally used with the assignment operator. Why are they called *shorthand operators?* Simple, because they enable you to write shorter code.

How does a shorthand operator work?

x=x+2 is equivalent to x+=2

x=x-2 is equivalent to x-=2

x=x/2 is equivalent to x/=2

x=x%2 is equivalent to x%=2

Therefore, the syntax for writing a shorthand operator is as follows:

operand operator=expression;

Here, *operand* is the one on which the operation is being applied. *Operator* is the operation being performed. And *expression* can be composed of a single value or a set of variables instead.

Following are the shorthand operators for arithmetic operators:

- +=
- –=

- *=
- /=
- %=

//Sample program to illustrate usage of shorthand operators

```
public class ShorthandOperatorDemo {

    public static void main(String[] args) {
        int x = 6;
        int y = 4;
        x += 5;
        y -= 2;
        System.out.println("x=" + x);
        System.out.println("y=" + y);
        x *= x+y;
        y /= x;
        System.out.println("x=" + x);
        System.out.println("y=" + y);

    }
}
```

```
Output:
x=11
y=2
x=143
y=0
```

```
public class OperatorDemo {

    public static void main(String[] args) {
        byte b = 5;
        int i = 6;
        b += i;             //works fine   (1)
        b = b + i;          //error!       (2)

    }
}
```

In the above code what do you think, are the two expressions equivalent? No. This is where the difference lies. Adding a byte variable to an integer variable will yield the result as an integer (following the type promotion rules). Therefore, the result should also be stored in an integer variable. This is the reason why the second expression yields an error. However, this is not the case when we use shorthand operators. Therefore, the reason why statement 1 executes correctly without giving a type mismatch error.

3.3 RELATIONAL OPERATORS

Relational operators are also *binary operators* since they work upon two operands.

Table 3.2 describes all the relational operators available in java.

Table 3.2 Relational operators

Operator	Operator Name	Operator type	Operation performed	Example
>	Greater than	Binary	Returns true if the left hand operand value is greater than the right hand operand value.	a>b
>=	Greater than equal to	Binary	Returns true if the left hand operand value is greater than or equal to the right hand operand value.	a>=b
<	Less than	Binary	Returns true if the left hand operand value is less than the right hand operand value.	a<b
<=	Less than equal to	Binary	Returns true if the left hand operand value is less than or equal to the right hand operand.	a<=b
==	Equal equal to	Binary	Returns true if the left hand operand value is equal to the right hand operand value.	a==b
!=	Not equal to	Binary	Returns true if the left hand operand value is not equal to the right hand operand value.	a!=b

All relational operators evaluate to a boolean value returning either a true value or a false value.

3.3.1 Comparison Operators

Comparison operators are >, >=, <, <=. They are normally used in expressions to evaluate their values.

//Sample program for relational operators

```
public class ComparisonOperator {
```

```
    public static void main(String[] args) {
        char a = 'A';
        char b = 'B';
        char c = 'A';
        boolean d = a>b;
        boolean e = a<b;
        boolean f = a>= c;
        boolean g = a<= c;
        System.out.println(d);
        System.out.println(e);
        System.out.println(f);
        System.out.println(g);
    }
}
```

Output:

```
false
true
true
true
```

In the above code, we are using the comparison operators to compare primitive types. The program compares the character variables based upon their ASCII values. As the ASCII value of 'A' is 65 whereas that of 'B' is 66, the expression *a>b* evaluates to false. All the other expressions are evaluated likewise.

3.3.2 Equality Operators

The = = and != operators come under the category of *equality operators*. They are named so as they are used to check the equality between the two types. These types can be primitive types as well as reference types. For now, we will only see the effect of this operator on primitive types.

```
public class EqualityOperator {
    public static void main(String[] args) {
        char c = 'a';
        int i = 97;
        if (c != i) {
            System.out.println("Not Equal");
        } else
            System.out.println("Equal");
    }
}
```

Output:

```
Equal
```

The above program portrays the effect of using the equality operators on primitive types. Observe, in the second case, the output comes out to be *equal* even though one of the primitive types is a char and the other is an int. Why? This is so because, despite the types being different, the == operator evaluates the value of variable *c* as an int. And since the ASCII value of *'a'(variable c)* and the value of *variable i* is same as 97, the output comes out to be *equal*.

3.4 BITWISE OPERATORS

Bitwise operators are the ones which perform operations on the bits. As you know, a bit is a binary digit either 0 or a 1. Data is stored in the form of bits in the memory. The number of bits allocated to the data depends upon the kind of operating system you have. For example, 14 can be represented as 00001101 in memory for a 8-bit processor.

Bitwise operators can be further divided into two categories:

3.4.1 Bitwise Logical Operators

This category includes the following operators as described in Table 3.3.

Table 3.3 Bitwise logical operators

Operator	Operator Name	Operator type	Operation performed	Example
&	Bitwise AND	Binary	Performs the bitwise AND on the bits of the two operands. Returns a 1 if both the operands have the value 1.	a&b
|	Bitwise OR	Binary	Performs the bitwise OR on the bits of the two operands. Returns a 1 if either of the two operands have the value 1.	a|b
~	Bitwise NOT	Unary	Performs the bitwise NOT on the bits of the operand. Returns the inverse value of operand.	~a
^	Bitwise XOR	Binary	Performs the bitwise XOR on the bits of the two operands. Returns a 1 if both the operands have dissimilar values.	a^b

- *Bitwise AND*

  Bitwise AND performs the AND operation on the bits of the given operands. Consider the two operands as 14 and 8, then the calculations can be done as follows:[2]

14	– 00001110
8	-- 00001000
8	00001000

  The bitwise AND operation gives a 1 as the output if both the bits of the operands is a 1 else it gives a 0.

- *Bitwise OR*

  Bitwise OR performs the OR operation on the bits of the given operands. So OR'ing the bits of the operands 14 and 8 would yield the following result:

14	– 00001110
8	-- 00001000
	00001110

  Bitwise OR operations produces a 1 when any one of the bits of operand is 1 else it gives a 0 as the output.

- *Bitwise NOT*

  Bitwise NOT is a *unary* operator (takes up only one operand) which performs the NOT operation on the bits of the operand. Performing the bitwise NOT operation on an operand, say 14, yields the ensuing outcome:

14	– 00001110
–15	11110001

  Bitwise NOT operation simply inverts or reverses the bits of the operand. This means wherever you encounter a 0 turn it into a 1 and for a 1 turn it into a 0.

- *Bitwise XOR*

  Bitwise XOR operation performs the XOR operation on the bits of the operands.

14	– 00001110
8	-- 00001000
6	00000110

[2] All calculations for bitwise operations in the book are done using 8 bits.

Bitwise XOR yields a 1 if the bits of the operand are different. For example 1 ^ 0=1 but 1 ^ 1=0.

Now, let us have a closer look at the bitwise operators through an example:

```
public class BitwiseOperator {

    public static void main(String[] args) {
            int a = 14;
            int b = 8;
            int AND = a&b;
            System.out.println("Decimal of a&b:" + AND);
            System.out.println("Binary of a&b:" + Integer.
            toBinaryString(AND));
            int OR = a | b;
            System.out.println("Decimal of a|b:" + OR);
            System.out.println("Binary of a|b:" + Integer.
            toBinaryString(OR));
            int NOT = ~a;
            System.out.println("Decimal of ~a :" + NOT);
            System.out.println("Binary of ~a:" + Integer.
            toBinaryString(NOT));
            int XOR = a ^ b;
            System.out.println("Decimal of a^b:" + XOR);
            System.out.println("Binary of a^b:" + Integer.
            toBinaryString(XOR));
    }
}
```

Output:

```
Decimal of a&b:8
Binary of a&b:1000
Decimal of a|b:14
Binary of a|b:1110
Decimal of ~a :-15
Binary of ~a:11111111111111111111111111110001
Decimal of a^b:6
Binary of a^b:110
```

The output clearly shows the use of bitwise logical operators. To convert the decimal output to binary, we have used the predefined *Integer* class and its method *toBinaryString()* which converts the decimal output as a binary string. Classes and methods will be taken up in detail later.

Bitwise binary logical operators can also be clubbed with various *shorthand operators* studied before.

```
public class BitwiseOperator {

    public static void main(String[] args) {
            int aAND = 14;
            int b = 8;
            int aOR = 14;
            int aXOR = 14;
            aAND &= b;
            System.out.println("Decimal of a&b:" + aAND);
            System.out.println("Binary of a&b:" + Integer.
            toBinaryString(aAND));
            aOR |= b;
            System.out.println("Decimal of a|b:" + aOR);
            System.out.println("Binary of a|b:" + Integer.
            toBinaryString(aOR));
            aXOR ^= b;
            System.out.println("Decimal of a^b:" + aXOR);
            System.out.println("Binary of a^b:" + Integer.
            toBinaryString(aXOR));
    }
}
```

Output:

```
Decimal of a&b:8
Binary of a&b:1000
Decimal of a|b:14
Binary of a|b:1110
Decimal of a^b:6
Binary of a^b:110
```

3.4.2 Bitwise Shift Operators

The bitwise shift operators are used to shift information either to the left or to the right. Table 3.4 lists the various shift operators available in java.

- *Right Shift Operator*

  The right shift operator shifts all the bits in a register to the right conserving the sign of the number. Since, it preserves the sign of the number even after shifting the bits, the operator is also called the signed right shift operator. Consider the following expression:

  a>>1

Table 3.4 Bitwise shift operators

Operator	Operator Name	Operator type	Operation performed	Example
>>	Right Shift	Binary	Shifts bits in a pattern to the right, to the number of times specified in the expression. It maintains the sign of the number even after shifting.	a>>2
<<	Left Shift	Binary	Shifts bits in a pattern to the left, to the number of times specified in the expression.	a<<2
>>>	Unsigned Right shift	Binary	Shifts bits in a pattern to the right, to the number of times specified in the expression. It always stuffs a 0 in the leftmost position of the number irrespective of the sign of the number.	a>>>2

The above expression shifts all the bits in the operand *a* to the right once. The operand on the right determines the number of times, the shifting has to take place. In our case, the shifting will be done only once which means all the bits in operand *a* will be shifted 1 bit to the right. Further, being a signed right shift, the leftmost bit (sign bit) in operand *a* will be a 1 if *a* is a negative or a 0 if it is positive. Whereas, the rightmost bit will be lost.

Assuming the value of *a* to be -2, let us see what happens after executing a>>1 expression.

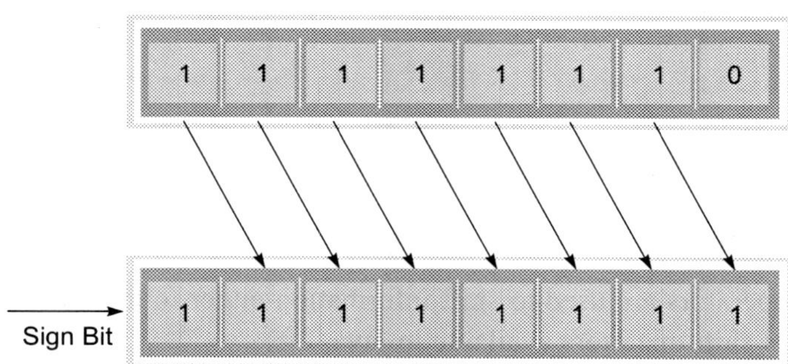

Fig. 3.1

In Figure 3.1 the value of the operand *a* is shifted 1 bit to the right. Since it is a negative number, the sign bit remains 1 even after the shifting has been done.

- *Left Shift Operator*

  The left shift operator shifts all the bits in a register to the left.

  a<<1

  The above expression will shift all the bits in the operand *a* to the left once. Assuming the value of *a* to be -2, and applying the left shift operator, the result would be as follows:

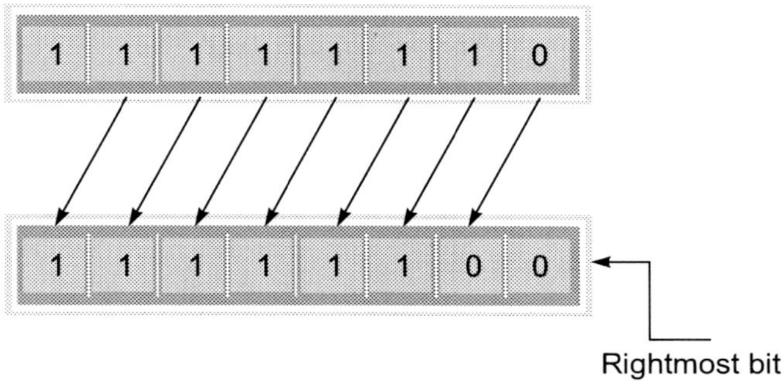

Fig. 3.2

  The left shift operator above shifts all the bits in the operand *a,* 1 bit to the left, stuffing a 0 in the rightmost bit. Observe that the rightmost bit is lost and replaced with a 0 instead.

- *Unsigned Right Shift Operator*

  The unsigned right shift operator also shifts the bits to the right just like a signed right shift operator. The difference being that unsigned right shift operator does not conserve the sign of the number after shifting has taken place. It stuffs a 0 in the leftmost bit of the number irrespective of the sign of the number. Taking the above example, the result would be as follows this time:

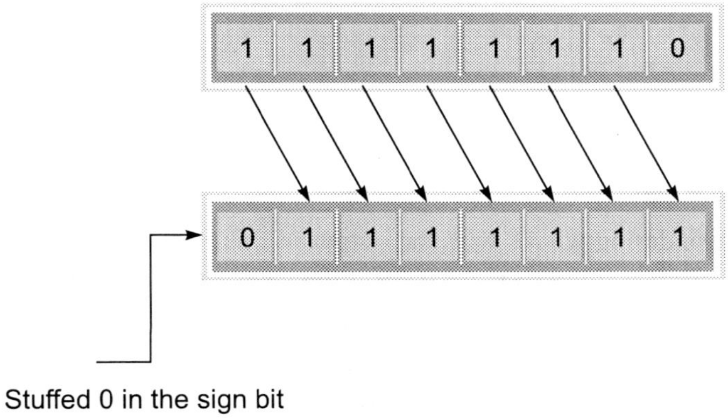

Fig. 3.3

Bitwise shift operators can also be used with shorthand operators.

//Program displaying the usage of shift operators

```
public class ShiftOperators {

    public static void main(String[] args) {
            int a = -2;
            int result_leftshift = a<< 1;
            System.out.print("Before Left Shift:");
            System.out.println(Integer.toBinaryString(a));
            System.out.print("After Left Shift:");
            System.out.println(Integer.toBinaryString(result_leftshift));
            System.out.print("Before Right Shift:");
            int result_rightshift = a>> 1;
            System.out.println(Integer.toBinaryString(a));
            System.out.print("After Right Shift:");
            System.out.println(Integer.toBinaryString(result_
            rightshift));
            System.out.print("Before unsigned right Shift:");
            System.out.println(Integer.toBinaryString(a));
            a>>>= 1;
            System.out.print("After unsigned right Shift:");
            System.out.println(Integer.toBinaryString(a));
    }
}
```

Output:

```
Before Left Shift:11111111111111111111111111111110
After Left Shift:11111111111111111111111111111100
Before Right Shift:11111111111111111111111111111110
After Right Shift:11111111111111111111111111111111
Before unsigned right Shift:11111111111111111111111111111110
After unsigned right Shift:1111111111111111111111111111111
```

Ok, so you are wondering what's with the output of this unsigned right shift? It should have a 0 in the leftmost bit. But it doesn't! Actually it does have a 0 in its leftmost bit, just that it is not shown here since putting a 0 in front of any number does not change its value.

3.5 BOOLEAN LOGICAL OPERATORS

Boolean logical operators are the operators that work upon boolean operands. Table 3.5 lists all the boolean logical operators available in java.

Table 3.5

<table>
<tr><th>Operator</th><th>Operator Name</th><th>Operator type</th><th>Operation performed</th><th>Example</th></tr>
<tr><td>&</td><td>Logical AND</td><td>Binary</td><td>Performs the logical AND on the two boolean operands. Returns true only if both the operands are true else false.</td><td>a&b</td></tr>
<tr><td>|</td><td>Logical OR</td><td>Binary</td><td>Performs the logical OR on the two boolean operands. Returns true if either of the two operands are true else false.</td><td>a|b</td></tr>
<tr><td>!</td><td>Logical NOT</td><td>Unary</td><td>Performs the logical NOT on the boolean operand. Returns the inverse value of the operand.</td><td>!a</td></tr>
<tr><td>^</td><td>Logical XOR</td><td>Binary</td><td>Performs the logical XOR on the two boolean operands. Returns true only if the two operands are not identical.</td><td>a^b</td></tr>
<tr><td>==</td><td>Equal equal to</td><td>Binary</td><td>Returns true if the left hand boolean operand value is equal to the right hand boolean operand value.</td><td>a==b</td></tr>
<tr><td>!=</td><td>Not equal to</td><td>Binary</td><td>Returns true if the left hand boolean operand value is not equal to the right hand boolean operand.</td><td>a!=b</td></tr>
<tr><td>&&</td><td>Short circuit AND/ Conditional AND</td><td>Binary</td><td>Returns true if both the clauses in the expression are true. Does not evaluate the second clause in the expression if the first clause is false.</td><td>(a|b&&b|c)</td></tr>
<tr><td>||</td><td>Short circuit OR/ Conditional OR</td><td>Binary</td><td>Returns true if either of the clauses in the expression is true. Does not evaluate the second clause in the expression if the first clause is true.</td><td>(a&b||b&c)</td></tr>
</table>

The following instance will clarify the above operators:

```
public class LogicalOperators {

    public static void main(String[] args) {
          boolean a=true;
```

```
            boolean b=false;
            boolean c=true;
            System.out.println("a:"+a);
            System.out.println("b:"+b);
            System.out.println("c:"+c);
            boolean result_AND=a&b;
            System.out.println("a&b:"+result_AND);
            boolean result_OR=a|b;
            System.out.println("a|b:"+result_OR);
            boolean result_NOT=!a;
            System.out.println("!a:"+result_NOT);
            boolean result_XOR=a^b;
            System.out.println("a^b:"+result_XOR);
            boolean result_Cond_AND=a|b&&b|c;
            System.out.println("a|b&&b|c:"+result_Cond_AND);
            boolean resut_Cond_OR=a&b||b&c;
            System.out.println("a&b||b&c:"+resut_Cond_OR);
            boolean result_Equal=a==b;
            System.out.println("a==b:"+result_Equal);
            boolean result_Not_Equal=a!=b;
            System.out.println("a!=b:"+result_Not_Equal);
      }
}
```

Output:

```
a:true
b:false
c:true
a&b:false
a|b:true
!a:false
a^b:true
a|b&&b|c:true
a&b||b&c:false
a==b:false
a!=b:true
```

3.6 ? OPERATOR (TERNARY OPERATOR)

The ? operator is also called the *ternary operator*. It works like an *if else* statement. The *if else* statement will be talked about in the next chapter. For now, understand the flow of an *if else* statement. The *if* clause evaluates an expression/variable, if its value is true, the statements falling under the *if* clause are executed otherwise, the statements under the *else* clause are executed.

The syntax for using a ternary operator is as follows:

Expression ? result1 : result2;

If the above *Expression* evaluates to true, *result1* is executed else *result2* is executed.

//Program demonstrating the use of ? operator

```
public class TernaryOperator {

public static void main(String[] args) {
int a = 64;
System.out.println((a % 2 == 0) ? a + " is an Even Number" : a
+ " is an odd Number");

}

}
```

Output:

```
64 is an Even Number
```

The above code, with the help of the ternary operator, checks if the value of variable *a* is divisible by 2 or not. If it is divisible, the output comes out to be an even number else it shows the variable value as an odd number.

3.7 OPERATOR PRECEDENCE

Table 3.6 shows a complete list of all the operators according to their precedence from highest to lowest. *All operators in the above table are evaluated from left to right except the assignment operator which is valued from right to left.* The precedence indicates the order in which the operators will be evaluated in an expression.

The array access operator ([]) is used to access the members of an array as discoursed earlier. And the Object member access operator (.) is used to access the members of a class through an object. This topic will be examined later at length.

```
public class OperatorPrecedence {

public static void main(String[] args) {
boolean a = true;
boolean b = false;
boolean c;
int d = 4;
```

Table 3.6

Operator	Operator Name	Operator Precedence
[] . () ++ --	Array access operator, object member access operator, post-increment, post-decrement operator.	Highest
++ -- + - ~ !	Pre-increment, pre-decrement, unary plus, unary minus, Bitwise NOT, Logical NOT operator.	
* / %	Multiplication, division, modulus operator.	
+ -	Binary Addition, Binary Subtraction operator.	
<< >> >>>	Left shift, Right shift, unsigned right shift operator.	
< > <= >=	Less than, Greater than, Less than equal to, Greater than equal to.	
== !=	Equal equal to, Not Equal to.	
& + -	Bitwise AND Binary Addition, Binary Subtraction operator.	
<< >> >>>	Left shift, Right shift, unsigned right shift operator.	
< > <= >=	Less than, Greater than, Less than equal to, Greater than equal to.	
== !=	Equal equal to, Not Equal to.	
&	Bitwise AND	
^	Bitwise XOR	
|	Bitwise OR	
&&	Logical AND	
||	Logical OR	
? :	Ternary Operator	
= += -= *= /= %= &= ^= |= <<= >>= >>>=	Shorthand operators	Lowest

```java
int e = 6;
boolean result = ((d<e) ? true : false) &&a;
System.out.println(result);
```

```
}
}
```

Output:

```
True
```

The program above shows the use of multiple operators and the order in which they are evaluated. At first, < operator is evaluated, not just because of its high precedence, but because it is enclosed within the braces. *So any expression enclosed within the braces is bound to be evaluated at priority.* The next operator to be evaluated according to the preference should be && operator, but ? : operator comes next in the line since it is enclosed within the braces. The last one to be evaluated is the && operator.

(d < e) ⟹ 4 < 6

((4 < 6) ? true : false) ⟹ true

((d < e) ? true : false) && a ⟹ true && true ⟹ True

SUMMARY

- An operand is the one on which the operation is performed.
- Operators define the type of operations to be performed on the operands.
- All operators are evaluated from left to right except the assignment operator which is evaluated from right to left.
- Operators can be broadly classified into three categories:
    - Unary Operator: which operate upon one operand only. Eg: ++, -- unary plus, unary minus.
    - Binary Operator: which works upon two operands. Eg: +, - , <<, >>, Bitwise AND etc.
    - Ternary Operator: which uses three operands to perform their operation. Eg: ? Operator which works like an "if else" statement.
- The assignment operator is a binary operator which assigns the value of operand on the right hand of an expression to the operand on the left side.
- Arithmetic operators are the operators capable of performing basic mathematical operations. The following operators fall under this category:
    - + : Addition operator
    - _ :Subtraction Operator
    - * : Multiplication Operator
    - / : Division Operator

  - % : Modulus Operator
  - + : Unary plus operator used to represent operands as positive.
  - - :Unary minus operator used to represent operands as negative.
  - ++, -- are called increment and decrement operators respectively.
  - ++ operator increments the value of an operand by one whereas -- decrements the value by one.

- Relational Operators are used for comparing the two operands. The following operators fall under this category:
  - > :Greater than operator
  - < :Less than Operator
  - >= : Greater than equal to operator
  - <= : Less than equal to operator
  - == : Equal equal to operator
  - != :Not equal to operator
- Bitwise Operators perform manipulations on the bits of the operands.
  - & :Bitwise AND
  - | :Bitwise OR
  - ~ : Bitwise NOT
  - ^ :Bitwise XOR
  - << :Left shift
  - >> :Right shift/signed right shift
  - >>> : unsigned right shift
- Boolean Logical Operators are the ones which work upon only boolean operands. The subsequent operators are the boolean logical operators:
  - & :Logical AND
  - | : Logical OR
  - ! : Logical NOT
  - ^ : Logical XOR
  - == : Equal Equal to
  - != : Not Equal to
  - && :Short circuit AND
  - || : Short circuit OR

- Shorthand operators are just a shorter way of using operators. The basic syntax of using a shorthand operator is as below:

  Operand operator=value;
- Operators are evaluated in the order of their precedence.

COMMON ERRORS

- The most common error we all make is that we forget which operator is compatible with what types. Always double-check, while using a specific operator, if it is compatible with the type of operands being operated upon. Example:

  ```
  int a=5;
  boolean b=true;
  System.out.println(a&&b);
  ```

  The above code will yield an error. Because && is defined only for boolean operands and "*a*" is not boolean in this case.
- DO NOT get confused with &, | and &&, ||. The former is a bitwise AND, bitwise OR operator and the latter is a boolean logical AND, boolean logical OR operator.
- >> stands for a signed right shift operator and will always fill up the sign bit depending upon the sign of the operand being shifted right. Whereas, >>> stands for the unsigned right shift that always stuffs a zero in the sign bit irrespective of the sign of the operand.

SELF-TEST

1. Explain the following terminologies with an example:
   - Binary operators
   - Unary operators
2. Write short notes on:
   - Arithmetic operators
   - Logical operators
3. What is a ternary operator? How does it work? How is it different from an "*if else*" statement?
4. What are shift operators? How many types of shift operators are available in java? Explain each of them via a small code snippet.
5. How are conditional/comparison operators different from equality operators? Explain.
6. Discuss the bitwise operators available in java.

PRACTICAL QUESTIONS

1. Produce the output for the following code snippets:

a)
```
public class SefTest {

public static void main(String[] args) {
int a=-10;
System.out.println(Integer.toBinaryString(a>>2));
System.out.println(Integer.toBinaryString(a<<3));
System.out.println(Integer.toBinaryString(a>>>2));

}

}
```

b)
```
public class SelfTest {

public static void main(String[] args) {
int a=10;
int b=5;
int c=2;
System.out.println(((a&b)|(a|c)));
System.out.println(((a|b)&&(b|c)));
System.out.println(!a&b|c);
System.out.println((a^b&~c));

}

}
```

c)
```
public class SelfTest {

public static void main(String[] args) {
int a = 34;
int b = 3;
int c = 2;
System.out.println(a % b / a>c);
System.out.println(a != b == c);

}

}
```

d)
```
public class SelfTest {

public static void main(String[] args) {
boolean a=true;
int b=32;
boolean c=false;
System.out.println((a&&b|b^c));
System.out.println((a||c&&a^c));
System.out.println(!a&&c|a&c);
}
}
```

4
CHAPTER

Control Structures

This chapter will enable you to learn the following:

- Defining and using the various selection statements like if, if-else and switch.
- Working with the iteration statements like for, while and do-while.
- Knowing the purpose and use of different jump statements like break, continue and return.

All the statements in any programming language are executed sequentially from top to down. But there might be times when we need to alter the flow of execution. Often, we need to decide or choose among two or more flows of execution that needs to be executed. Consider an example where we want to determine which all people can vote in an election. In such a case, our *condition* would be to check the *age* of the person. If the age is greater than equal to 18, the person is eligible to vote else not.

Control structures in java help us do all such things. Control structures are nothing but structures that control the flow of execution. Controlling here can refer to *branching*, *iterating* or *employing decision making* while executing a piece of code. Discussed below are some of the control structures available in java.

4.1 JAVA SELECTION STATEMENTS

Java Selection Statements are also called *Conditional Statements* or *Decision Statements* as these statements execute blocks of code (branch to a specific code) depending upon certain conditions. These statements can be further separated into the following:

4.1.1 If and If-Else Statement

- **If Statement:** *If* statement executes a set of statements based upon certain conditions.

  Syntax:

  if(condition)

{

Statements to be executed

}

Working:

The *if* clause accepts a condition and executes the set of statements falling under it only when the condition evaluated is true. Example, *displaying a number as positive (statement) if the number is greater than zero(condition)*. Figure 4.1 depicts the flow for an *If-Then* statement.

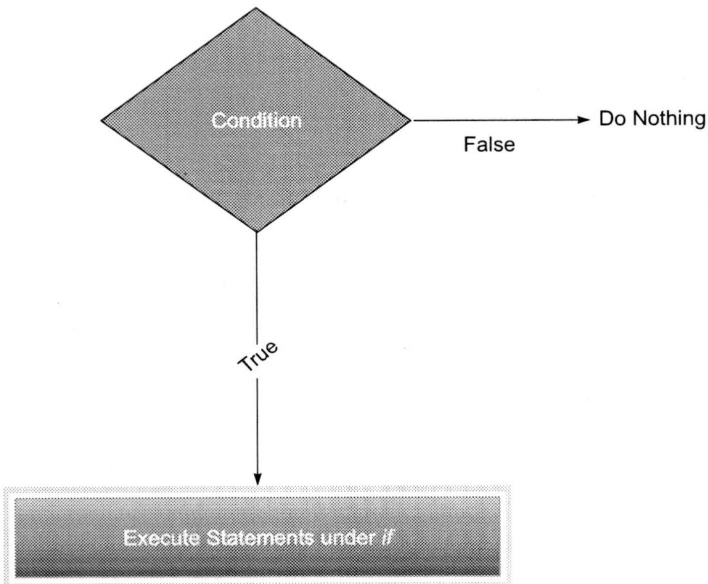

Fig. 4.1 If statement

//program illustrating If Statement

```
public class IfStatement {

public static void main(String[] args) {
double a=0.5;
if(a>0)
      System.out.println(a+" is a positive number");

      }
}
```

Output:

```
0.5 is a positive number
```

- **If-Else Statement**

The *If -Else* statement works in a similar fashion as an *If* statement. It is said to be a control structure that selects or chooses a set of statements depending upon certain conditions. Take, for an example, displaying a number as *positive* or *negative* based upon the *condition*: if the number is greater than zero or not.

The syntax for an *if-else statement* is as follows:

if(condition)

statement1;

else

statement2;

In the above syntax, the *if clause* evaluates an expression.[1] If it comes out to be true, *statement* 1 is executed else *statement 2* is executed. So, if you observe carefully here you will see that depending upon the condition some set of statements are executed and some are bypassed. Also, note that, an *else* statement should always succeed after an *if* statement. If not, the compiler will generate an error stating "*Misplaced Else*". Figure 4.2 demonstrates the *if-else* clause.

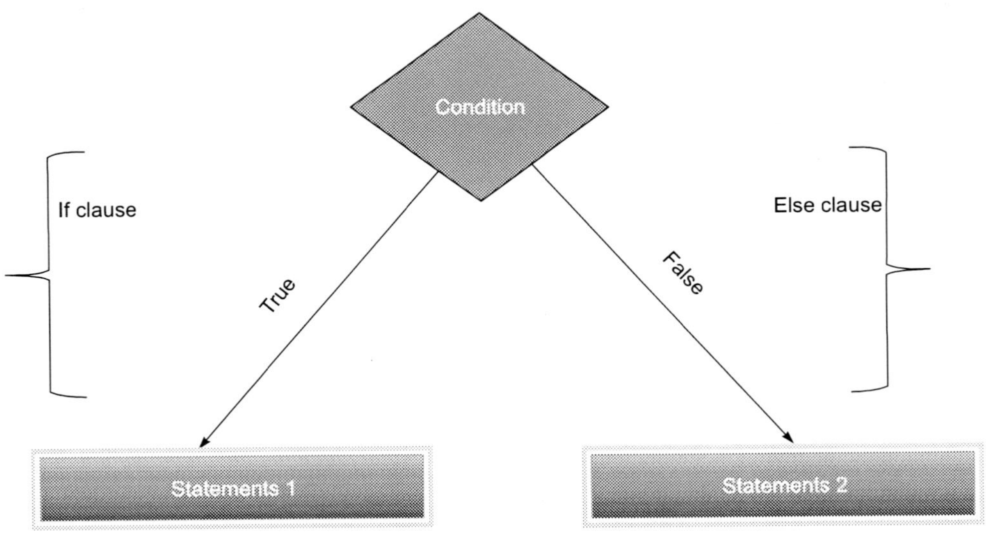

Fig. 4.2 If-else statement

//A program portraying the concept of an if-else statement

```
public class IfElseStatement {
```

[1] The if clause always evaluates an expression to a boolean value. A true value means any non-zero value whereas a false value means a zero value.

```
public static void main(String[] args) {
double a=0.5;
if(a>0)
    System.out.println(a+" is a positive number");
else
    System.out.println(a+" is a negative number");
    }

}
```

Output:

```
0.5 is a positive number
```

The program uses a double variable. If the value of the variable is greater than zero (condition), it displays the message that the number is positive else it displays the message that the number is negative.

4.1.1.1 Nested If-Else Statements

The nested *if-else statements* are the statements that incorporate more than one *if-else* clause. The subsequent code clarifies the concept.

```
public class NestedIfElse {

    public static void main(String[] args) {
        double total_marks=472;
        char grade;
        double perc=(total_marks/500)*100;
        if(perc>=80)
        {
            grade='A';
        }
        else if(perc>=70&&perc<80)
        grade='B';
        else if(perc>=60&&perc<70)
            grade='C';
        else
            grade='D';
        System.out.println("The percentage of the student is:"+perc);
        System.out.println("The grade of the student is:"+grade);
    }

}
```

Output:

```
The percentage of the student is:94.39999999999999
The grade of the student is:A
```

The program above uses a nested if-else statement structure. In the first case, it checks if the percentage of the student is greater than or equal to 80, it displays the grade of the student as 'A'. In the else clause, it checks again if the percentage falls between 70 to 80, it displays the grade as 'B'. Further, if the percentage is greater than equal to 60 or less than 70, the grade is set to 'C'. The last *else* denotes that the percentage did not fall in any of the above cases and sets the grade to 'D'.

//Program displaying a Misplaced if-else

```
public class MisplacedElseDemo {

    public static void main(String[] args) {
    boolean b=false;
    if(b);
    System.out.println("Will always execute");
    else
        System.out.println("Error:Misplaced Else");
    }
}
```

The above code will generate an error. Why? The program uses a boolean variable *b* initialized to false. It then uses an *if-else* construct to evaluate the value of *b*. But notice, we have a semicolon at the end of the *if statement.* A semicolon denotes the termination of *if statement* here. What comes next is always executed since it is a normal statement and does not come under the *if construct.* The *else statement* comes up as an error since we should always have an *else* immediately after an *if statement* which is not the case here. Hence, the compiler shows an error here since it does not correspond to an *if statement.*

```
public class IfElseDemo {
        public static void main(String[] args) {
                byte b = 5;
                int a = -1;
                if (b)
                        System.out.println("Type mismatch:Cannot convert
                        from byte to boolean");
                else
                        System.out.println("No Error");
        }
}
```

The above code will yield an error of Type mismatch. However, this code will run perfectly fine for C/C++.

*The reason is that the statement **if(b) is equivalent to if b is true**.Since b is a byte variable and cannot be initialized a boolean value: true, the compiler gives us an error of **type mismatch: cannot convert from byte to boolean.** Therefore, in java, we have to explicitly write the below statement to get it executed:*

if(b==5)

4.1.2 Switch Statement

A *switch* statement is much like an *if-else* statement in the sense that it is also a selection statement and selects a particular path of execution based upon certain criteria. The difference being here is that an *if-else* statement has only two possible paths of execution. It either goes into an *if* or into an *else*. But the *switch* statement can have multiple paths of execution. Also, an *if-else* construct always evaluates an expression to a boolean value but a switch statement may evaluate an expression to some of the primitive types or class types and match their value with its cases.

A *switch* can well work with *byte*, *char*, *short*, and *int* primitive types along with its wrapper classes. Wrapper classes will be discussed in the upcoming chapters. It can also work with Strings.

Syntax:

```
switch(Expression)
{
 case value1:  statement 1;
 case value2:  statement 2;
 .
 .
 .
 .
 .
 case valuen: statement n;
 default: default statement;
}
```

The *switch* statement accepts an *expression*. This expression value can be one of the primitive/class types discussed above. The *switch* statement can encompass a number of cases with specific values, for example, *value1*, *value2 ....valuen*. The *value* in the switch is compared with the values of different cases falling under the switch. If a match is found, then the statements under the specific case are executed. If not, a default case is executed. If the default is not present inside a switch, then no statements are executed. Example, if the *value* in the switch matches with say *value1* then *statement1* is executed. If it matches with *value2* then *statement 2* is executed and so on. If it does not match with any of the cases then the *default statement* is executed. Figure 4.3 diagrammatically illustrates the concept.

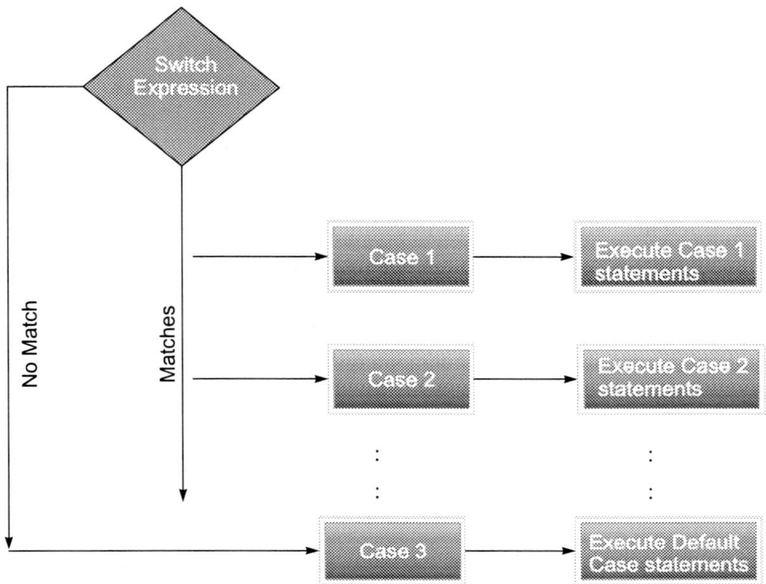

Fig. 4.3 Switch statement

The program below explains the switch statement:

```
public class SwitchDemo {

    public static void main(String[] args) {
            char a = 'A';
            switch (a) {
            case 'A':
                    System.out.println("A");
            case 'C':
                    System.out.println("C");
            case 'D':
                    System.out.println("D");
            default:
                    System.out.println("default");

            }
    }
}

Output:
A
C
D
default
```

In the above program, the *switch* statement accepts a char variable and matches its value with its cases. Since the value of the char variable matches with its first case, ideally our output should have been *A*. But oops! What do we see here? Our output is *A, C, D, default*. That means, despite the value of the char variable not matching with the other cases, our output *falls through* the other cases as well. This happens because the *switch* statements are executed in a sequential manner just like the other programming statements. This is the reason why the flow of execution does not stop even after matching the first case and prints the other cases as well. To alter the flow of execution, we need something which can take us out of the switch cases as soon as we match with our specific case. To our saviour, now comes a *break statement* discussed in the next section.

4.1.2.1 Using break with Switch

A break statement is also called a *jump statement* since it can alter the flow of execution and jump to a new set of statements. A break when used in a switch statement bypasses all the other cases and jumps out of a *switch*. The program below alters the above program with a break statement.

```
public class SwitchBreakDemo {

    public static void main(String[] args) {
            char a = 'A';
            switch (a) {
            case 'A':
                    System.out.println("A");
                    break;
            case 'C':
                    System.out.println("C");
                    break;
            case 'D':
                    System.out.println("D");
                    break;
            default:
                    System.out.println("default");

            }
            System.out.println("outside switch");
    }
}
```

Output:

```
A
outside switch
```

Using a break inside a *switch* now helps us achieve our desired output. As soon as our matching case is found, the statements under it are executed. And the break statement helps us bypass all the other cases bringing us out of the *switch* block to the statement "*outside switch*".

4.1.2.2 *Multiple case labels in a switch*

We can have multiple case labels in a switch statement. This type of switch case labels are required when we want to perform the same task for a set of cases. The following example illuminates the concept:

```
public class MultipleCaseLabelDemo {
    public static void main(String[] argv) {
            char a = 'B';
            switch (a) {
            case 'B':
            case 'b':
                    System.out.println("Letter B");
                    break;
            case 'C':
            case 'c':
                    System.out.println("Letter C");
                    break;
            default:
                    System.out.println("Default case:No letter matched!");
            }

    }
}
```

Output:

```
Letter B
```

4.1.2.3 *if-else vs switch*

Table 4.1

	If-else	Switch
Flow of execution	Can have only two possible paths of execution.	Can have multiple paths of execution.
Type of outcome	Always evaluate an expression to a boolean value.	Can evaluate an expression to a byte, short, char, int primitive type values.
Readability	Less readable in case of multiple if-else.	More readable in case of multiple cases.
Efficiency	Less efficient in case of multiple if-else since it checks for every if/else and evaluates the corresponding statements.	More efficient because once a valid match is found the other cases are bypassed if handled carefully with a break statement.

4.2 ITERATION STATEMENTS

Now, imagine a scenario wherein you want to execute a statement repeatedly. Say, you want to print all even numbers ranging between 1-10. Then, in this range you will be required to check again and again, the numbers divisible by two and then print those numbers only. And this is going to take hell lot of your time and effort! To save us from this turmoil, we have a set of *iteration statements.* The iteration statements are the ones which help us perform a task repeatedly so that we don't have to write the code explicitly again and again. This is why they are also called as *loops* since they work in a loop to complete a task.

Discussed below are the iteration statements available in java:

4.2.1 For Statement

A *for* statement is used to iterate over a collection of values. These values can be of different types. The basic syntax for a *for loop* is as follows:

for(initialization; termination condition; increment/decrement)

{

Set of statements to be executed repeatedly

}

- The initialization in a *for loop* is done to start the loop with an initial value. It serves as an entry point value for the loop.
- The termination condition acts as the exiting condition for the loop. The condition always evaluates to a boolean value. So, the loop runs till the time this condition is true. The flow exits from the loop as soon as the condition turns false.
- The increment/decrement operation is applied to progressively execute the loop so that it can proceed onto its next iteration.
- The beginning and ending curly braces indicates the statements that will be executed as a part of the *for loop.*
- A *for loop* without a curly brace simply means that there is only one statement under the loop which happens to be the immediate next statement.
- The three conditions of the *for loop* are optional.

The below program below prints all the even numbers in the range of 1-10.

```
public class ForLoopDemo {

    public static void main(String[] args) {
          for (int i = 1; i<= 10; i++) {
                if (i % 2 == 0) {
                      System.out.println(i);
```

```
                }
            }
            System.out.println("Loop Ended");

        }

}
```

Output:

```
2
4
6
8
10
Loop Ended
```

The loop above is initialized with a value 1. It executes ten times checking every time if the value of *i* is divisible by 2 or not; if it is, it displays the number else it does not do anything. Finally, it prints the statement *Loop Ended* on exiting the *for loop*.

Dry Run for the above *for loop*

Ist iteration

i=1

The value of i=1 and is less than equal to 10, so we enter into the loop executing the *if* statement. Since, 1 mod 2 is not equal to 0, 1 is not printed.

2nd iteration

i=2

The value of i is now incremented to 2 and is still less than equal to 10. Therefore, we check again if 2 mod 2 is equal to 0 and yes, it is, this time. So, 2 is printed as a result on the console.

3rd iteration

i=3

The value of i now becomes 3 which is less than equal to 10 and 3 mod 2 is not equal to 0 therefore, 3 is not printed.

.....

11th iteration

i=11

The value of i is now 11 which violates our terminating condition: i<=10. So, the flow of control now comes out of the *for loop* and jumps to the statement "*Loop Ended*".

4.2.1.1 Using semicolon with for loop

Using a semicolon with a *for loop* can have varied interpretations when used at different places.

- *Semicolon inside the for statement*: There can be times when you want to run your *for loop* infinitely. In such a condition, follow the below version of the *for loop.*

  ```
  for(; ;)
  {
          Statements to be executed infinitely
  }
  ```

  Such a *for loop* is without any of the three expressions defined above. And the statements coming under it are executed infinitely. So, are you wondering, will we get stuck up in this loop forever and never come out! No, that's not the case. We can use one of the jump statements; like *break* to come out of loop. Jump statements are discussed in the next section.

  ```
  for(; ;)
  {
          if(condition is true)
                  break;
  }
  ```

- *Semicolon after the **for** statement:*

  ```
  for(; ;);
  {
  Statements that will be executed only once rather than getting executed infinitely
  }
  ```

  Using a semicolon immediately after the *for* statement means terminating the loop indicating that the loop has no definition. As a result, no statements are iterated. And the statements inside the curly braces are treated as just a set of statements inside a block which will be executed once.

4.2.1.2 For each loop

The *for loop* has an alternative form of syntax wherein we call it a *for each loop.* This loop is generally used to iterate over a group of elements like arrays. Use this loop when you want to traverse each element of the array. The syntax for the loop is as given below:

for(int i : array_name)

{

statements to be iterated

}

The variable *i* is used to iterate over the array named *array_name*. The subsequent example can be used to describe a *for each loop*.

```
public class ForEachDemo {

    public static void main(String[] args) {
          int[] digits = { 2, 3, 4, 6, 7, 8, 9 };
          for (int i : digits) {
                System.out.println(i);
          }
    }

}
```

Output:

```
2
3
4
6
7
8
9
```

Here, the variable *i* is used to iterate over the array named *digits*. It prints as a result all the elements in the array.

4.2.2 While Statement

The *while loop* is another iteration statement which can be used to iterate over different types. The syntax for the loop is as follows:

while(condition)

{

Execute a set of statements

}

The while loop accepts a condition and evaluates it to a *boolean* value. If the value is true, only then, the statements under the loop are executed else the control jumps out of the loop. This loop is also called the *entry control loop* since you cannot enter into the loop until the condition evaluated by the loop is true. The next program will help you get a glimpse of the *while loop.*

//Program to print even numbers ranging from 1-10 using a while loop

```
public class WhileLoopDemo {

    public static void main(String[] args) {
            int i = 1; // initialization of the loop
            while (i<= 10) { // condition for entry into the loop
                    if (i % 2 == 0) {
                            System.out.println(i);

                    }
                    i++; // increment of the loop
            }
    }
}
```

Output:

```
2
4
6
8
10
```

The above loop is initialized with an initial value of 1 and prints even numbers ranging from 1-10.

Dry run for the above while loop

Ist iteration

i=1

In the first iteration, the condition: *i<=10*, is checked. Since, the value of *i=1*, the condition evaluates to true and so we enter into the loop. The code under the loop then checks using the *if statement,* if the value of *i* is divisible by 2. If it is, the loop prints the value of *i* on the console. If not, it does not do anything. In this iteration, it just increments the value of *i* by 1 making *i=2* since the value of *i* is not divisible by 2.

IInd iteration

i=2

The value of *i* now turns 2. The condition of the *while loop* again evaluates to true. And this time, the condition for the *if statement* also turns true which prints the value of *i*. The next statement increments the value of *i* to 3.

...

....

...

11th iteration

```
public class LoopScopeDemo {

    public static void main(String[] args) {
          for (int i = 1; i<= 4; i++)           (2)
                System.out.println(i);
          i = i + 4;   //error! i cannot be resolved to a variable

    }
}
```

The above code will produce an error stating " i cannot be resolved to a variable".

Can you think of why did this happen in spite of declaring the variable i at line 2.

To think about its solution, you need to rush back to ***chapter 2*** *where you learnt about the scope of variables. The scope of a variable only exists within the block in which it is declared. The variable i is declared within the for loop here, so using it outside the loop will prompt an error.*

i=11

The value of *i=11* now. The condition: *i<=10*; evaluates to false this time, controlling the entry into the *while loop*; thereby terminating the loop.

4.2.2.1 Infinite while loop

An infinite *while loop* can be implemented by using the following code:

while(true)

{

Statements to be executed infinitely

}

Just as we discussed for the *for loops*, jump statements can be used to come out of an infinitely running loop.

4.2.2.2 Using a semicolon with a while loop

Using a semicolon with a *while loop* indicates that the loop does not have any definition.

The following code does not print anything.

```
public class WhileLoopDemo {

    public static void main(String[] args) {
        int i = 1;
        while (i< 10);
        {
            System.out.println(i);
            i++;
        }
    }
}
```

You might be wondering that where are we going wrong here? The value of *i* is definitely less than 10 since it is equal to 1. But then also, our *while loop* is not executing its statements. The reason behind is that we have done a *small* but *deadening* mistake here of putting a *semicolon* after the *while loop*. As we have already discussed in case of *for loops*, a semicolon implies termination of a statement and here, it means termination of the *while loop*. This further infers that the *while loop* does not have any definition. Therefore, the next set of statements is treated as just another set of statements inside a block.

But, then why did this block of statements not execute then? The above *while loop* can be interpreted as: if the value of the variable *i* is less than 10, *do nothing*. Now, the problem is the value of i=1, which will always be less than 10 and we will be stuck in an *infinite loop*!

Figure 4.4 displays the general flow of *for* and *while loops*.

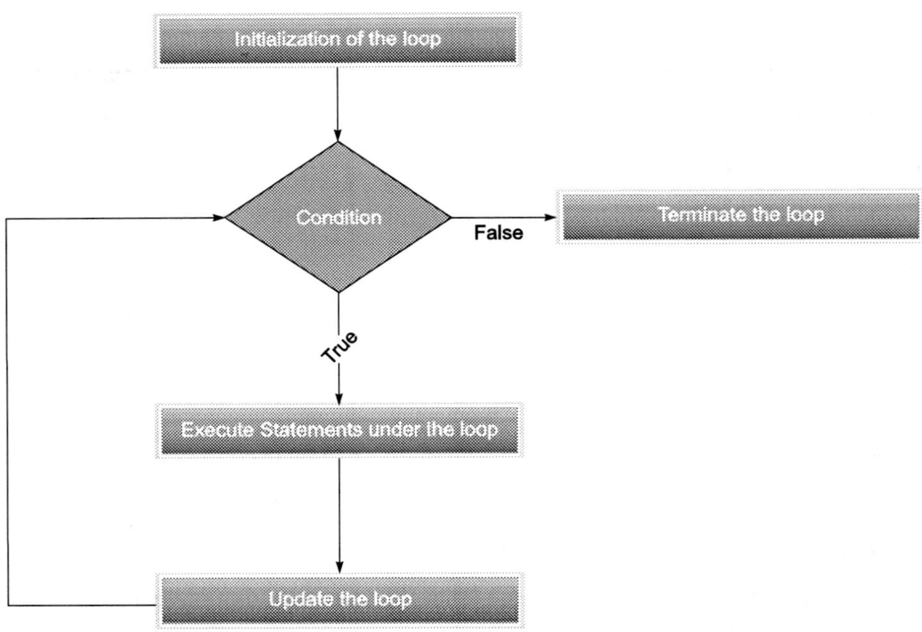

Fig. 4.4

4.2.3 Do-while Statement

A *do-while* statement is much similar to a *while loop* statement. The basic syntax for a *do-while* loop is as given below:

do

{

Statements to be iterated

}

while(condition);

The condition for a *do-while* loop always evaluates to a boolean value and is checked in the end of the loop. This means, that the statements under the loop will be executed at least once even if the condition evaluates to false. Hence, the reason why we call a *do-while loop* an *exit controlled loop.*

One of the major differences between a *while* and a *do-while loop* is that a *while loop* does not run if the condition evaluates to false whereas a *do-while loop* executes at least once even if the condition evaluated is false.

Figure 4.5 illustrates the flow of *do-while loop*.

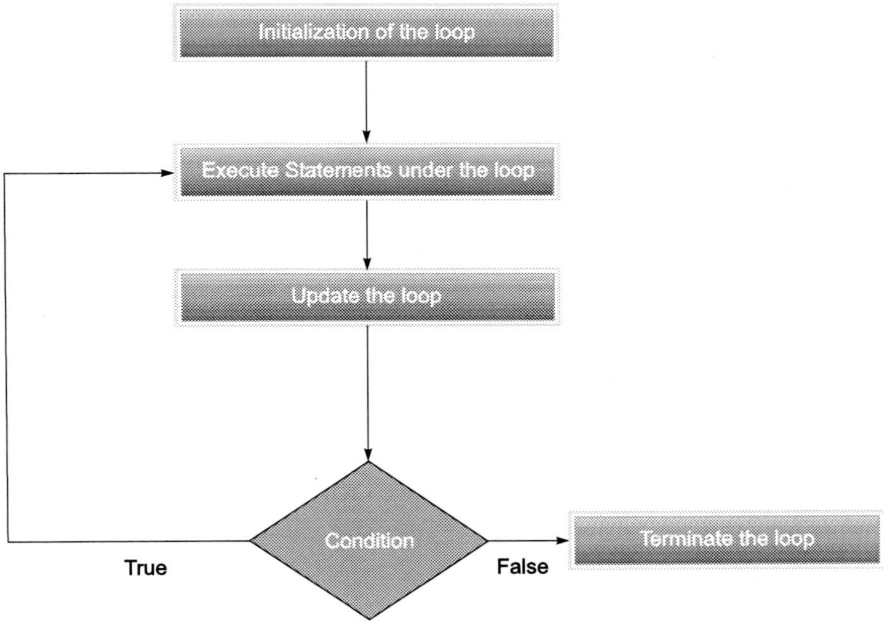

Fig. 4.5

//Implementing the above program using a do-while loop

```
public class DoWhileDemo {

    public static void main(String[] args) {
        int i = 1; // initialization of the loop
        do {
            if (i % 2 == 0)
                System.out.println(i);
            i++; // increment of the loop
        } while (i<= 10); // condition of the loop
    }
}
```

Output:

```
2
4
6
8
10
```

The above program implements a *do-while loop* to print even numbers in the range of 1-10.

//Another program using a do-while loop

```
public class DoWhileDemo {

    public static void main(String[] args) {
        int i = 11;
        do {
            System.out.println(i);
        } while (i % 2 == 0);
    }
}
```

Output:

```
11
```

The above code prints the value of variable *i* even when its value is not divisible by 2. Had it been a *while loop* instead, this code would never have executed.

4.2.3.1 *Infinite do-while loop*

An infinite *do-while loop* can be implemented in a similar fashion to a *while loop.*

do

{

Statements to be iterated infinitely

}

while(true);

4.2.4 Nested Loops

A nested loop refers to a loop inside a loop. All the above loops can be implemented as nested loops.

- *Nested for loop*

  A nested *for loop* encompasses another *for loop* inside it.

  Working of a nested for loop

  A nested *for loop* contains an *outer* loop and an *inner* loop. The outer loop is responsible for initializing the inner loop again and again till the time its condition for execution is met. In other words, for each iteration of the outer loop, all the iterations for an inner loop are executed.

//Program implementing a nested for loop

```
public class NestedForDemo {

    public static void main(String[] args) {
        for (int i = 0; i< 3; i++) {    //outer loop
            for (int j = 0; j< 2; j++)      //inner loop
                System.out.print(i + "\t");
            System.out.println();

        }

    }
}
```

The above program uses two *for loops* to print elements in a matrix form. The outer loop of *i* runs thrice from 0 to 2. The inner loop of *j* being a part of the outer loop is executed twice from 0 to 1 in each of the iterations. Therefore, the *outer loop* runs for a totality of *three* times whereas the *inner loop* runs for *six* times. Each of the time when the outer loop executes, it reinitializes the inner loop twice printing the element with a tab. At the end of every iteration of the outer loop, it also prints a new line on the console.

Dry run for the program

Ist iteration for the outer loop

i=0

j=0, j=1

The outer loop initializes *i=0*; checks the condition *i<3* which comes out to be true. It then enters into the inner loop. The inner loop further initializes *j=0*; checks the condition: *j<2* which is again true and starts executing the inner loop. It then prints the value of *i* with a tab. The inner loop is now incremented, and the value of *j* turns out to be 1 this time. Satisfying the loop condition, it prints the value of *i* with a tab. Next, the inner loop increments *j* to 2 which no more fulfils our condition for the loop as *j*<2, therefore, we exit out of the inner loop of *j*. Exiting the inner loop, the next statement inside the outer loop prints a new line on the console using the *println* function.

Current Status of the output

0 0

IInd iteration

i=1

j=0, j=1

Remember, we have just exited out of the loop of *j*, our outer loop of *i* is still running. So, the value of *i*=1 in this iteration. The value still satisfies the condition; *i*<3, so we move to our inner loop of *j* once again. The inner loop reinitializes *j* to 0 and 1 as discussed above and follows the above procedure. Consequently, printing the value of *i* twice with a tab followed by a newline.

Current Status of the output

0 0
1 1

....

....

....

IVth iteration

i=3

j not initialized

The value of *i*=3 here which does not satisfy the condition for execution of the loop. Therefore, we do not enter into any of the loops inside as the outer loop contains the inner loop.

Final Status of the output

0 0
1 1
2 2

Nested *while* and *do-while* loops can be implemented in a similar fashion.

4.3 JUMP STATEMENTS

In the above sections, we have seen that the normal flow of execution for programming statements is sequential. And to alter the flow of execution, several statements like *Selection Statements*, *Iteration Statements* are available in java. Another such set of statements is called *Jump Statements* or *Branching Statements*. These statements help us amend the flow of execution by jumping to another piece of code in your program. *break*, *continue* and *return statements* fall under the category of jump statements.

4.3.1 Break Statement

The *break* statement in java can be used in three ways:

- *In a switch case:* The above sections clearly demonstrate how a *break statement* can be used to come out of a *switch* case when a matching case has been found.
- *Exiting a loop:* A break statement can also be used to exit a loop, specially an infinite loop. The following code will explain how to use a *break* to exit a loop.

```
public class UnlabelledBreakDemo {

    public static void main(String[] args) {
        int i = 5;
        for (;;) {
            if (i == 5)
                break;

        }
        System.out.println(i);                    (1)
    }
}

Output:
5
```

The *for loop* above indicates that it is an infinite loop. But this loop does not run infinitely because of the inclusion of the *break* jump statement in it. The loop checks for the value of variable *i* here. Since *i* is equal to 5 we break out of the loop and directly come to the statement (1).

The above *break* statement used with switch and loops is also called the *unlabelled break.*

- *As a form of goto*

  Goto was used in traditional programming languages like C. This programming construct was used to transfer control from one part of program to another. The syntax of *goto* is given below:

  goto label;

The above statement branches control to a block of statements named *label*. Statements falling under *opening curly brace* and *ending curly brace* are said to be inside a *block*. And a block that has a name attached to it is called a *label*. Java does not use *goto* statement as it generates a lot of unmaintainable codes.

Instead, it uses *break* statement as a form of *goto*. Mentioned below is the syntax for the break statement:

break label;

Here, the *break* statement is used to break out of the label named *label*. Since, label is nothing but a named block of statements, so using *break* with a label will help us come out of that block of statements. This kind of *break* statement is also called a *labelled break* as it is used with a label.

//Program using break as a form of goto

```
public class LabelledBreakDemo {

    public static void main(String[] args) {
            label1: {
                    label2: {
                            label3: {
                                    for (int i = 0; i< 100; i++) {
                                            System.out.println("In label3");
                                            if (i == 3)
                                                    break label3;

                                    }

                            }
                            System.out.println("In label2");

                    }
                    System.out.println("In label1");
            }
    }
    }
```

Output:

```
In label3
In label3
In label3
In label3
In label2
In label1
```

The above code uses three labels: *label1, label2, label3; label1* being the outermost label. The innermost label *label3*, consists of a *for loop*, which should run for 100 times. But, as we are using a *break* statement, this loop runs only for *four* times printing *label3* every time. The loop breaks out from the *label3*, as soon as the value of *i* becomes 3. Consequently, the *break* statement jumps out of the *label3* block and prints the statements outside it.

//break used in nested loops

```
public class LabelledBreakDemo {

     public static void main(String[] args) {
          int a = 5;
          label1: {
               for (int i = 0; i< 100; i++) { // outer loop
                    System.out.println("In the loop of i");
                    for (int j = 0; j< 200; j++) { // inner loop
                         System.out.println("In the loop of j");
                         if (a == 5)
                              break label1;
                    }
               }
          }
          System.out.println("Break out from the label");
     }
}
```

Output:

```
In the loop of i
In the loop of j
Break out from the label
```

The program above makes use of nested loops inside a block labelled *label1*. The *outer* loop is supposed to execute for *100 times* whereas the *inner* loop should run for *200 times*. But both the loops run only *once*. Why? In the first iteration of *i,* the statement *"In the loop of i"* is printed on the console. Then, the inner loop of *j* is executed to print the statement *"In the loop of j"*. The loop then checks if the value of variable *a* is equal to 5. Since the condition is true, we break out from the label *label1* and jump onto the statement *"Break out from the loop"*.

4.3.2 Continue Statement

The *continue* statement in java also serves as a *jump statement*. **It can be used only with loops**. Unlike *break*, it does not come out from a block, instead it forces the next iteration of the loop bypassing all the statements that fall after it. The *continue* statement when used without a *label* is called an *unlabelled continue* whereas when used with a *label* is also called the *labelled continue.*

Let us have a look at the below program to get the concept more vividly.

```
public class UnlabelledContinueDemo {

    public static void main(String[] args) {
            for (int i = 0; i< 10; i++) {
                    if (i< 5)
                            continue;
                    System.out.println("Not executed every time");
            }
    }
    }
```

Output:

```
Not executed every time
Not executed every time
Not executedevery time
Not executed every time
Not executed every time
```

Observe the output carefully. The above loop runs for *ten* times but prints the statement *"Not executed every time"* only *five* times. This is because we are using the *continue* statement inside our loop. The loop checks in each iteration if the value of variable *i* is less than *five*, if it is, it forces the next iteration of the loop bypassing any of the statements after it. Only when the *if* condition becomes false, the statement gets printed on the console.

//Modifying the above program to show the use of labelled continue

```
public class LabelledContinueDemo {

    public static void main(String[] args) {
            label1: for (int i = 0; i< 10; i++) {
                    if (i< 5)
                            continue label1;
                    System.out.println("labelled continue");
            }
    }
}
```

Output:

```
labelled continue
labelled continue
labelled continue
labelled continue
labelled continue
```

4.3.3 Return Statement

The last jump statement that we will be covering under this section is the *return* statement. It can be used inside methods only. Any code written after a return statement might be treated as an *unreachable code* by the compiler. A return statement, terminates the execution of the current method and passes the control to the calling method. It can exist in two forms:

- *Return with a value*: This type of return statement returns a value to the calling method. The value can be either a primitive type or a reference type.

  Syntax:

  return value;

  Such type of return statements will be talked about at length in the chapter *classes and objects.*

- *Return without a value:* This type of return statement simply transfers the control back to the calling method without sending any value.

  Syntax:

  return;

  //program illustrating return without a value

```
public class ReturnDemo {

        public static void main(String[] args) {
                int age = 12;
                System.out.println("Using return");
                if (age< 18)
                        return; // terminates the method
                System.out.println("Will not execute");
        }
}
```

Output:

```
Using return
```

The above code after printing the statement "Using return", terminates the main method and transfers the control to its calling method (as the value of age is less than 18) which is the *java run time system* in this case. As a result, the last statement is not executed.

SUMMARY

- A control statement is a statement which lets you alter the flow of execution rather than following a sequential execution.

- A control statement can amend the execution flow by using decision statements, iteration statements and branching statements.
- Decision statements use if, if-else and switch statements to employ a decision based upon certain condition.
- An *else statement* always follows immediately after an *if statement*.
- Iteration statements are the statements used to perform a task repeatedly. Java uses *for*, *while*, and *do-while* loops to implement iteration.
- The *for loop* executes with an initial value and keeps incrementing or decrementing that value till the termination condition is met.
- The *while loop* evaluates a condition expression to a boolean value. If it comes out to be true, the loop is executed else not.
- The *do-while loop* executes the statements inside the loop first and then checks for the condition expression if it is true. Therefore, it executes at least once, even if the condition evaluated is false.
- A semicolon present at the end of any loop denotes termination of the loop.
- Jump statements are also called *branching statements* as they are used to branch from one piece of code to other.
- The jump statements available in java are: break, continue and return.
- The break statement is used to break out from a block. It can work with loops, switch and as a form of goto.
- The continue statement skips the current iteration of a loop bypassing all the statements that occur after it and forces the next iteration of the loop.
- The return statement is used to terminate the current method and return the flow of execution to the calling method.

```
public class UnreachableCodeDemo {

    public static void main(String[] args) {
          int age = 12;
          System.out.println("Using return");
          return; // terminates the method
          System.out.println("Will not execute"); // unreachable code
    }
}
```

The use of return statement in the code above terminates the execution of the program in all cases thereby making the last statement unreachable. Hence, the error: unreachable code. However, in the previous example, as the execution of the return statement was conditional, the last statement was not treated as unreachable code.

COMMON ERRORS

- One of the most common errors is to put a semicolon after an *if-else statement.* As discussed above, a semicolon tends to terminate the *if statement* thereby producing a *Misplaced Else error.*
- The if condition always evaluates to a boolean value. Therefore, *if(b)* would result into a *Type Mismatch* error if b is not a boolean value.
- Absence of the *break* statement in a *switch* case will result in execution of all cases.
- Presence of a semicolon at the end of a loop simply means iterating the loop and not doing anything.
- Writing statements after the return statement may lead to the *unreachable code* problem.

SELF-TEST

1. Discuss the selection statements available in java.
2. State the differences between if-else statement and switch statement.
3. What are iteration statements? Describe each of them with examples.
4. Which of the loops execute at least once even if the condition evaluated is false? Also explain why.
5. List and discuss the branching statements in java.
6. Differentiate between labelled and unlabelled continue.

PRACTICAL QUESTIONS

1. State the output for the following:

a)
```
class SelfTest {
public static void main(String[] args)
    {
int a=5;
if (a != 5);
            System.out.println("Inside If Condition");
else if (a==5)
        {
            System.out.println("Inside Else If Condition");
        }
else
            System.out.println("Inside Else Condition");
    }
}
```

b)
```
public class SelfTest {

    public static void main(String[] args) {
        int var = 6;
        switch (var) {
        case 2:
                System.out.println("2");
        default:
                System.out.println("default");
        case -1:
                System.out.println("-1");
        case 10:
                System.out.println("10");

        }
    }
}
```

c)
```
public class SelfTest {
public static void main(String[] argv) {
for (int i = 0; i< 2; i++) {
for (int j = 0; j< 4; j++) {
if (i == j) {
continue;
                }
                System.out.println("i = " + i + " j = " + j);
            }
        }

    }
}
```

d)
```
public class SelfTest {
public static void main(String[] argv) {
        int i=20;
        while(i>10)
        {
                System.out.println("i=" + i);
        }
    }
}
```

e)
```
public class SelfTest {
public static void main(String[] argv) {
    int a[] = { 23, 21, 33, 45 };
    int element = 33, flag = 0, i;
    for (i = 0; i<a.length; i++) {
            if (element == a[i]) {
```

```
                        flag = 1;
                        break;
                } else
                        flag = 0;

        }
        if (flag == 1) {
                System.out.println("The element " + element
                                + " is present at location " + i);
        } else
                System.out.println("Search Unsuccessful!");
    }
}
```

2. Which of the following is not a nested loop?

```
a)  for (int i = 0; i< 3; i++)
    for (int j = 0; j< 5; j++)

b)  for (int i = 0; i< 3; i++)
    System.out.println("Statement 1");
    for (int j = 0; j< 5; j++)
    System.out.println("Statement 2");

c)  int i = 1;
    while (i< 10) {
    for (int j = 0; j< 2; j++)
    System.out.println(j);

    }
```

3. Write the equivalent while and do-while loop for the following:

```
a)  for (int i = 20; i> 10; i--) {
                System.out.println("i=" + i);
                }
```

5
CHAPTER

Fundamentals of Classes and Objects

This chapter will enable you to learn the following:

- Modelling classes and objects.
- Understanding constructors and methods.
- Learning passing of arguments to a method/constructor.
- Using *this* keyword in our examples.
- Defining garbage collection using the *finalize()* method.

Till now, we have been talking about and working strictly inside classes as java being a pure object oriented language, but we have not yet seen how our program will behave when we have multiple classes and how would they be interacting with each other. So before coming to answer all these questions, let us first define classes and objects.

5.1 CLASS

A class is a *blueprint* or a *template* available through which we can build objects. An object is said to be an *instance* of a class.

The syntax for writing a class is discussed below:

```
class class_name
{
        instance variables
        methods
}
```

A class has a *name* and is created by using the keyword *class* preceding it. It encompasses *instance variables* and a set of *methods*. The instance variables are the variables defined directly inside a class. And the methods are used to manipulate or change the value of these instance variables.

An object is characterized by its state[1] and behaviour. The state of an object is represented by the value of instance variables whereas the behaviour is depicted by the methods of that class. Think about your daily routine and you will be able to spot a lot of objects. Examples can be air conditioner, animals, chair, etc. The air conditioner can have properties like its current temperature, make, model, year of manufacture which can serve as its instance variables. Its behaviour can be depicted by methods like increase temperature, decrease temperature, power toggle and auto-swing. On the other hand, the state of the animals can be defined by its breed and colour whereas its behaviour can be eating and sleeping.

Therefore, the instance variables inside a class are generally used to show the properties its object will exhibit. And the methods depict what task its object is capable of performing. As, there can be several instances/objects of a class that can be made, each object will have its own copy of the instance variables. Let us now have a closer look at how to write a class with some instance variable inside it.

```
public class Rectangle {
     double length;
     double breadth;
}
```

The class *Rectangle* contains the instance variables *length* and *breadth*. Currently, the class has not been instantiated. A class is instantiated when we declare its objects. Always remember, that the class just represents a template, *no memory is allocated to the instance variables till the time we instantiate a class or declare objects of a class.*

5.2 DECLARING OBJECTS

As we saw in the previous section, a class in itself does not serve the complete purpose. One needs to instantiate a class or declare objects of the class in order to use its instance variables. An object for the class *Rectangle* can be created in the following manner:

Rectangle myrec=new Rectangle();

The above statement performs an assignment operation so the evaluation of the expression takes from right to left. The new operator used here, is responsible for allocating memory for the *Rectangle* type. Allocating memory for the *Rectangle* type simply means allotting memory to the instance variables of the class *Rectangle*. The left hand side of the expression creates a reference *myrec* of *Rectangle* type which refers to the memory allocated above. The parenthesis in the end of the statement determines the type of the constructor that is invoked. Constructors will be explained in the later sections of the book. Figure 5.1 clearly explains the concept.

[1] The object state is also called its attributes or properties. The words may be used interchangeably throughout the book.

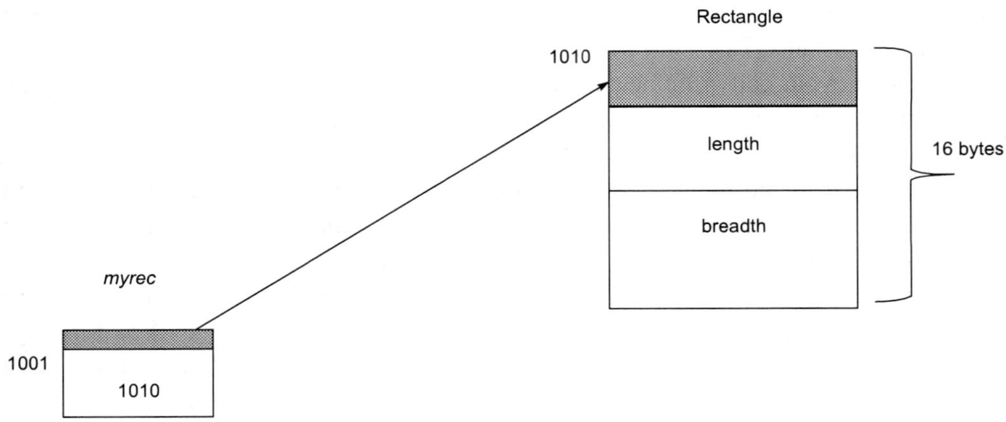

Fig. 5.1 Memory picture for a class and object

Let us hypothetically assume that the new operator allocates memory to our instance variables at the memory address 1010. As each of the instance variables are of type double, a total of 16 bytes of memory is allocated. This memory is referred by a reference named *myrec* of type *Rectangle*. Note that the *type of reference should match or be compatible with the type of memory it refers to*. Since the reference variables are variables that hold the memory address of some other location; therefore in our case, it holds the address 1010. Now, using *myrec*, we can access *length* and *breadth* instance variables with a dot operator as *myrec* now becomes an instance or object of the class *Rectangle*.

The following program instantiates the above class.

```
public class Rectangle {
    double length;
    double breadth;
}

public class RectangleDemo {
    public static void main(String[] argv) {
        Rectangle myrec = new Rectangle();
        myrec.length = 20;
        myrec.breadth = 10;
        double area;
        area = myrec.length * myrec.breadth;
        System.out.println("The area of the rectangle is:" + area);
    }
}
```

Output:

```
The area of the rectangle is:200.0
```

This is what happens in memory after the execution of the above statements.

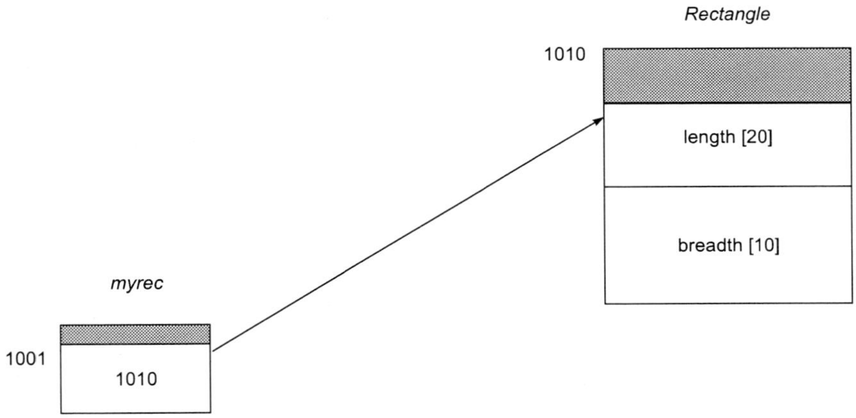

Fig. 5.2

5.2.1 References and Objects

Most of you, by now must be having this confusion as to what is an object and what is a reference.

So, let us consider the two statements below and their effects in memory.

Statement 1:

Rectangle myrec;

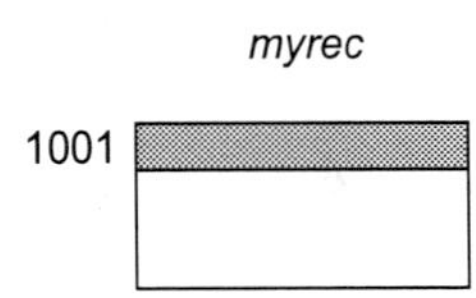

Fig. 5.3 Modelling a reference

Right now, *myrec* is a reference of type *Rectangle*. Though it has its own address in memory (1001), it does not refer to any memory location currently i.e., it does not hold any memory address. Any attempt to execute the following statements at this point of time will result in a compile time error: *"The local variable myrec might not have been initialized"*.

myrec.length=20;

myrec.breadth=10;

Presently, *myrec* does not refer to the memory location containing *length* and *breadth* instance variables. Therefore, any such attempt to access the instance variables of class Rectangle will yield an error.

Statement 2:

Rectangle myrec=new Rectangle();

Or

Rectangle myrec;

myrec=new Rectangle();

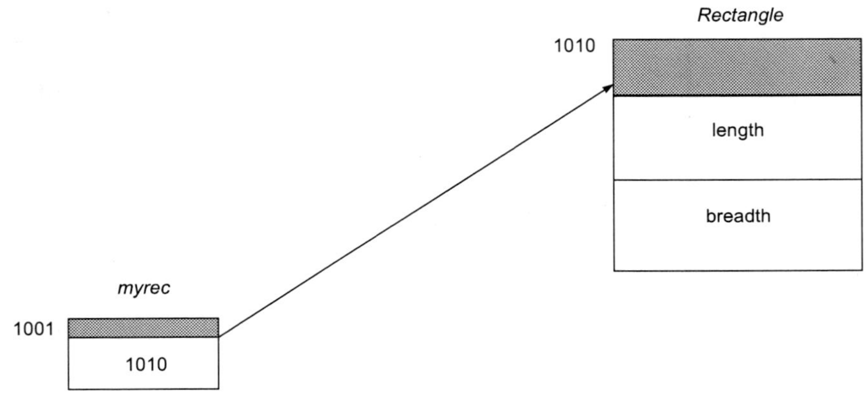

Fig. 5.4 Modelling an object

The reference *myrec* now starts pointing or referring to the memory location of type *Rectangle* allocated by the new operator. *myrec* now becomes an instance or an object of type Rectangle and is capable of accessing *length* and *breadth* instance variables.

5.3 USING METHODS

In the previous section, we have seen what instance variables are and how they are allocated memory. The next element, a class, has, is its *methods*. A method in a class is used to define the behaviour of its object. In other words, it describes what operations its objects are capable of performing. The syntax for defining a method is as follows:

return_Type methodName(parameter_List)

{

definition/implementation/body of the method

}

The *return_Type* of a method specifies the type of value that is returned from a method. The return type can be any primitive type or a reference type. If a method does not return any value, its return type is marked as *void.* The *method_Name* specifies the name of the method and the *parameter_List* is the list of arguments or parameters that the method receives. These parameters serve as input parameters for a method. Lastly, the *definition* of the method defines what operations it will perform. The next example will demonstrate how a method works in a class.

```
class Rectangle {
    double length;
    double breadth;

    void calculateArea() {    //method definition
        double area = length * breadth;
        System.out.println("The area of the reactangle is" + area);
    }
}
```

```
class RectangeDemo {
    public static void main(String[] argv) {
          Rectangle myrec = new Rectangle();    //First object of type
          //Rectangle
          Rectangle myrec1 = new Rectangle();//Second object of type
          //Rectangle
          myrec.length = 20;
          myrec.breadth = 10;
          myrec1.length = 30;
          myrec1.breadth = 20;
          myrec.calculateArea();  //invokes calculateArea() with myrec
          myrec1.calculateArea(); //invokes calculateArea() with myrec1

    }
}
```

Output:

```
The area of the rectangle is 200.0
The area of the rectangle is 600.0
```

The above code uses a method named `calculateArea`*()* to calculate the area of the rectangle using instance variables—length and breadth. The return type of the method here is *void* as it does not return any value to its calling method. And it does not accept any parameters. As soon as the *calculateArea*() method is called, the flow of control jumps to the definition of the method and returns back to its calling method(main, in our case) when the definition ends. Notice carefully, we have two objects working here; *myrec* and *myrec1*. The two objects access instance variables as well as the method `calculateArea`*()* with a dot operator. The memory picture for the two objects looks something like this:

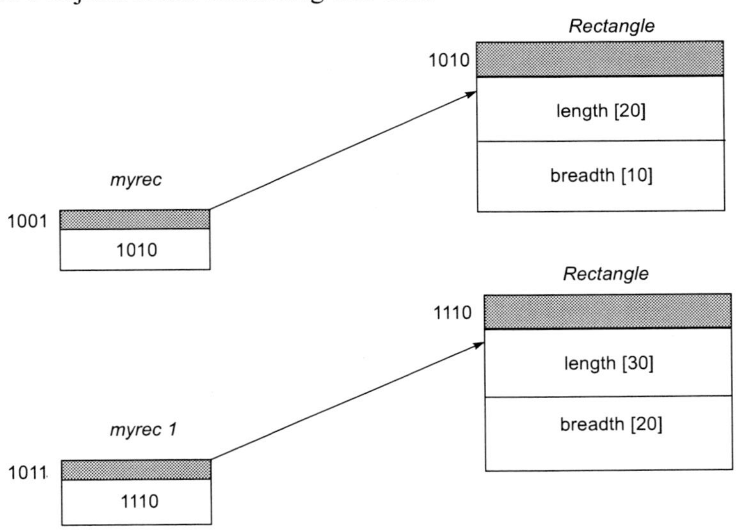

Fig. 5.5

As discussed earlier, the new operator allocates memory. Since, the new operator is used twice here, we have two memory allocations being done, both of the type *Rectangle*. One of the memory location is referred by the reference *myrec* whereas the other one by *myrec1*. Both the objects have different values for the instance variables—length and breadth. This is the reason why the statements *myrec.calculateArea()* and *myrec1.calculateArea()* yield different results for the area of rectangle.

Note: The instance variables and methods are associated with an object. Each object will have a separate copy of the instance variables. Also, memory allocation is done only for instance variables and not for methods.

5.3.1 Returning Values from a Method

Till now, we have seen methods that did not return any value. But, sometimes, the calling method may require the results processed by the called method for further computation. In such a case, the return types would not be void. The next example modifies the above method *calculateArea*() to showcase the returning values from a method.

```
class Rectangle {
     double length;
     double breadth;

     double calculateArea() {
            return length * breadth;
     }
}

class RectangleDemo {
     public static void main(String[] argv) {
            double area;
            Rectangle myrec = new Rectangle();
            Rectangle myrec1 = new Rectangle();
            myrec.length = 20;
            myrec.breadth = 10;
            myrec1.length = 30;
            myrec1.breadth = 20;
            area = myrec.calculateArea(); //control goes to the
            //calculateArea()
            System.out.println("The area of the first rectangle is " +
            area);
            area = myrec1.calculateArea();
            System.out.println("The area of the second rectangle is " +
            area);

     }
}
```

Output:

```
The area of the first rectangle is 200.0
The area of the second rectangle is 600.0
```

The example above uses the method *calculateArea*() with the return type of double. In this method, the value of *length*breadth* is being returned to the calling method*main*() with the help of the return statement. The syntax for returning a value form a method is:

return value;

The return statement should preferably be the last statement of a method as the control of execution jumps to the calling method as soon as the return statement is encountered. The value returned to the calling method must be captured in a type compatible to the return type of the method. This is why, the value returned from *calculateArea*() is captured in the variable *area* of *double* type.

Rules for returning values from a method

- The value returned from a method must match its return type. Else, the compiler will generate an error.
- The value being returned to the calling method is a local value and will be lost as soon as we exit the method. Therefore, this value must be caught in the calling method in a type compatible to the return type of the method.

5.3.2 Parameterized Methods

Methods that receive parameters or arguments are called parameterized methods. Normally, a method accepts parameters because these parameters are needed by the method to process upon them. For example, a method that needs to calculate simple interest will require principal amount, rate and time as the method parameters. The following example uses a method *calculateInterest*() to calculate the simple interest given the principal, rate and time as input parameters. The parameters passed while invoking the method are called *actual parameters* whereas the parameters passed in the method definition are called *formal parameters.* Based on the value of formal parameters, the result of the method varies.

```
public class SimpleInterest {
    public double calculateInterest(double principle, double rate, double
    time) // formal parameters

    {
          return principle * rate * time;
    }
}
public class MethodDemo {
    public static void main(String[] args) {
          // TODO Auto-generated method stub
```

```
            SimpleInterest si = new SimpleInterest();
            // actual parameters
            double interest = si.calculateInterest(20000.50, 0.8, 1.4);
            System.out.println("The interest calculated is " + interest);
            interest = si.calculateInterest(5000, 0.3, 1.5);
            System.out.println("The interest calculated is " + interest);

    }

}
```

Output:

```
The interest calculated is 22400.56
The interest calculated is 2250.0
```

How does the above method call work?

When the compiler comes to the statement where the method *calculateInterest* is invoked, it tries to find a method with the name *calculateInterest* in the class *SimpleInterest* as the method is invoked with an object of class *SimpleInterest*[2]. While searching for the method in the class, it matches the method name, number and type of parameters in the method declaration (if any). On finding the correct method, the control of the program branches to the method. The actual parameters are then mapped on to the formal parameters. Consider the two statements given below:

```
double interest = si.calculateInterest(20000.50, 0.8, 1.4);

public double calculateInterest(double principle, double rate, double time)
```

The formal parameter 20000.50 is copied into principal, 0.8 into rate and 1.4 into time. So, internally, the compiler reads the above statements as:

```
double principle=20000.50
double rate=0.8
double time=1.4
```

Remember, these variables are local variables for the method. Only the values are copied from actual parameters into formal parameters.

Once the method definition ends, the flow of control branches back to the caller method(*main,* in our case).

//Modifying the Rectangle program to show the use of parameterized methods

```
public class Rectangle {
    double length;
    double breadth;
```

[2] The methods are always searched in the class, whose object we use to call it.

```
    void setDimension(double l, double b) {
          length = l;
          breadth = b;
    }

    double calculateArea() {
          return length * breadth;
    }

}

public class RectangleDemo {
    public static void main(String[] argv) {
          double area;
          Rectangle myrec = new Rectangle();
          Rectangle myrec1 = new Rectangle();
          myrec.setDimension(20, 30);
          myrec1.setDimension(10, 20);
          area = myrec.calculateArea();
          System.out.println("The area of the first rectangle is " +
          area);
          area = myrec1.calculateArea();
          System.out.println("The area of the second rectangle is " +
          area);

    }
}
```

Output:

```
The area of the first rectangle is 600.0
The area of the second rectangle is 200.0
```

The program above uses a parameterized method *setDimension* to set the values of length and breadth. The values 20 and 30 are copied into formal parameters length and breadth respectively.

5.4 CONSTRUCTORS

To understand this section, let us drive back to the section which taught us to create objects. Following is the syntax to create an object:

ClassName objectName=new ClassName();

We learnt that the new operator is used to allocate memory to the instance variables of a class. But we didn't talk much about the parenthesis at the end. So, what actually happens when we create an object of a class? Besides, the instance variables getting memory, a special method called a *constructor* is also called. This parenthesis is actually used to pass parameters to a constructor.

What is a constructor and why do we need it?

A constructor is a special method (member of a class) which has a name as that of the class name, a list of parameters (optional), but no return type. It cannot even have a return type of void. It is needed to initialize the instance variables. Yes, we can also use methods (like, *setDimension* used in the previous section), to initialize instance variables. But it is easier to let the constructors do this job as the methods need to be invoked every time. But in the case of constructors, *they are called at the time of object creation.*

Syntax of a constructor:
ClassName(param_List[optional])
{
//code to initialize instance variables
}

Constructors can be broadly classified into the following types:

- No-Argument Constructor:
- Parameterized Constructor
- Default Constructor

5.4.1 No-Argument Constructor

These constructors do not accept any parameters/arguments. They are invoked when the object of the class is created. Reworking the above Rectangle program, we can replace the *setDimension* method with our *no-argument* constructor.

```
public class Rectangle {
    double length;
    double breadth;

    Rectangle() {
          length = 15.4;
          breadth = 10.3;
    }

    double calculateArea() {
          return length * breadth;
    }
}

public class RectangleDemo {
    public static void main(String[] argv) {
          double area;
```

```
            Rectangle myrec = new Rectangle();
            Rectangle myrec1 = new Rectangle();
            area = myrec.calculateArea();
            System.out.println("The area of the first rectangle is " +
            area);
            area = myrec1.calculateArea();
            System.out.println("The area of the second rectangle is " +
            area);
      }
      }
```

Output:

```
The area of the first rectangle is 158.62
The area of the second rectangle is 158.62
```

Notice the lines where the object of class *Rectangle* is created:

```
Rectangle myrec = new Rectangle();
Rectangle myrec1 = new Rectangle();
```

The parentheses actually indicate what type of constructor will be called here. As we are not passing any arguments to the constructor, the compiler will search a *no-arg* constructor in the class *Rectangle*.[3] Also, observe, the two objects, i.e., *myrec* and *myrec1*, have the same value for the instance variables *length* and *breadth (15.4 and 10.3)* as the *no-arg* constructor is called here twice.

Therefore, whenever a new operator is used to create an object of a class, its constructor will be called. And the type of constructor that has to be called will be decided upon whether we send any arguments after the ClassName or not.

5.4.2 Parameterized Constructors

Parameterized constructors are the constructors that accept parameters. They are also invoked upon object creation. The number and the type of arguments passed at the time of object creation (after the class name) decides which type of parameterized constructor will be called.

Why do we need it?

The no-argument constructor discussed above initializes all the objects with the same value. This is the reason, why we have the same area for both the objects above. But what if we need to create rectangles with different dimensions? In such a case, we can use separate parameterized constructors which will be capable of passing different values to the objects.

[3] Constructors are always searched in the class whose objects have been created.

The following program integrates parameterized constructor in the above *Rectangle*program:

```
public class Rectangle {
    double length;
    double breadth;

    Rectangle() {
            length = 15.4;
            breadth = 10.3;
    }

    Rectangle(double l, double b) {
            length = l;
            breadth = b;
    }

    double calculateArea() {
            return length * breadth;
    }
}

public class RectangleDemo {
    public static void main(String[] argv) {
            double area;
            Rectangle myrec = new Rectangle(20, 30);
            Rectangle myrec1 = new Rectangle(40, 50);
            area = myrec.calculateArea();
            System.out.println("The area of the first rectangle is " +
            area);
            area = myrec1.calculateArea();
            System.out.println("The area of the second rectangle is " +
            area);
    }
}
```

Output:

```
The area of the first rectangle is 600.0
The area of the second rectangle is 2000.0
```

The output above clearly shows that the area of the two rectangles is now different. How? As we are passing arguments at the time of object creation (*myrec* and *myrec1*), parameterized constructors of the class *Rectangle* are called, but with different arguments (*20, 30 and 40, 50*). These arguments are copied into the constructor's *local variables (l and b)*. The definition of the constructor simply copies the values of *l* and *b (local variables) into length and breadth (instance variables).*

So, the definition becomes something like this for both the objects:

length=20;
breadth=30;

And

length=40;
breadth=50;

In the next step, a call to the *calculateArea*() is made, which calculates the area for the two rectangles as 600.00 and 2000.00 respectively.

Note: The no-argument constructor will not be invoked here.

```
public class Rectangle {
     double length;
     double breadth;

     Rectangle() {
            length = 15.4;
            breadth = 10.3;
     }

     Rectangle(double l, double b) {
            l = length;
            b = breadth;
     }

     double calculateArea() {
            return l * b;
     }
}
```

This code snippet will generate a logical error and a syntactic error stating "*l and b cannot be resolved to a variable*".

1.
```
Rectangle(double l, double b) {
       l = length;
       b = breadth;
}
```

The above constructor contains a *logical error*. In the assignment operation, we are trying to assign the value of *length* and *breadth* to the local variables *l* and *b* respectively. But, *length* and *breadth* instance variables have not been initialized yet. Therefore, the correct way would be to do the following:

```
Rectangle(double l, double b) {
          length = l;
          breadth = b;
     }
```

2.
```
double calculateArea() {
        return l * b;
}
```

The method *calculateArea*() contains a syntactic error. The variables *l* and *b* are local variables declared inside our parameterized constructor. They are not known outside the constructor. So, to correct it we have the following code:

```
double calculateArea() {
        return length * breadth;
}
```

5.4.3 Default Constructors

The next thing that will come to your mind will be:

Ok, we now know that an object creation done without parameter will call a *no-argument constructor* of the class and object creation done with parameters will invoke the *parameterized constructor* of the class. But *what if, we do not have any constructors in our class?* In such a case java's *default constructor* is invoked which initializes all instance variables to their default values. For example, the default value for an *int* is 0 whereas for a *double* is 0.0.

Let us have a look at it through a program:

```
public class Rectangle {
    double length;
    double breadth;

    double calculateArea() {
        return length * breadth;
    }

}

public class RectangleDemo {
    public static void main(String[] argv) {
        double area;
        Rectangle myrec = new Rectangle();
        area = myrec.calculateArea();
        System.out.println("The area of the first rectangle is " +
        area);
    }
}
```

In the program above, as we do not have any constructor, java runtime system invokes the default constructor which initializes instance variables; *length* and *breadth* to 0.0 (as they are double values), thereby calculating the area as 0.0.

```
public class Rectangle {
     double length;
     double breadth;

     Rectangle(double l, double b) {
            length = l;
            breadth = b;
     }

     double calculateArea() {
            return length * breadth;
     }

}
public class RectangleDemo {
     public static void main(String[] argv) {
            double area;
            Rectangle myrec = new Rectangle();   //compile time error
            Rectangle myrec1 = new Rectangle(2,3);
            area = myrec.calculateArea();
            System.out.println("The area of the first rectangle is " +
            area);
     }
}
```

This code will generate a compile time error at the above-mentioned line. No default constructor is called for this code. The reason behind is, default constructors are called only when there exist NO constructors in the class. As we have a parameterized constructor available in our class, the java runtime system fails to invoke the default constructor.

5.5 RETURNING OBJECTS FROM A METHOD

The return type of a method can be a *primitive type* as well as a *class type*. Return type being that of a class type means that the method is returning an object of that class. The syntax for the same is given below:

ClassName methodName(param_List[optional])

Let us have a closer look at returning objects through a program:

```
public class Rectangle {

     double length;
     double breadth;
```

```
    Rectangle(double l, double b) {
            length = l;
            breadth = b;
    }

    Rectangle meth() {
            Rectangle r = new Rectangle(length * 10, breadth * 10);
            return r;
    }
}

public class RectangleDemo {
    public static void main(String[] argv) {
            Rectangle myrec = new Rectangle(2, 3);
            Rectangle ob;
            System.out.println("The original length an breadth are: "
                        + myrec.length + " and " + myrec.breadth);
            ob = myrec.meth();
            System.out.println("The modified length an breadth are: " +
            ob.length + " and " + ob.breadth);

    }
}
```

Output:

```
The original length and breadth are: 2.0 and 3.0
The modified length and breadth are: 20.0 and 30.0
```

As you can see, the *myrec* object creation gives a call to the parameterized constructor of the class *Rectangle* which initializes the instance variables as 2 and 3. Next, a call to the method *meth* is made. Every time, this method is called, a new object, r, of the class *Rectangle* is created which again invokes the parameterized constructor of the class with a modified length and breadth (2*10, 3*10). The method returns this object to the calling method *main*. *main* method then captures a reference to this object in *ob*. This is why, *ob.length* and *ob.breadth* equals *20* and *30* respectively.

5.6 ARGUMENT PASSING

In java, an argument refers to the actual parameters, i.e., values we send at the time of invoking a method/constructor. Arguments can be passed to a method by two ways; *call by value* and *call by reference*. In call by value, the arguments are passed by value which means a copy of the arguments are passed and not their references. Therefore, any changes done to the arguments are made in their copies and not at their original location. Whereas, in call by reference, a reference to the argument is passed. Any changes done, are recorded in the original location of the arguments and not their copies.

By default, all primitive types in java are passed by value whereas objects and arrays are passed by reference.

5.6.1 Call by Value

As discussed above, in call by value approach, a copy of actual parameters is passed into formal parameters of a method. Therefore, any changes done to these formal parameters have no effect outside its block where they are defined.

```
public class CallByValue {

    public void swap(int a, int b)   //formal parameter {
          int temp;
          temp = a;
          a = b;
          b = temp;

    }
}

public class SwapDemo {
    public static void main(String[] argv) {
          CallByValue c = new CallByValue();
          int a, b;
          a = 20;
          b = 15;
          System.out.println("Values before method call:");
          System.out.println("a=" + a + " b=" + b);
          c.swap(a, b);  //actual parameter
          System.out.println("Values after swapping are:");
          System.out.println("a=" + a + " b=" + b);
    }
}
```

Output:

```
Values before method call:
a=20 b=15
Values after swapping are:
a=20 b=15
```

The above program intends to swap two variables but fails to do so because, the variables are passed by value. The class *CallByValue* has a method *swap* which is responsible for swapping two values. The mapping of the actual parameters to formal parameters takes place in the below given manner:

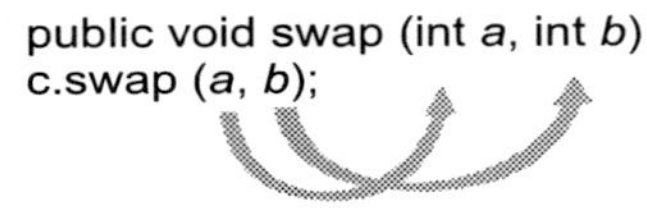

The value of actual parameters *a* and *b* is copied into the formal parameter *a* and *b* respectively.

Note: The actual parameters a and b are local variables inside the main method and the formal parameters a and b are local variables inside the method swap. As only the values are being copied, the moment we come out of the swap method and return to the main, all the changes done to the formal parameters are lost because their scope ends with the closing of swap method.

5.6.2 Call by Reference

In this approach, instead of passing primitive types (by value), we pass parameters by reference. Let us see this via an example.

```
public class CallByReference {

    int a, b;

    public CallByReference(int a, int b) {
            this.a = a;
            this.b = b;
}
            public void swap(CallByReference c1) {
            int temp;
            temp = c1.a;
            c1.a = c1.b;
            c1.b = temp;

    }
}
public class SwapDemo {
    public static void main(String[] argv) {
            CallByReference c = new CallByReference (20,15);
            System.out.println("Values before method call:");
            System.out.println("a=" +c. a + " b=" + c.b);
            c.swap(c);
            System.out.println("Values after swapping are:");
            System.out.println("a=" + c.a + " b=" + c.b);
    }
}
```

Output:

```
Values before method call:
a=20 b=15
```

```
Values after swapping are:
a=15 b=20
```

This approach passes an object c of class *Call By Reference* to the swap method. The mapping of actual to formal parameters takes place as follows:

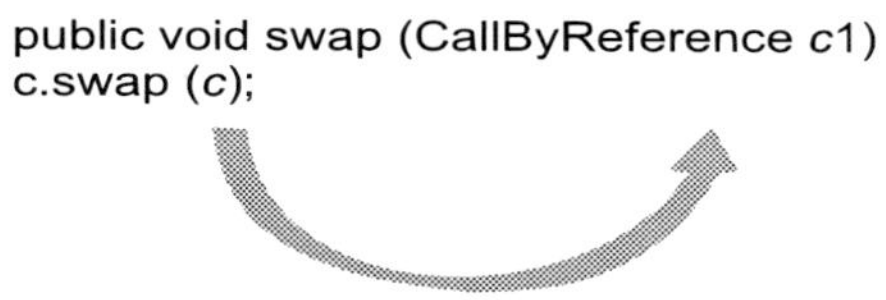

i.e c1=c

where c1 is a reference of class *CallByReference*. Therefore, the reference c1 now refers to the memory location where the reference *c* refers.

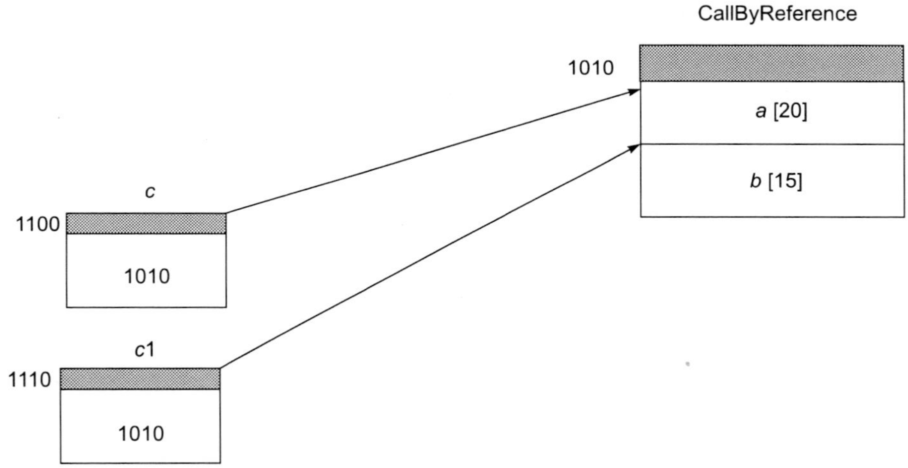

Fig. 5.6

Now, when we refer to c1.a and c1.b, and swap the two values, these changes are being done at the original location (1010) where the instance variables are stored and not in temporary or local copies. This is the reason why the swapped values are reflected even when we refer to them outside the swap method.

5.7 THIS KEYWORD

This is a keyword in java which is capable of referring to the *current object*. It has the following uses:

- *Using this with an instance variable*

  Sometimes, the local variables in a constructor, or a method can shadow (hide) the instance variables. In such a case, we use *this* keyword to distinguish between them. *this* when used with a variable simply means that the variable is an instance variable and belongs to the current object, i.e., the object which was responsible for calling the constructor or the method.

The below given code snippet clarifies the usage:

```
public class Rectangle {
    double length;
    double breadth;

    Rectangle(double length, double breadth) {
        length = length;    //assignment has no effect
        breadth = breadth;
    }

    double calculateArea() {
        return length * breadth;
    }

}

    public class RectangleDemo {
    public static void main(String[] argv) {
        double area;
        Rectangle myrec = new Rectangle(2,3);
        area = myrec.calculateArea();
        System.out.println("The area of the first rectangle is " +
        area);
    }
}
```

The above assignment in the constructor has no effect because the names of the local variables and the names of the instance variables are the same. In such a case, the local variables tend to hide the instance variables of the class. To solve this confusion, we use *this* keyword with the variables to indicate that they are instance variables.

```
Rectangle(double length, double breadth) {
        this.length = length;
        this.breadth = breadth;
}
```

this.length and this. breadth are now the instance variables belonging to the *myrec* object. Therefore, their values are 2 and 3 respectively.

- *Using this inside a constructor to call another constructor*

  this keyword can also be used to call the current class constructor from within a constructor.

```
public class Rectangle {
    double length;
```

```
    double breadth;

    Rectangle() {
          System.out.println("No-argument constructor called");
    }

    Rectangle(double length, double breadth) {
          this();
          this.length = length;
          this.breadth = breadth;
    }

    double calculateArea() {
          return length * breadth;
    }

}

public class RectangleDemo {
    public static void main(String[] argv) {
          double area;
          Rectangle myrec = new Rectangle(2,3);
          area = myrec.calculateArea();
          System.out.println("The area of the first rectangle is " +
          area);
    }
}
```

Output:

```
No-argument constructor called
The area of the first rectangle is 6.0
```

The call to *this*() inside the parameterized constructor gives a call to current class (*Rectangle*) no-argument constructor, printing the statement "*No-argument constructor called*" on the console. *Note: The call to this keyword should be the first statement inside the constructor else it yields a compile time error.* It is mainly used for the purpose of code reusability.

- *Using this to call the current class method*

  this keyword is also used to call a method of the current class.

```
public class Rectangle {
    double length;
    double breadth;
```

```
      Rectangle(double length, double breadth) {
            this.length = length;
            this.breadth = breadth;
      }

      void calculateArea() {
            double area = length * breadth;
            System.out.println("The area is:" + area);
      }

      void callMethod() {
            calculateArea(); // equivalent to
                             //this.calculateArea()

      }

}

public class RectangleDemo {
      public static void main(String[] argv) {
            Rectangle myrec = new Rectangle(2, 3);
            myrec.callMethod();
            Rectangle myrec1 = new Rectangle(4, 5);
            myrec1.calculateArea();
      }
}
```

Output:

```
The area of the first rectangle is 6.0
The area of the second rectangle is 20.0
```

The call to the method *calculateArea*() by *callMethod()* is actually interpreted by the compiler as *this.calculateArea()* (the compiler adds *this* keyword implicitly even if we do not write explicitly). As *this* refers to the current object, so here it means *myrec.calculateArea()* for the first time and *myrec1.calculateArea()* for the second time.

- *Passing this to a method*

  this can also be passed as an argument to a method which again refers to the current object.

```
public class Rectangle {
      double length;
      double breadth;

      public Rectangle(double l,double b) {
            length=l;
            breadth=b;
      }
```

```
    void calculateArea(Rectangle obj) {
            System.out.println("The area is: "+ obj.length * obj.breadth);
    }
    void callMethod()
    {
            calculateArea(this);
    }

}

public class RectangleDemo {
    public static void main(String[] argv) {
            Rectangle myrec = new Rectangle(2, 3);
            myrec.callMethod();
            Rectangle myrec1 = new Rectangle(4, 5);
            myrec1.callMethod();
    }
}
```

Output:

```
The area is: 6.0
The area is: 20.0
```

The program above, gives a call to a method *callMethod* using two objects *myrec* and *myrec1*. The *callMethod* method, in turn, gives a call to *calculateArea* method which passes *this* as an argument. *this* here refers to the current object *myrec* (for the first time) and therefore is mapped to the reference *obj* of class Rectangle.

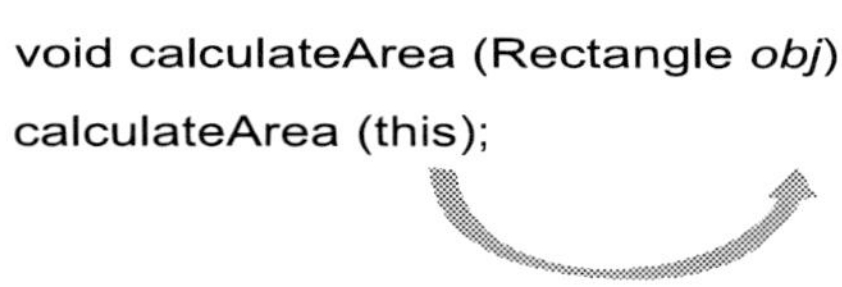

This is why obj.length and obj.breadth is 2 and 3 respectively calculating the area for the first rectangle as 6.0 and 20.0 for the second rectangle.

Note: this keyword refers to myrec in the first call to calculateArea() and to myrec1, the second time.

- *Passing this to a constructor*

  Just as we saw in the above example, this can also be passed as an argument to a constructor.

```
public class Rectangle {
    double length;
    double breadth;
```

```
    public Rectangle() {
            Rectangle r = new Rectangle(this);
    }

    Rectangle(Rectangle o) {
            o.length = 2;
            o.breadth = 3;
    }

    double calculateArea() {
            return length * breadth;
    }

}

public class RectangleDemo {
    public static void main(String[] argv) {
            Rectangle myrec = new Rectangle();
            double area = myrec.calculateArea();
            System.out.println("The area of the rectangle is: " + area);
    }
}
```

Output:

```
The area of the rectangle is: 6.0
```

The creation of *myrec* object invokes the *no-argument* constructor of the class *Rectangle*. The *no-arg* constructor further creates an object *r* of *Rectangle* and is passed *this* as a parameter (referring to *myrec* here) which gives a call to the parameterized constructor of class *Rectangle* on *myrec*. *myrec* is then mapped to the reference *o* initializing the instance variables *length* and *breadth* as 2 and 3 respectively, thereby printing the area as 6.0.

- *Using this as the return type of a method*

  As discussed earlier, a method is also capable of returning objects from itself to the calling method. In such a case, the return type of the method is the class name. Using *this* as the return type of a method simply means it is returning the current instance of the class.

```
public class Rectangle {
    double length;
    double breadth;

    Rectangle(double l, double b) {
            length = l;
            breadth = b;
    }
```

```
    Rectangle meth() {
        Rectangle r = new Rectangle(length * 10, breadth * 10);
        return this;
    }
}

public class RectangleDemo {
    public static void main(String[] argv) {
        Rectangle myrec = new Rectangle(2, 3);
        Rectangle ob;
        System.out.println("The original length an breadth are: "
                + myrec.length + " and " + myrec.breadth);
        ob = myrec.meth();
        System.out.println("The modified length an breadth are: " +
        ob.length
                + " and " + ob.breadth);
    }
}
```

Output:

```
The original length and breadth are: 2.0 and 3.0
The modified length and breadth are: 2.0 and 3.0
```

In the example above, the *meth* method returns *this* to its calling method *main. this* here refers to the current instance of *Rectangle,* i.e., *myrec* and not *r*. Therefore, the original and the modified length and breadth come out to be the same.

5.8 GARBAGE COLLECTION

Garbage Collection in programming languages means collecting the garbage in an executing program. Garbage refers to the unreachable or unreferenced memory blocks. Therefore, *garbage collection is the process of reclaiming memory that is unreachable*. Memory is an expensive resource for us and we just can't let it be wasted like that. So, every programming language has a process of memory management by which we can manage the available memory, reclaim such memory blocks and use it for some other purpose. In languages like C and C++, garbage collection is done manually by using *free*() and *delete*() respectively. But, as it is done manually, there are chances of creating memory leaks in the system. Memory leak is a situation where these memory blocks might not be reclaimed properly or may be lost forever. Therefore, due to unavailability of sufficient memory, our programs may crash over the time.

However, java provides *automatic garbage collection.* The automatic garbage collector in java periodically looks up for objects that have no references pointing to it, takes up the memory occupied by these objects and frees them.[4] The garbage collector may be called in case

[4] The objects in java are allocated memory on the heap.

the system memory is getting low but it is purely a JVM decision when to call it. One cannot predict the time when it will be invoked. However, we can use the *gc*() to invoke the garbage collector. The syntax for the method is defined below:

public static void gc() { }

To understand when the objects become eligible for garbage collection, consider the below code snippet:

```
Rectangle ob1=new Rectangle();
Rectangle ob2=new Rectangle();
Rectangle ob3=new Rectangle();
```

In the above code snippet, we have created three objects named ob1, ob2, ob3 respectively using the new operator. The memory picture at this step is as follows:

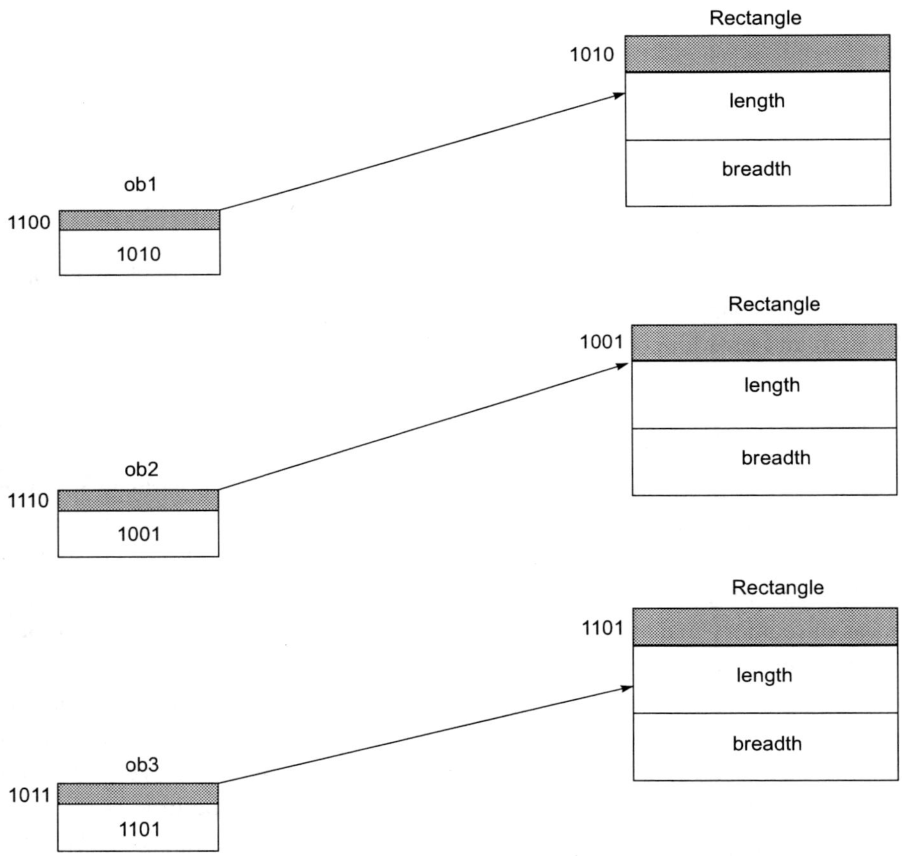

Fig. 5.7

```
ob1=null;
ob2=ob3;
```

After executing the above statements, the memory pointed to by the reference ob1 is now eligible for garbage collection as ob1 refers to null. Also, the reference ob2 refers to the memory pointed to by ob3. Therefore, it is also eligible for garbage collection.

The memory picture for the above becomes somewhat as follows:

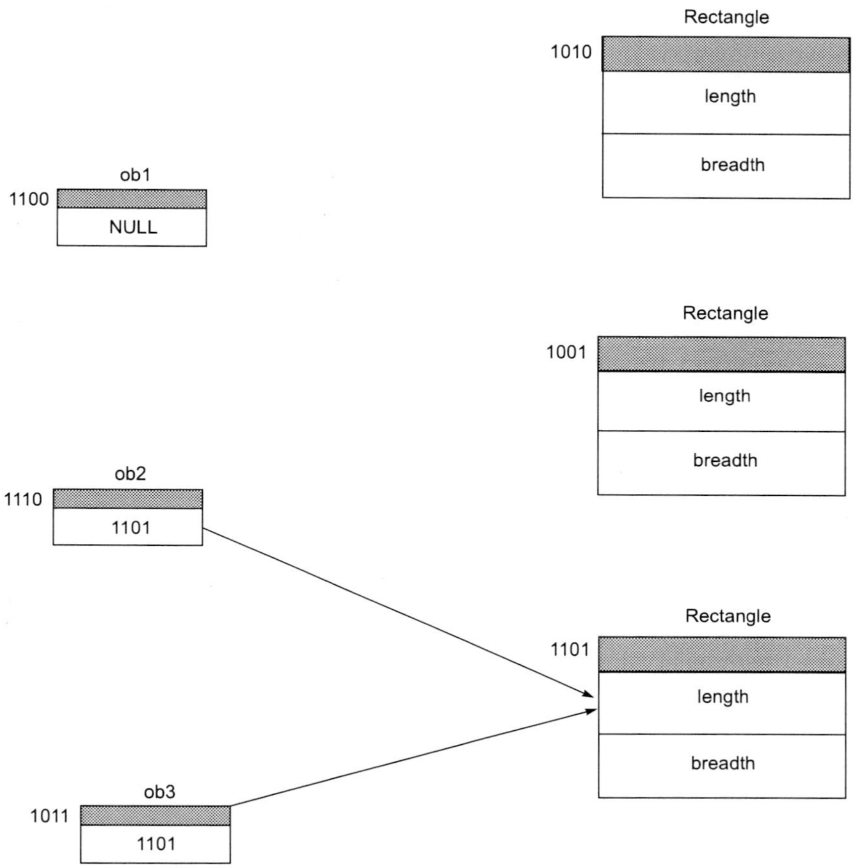

Fig. 5.8

5.9 FINALIZE METHOD

There might be times when we want an object to perform some task just before it is about to get garbage collected. For example, an object might be working on some resources like reading or writing from a file. In such a case, before it is destroyed, we would like to close the file so that no inconsistent changes are recorded on the file. Such operations can be written inside a method called *finalize()* method. The syntax for the same is mentioned below:

protected void finalize()

{

}

This method is actually available in the Object class and we can override or redefine this method in our code. Overriding a method will be talked about in detail in the coming chapters. Also, notice the prototype of the method contains the keyword *protected.* This keyword determines the accessibility of the method, limiting its access only in its class and its sub-class. The protected keyword will be discussed at length in the upcoming chapters. Despite the fact, that we can write any code inside the finalize method, there is no guarantee the method will be invoked before garbage collection. Therefore, it is recommended, not to write this method in your code.

Note: finalize method is called only once for every object.

SUMMARY

- A class is a blueprint by which we can build objects. An object is an instance of a class.
- A class comprises instance variables and methods. The instance variables define the properties or attributes for an object whereas the methods define the behaviour adopted by them.
- Every method is characterized by its three elements: return type, method name, and list of parameters (optional).
- A constructor is a special member method of a class which has no return type, not even void and is mainly used to initialize instance variables with a value.
- Constructors are broadly of two types: no-argument constructor and a parameterized constructor and is invoked upon object creation.
- In case a class has no explicit constructor defined, the default constructor is invoked which initializes all instance variables with their default values.
- Arguments can be passed into a function by two ways: call by value and call by reference.
- The call by value method copies the values of actual parameters into formal parameters, therefore, any changes done to the copies do not persist.
- The call by reference approach passes an object into the actual parameters which is captured by a reference in the formal parameters. Changes done to these parameters reflects in the passed object.
- *this* keyword refers to the object in use.
- Java supports automatic garbage collection wherein the garbage collector looks for memory locations that are not referenced by any reference and frees them.
- The *finalize()*method is called just before an object is about to get garbage collected. The method definition consists of any important tasks that we want the object to perform before getting garbage collected.

COMMON ERRORS

- The most common error made is the use of *reference* and not an *object.* A reference in itself does not point anywhere. It starts pointing to a location when the new operator allocates memory for its instance variables.
- The number and type of actual parameters and formal parameters do not match. Make sure the number and the type of parameters passed in the method call must match with that of formal parameters defined in method definition.
- The return type of a method when returning an object of a class is the class name and not the object name.
- In case a class has no no-argument constructor but has a parameterized constructor defined, a call to the no-argument constructor will not invoke the default constructor for the class. Default constructors for a class are invoked only when there are NO constructors defined in a class.

SELF-TEST

1. Define different types of constructors. How are they different from member functions. Explain with an example.
2. What is a reference variable?
3. "One object in java can be assigned as a reference to another object of the same type". To explain this concept write a complete java program and explain how a reference objects works?
4. Discuss the use of finalize and this keywords with examples.
5. Explain call by value and call by reference methods in java using examples.
6. What is a constructor? Does java provide default constructor? Does it provide a default copy constructor?
7. Define what is a class and an object in java. How do we declare them?
8. Discuss with an example the process of garbage collection in java and when does an object become eligible for garbage collection diagrammatically.

PRACTICAL QUESTIONS

1. Try modelling the classes for an online shopping system.
2. What output the following code will generate?

a)
```
class Loan {
double interest;
String type;
```

```
    public Loan() {
        this("personal loan");
    }

    public Loan(String type) {
        this.type = type;
        this.interest = 10.0;
    }
    }

    public class SelfTest {
    public static void main(String[] args) {
        Loan l = new Loan();
        System.out.println("Interest=" + l.interest);
        System.out.println("Loan Type=" + l.type);
    }
    }
```

b)

```
class A {
int a;

A(int a) {
    this.a = a;
}

void meth3() {
    System.out.println("The value of a is:" + a * 3);

}

void meth2() {
    this.meth3();
}

void meth1() {
    meth2();
}

public static void main(String args[]) {
    A o = new A(10);
    o.meth1();
    A o1 = new A(20);
    o1.meth1();
}
}
```

c)
```
class A {
    String s;

    A(String s) {
        this.s = s;
    }

    void meth2(A obj) {
        System.out.println(s);
    }

    void meth1() {
        meth2(this);
    }

    public static void main(String args[]) {
        A o = new A("First String");
        o.meth1();
        A o1 = new A("Second String");
        o1.meth1();
    }
}
```

d)
```
class A {

    public static void main(String args[]) {
        A ob1 = new A();
        A ob2 = new A();
        A ob3 = new A();
        ob1 = ob3;
        ob2 = ob3;
        System.gc();
    }

    protected void finalize() {
        System.out.println("Object garbage collected");
    }
    }
```

6

CHAPTER

More about Classes

This chapter will enable you to learn the following:

- Getting a closer look at classes and objects.
- Reading and comprehending concepts like polymorphism, static variables and methods, access control.
- Learning to write recursive methods.
- Passing command line arguments through command prompt.

6.1 POLYMORPHISM

As discussed earlier, *polymorphism* is the ability of an object to acquire many forms. Some of the ways in which java implements polymorphism is by *overloading methods* and *constructors*.

6.1.1 Overloading Methods

Method overloading is a process by which we can have multiple methods with the same name but different arguments. Overloaded methods give you an ability to reuse the method with the same name over and over again, though this method could be performing different tasks every time. Java achieves compile time polymorphism by method overloading. Some of the valid method overloads are given below:

```
void meth1();
void meth1(int a);
double meth1(double b);
```

And some invalid ones are:

```
void meth(int a);
double meth(int a);
void meth(int b);
```

To overload a method, keep the following in mind:

- The type or number of arguments *must* vary in each of the overloaded version of the method.
- The return type of the method *may or may not* vary.
- The method name *must* be the same in all the overloaded versions.

Which version to call when?

The compiler decides which version of the overloaded method to call depending on the type and number of arguments present.

Let us quickly browse through an example showing method overloading.

```
public class MethodOverload{
    void meth1() {
        System.out.println("Method without arguments");
    }

    void meth1(int a) {
        a += 5;
        System.out.println("a=" + a);

    }

    double meth1(double c) {

        return c * c;
    }
}

public class MethodOverloadDemo {
    public static void main(String[] argv) {
        Test o = new Test();
        o.meth1();  //calls meth1()
        o.meth1(5); //calls meth1(int)
        double a = o.meth1(5.2); //calls meth1(double)
        System.out.println("a=" + a);
    }
}
```

Output:

```
Method without arguments
a=10
a=27.040000000000003
```

In the code above, we have three overloaded methods named *meth1* with varying arguments. The first one does not accept any argument, the second accepts an integer argument whereas the third one accepts a double argument. On invoking the method *meth1*, the compiler checks the *type* and the *number* of arguments being passed to the method call, and then invokes the correct version of the method. This is why, *meth1(5)* invokes the version of *meth1* accepting an *int* argument.

```
public class MethodOverload{
     void meth1() {
          System.out.println("Method without arguments");
     }

     void meth1(int a) {
          a += 5;
          System.out.println("a=" + a);

     }

     double meth1(double c) {

          return c * c;
     }
}

public class MethodOverloadDemo {
     public static void main(String[] argv) {
          MethodOverloado = new MethodOverload();
          o.meth1();
          o.meth1(5);
          double a = o.meth1(5.2);
          o.meth1("Hello");    //error!
          System.out.println("a=" + a);
     }
}
```

The above code generates an error because the compiler is unable to find a method named *meth1* with *String* parameters.

6.1.2 Overloading Constructors

Just as we saw methods getting overloaded, we can also overload constructors. If you remember, we have already seen some examples (in Chapter 5), of constructors getting overloaded. Constructor overloading is having multiple constructors in a class with the same name *(they ought to have the same name)* with different type and number of arguments. Here also, the compiler checks to see the type and number of arguments and then calls the appropriate version. Let us see it through an example:

```
public class Rectangle {
    double length;
    double breadth;

    Rectangle() {
          length = 0.0;
          breadth = 0.0;
    }

    Rectangle(double l, double b) {
          length = l;
          breadth = b;
    }

    Rectangle(Rectangle o) {
          length = o.length;
          breadth = o.breadth;
    }

    double calculateArea() {
          return length * breadth;
    }
}

public class RectangleDemo {
    public static void main(String[] argv) {
          Rectangle r = new Rectangle();  //calls Rectangle()
          double area = r.calculateArea();
          System.out.println("The area for the first rectangle is:" +
          area);
          //calls Rectangle(double,double)
          Rectangle r1 = new Rectangle(2, 3);
          area = r1.calculateArea();
          System.out.println("The area for the second rectangle is:" +
          area);
          Rectangle r2 = new Rectangle(r1); //calls Rectangle(Rectangle)
          area = r2.calculateArea();
          System.out.println("The area for the third rectangle is:" +
          area);

    }
}
```

Output:

```
The area for the first rectangle is:0.0
The area for the second rectangle is:6.0
The area for the third rectangle is:6.0
```

The program above shows three overloaded versions of the constructor Rectangle. The first one does not accept any argument, the second accepts two arguments of double type whereas the third accepts a Rectangle reference.

6.2 STATIC KEYWORD

The static keyword is one of the most important keywords used in java. This modifier can be used with *variables, methods,blocks and classes.*

- *Static Variables*

  Static when used with a variable makes it a global variable as they do not belong to any specific instance of a class, rather they belong to the class. Therefore, all the objects of the class share the same copy of the static variable.

  One of the classic examples for explaining the static modifier is when we have to count the objects created from a class. Let us see this through an example.

```
class StaticDemo {
    static int count; // static counter to count number of objects
                  //created
    StaticDemo() {
          count++;
    }

}

public class Main {
    public static void main(String[] argv) {
          new StaticDemo();
          new StaticDemo();
          new StaticDemo();
          System.out.println("The total number of objects created are:"
                      + StaticDemo.count);


    }
}
```

Output:

```
The total number of objects created are:3
```

The above class *StaticDemo* defines a static variable named *count* with a default initial value as 0. It also has a constructor which keeps on incrementing the value of *count* every time an object is created. (Do not forget! Constructors are called when an object is created for the class.) In the main method, we introduce here a new way of defining objects. As we know, static variables do not belong to any specific instance but to the class, therefore, we do not need the name of objects here. Thus:

new StaticDemo();

is actually equivalent to:

StaticDemo ob1=new StaticDemo();

Hence, the main method defines three *anonymous* objects here and every time one is created, the constructor is called incrementing the value of *count*. As all the objects share the same copy of the static variable, the total count comes out to be 3. Also notice the line:

```
StaticDemo.count
```

This is so because static members are invoked on the class name than on any object name.

Let us see what would happen if *count* had been an instance variable and not a static variable.

```
class NonStaticDemo {
int count ; // counter to count number of objects created

NonStaticDemo() {
    count++;
}

}

public class Main {
    public static void main(String[] argv) {
          NonStaticDemo ob1 = new NonStaticDemo();
          NonStaticDemo ob2 = new NonStaticDemo();
          NonStaticDemo ob3 = new NonStaticDemo();
          System.out.println("The total number of objects created are:"
                      + ob1.count);
          System.out.println("The total number of objects created are:"
                      + ob2.count);
          System.out.println("The total number of objects created are:"
                      + ob3.count);

    }
}
```

Output:

```
The total number of objects created are:1
The total number of objects created are:1
The total number of objects created are:1
```

The above program now uses a non-static variable *count* (default initial value: 0). Each object now has a separate copy of *count*. Every time an object is created its value is incremented. Therefore, *ob1.count, ob2.count, and ob3.count* all give the value as *1*.

- *Static methods*

  Static modifier can also be used with a method as they too are not invoked upon any specific instance of a class. Our very own main method is also declared as static because we want these methods to be invoked before any objects are created.

  We invoke methods upon specific objects because invoking methods on different objects yields different behaviour as the behaviour depends on the values of instance variables. Such methods are called non-static methods. Imagine if you have a method which works exactly the same way irrespective of the values of instance variables, i.e., it is independent of the instance variables values. Such a member can be marked static. One of the examples is when we use the utility methods like finding out the square root of a number *(sqrt()),* or finding out the absolute value of a number*(abs())*. These methods are available in a predefined class named *Math* and are marked as static as they behave the same way irrespective of the instance variable values.

Restrictions on Static Methods

1. Static methods can only call static methods directly. (You must be wondering *main*, being a static method, has called so many non-static methods till now, but remember, it has done so using an object of the class).
2. Static methods can access static data members only.
3. Static methods cannot refer to *this* or *super*. This is because, *this* refers to the current object. But static methods know nothing about objects as they belong to the class.

   The super keyword will be discussed in the next chapter and also its relation with static.

   Let us see how our static method main calls another static method meth.

```
public class StaticMethodDemo {
    public static void main(String[] argv) {
          meth();
    }

    static void meth() {
          System.out.println("Inside static method meth");
    }
}
```

Here, we see how our static method *main* invokes the other static method *meth* directly. Since both the methods are inside the same class, the method *meth* can be called directly without the use of the class name. Had *meth* been in some other class we would have used the class name to call it! Removing the static keyword from *meth* would yield a compile time error as it will become a non-static method. And we just read that static methods can only invoke other static methods only.

- *Static Blocks*

  A block starts from a curly brace and ends on a curly brace. It defines the scope of variables. Preceding the *static* keyword with a block makes it a *static block*. Static blocks are executed even before the *main* method is called. The following example shows static blocks and methods in the same class.

```
public class StaticBlockDemo {
    static int var;
    static// static block
    {
        var++;
        System.out.println("Inside static block: \n var=" + var);
    }

    public static void main(String[] argv) {
        System.out.println("Inside main: \n var=" + var);
        meth();
    }

    static void meth() {
        System.out.println("Inside static method meth: \n var=" + var);
    }
}
```

Output:

```
Inside static block:
var=1
Inside main:
var=1
Inside static method meth:
var=1
```

The output shows clearly the flow of execution. The static variables are initialized just as the class is loaded. Next, the static block is executed followed by the *main* method and then by the *meth* method.

- *Static classes*

  Java does not provide a top-level static classes but it does have static nested classes which we will be talking about in detail in the coming chapters.

Have a look at the code snippet below and think how it will behave:

```
class StaticDemo {
    int count ; // counter to count number of objects created

    static StaticDemo() {
            count++;
    }

}
```

This class has a static constructor! Is it possible to have static constructors in java? No. There is no point making a constructor static as constructors are invoked upon specific objects and static has no idea about the objects. Thus, the above code yields an error stating "*Illegal modifier*."

6.3 ACCESS CONTROL

Access control means controlling the visibility or accessibility of a program. In other words, it defines what parts of program like classes, methods, etc., will be accessible to the other parts. As we know from the earlier chapters, encapsulation is the process wherein we bundle up the data (instance variables) and the code (methods) together. So, access control is something which comes along with encapsulation.

Why do we need it?

The answer is simple. If you allow your code to be publicly available, it might undergo undesired changes. To avoid such situations, we limit the access of our data to the external world.

Java provides various access specifiers to achieve access control which can be applied on the following entities:

- *Classes:* We can apply either *public* or *package-level (default)* access specifier with a class. A class with *no access specifier* is said to have a *package level/package private or a default access specifier.*
    - *public*: If a class has a public specifier before it, it simply means *"this class is accessible to every other class"*. Note that *if a class is public, it does not mean that the enclosing data members and methods are also available outside the class. It just means that we will be able to instantiate the class anywhere outside.*
    - *Package-level(default):* If no access specifier is used before a class, it means that the class access specifier, by default, is of package-level. What are packages now? For now, just view packages as a folder which contains collection of related classes. Package-level accessibility of a class means that the class is accessible only within

the same package where it is defined. This type of accessibility will be discussed while discussing packages.

Till now, all the classes we have declared have a public access specifier.

Syntax for declaring a public class:

```
public class A {
}
```

Syntax for declaring a package private class:

```
class A {
}
```

- *Data members and methods:* The access specifiers used with data members and methods are *public*, *private*, *protected* and *package-level (default).*
    - *public:* The public access specifier when used with a data member or a method makes it accessible everywhere, even outside the class.
    - *private:* The private data members and methods are available only in the class where they are defined.
    - *protected:* The protected data members and methods are visible in their own class and in their inherited class. Inheritance and protected members will be taken up in the next chapter.
    - *package-level:* Package level is the default access specifier for methods and data members also. These types are accessible within the package (folder) where they are defined only. The package may consist of several other classes as well. Thus, these members will be available in all these classes.

Let us now understand public and private access specifiers through an example.

```
class AccessSpecifierDemo {
    private int a;
    public int b;

    public void setVal() {
            a = 5;
            b = 2;
    }

    public void getval() {
            System.out.println("a=" + a);
            System.out.println("b=" + b);
    }

}
```

```
public class Main {
    public static void main(String args[]) {
            AccessSpecifierDemo ob = new AccessSpecifierDemo();
// Error! Cannot access private variable a
            System.out.println("The value of a=" + ob.a);
            ob.setVal(); // public setVal() works fine
            ob.getval(); // public getVal() works fine


    }
}
```

The above program clearly shows that private variables can be accessed inside their own class but not anywhere outside the class. Whereas public members (instance variables or methods are accessible everywhere even outside the class.

Note: As a rule for programming, you should always try and keep all the instance variables as private and access them through public methods. In this way, nobody can tamper with the instance variables directly.

6.4 PRIVATE CONSTRUCTORS

So, what do you think a private constructor is? We have studied till now public constructors or package-level constructors. These constructors were either available everywhere or inside their package only. But what about the private constructors? Constructors which are private to a class are called private constructors. Just like private instance variables and methods, they are also accessible inside the class where they are defined. This further means only the class which encompasses the private constructor is allowed to instantiate it. *No other class is allowed to instantiate this class.*

What is the use of having a private constructor?

When a class wants its objects to be created internally only, it makes use of *private constructors*. In such a case, no other class is allowed to instantiate this class. This ensures security and access control. One of its applications is already used in java in the Singleton design pattern. The following program will give a glimpse of how to create private constructors in java:

```
public class MySingleton {

private static MySingleton obj;   //private static MySingleton obj
                                  //reference


    /**
     * Create private constructor
     */
    private MySingleton() {

    }
```

```
    /**
     * Create a static method to get instance
     */

    public static MySingleton getInstance() {    //ensuring single object
                                                 //creation
          if (obj == null) {
                obj = new MySingleton();
          }
          return obj;
    }

    public static void main(String a[]) {
          MySingleton st = MySingleton.getInstance();
          }
}
```

In the above code, we have created a *private static reference*[1] of the class *MySingleton*. As this reference is private and static, this will be accessible only inside the class and that too by a static method. We then have a private constructor which will limit all the callers to instantiate the class from outside.

Next, we have a public static method, *getInstance*() and it returns an instance of the class *MySingleton* to its caller method *main*. In this method, we are checking if the reference *obj* is currently null (has not been allocated memory), only then we create an object of the class *MySingleton*, returning the object to its caller method *main* and ensuring single object creation only.

6.5 RECURSION

Recursion is a process where a method calls itself. The next question that comes to our mind is, does the method then fall into an infinite loop? No, but only when handled carefully. A recursive method needs to have a base case where its execution terminates else it can fall into an infinite loop. Consider the following recursive loop which falls into an infinite one:

```
public class A {
    public void meth() {
          meth();
    }
}
```

[1] Instance variables of a class can also be references of some class besides being primitive types only. In such a case, we say, class MySingleton contains a reference of MySingleton.

```
public class Main {
    public static void main(String args[]) {
            A ob = new A();
            ob.meth();
    }
}
```

Output:

```
Exception in thread "main" java.lang.StackOverflowError at A.meth(A.java:3)
```

The code will generate a *StackOverflowError* exception. Exceptions (will be discussed in the upcoming chapters) are abnormal situations that occur in your program and can be handled, if needed, in java. As you can see above, *meth* gives a recursive call to itself but there is no termination point at which the execution stops so we need a base case here at which the execution will stop.

Let us now examine an example of a recursive method with a base case condition.

> *What is a stackoverflow error?*
>
> Every process, when executes, is given memory. The local variables and method parameters reside on the stack memory whereas reference types like objects live on the heap memory. Every time a method is called, its parameters and local variables are pushed on the stack. In case of the above recursive call where we do not have any termination condition for the method to stop executing, these parameters are again and again pushed on the stack causing the stack memory to overflow instigating the JVM to throw the *StackOverFlowError* exception.

```
public class RecursionDemo {
    public int factorial(int num) {
            if (num == 1)
                    return 1;
            else
                    return (num * factorial(num - 1));
    }
}

public class Main {
    public static void main(String args[]) {
            RecursionDemo ob = new RecursionDemo ();
            int fact = ob.factorial(4);
            System.out.println("The factorial is:" + fact);
    }
}
```

Output:

```
The factorial is:24
```

The above program is an example of a good recursive call with a terminating condition to stop the execution of the method. A call to the *factorial()* method checks the value of the number being passed to it. As the value of *num* is 4, the flow goes to the *else* part and executes the statement as follows:

4 factorial(4-1)*

This gives a recursive call to the *factorial()* method but with a different parameter this time, i.e., 3. And now the statement becomes something like this:

*4*3*factorial(3-1)*

This time the method is again called but with the parameter as 2, thus, the definition becomes:

*4*3*2*factorial(2-1)*

This call invokes the *factorial()* one more time, with the parameter as 1. As the value of *num* now becomes 1, the method returns 1 to itself (as it is its own calling method right now) to generate the following code:

*4*3*2*1=24*

This value is finally returned to its original calling method *main* which displays the factorial on the console.

Therefore, the base case condition for the factorial method is:

```
if (num == 1)
    return 1;
```

as it helps terminating the recursive call to the method.

Figure 6.1 helps summarize the method calls for the above program. Have a look:

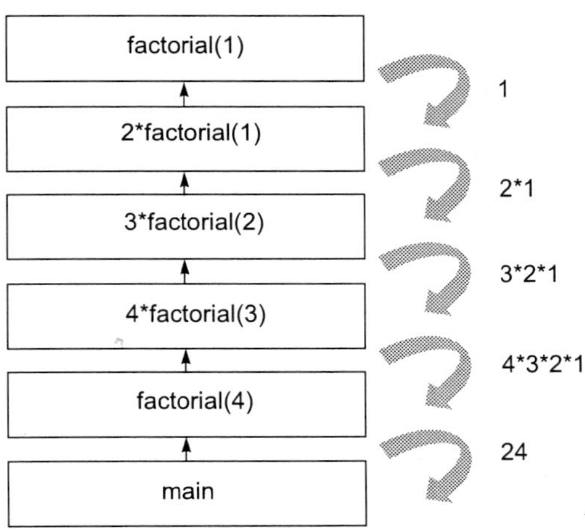

Fig. 6.1

So, now we know what recursion is, and how we can make recursive calls to a method correctly. But why do we need recursion? Does it make our code faster or does it consume lesser memory? No, in every call to the recursive method, the parameters are pushed on the stack thus, taking more time and space to compute the results for each call. It is simply easier to write recursive versions of a method than to write an iterative one. (The methods which use loops to perform their task are called iterative methods.)

Following is the iterative version of factorial program:

```
public class IterativeMethodDemo {
    public int factorial(int num) {
        int fact = 1;
        for (int i = 1; i<= num; i++) {
            fact = fact * i;
        }
        return fact;
    }
}
```

The iterative methods are more efficient in terms of memory and space than a recursive method.

6.6 COMMAND LINE ARGUMENTS

Command line arguments in java are the arguments which are passed at runtime (while the program is executing). These arguments can be captured in our java program and used for further processing. They are stored in the array of references of String type which is passed in the main method. All the command line arguments are of String type and can be type cast to any other type. Consider the following example for further clarification:

```
public class CommandlineArgumentDemo {
    public static void main(String args[]) {
        System.out.println("The first command line argument is:" +
        args[0]);
    }
}
```

Compiling and running the program on command prompt:

C:\>javac CommandlineArgumentDemo.java

C:\>java CommandlineArgumentDemo10

Output:
The first command line argument is: 10

We have already seen in the earlier chapters how to compile and run a java program from command prompt. The command line arguments can be specified at the time of running the program and can be any in number. Here, 10 is specified as the command line input and is stored in the array of references of class String, *args*. As, *args* is an array, the first command line argument is stored in the 0th position of the array and can be referred as *args[0]*. The next argument can be accessed as *args[1]* and so on. Hence, the output.

//Another program depicting the use of more than one command line argument

```
public class CommandlineArgumentDemo {
    public static void main(String args[]) {
        System.out.println("The command line arguments for the program
        are:"
                    + args[0] + " " + args[1]);
    }
}
```

```
public class CommandlineArgumentDemo {
    public static void main(String args[]) {
        int result = args[0] + args[1];
        System.out.println("The addition of the command line argu-
        ments is:"
                    + result);
    }
}
```

The above code will generate a compile time error stating: *"Type Mismatch: cannot convert from String to int"*. This is because by default, all the command line arguments are of string type. Arithmetic operations cannot be performed on them. To do so, we will have to parse them into integers which can be done using wrapper classes. Wrapper classes will be talked at length in the coming chapters. So till then wait and remember arithmetic operations cannot be done on the command line arguments directly.

Compiling and running the program from command prompt:

C:\>javac CommandlineArgumentDemo.java

C:\>java CommandlineArgumentDemo 10 20

Output:

The command line arguments for the program are:10 20

SUMMARY

- Polymorphism is the capability of an object to attain multiple forms. Broadly, it is of two types: method overloading and constructor overloading.
- Method overloading is an approach wherein we can have multiple methods with the same name but differing parameters. The sufficient condition for method overloading is that the number or type of arguments should be different in the two versions of the method.
- Constructor overloading is where we can have multiple constructors of the same class with different arguments.
- The static modifier can be used with methods as well as data members.
- Static data members are in a way, global variables which are shared by all the objects of the class.
- Static methods and data members belong to the class and not to any specific object, thus static methods are called upon the class name and not upon any object.
- Static methods can only access static members and cannot refer to *this* keyword.
- Java provides access specifiers, *public, private, protected* and *package-level* to ensure limited access and facilitate code security.
- Public members of a class are accessible outside their class also.
- Private members are visible only in their class.
- Protected members are used in inheritance.
- Package-level members are available inside their own package (within every class). It is also the default access specifier.
- Classes which have a private constructor can only be instantiated in their own class. It is beneficial when we want to restrict object creation by any other class. They are used in the Singleton design pattern.
- Recursion is a feature of java where one method is a class itself. The method should have a base case condition to terminate its execution. Java uses stacks to implement recursion.
- Command line arguments are the arguments or inputs, a program receives at runtime. These arguments are stored in *args* array of type *String* which is passed to the main method and can be accessed like any other array element.

COMMON ERRORS

- The most common mistake an user will do is in overloading methods.

```
public int meth1(int a)
{

}
```

```
public void meth1(int b)
{

}
```

These are not overloaded versions of the method *meth1*. Remember, a different return type is not a sufficient condition for two methods to be overloaded. The two methods should have differing numbers or type of arguments.

- Overloading can be done in the same class only.
- We often make a mistake of calling a non-static method from a static method. This cannot be done as static methods can only access static data members.
- Use of *this* keyword and *static* keyword together. As *this* belongs to a specific instance and static members belong to the class, they can never be used together.
- Another error can be to create static constructors. Constructors are called upon creation of specific objects whereas static members do not belong to any specific object. Therefore, having a static constructor is not allowed in java.
- Errors in accessing data members/methods. Make sure you see the data type of members before accessing them. A common error for the same is *"call to method could not be resolved"*.This type of error comes up when the compiler fails to find the specific method as the method might not be accessible in your class.
- Recursive methods must have a base condition on which the termination of the method ends else you may fall into an infinite loop.
- The command line arguments are of string type. Make sure you cast them into compatible types before performing any arithmetic operations on them.

SELF-TEST

1. What is overloading? Differentiate between a method and a constructor overloading.
2. What is the purpose of a static block?
3. What are static methods and variables? Can we have static constructors? Why or why not? Support your answer with an example.
4. What is access control in java? What does the language provide to facilitate access control?
5. What is recursion in java? Which data structure is used to implement recursion? Explain with an example.

PRACTICAL QUESTIONS

1. Predict the output for the following:

a)
```
public class Count {
```

```
    public int getCount() {
        return 3;
    }

    public String getCount() {
        return "Total count is 4";
    }

    public static void main(String[] args) {
        Count c = new Count();
        System.out.println(c.getCount());
    }

}
```

b)
```
public class A {
public static void meth() {
    System.out.println("In static method");
}
}

public class SelfTest {
    public static void main(String[] args) {
        A o = new A();
        o.meth();
    }
}
```

c)
```
public class A {
static int a = 5;
public static void meth() {
    a++;
System.out.println("The value of a is:"+a);
}
}

public class SelfTest {
    public static void main(String[] args) {
        A o = new A();
        A o1 = new A();
        A o2 = new A();
        o.meth();
```

```
                o1.meth();
                o2.meth();
                A.meth();
                A.meth();
        }
    }
```

2. Write a recursive method to find the power of a number.
3. Write recursive methods to implement stack operations: *push and pop.*

7

CHAPTER

Inheritance

This chapter will enable you to learn the following:

- Basics of inheritance with clear examples.
- Using the super keyword.
- Learning the types of inheritance.
- Implementing runtime polymorphism using method overriding.
- Building abstract classes.
- Using the final keyword with variables, methods and classes.

7.1 INTRODUCTION

The literal meaning of inheritance is to *acquire*. In java, it means one entity acquiring properties or attributes of another entity. Inheritance is used to define "IS A" relationship between two entities. For instance, BANANA "IS A" FRUIT, DOG "IS A" ANIMAL, CAR "IS A" VEHICLE, etc. In the above examples, BANANA acquires properties of a FRUIT through the process of inheritance but the vice versa is not true.

Java establishes inheritance between two classes using the *extends* keyword. The class whose attributes are inherited is called a *super class* or a *parent class* whereas the class which inherits the properties is called a *subclass* or *child class*. In the above example, FRUIT is a superclass and BANANA is a subclass as BANANA inherits the properties of a FRUIT. Using inheritance in our code facilitates *code reusability* to a greater extent which further saves development time and eases debugging efforts.

As discussed earlier, a class can have members at public, private, protected and package level. During the process of inheritance, these members behave differently according to their access level, the detail of which is given below:

Members	Availability in subclass
Private	Not visible
Public	Visible
Protected	Visible
Package-level	Visible only in same package

Fig. 7.1

Let us see an example for the same now:

```
public class A {
    int a = 5;

    void inheritMe() {
          System.out.println("Hi! I just got inherited");
    }
}

public class B extends A {
    int b = 6;

    void bMethod() {
          System.out.println("Hi! I am in class B");
    }

}

public class InheritanceDemo {
    public static void main(String[] args) {
          B b = new B();
          System.out.println("a=" + b.a);// inherited from class A
          System.out.println("b=" + b.b);
          b.inheritMe(); // inherited from class A
          b.bMethod();
    }
}
```

```
Output:

a=5
b=6
Hi! I just got inherited
Hi! I am in class B
```

The above code shows how members of the super class *A* gets inherited in the subclass *B*. The *extends* keyword actually alters the definition of subclass *B* which now looks something like this:

```
public class B extends A {
    int a = 5; // inherited member
    int b = 6;

    void inheritMe() // inherited member
    {
          System.out.println("Hi! I just got inherited");
    }

    void bMethod() {
          System.out.println("Hi! I am in class B");
    }

}
```

As you can see now, instance variable *a* and the *inheritMe()* method belonging to the superclass A now becomes the members of subclass B as well. Therefore, can be called by using an object of class B.

Let us now alter our Rectangle program which we have been discussing till now and see how inheritance can work here.

```
public class Figure {
    double dimension1, dimension2;

    Figure() {
          dimension1 = 5;
          dimension2 = 4;
    }

    double calculateArea() {
          return dimension1 * dimension2;
    }
}

public class Rectangle extends Figure {

    Rectangle(double l, double b) {
          dimension1 = l;
          dimension2 = b;
    }

}

public class InheritanceDemo {
    public static void main(String[] args) {
          Rectangle r = new Rectangle(3, 4);
          double area = r.calculateArea();
```

```
            System.out.println("The area of the rectangle is:" + area);
      }
}
```

Output:

```
The area of the rectangle is:12.0
```

As Rectangle "IS A" figure, the Rectangle class inherits properties of the figure class. Notice, we have constructors working here (constructors do not get inherited) to initialize the instance variables. The Rectangle object r calls the constructor for the Rectangle class[1] and initializes the instance variables to 3 and 4. Note that *dimension1* and *dimension2* are available in the Rectangle class as well, as they have been inherited. Hence, the inherited method *calculateArea*() yields the result as 12.

7.2 INHERITANCE AND MEMBER ACCESS

As discussed in Fig. 7.1, not all the members of a class get inherited in their subclass. It depends on the access level of the member as to where all it will be accessible. According to Fig. 7.1, the private members of a class do not get inherited and therefore are accessible inside their class only. The public members of a class are always inherited in its child class and are visible in every other class too. The protected members on the other hand, are visible inside their class and its subclass. These members will become clearer in the next chapter when we discuss packages. Lastly, the members with default access are visible inside their package (folder) only. The following example will demonstrate how private and public members of a class behave in the inheritance process:

```
public class A {
      private int a;

      void setA() {
            a = 5;
      }
}

public class B extends A {
      public int b = 7;

      void setB() {
            b = b * 5;
      }
}
```

[1] During the process of inheritance the constructors behave a little differently which will be explained in the coming sections.

```
public class InheritanceDemo {
    public static void main(String[] args) {
        B b = new B();
        b.setA(); //valid
        System.out.println("a=" + b.a);   //error!
        b.setB(); //valid
        System.out.println("b="+b.b); //valid

    }
}
```

The above program generates an error: *"The field A.a is not visible"*. The methods *setA*() and *setB*() are of default access level and therefore are available in the *InheritanceDemo* class (assuming it is in the same package or folder). The instance variable *a* does not get inherited in class B as it is a private member of the class A whereas the instance variable *b* being a public member is visible outside the class also in the main method.

7.3 SUPER KEYWORD

One of the most significant keywords you will study in this chapter is the *super* keyword. The super keyword has two usages in inheritance:

1. *Calls super class constructor:* In the Rectangle example discussed above, we said (in the footnote) that *constructors behave a little differently when used in the inheritance process.* This is so because when we have a super class and a subclass constructor available at the same time, it is always the super class constructor that is called the first. To facilitate this, the first statement written inside any subclass is a call to *super* which means calling the super class constructor. One can also give a call to *super* explicitly by using the *super* keyword. The following example shows how *super* can be used to call the super class constructor:

```
public class Figure {
    double dimension1, dimension2;

    Figure(double d1,double d2) {
        dimension1 = d1;
        dimension2 = d2;
    }

    double calculateArea() {
        return dimension1 * dimension2;
    }
}

public class Rectangle extends Figure {

    Rectangle(double l, double b) {
        super(l, b);          //call to Figure class constructor
```

```
    }
}
public class SuperDemo {
    public static void main(String[] args) {
            Rectangle r = new Rectangle(3, 4);
            System.out.println("The area is:" + r.calculateArea());
    }
}
```

Output:

```
The area is:12.0
```

Let us closely examine what is happening here. The main method creates an object of class Rectangle. The object creation, in turn, calls the parameterized constructor for the class Rectangle. The parameterized constructor further gives a call to the super class constructor; *Figure* by passing 3 and 4 as *l* and *b* respectively. The *Figure* class constructor then assigns the value of *l* and *b* to the instance variables *dimension1* and *dimension2 respectively* (*dimension1* and *dimension2* are available to the *Rectangle* class as they just got inherited). Therefore, the object *r* now, has the value of *dimension1* as 3 and *dimension2* as 4. Hence, the area comes out be 12.

2. *Access super class members*

   The super keyword is also used to access super class or base class members in its subclass. The following example demonstrates the use of *super* in accessing super class members.

```
public class A {
    int a;
    A() {
            a = 5;
    }
}
public class B extends A {
    int a;
    B() {
//gives a call to super()
            a = super.a * 5;
    }
    void setB() {
            System.out.println("The super class version of a is:" +
            super.a);
```

```
            System.out.println("The subclass version of a is:" + a);

        }
    }

public class SuperDemo {
    public static void main(String[] args) {
            B ob=new B();
            ob.setB();

        }
    }
```

Output:

```
The super class version of a is:5
The subclass version of a is:25
```

The example above shows the presence of two instance variables in the super class and subclass with the same name. When class B inherits class A, the inherited instance variable *a* from the super class is shadowed by the instance variable *a* of class B, as they are of the same name. To distinguish between these two variables, we use the super keyword by writing *super.a*. Therefore, *a* refers to the subclass version of the instance variable *a* and *super.a* refers to the super class version of *a*.

Remember, the object creation of class B calls the super class constructor first initializing *super.a* as 5 and then calls its own constructor as the first line written in any subclass constructor is *super()*.

Static and Super

As discussed earlier, static methods cannot refer to *this* or *super* in any way. The reason being, *this* refers to current object whereas *super* refers to super class of the current object. And as you all know static methods are not tied to any object, therefore it cannot refer to *super*.

7.4 RELATION BETWEEN A SUPER CLASS AND A SUBCLASS REFERENCE VARIABLE

The subclass is a *type of* or a *specialization* of the super class. For instance, Dog IS An Animal which implies that a subclass reference is also a type of super class reference variable and hence can be assigned to a super class variable. But the vice versa is not true as all animals are not dogs. Now, let us take our Figure class example to explain this concept:

```
public class Figure {
    double dimension1, dimension2;
```

```
    Figure(double d1, double d2) {
        dimension1 = d1;
        dimension2 = d2;
    }
    double calculateArea() {
        return dimension1 * dimension2;
    }
}
public class Rectangle extends Figure {
    Rectangle(double l, double b) {
        super(l, b);
    }
    void meth() {
        System.out.println("In method meth");
    }
}
public class FigureDemo {
    public static void main(String[] args) {
        Figure f = new Rectangle(3, 4);
        System.out.println("The area is: " + f.calculateArea());
    }
}
```

Output:

```
The area is: 12.0
```

As we can see in the main method, a *Figure* class (*super class*) reference variable points to the *Rectangle* class object (*subclass*). *The key point to remember here is when a super class reference variable points to a subclass object, then this reference variable can be only used to invoke methods and members of its type.* This means, the Figure class reference variable *f* can only invoke members that are available in its class and have been inherited in the subclass. *It cannot access members of Rectangle class that are not defined in Figure class.* Therefore, the following statement will produce an error:

```
f.meth();
```

as *meth* is not available in the Figure class.

Note: The subsequent statement is invalid for the reasons discussed above:

```
Rectangle r = new Figure(3, 4);
```

```
public class Figure {
    double dimension1, dimension2;

    Figure(double d1, double d2) {
        dimension1 = d1;
        dimension2 = d2;
    }

    double calculateArea() {
        return dimension1 * dimension2;
    }
}
public class Rectangle extends Figure {
    Rectangle(double l, double b) {   //error!
        dimension1 = l;
        dimension2 = b;
    }

}
public class InheritanceDemo {
    public static void main(String[] args) {
        Rectangle r = new Rectangle(3, 4);
        System.out.println("The area is:" + r.calculateArea());
    }
}
```

What do you think about the output of the above code? At first sight, there might not seem any problem. But it does generate an error saying *"Implicit super constructor Figure() is undefined. Must explicitly invoke another constructor"*. This happens because the first statement inside a subclass constructor is a call to *super*. If the super statement is specified explicitly in the subclass constructor, it calls the corresponding version of the super class constructor. Otherwise, it gives a call to the no-argument super class constructor by default, issuing *super()*. In the code above, we have not given a call to the super class constructor explicitly. Therefore, it gives a call to the no-arg constructor of Figure class implicitly. And alas! there does not exist a no-arg constructor for the Figure class. Hence, the error.

7.5 TYPES OF INHERITANCE

There are several types of inheritance supported in java which as given below:

1. *Single Inheritance:* The inheritance in which there exist one super class (parent class) and one subclass (child class) is called *Single Inheritance*. Figure 7.2 depicts the same:

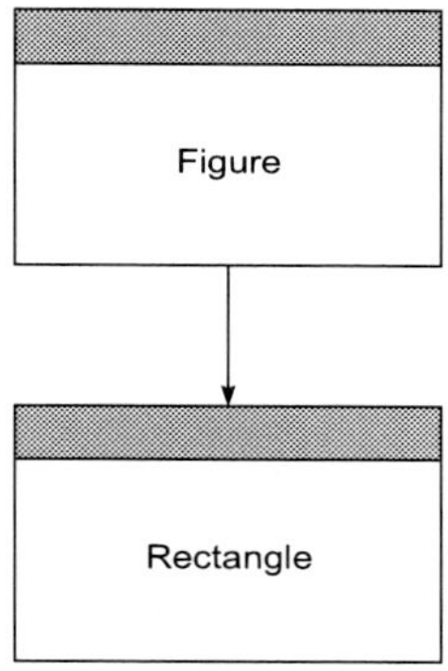

Fig. 7.2

The examples taken up till now in this chapter are that of single inheritance.

2. *Multilevel Inheritance:* The inheritance in which we have multiple levels of single inheritance is called a *Multilevel Inheritance.* Figure 7.3 portrays the same:

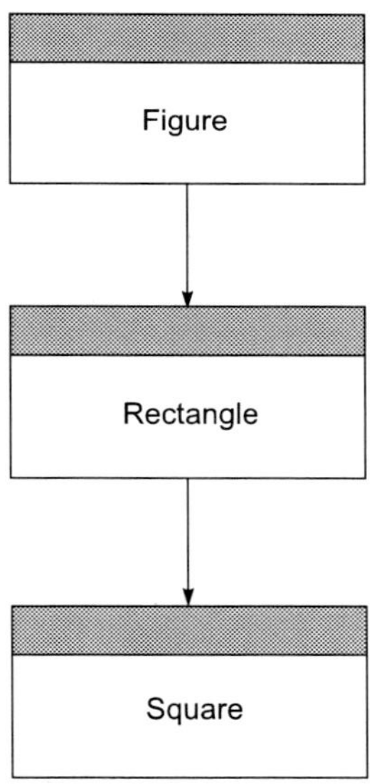

Fig. 7.3

The following example illustrates multilevel inheritance:

```
public class Figure {
    double dimension1, dimension2;

    Figure(double d1, double d2) {
           dimension1 = d1;
           dimension2 = d2;
    }
```

```
        double calculateArea() {
                return dimension1 * dimension2;
        }
}

public class Rectangle extends Figure {
        Rectangle(double l, double b) {
                super(l, b);
        }
}

public class Square extends Rectangle {

        Square(double size)
        {
        super(size,size);
        }

}

public class FigureDemo {
        public static void main(String[] args) {
                Figure f = new Rectangle(3, 4);
                System.out.println("The area of the rectangle is: " +
                f.calculateArea());
                Square s = new Square(3);
                System.out.println("The area of the square is:" +
                s.calculateArea());

        }
}
```

Output:

```
The area of the rectangle is: 12.0
The area of the square is:9.0
```

The square constructor calls the Rectangle constructor with the help of *super* which further calls the Figure class constructor initializing the instance variables and thus calculating the area.

Note: An object can be referred to, by a reference variable of its type or of its super class type. In the example above, Square object is referred by a reference variable of Square type and Rectangle object by a reference variable of Figure type.

3. *Hierarchical Inheritance:* is the inheritance where a super class can have more than one subclass or child class. This is well depicted in Fig. 7.4.

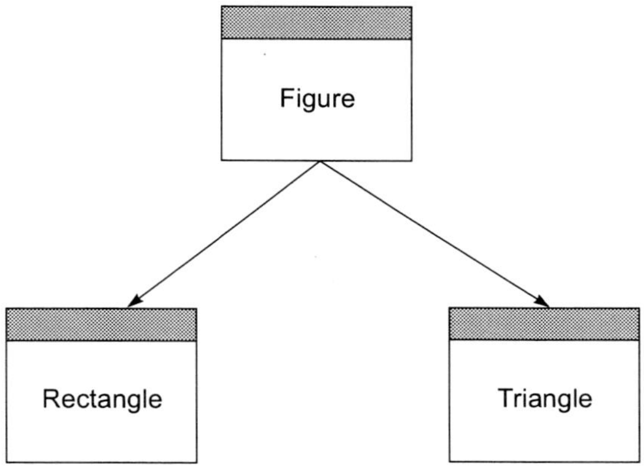

Fig. 7.4

The subsequent program demonstrates hierarchical inheritance:

```
public class Figure {
    double dimension1, dimension2;

    Figure(double d1, double d2) {
          dimension1 = d1;
          dimension2 = d2;
    }

}

public class Rectangle extends Figure {
    Rectangle(double l, double b) {
          super(l, b);
    }
}

public class Triangle extends Figure {
    Triangle(double base, double height) {
          super(base, height);
    }
}

public class FigureDemo {
    public static void main(String[] args) {
          Rectangle r = new Rectangle(3, 2);
          System.out.println("The length of the rectangle is: " +
          r.dimension1);
          System.out.println("The breadth of the rectangle is: " +
          r.dimension2);
          Triangle t = new Triangle(4, 3);
          System.out.println("The base of the triangle is: " +
          t.dimension1);
```

```
            System.out.println("The height of the triangle is: " +
            t.dimension2);
        }
}
```

Output:

```
The length of the rectangle is: 3.0
The breadth of the rectangle is: 2.0
The base of the triangle is: 4.0
The height of the triangle is: 3.0
```

4. *Multiple Inheritance:* It is the inheritance in which one child or subclass can have multiple super classes as shown in Fig. 7.5.

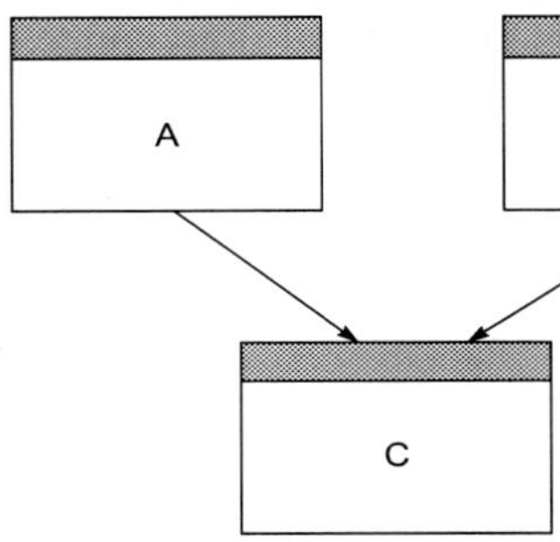

Fig. 7.5

5. *Hybrid Inheritance:* is a combination of hierarchical and multiple inheritance as shown in Fig. 7.6.

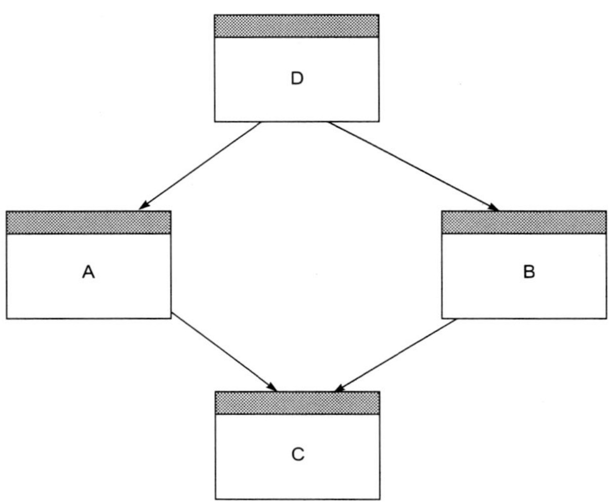

Fig. 7.6

Note: Java does not support multiple and hybrid inheritance. Instead, it uses interfaces achieve its functionality. (Interfaces will be discussed shortly.)

7.6 ORDER OF CONSTRUCTOR CALLING IN INHERITANCE

Now, let us take up the question that has been hovering our minds from the beginning of this chapter. *"In what order the constructors in an inheritance hierarchy are invoked?"* In an inheritance hierarchy, the constructors are invoked in the order of their creation, i.e., from super class to subclass and the *super* keyword assures the same. Let us examine this through an example:

```
public class X {
     X() {
               System.out.println("Inside X's Constructor");
     }
}

public class Y extends X {
     Y() {
               System.out.println("Inside Y's Constructor");
     }

}

public class Z extends Y {
     Z() {
               System.out.println("Inside Z's Constructor");
     }

}

public class ConstructorOrderDemo {
     public static void main(String[] args) {
               Z ob=new Z();
     }
}
```

Output:

```
Inside X's Constructor
Inside Y's Constructor
Inside Z's Constructor
```

Let us now understand how the above program works. The main method defines an object of class Z which calls its own constructor. But as we all know, the first statement written inside any subclass constructor is a call to its super class constructor, therefore the Z class constructor invokes the Y class constructor. Memorize, we talked in the previous sections of this chapter, that *if the super keyword is missing inside the subclass constructor, the compiler issues a call to the no-argument super class constructor by default.* Coming inside the Y's constructor, there is again an implicit call to its super class X constructor. Hence, the messages are printed in the reverse order.

//Another example showing the order of constructor calling in hierarchical inheritance

```
public class X {
     X() {
             System.out.println("Inside X's Constructor");
     }
}

public class Y extends X {
     Y() {
             System.out.println("Inside Y's Constructor");
     }

}

public class Z extends X {
     Z() {
             System.out.println("Inside Z's Constructor");
     }

}

public class ConstructorOrderDemo {
     public static void main(String[] args) {
             Z ob = new Z();
     }
}
```

Output:

```
Inside X's Constructor
Inside Z's Constructor
```

The example above prints the messages only in X and Z's constructor as the call to Z's constructor invokes its super class X's constructor only and hence, there is no call to Y class constructor.

7.7 METHOD OVERRIDING

Method Overriding is a mechanism to achieve *runtime polymorphism* in java. Runtime polymorphism is an ability of a method to behave differently (with different definitions) at runtime.

Method overriding is a process in which a method of the super class is redefined in one of its subclasses. A necessary condition for a method in a superclass to be overridden is that the method should have the *same return type, method name and parameter list* in its subclass. If the super class method is not overridden (redefined) in its subclass, then the superclass version of the same is used. Let us understand this by an example:

```
public class A {
    void meth() {
            System.out.println("I am in A");
    }
}

public class B extends A {
    void meth() {           //overridden version of meth()
            System.out.println("I am in B");
    }
}

public class C extends A {
        //no overridden version of meth() available
        void call() {
        System.out.println("Call me");
        }
}

public class OverridingDemo {
    public static void main(String[] args) {
            A a=new A();
            a.meth();   //calls meth() in A
            A ab=new B();
            ab.meth(); //calls meth() in B
            A ac=new C();
            ac.meth(); //calls meth() in A
    }
}
```

The above code shows how one can override a method of the superclass in its subclass. This program overrides the method *meth()*(defined in *A*) by redefining it in the subclass *B*. Notice that the method has the same signature(type, name and parameters) in its subclass too.

Now let us examine how the Java Run Time system decides which version of *meth()* to call on run time.

Whenever an overridden method like *meth()* is invoked via a superclass reference, the JVM checks to see on runtime where the superclass reference currently points to. If the reference points to its own type (class A in our case), it invokes its own version of *meth()*. Else if it points to one of its subclass objects, it invokes the subclass version of *meth()*. And if the subclass does not override the method, then the superclass version of *meth()* is called. Lastly, an error is generated if the method is not even found in its super class.

Therefore, the below statements

```
A a=new A();
a.meth();
```

invoke *meth()* in class A as the superclass reference points to its own object whereas the statements

```
A ab=new B();
ab.meth();
```

call *meth()* in B since the reference points to an object of class B but the statements

```
A ac=new C();
ac.meth();
```

Invokes *meth()* in A as C does not provide an overridden version of meth(). Therefore, the JVM looks for the same in its super class A.

Note: Overridden method calls are made based upon the type of object used to invoke them and not on the type of reference.

```
//Implementing the Figure Class example using Method Overriding
public class Figure {
    double dimension1, dimension2;

    Figure(double d1, double d2) {
          dimension1 = d1;
          dimension2 = d2;
    }

    void calculateArea() {
          System.out.println("Area is undefined");
    }
}

public class Rectangle extends Figure {
    Rectangle(double l, double b) {
          super(l, b);
    }

    void calculateArea() {
          System.out.println("The area of the rectangle is: " + dimension1
                      * dimension2);
    }
}

public class Triangle extends Figure {
    Triangle(double base, double height) {
          super(base, height);
    }
```

```
    void calculateArea() {
          double area = 0.5 * dimension1 * dimension2;
          System.out.println("The area of the triangle is: " + area);
    }
}
public class MethodOverridingDemo {
    public static void main(String[] args) {
          Figure f = new Figure(2, 3);
          f.calculateArea();    //calls area in Figure
          Figure fr = new Rectangle(4, 3);
          fr.calculateArea(); //calls area in Rectangle
          Figure ft = new Triangle(4, 5);
          ft.calculateArea();//calls area in Triangle
}
}
```

Output:

```
Area is undefined
The area of the rectangle is: 12.0
The area of the triangle is: 10.0
```

Method overriding and Method Overloading

Method overloading is having two or more methods in a class with the same name but different parameters whereas Method Overriding is redefining a superclass method with the same name, type and parameters in a subclass.

//A Program differentiating between method overriding and method overloading

```
public class A {
    void meth() {
          System.out.println("I am in A");
    }

}
public class B extends A {
    void meth() {              //overridden version
          System.out.println("I am in B");
    }
    void meth(int a) {      //overloaded version
          System.out.println(a);
    }
}
```

```
public class Main {
    public static void main(String[] args) {
            A a = new A();
            a.meth();              //calls meth() in A
            A b = new B();
            b.meth();              //overridden method, calls meth() in B
            b.meth(5);             //Error!
    }
}
```

This program demonstrates some of the most important points about method overriding and overloading. The below statements

```
A a = new A();
a.meth();
```

give a call to the overridden method in class A whereas the statements

```
A b = new B();
b.meth();
```

invoke the overridden version of *meth* present in class B.

But the statement below generates a compile time error stating *"The method meth in the type A is not applicable for the arguments (int)"*

```
A b = new B();
b.meth(5);
```

The reason behind is the above version of *meth* is an overloaded version and not an overridden version. *Overloaded method calls are resolved at compile time and these methods are searched in the class whose reference is created.* In the above call, a reference of class A is created which points to an object of class B. Therefore, the method is searched in class A and not in class B. But unfortunately, the method *meth(int)* does not exist in class A, hence the error!

Note: The above process of method overriding and resolving method calls at runtime is also called Dynamic Method Dispatch.

7.8 ABSTRACT CLASSES AND METHODS

The literal meaning of *abstract* means something which is not defined. As we saw in the previous example of overriding, sometimes, the same operation say, finding the area of a figure can be performed differently for different figures. But in general, a figure is abstract in itself and does not have any area till the time we give a specific implementation to the figure. Such cases can be handled efficiently by using abstract methods. An abstract method is a method which does not have any definition. It is the responsibility of the subclass methods to give a concrete implementation of such methods. In doing so, every subclass (example, Rectangle or Triangle) is free to give its own implementation of the abstract method.

Below is the syntax for declaring an abstract method:

abstract ret_Type method_Name(param_List);

The semicolon denotes that the method has no definition.

An abstract class on the other hand is a class which *may* contain some abstract methods. Abstract classes can also have concrete methods along with some abstract ones in them. To declare an abstract class or an abstract method, all we need to do is precede them with the keyword *abstract*.

Let us now go through an example for the same:

```
abstract public class Figure {
    double dimension1, dimension2;

    Figure(double d1, double d2) {
          dimension1 = d1;
          dimension2 = d2;
    }

    abstract void calculateArea();  //abstract method
}

public class Rectangle extends Figure {
    Rectangle(double l, double b) {
          super(l, b);
    }

    void calculateArea() {          //implementing abstract method
          System.out.println("The area of the rectangle is: " + dimension1
                      * dimension2);
    }
}

public class Triangle extends Figure {
    Triangle(double base, double height) {
          super(base, height);
    }

    void calculateArea() {       //implementing abstract method
          double area = 0.5 * dimension1 * dimension2;
          System.out.println("The area of the triangle is: " + area);
    }
}

public class AbstractDemo {
    public static void main(String[] args) {
          Figure f;//reference of Figure class
          f = new Rectangle(3, 4);
          f.calculateArea();       //calls calculatArea() in Rectangle
          f = new Triangle(4, 5);
```

```
            f.calculateArea();//calls calculatArea() in Triangle
      }
  }
```

Output:

```
The area of the rectangle is: 12.0
The area of the triangle is: 10.0
```

If you observe carefully in the above example, the Figure class was not instantiated. This is because, abstract classes may contain abstract methods (which does not have any definition) and calling such methods is of no use. *Therefore, the java compiler prohibits us to instantiate any abstract class.* The example once more shows runtime polymorphism being implemented by using a Figure class reference variable. And calls to the *calculateArea()* method are resolved based upon where the Figure class reference variable points to, at the runtime.

Overriding and Overloading with Static methods

It is perfectly legal to overload static methods of a class, but overriding a static method yields a compile time error. This is because, the static methods belong to the class, not to an object and calls to an overridden method are resolved based upon where the super class reference points to at runtime.

Key points to remember regarding the Abstract keyword

- Abstract classes *can have* concrete methods in them.
- A class containing an abstract method is indeed abstract but an abstract class may or may not contain an abstract method.
- Only references for an abstract class can be created.
- If a subclass does not override an abstract method defined in its super class, then the compiler reports an error. In such a case, one should either implement the inherited abstract method or should define the subclass as abstract.
- There are no abstract constructors available in java. Having an abstract constructor in a class will make the class as abstract which means no objects can be created out of it. In such a case, the abstract constructor will never be invoked as constructors are not inherited.
- We cannot have abstract static methods. Having an abstract static method in a class means this method needs to be overridden in one of its subclasses but as we showed in the previous section, static methods cannot be overridden, hence the above statement holds true.

7.9 FINAL KEYWORD

Another significant keyword available in java is the *final* keyword. This keyword behaves differently when used with *classes, methods* and *variables*. Let us study the effect of using the final keyword with each of them:

- *Final Keyword with variables:* Final Keyword when used with a variable makes it a constant variable. Its value cannot be changed once assigned. The below example explains the same:

```
public class A {
        final int a=5;

        void meth() {
                a = 10; // not allowed
        }
}
```

The above code yields an error as there is an attempt to change the value of a final variable.

- *Final Keyword with methods:* Final when used with a method prevents that method to be overridden.

```
public class A {
        final void meth() {
                System.out.println("I am a final method");
        }
}

public class B extends A {
        void meth() { // error! cannot override a final method
                System.out.println("I am in B");
        }
}
```

This code generates an error as *"meth() being a final method in the superclass A cannot be overridden in subclass B"*

- *Final Keyword with classes:* Final classes are the classes that cannot be inherited.

```
final public class A {
        void meth() {
                System.out.println("I am a final method");
        }
}
public class B extends A {// error! cannot inherit from a final class A
        void meth() {
                System.out.println("I am in B");
        }
}
```

The code snippet above prevents class A to be inherited as A has been declared as a final class.

SUMMARY

- Inheritance is a process where one class acquires (inherits) properties/attributes of another class. The class from which the properties are inherited is called a *super class* and the class which inherits the properties of the other class is called a *subclass*.
- Inheritance is defined as "IS A" relationship between two classes.
- The private members of a class are not inherited into their subclass whereas the public members are available everywhere outside the class. The protected members on the other hand are only visible in their class and their subclass and the package level members are accessible inside their package only.
- The *super* keyword in java is used to call super class constructor and access super class members.
- The first statement written inside any subclass constructor is a call to *super* which calls the no-argument constructor of the super class by default.
- Multiple and hybrid inheritance in java is supported through interfaces.
- A superclass reference variable can point to a subclass object but the reverse is not true.
- A superclass reference variable can only invoke those methods that are of its own type. It cannot access members of its subclass type.
- The superclass constructor is always the first to be invoked in a constructor hierarchy.
- Method overriding is a mechanism by which one can redefine an inherited method in a subclass. It is a way by which java implements *runtime polymorphism.*
- Overridden method calls are resolved based upon which object, the super class reference points to, at run time.
- Overloaded method calls are resolved based upon the type of reference created and not the object.
- Abstract methods are the methods which do not have any definition.
- Abstract classes are those which may contain abstract methods.
- There does not exist any abstract constructor and abstract static method.
- It is the responsibility of the class inheriting an abstract class to give concrete implementations for all the abstract methods present in it. In case it is unable to do the same, then the class should be declared abstract.
- A *final* variable behaves as a constant variable, a *final* method cannot be overridden and a *final* class cannot be inherited.

COMMON ERRORS

- Accessing the members of a class at a place where they are not visible. Example: accessing private members outside their class.
- Missing no-argument constructor in a super class when invoked via super keyword.
- *Type mismatch error*, where a subclass reference points to a super class object.
- Using a super class reference variable to access subclass members which are not available in the super class.
- Getting confused between method overriding and method overloading.
- Not making a class as abstract even in the presence of certain abstract methods in it. A class has to be declared as abstract explicitly in such a case.
- Improper use of final keyword can lead to programming errors (see section 7.9).

SELF-TEST

1. What is inheritance? Can all members of a class be inherited in their subclass?
2. Explain the types of inheritance available in java with suitable examples and diagrams.
3. What are abstract classes? How does they differ from concrete classes? Can an abstract class be instantiated? Can there be an abstract constructor of a class? Explain with suitable examples.
4. How is method overloading different from method overriding? Explain.
5. Method overloading calls are resolved based upon the reference type whereas method overriding calls are based on the object type. Discuss.
6. Discuss the significance of super and final keywords in java.

PRACTICAL QUESTIONS

1. Will the code compile? If yes, what will be the output?

a)
```
public class Base {
   void callMe() {
         System.out.println("I am in Base");
   }
}

public class Sub extends Base {
   void callMe() {
          System.out.println("I am in Sub");
   }
}
```

```
public class SelfTest {
    public static void main(String[] args) {
          Sub s = new Base();
          s.callMe();
    }
}
```

b)
```
public class Base {
    void callMe() {
          System.out.println("I am in Base");
    }
}

public class Sub extends Base {
 void callMe() {
    System.out.println("I am in Sub");
    }

void callMeToo() {
    System.out.println("Called in sub class");
    }
}

public class SelfTest {
    public static void main(String[] args) {
         Base b = new Sub();
         b.callMeToo();
    }
}
```

c)
```
public class Base {
    void callMe() {
          System.out.println("I am in Base");
    }
}

public class Sub extends Base {
    void callMe() {
          System.out.println("I am in Sub");
    }

    void callMe(String msg) {
          System.out.println("Called with a message: " + msg);
    }
}

public class SelfTest {
    public static void main(String[] args) {
         Base b = new Sub();
         b.callMe();
         b.callMe("Hello");
```

```
    }
}
```

d)
```
public class Base {
void message() {
System.out.println("Parent");
}
}

public class Sub extends Base {
    void message() {
            System.out.println("Child");
}
}

public class SelfTest {
     public static void main(String[] args) {
           new Base().message();
}
     }
```

e)
```
public class Base {
     void message() {
           System.out.println("I am a static method");
     }
}

public class Sub extends Base {
     static void message() {
          System.out.println("I am a child method");
}
}
```

8 CHAPTER

Packages and Interfaces

This chapter will enable you to learn the following:

- Defining and executing a package.
- Learning about the accessibility of class members with respect to packages.
- Defining and understanding the need of interfaces.

A package can be viewed as a directory/folder which comprises a set of related classes and interfaces. They were introduced as a way of organizing various java resources. They are also used to avoid name space collisions as it allows us to create two classes with the same name as far as they reside in a different package.

Interfaces on the other hand, provide complete flexibility to a programmer to implement an application programming blueprint in different ways. This allows a blueprint or an interface to take up multiple forms as and when required.

8.1 DEFINING A PACKAGE

As said above, packages are a way of grouping a set of associated classes and interfaces. It is similar to the concept of folders that we have in our systems. For instance, one can create a *development* folder which comprises all the development tools for a specific language. Packages in java were also introduced to avoid name space collisions. They facilitate us to ensure no two names and locations of two classes collide with each other. One can use the same name for two classes till the time they reside in different packages.

We have been using the user defined class *Rectangle* in all our examples, whereas there exists a predefined class *Rectangle* too in java! The two class names used here do not conflict with each other because both of them belong to separate packages. The *Rectangle* class used in the above examples fits into the default package (as no package statement was included in its source file) whereas the predefined *Rectangle* class falls under the *java.awt* package.

How to define a package for a class?

A package can be defined using the keyword *package*. The following statement creates a package named *pkg* and puts *class A* under it.

```
package pkg;
class A
{
}
```

This statement ensures that all the classes written in this java source file fall under the package *pkg. The package statement must be written at the top of every java source file, omitting which these resources will be put under a default package which has no name. (This is why, you didn't care about packages till now while creating classes.) The naming convention to name a package in java is to choose a name with all lowercase letters.*

Hierarchy of Packages

One can create a hierarchy of packages by building packages inside other packages. For example, the predefined package *awt(abstract window toolkit)* resides inside another predefined package *java*. To access such packages, we specify a *dot* in between the two packages. Have a look at the below example:

java.awt denotes an access to the *awt* package inside the *java* package.

java.event denotes an access to event package inside the java package.

Therefore, to create a multilevel hierarchy of packages one can use the following syntax:

package pk1.pk2.pk3;

All the classes and interfaces using the above package statement will be a part of *pk3* package residing inside the *pk2* package which is under the *pk1* package as shown in Fig. 8.1.

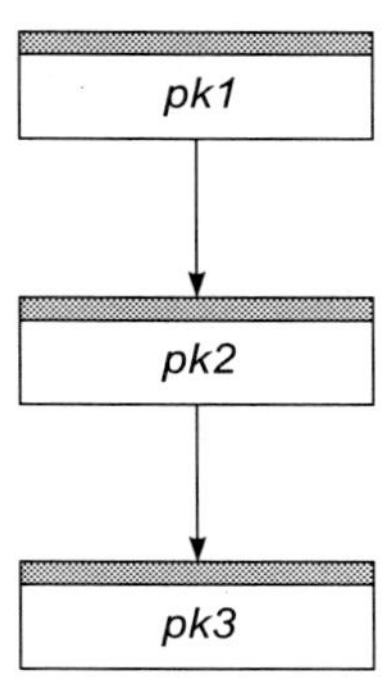

Fig. 8.1

8.2 ACCESSING PACKAGE MEMBERS

There can be times when members of one package are to be used in another package. In such a case, we can follow one of below given approaches:

- *Accessing a package member using its fully qualified name*

  A fully qualified name refers to the package name along with the member name. Take for an example the below code:

```
package pkg1;

public class A {
 public int a=10;   //public member in package pkg1
}

package pkg;

public class B {
     int b;    //member of package pkg with default access

     void setB() {     //member of package pkg with default access
          pkg1.A ob = new pkg1.A();   //accessing class A using
                                      //fully qualified name
          b = 2 * ob.a;
          System.out.println("The value of a is:" + ob.a);
          System.out.println("The value of b is:" + b);

     }
}
```

  As you can see above, we have two classes here,*A* and *B*, both belonging to different packages *pkg1* and *pkg* respectively. To access the member *a* of package *pkg1*, one needs to create an object of class *A* which has been done above using the fully qualified name of class *A*along with its package.

```
pkg1.A ob = new pkg1.A();
```

  Note that the member 'a' of package pkg1 could be accessed outside its own package because of its public nature.

- *Importing a package member*

  In the above case, one can also import the package member which has to be used or accessed in the other package. This can be done using the *import* statement[1]. The below given code explains the concept more vividly:

```
package pkg1;

public class A {
      public int a=10;   //public member in package pkg1
}
```

[1] The java.lang package is the package that gets implicitly imported in all our programs.

```
package pkg;
import pkg1.A;   //importing class A from the package pkg1
public class B {
      int b;   //member of package pkg with default access
      void setB() {     //member of package pkg with default access
            A ob = new A();   //accessing class A directly
            b = 2 * ob.a;
            System.out.println("The value of a is:" + ob.a);
            System.out.println("The value of b is:" + b);
      }
}
```

The import statement in the above code imports class *A* from the package *pkg1* into the package *pkg*. Once we have imported the member of the package we can use it directly without using its fully qualified name.

Note that the above program only imports class A from the package pkg1. If there would have been more members of the package, they would have not been imported inside package pkg.

- *Importing the entire package*

  Another case can be when one has to import all the classes/members of a package. In such a scenario, it is best to import the entire package rather importing all the members separately using different import statements. The below given example shows clearly how to import an entire package.

```
package pkg1;

public class A {
    public int a=10;   //public member in package pkg1
}

package pkg;
import pkg1.*;   //importing all members of the package pkg1
public class B {
    int b;   //member of package pkg with default access
    void setB() {     //member of package pkg with default access
        A ob = new A();   //accessing class A directly
        b = 2 * ob.a;
        System.out.println("The value of a is:" + ob.a);
        System.out.println("The value of b is:" + b);
    }
}
```

Note that the below given statement imports only classes and interfaces in the package *pkg1*.

```
import pkg1.*;
```

It does not import any packages inside *pkg1*. Take, for example, the following structure of a package *pkg1*:

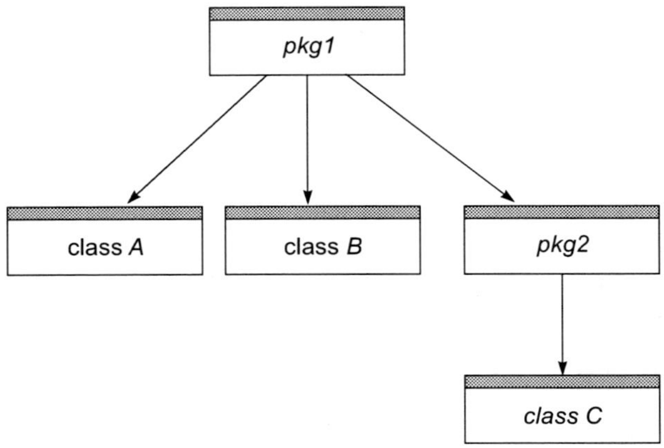

Fig. 8.2

According to the Fig. 8.2, the above import statement will import only the classes *A* and *B*. It will not import the package *pkg2* or class *C* in that case. To import class *C*, one needs to write the subsequent import statement:

```
import pkg1.pkg2.C;
```

8.3 COMPILING AND EXECUTING A PACKAGE

This section deals with how to compile and execute classes inside specific packages from command prompt/terminal. As we have talked earlier, packages are analogous to folders/directories. *When we define a new package, it should be put into a folder of the same name as that of the package.*

At the time of compilation of such classes, we can have two scenarios:

1. *Compiling the classes specifying the complete path:* For example, let us assume, a class *A* is stored under a package named *pkg1* (given in the below example). This implies that class A should be kept under a folder with the same name i.e., *pkg1*. Say, the complete path to A.java is D:\example\pkg1\A.java, so to compile the above class we can issue the command as below:

   D:\javac example\pkg1\A.java

   This creates the corresponding .class file for the same.

To execute the above class, we can issue the below given command indicating the complete path to A.java:

D:\java example\pkg1\A

Or

D:\java example\pkg1.A

Note that if we do not specify the complete path to A.java, the class will be searched in the current directory you are into at that point of time which can be denoted by a dot(.). If the file does not exist in the current directory, a *"file not found"* error will show up.

2. *Compiling the classes using classpath:* The *classpath* indicates the path where a class resides. One of the use cases where the *classpath* can be used is, when a class inside a package uses a *jar* file. A jar file is nothing but a java archived file which consists of .class files packaged together. Let us take up our previous example, where the class *A* now imports a class named *org.apache.commons.io.IOUtils* existing in the *commons-io.jar* file. Now the .class files inside this jar needs to be put on the *classpath* so that the JVM knows where to find it to compile A.java. In such a case we can use the below two approaches:

    - *Setting the classpath Environment Variable:* The *classpath* environment variable can be set up in a similar fashion as to how we set the *path* environment variable (discussed in the initial chapters). The value of this variable will be the path where we want the JVM to search for this jar. The name of the *classpath* variable is not case sensitive.
    - *Using the –cp or –classpath command:* One can also issue a *–cp* or *–classpath* command on the terminal as given below:

      D:\ javac –cp .* example\pkg1\A.java

      Or

      D:\javac –classpath .* example\pkg1\A.java

      This ensures to put all the files in the current directory on the *classpath* which are needed to compile A.java file (assuming our jar is kept in the current directory).

//Class A under package pkg1;

```
package pkg1;
import org.apache.commons.io.IOUtils;   //jar to be put on classpath
public class A {
    public static void main(String[] args) {
    }
}
```

8.4 ACCESS CONTROL IN PACKAGES

As deliberated in the earlier sections, java provides access control mechanism on *classes* as well as on *members* of classes. With packages coming into picture, access control mechanism can be seen from a new perspective.

The members of the class can be categorized into access levels of private, public, protected and default access level, ones with no access specifier (also called package private). The private members of a class are only visible inside their class. The public members on the other hand, are accessible to all the classes outside. The protected members are available inside their own package and to their immediate subclasses outside their package. Lastly, the default access members are visible inside their own package only. The access control of these members can be described clearly in Table 8.1 with respect to packages:

Table 8.1

Accessibility	Private members	Public members	Protected members	Package Private members (default access)
Within the class	√	√	√	√
Within the package	X	√	√	√
Outside the package in the subclass	X	√	√	X
Outside the package	X	√	X	X

The above table shows four levels of accessibility for the members of a class. The first level specifies whether the members of the class are available inside their own class and as we all know, all the members of a class are visible inside the class in which they are defined. The second level shows whether the members are accessible inside their own package. Baring the private members, all the members are available inside their own package. The third level indicates whether the members of a class are reachable outside their packages restricted to their immediate subclasses. And the fourth level demonstrates whether the members are obtainable outside their packages anywhere. The protected and pubic members are visible outside their packages with a constraint for protected members being seen in only their direct subclasses.

Let us now study an example illustrating the access mechanism for all the members of a class with respect to packages:

//A.java

```
package pkg1;

public class A {
    int defVar = 10; // default access member in package pkg1
    protected int protVar = 34; // protected member in package pkg1
```

```
    private int priVar = 23; // private member in package pkg1

    public void disp() {
           System.out.println("I am a public method");
    }
}
```

//B.java

```
package pkg1;

public class B {
    public void samePackage() {
           A o = new A();
           System.out.println(o.defVar); // accessing default variable in
                                                    //the same package
           System.out.println(o.protVar); // accessing protected variable
                                                      //in the same package

           /*
            * Error! No access to private variable in the same package
            */
           System.out.println(o.priVar);

           o.disp(); // accessing public member in the same package
    }
}
```

//C.java

```
package pkg2;

import pkg1.A;// importing class A of package pkg1
public class C extends A {
    public void diffPackage() {
           System.out.println(protVar); // accessing protected variable
                                        //outside its package in a subclass

           /*
            * Error! No access to private variable outside the package
            */
           System.out.println(priVar);

           /*
            * Error! No access to default variable outside the package
            */
           System.out.println(defVar);

    }

}
```

//Main.java

```
package pkg2;
import pkg1.*;// importing all the classes of package pkg1
public class Main {
    public static void main(String[] args) {
            A a = new A();
            a.disp(); // public members accessed anywhere
            /*
            Error! Cannot access protected, private and default variable
            outside the package
             */
            System.out.println(a.protVar);
            System.out.println(a.priVar);
            System.out.println(a.defVar);

    }
}
```

In the above example, we have two packages *pkg1* and*pkg2*. The package *pkg1* contains classes *A* and *B* whereas, the package *pkg2* consists of classes *C* (a subclass of A) and *Main*. The private members of classes *A* and *B* are confined to their class only whereas the protected members of class *A* are accessible inside its direct subclass *C* and also within the same package in class *B*. The public members are visible in every class inside any package. The members with no access specifier in class *A* are available within its own package, i.e in classes *A* and *B*.

8.5 INTERFACES

Interfaces is one of the most significant and beneficial topics in java used extensively today. To start with, let us first understand as to *what is an interface.*

All of us today cannot imagine our lives without the mobile phones wherein we have ample of applications to keep ourselves occupied and entertained. The dialler application in our phones provide us with a means to *make a call, disconnect a call, put a call on hold*, etc. This is possible because the application gives us an interface to interact with it. Therefore, what you see on your mobile screen is nothing but an interface through which you can communicate with all the applications. The speciality of an interface is that it is like a skeleton which can be given any shape or implementation. Such an interface enables different mobile phone manufacturers like Apple, Samsung, Nokia, etc., to have varied implementations for the same interface of their dialler application. For example, the conference call feature was not available in the earlier phones of Nokia but is available in Samsung and Apple now.

In java, an interface is a reference type, defined as similar to a class but consisting of only *abstract* methods. Put in other words, an interface cannot have any concrete methods inside it due to which *they cannot be instantiated.* Even the *variables inside an interface are final and static* implicitly. Different classes can implement this interface and provide their set of implementations to the abstract methods. *It is the responsibility of the implementing class to provide definitions for all the abstract methods available in the interface.*

Syntax for declaring an interface

```
public interface Name {
     data_Type var1;   //implicit public final static variables
     ....
     data_Type varN;
       ....
     ret_Type methodName(arg); //abstract methods
}
```

Name specifies the name of the interface including implicit public final static variables and a set of abstract methods.

//A concrete example for an interface

```
public interface Phone // interface named Phone
{
     void dialNumber(String number); // abstract method
     void disconnectCall();          // abstract method

}

//implementing class
public class MobilePhone implements Phone {
     public void dialNumber(String number) {
           System.out.println("Connecting to Mobile number " + number);
     }

     public void disconnectCall() {
           System.out.println("Disconnecting the wireless connection");
     }

}

public class LandLine implements Phone{
     public void dialNumber(String number) {
           System.out.println("Connecting to Landline Number " + number);
     }

     public void disconnectCall() {
           System.out.println("Disconnecting the wired connection");
     }
}
```

```
public class InterfaceDemo {
    public static void main(String[] args) {
        /*
         * error! cannot instantiate an interface
         * Phone phone=new Phone();
         */
        Phone phone; // valid
        phone = new MobilePhone();
        // calling MobilePhone methods
        phone.dialNumber("91+9823455111");
        phone.disconnectCall();
        phone = new LandLine();
        // calling LandLine methods
        phone.dialNumber("91+8676543218");
        phone.disconnectCall();

    }
}
```

Output:

```
Connecting to Mobile number 91+9823455111
Disconnecting the wireless connection
Connecting to Landline Number 91+8676543218
Disconnecting the wired connection
```

The above example defines an interface named *Phone* with the given below abstract methods:

```
void dialNumber(String number);
void disconnectCall();
```

A semicolon after a method signifies that they do not have any definition and are therefore abstract.

The two implementing classes *MobilePhone* and *LandLine* give their set of implementations for the abstract methods of the interface *Phone*. As we already know that interfaces cannot be instantiated, therefore, we declare a reference (*phone)* of the same. The JVM then checks where this reference points to at *runtime*. If it points to an object of *MobilePhone*, methods inside this class are called "else methods" inside *LandLine* class are invoked.

Observe, we have a string parameter inside the `dialNumber(String number)` method. String is a class (introduced in the first chapter) in java and the *number* refers to its object here which receives its corresponding value from the main method (example, `"91+9823455111")`. Also, spot that the methods inside the implementing classes are public. This is because all the methods of an interface are implicitly public and it is compulsory for an implementing class to define all the abstract methods as public.

Note that in the above example, it is mandatory for *MobilePhone* and *LandLine* classes to give complete implementations for all the abstract methods in the *Phone* interface missing which the compiler would issue an error.[2]

8.5.1 Interfaces and Multiple Inheritance

Interfaces in java facilitate us to have multiple inheritance. Multiple Inheritance as we talked in the previous chapter is the one, wherein we can have one child class inheriting from multiple base classes. Let us see this through an example given below:

```
public interface A {
     void meth1();
}

public interface B {
     void meth2();
}

public class ConcreteClass implements A, B // multiple inheritance through
// interfaces
{
     public void meth1() {
            System.out.println("I am from interface A");
     }

     public void meth2() {
            System.out.println("I am from interface B");
     }
}

public class InterfaceDemo {
     public static void main(String[] args) {
            A ar; //reference of interface A
            B br; //reference of interface B
            ar = new ConcreteClass();
            br = new ConcreteClass();
            ar.meth1(); //ar calls methods only in A
            br.meth2(); //br calls methods only in B

     }
}
```

This code clearly shows how a class can implement from multiple interfaces. *The important thing to observe here is that a reference of an interface is only capable of accessing members of its type. Therefore, ar could access meth1() and br could access meth2() only.*

---

[2] The check whether the implementing classes implement all the abstract methods of an interface or not, is done at compile time.

8.5.2 Extension of Interfaces

```
public interface A {
    void meth1();
}
public interface B extends A
{
    void meth2();
}
public class ConcreteClass implements B// multiple inheritance through
// interfaces
{
    public void meth1() {
        System.out.println("I am from interface A");
    }
    public void meth2() {
        System.out.println("I am from interface B");
    }
}
public class InterfaceDemo {
    public static void main(String[] args) {
        B br; //reference of interface B
        br = new ConcreteClass();
        br.meth1();
        br.meth2();
    }
}
```

We have an interface *B* in our example which extends from another interface *A*. Now when the class *ConcreteClass* implements an extended interface *B*, then it has to provide definitions for both the abstract methods: *meth1()* and *meth2()* as interface *B* now comprises two abstract methods after extending from *A*. This is why, the reference *br* of type *B* is able to call both the methods.

```
public interface A {
        void meth1()
}
public interface B implements A{
        void meth2()
        {
        }
}
```

This code generates a syntactical error as an interface in itself is abstract therefore, it cannot implement another interface. Implementing an interface would mean providing the definitions for all the abstract methods in that interface, which an interface is incapable of providing. Hence, the error.

8.5.3 Interface Variables

The variables inside an interface are *public, final and static* implicitly. Implicitly here means, whether we write it or not, the variables are so, by default. As you can recall, a public variable will be available everywhere inside and outside the class. A final variable acts like a constant variable whose value cannot be changed. *Therefore, remember to initialize the variables in the interface with a value else you will get a compile time error!* Finally, the interface variables are also marked as static because we do not want an interface to be instantiated. Hence, the static modifier, as it belongs to the class and not to particular objects. The following example elaborates this concept:

```
public interface Phone {
    int lock=1;//public static final by default
    int unlock=0;//public static final by default
    void checkStatus(int s);

}

public class Nokia implements Phone {
    public void checkStatus(int st) {
          if (st == lock) {
                System.out.println("Phone locked");

          } else
                System.out.println("Phone unlocked");
    }

}

public class Samsung implements Phone{
    public void checkStatus(int st) {
          if (st == lock) {
                System.out.println("Draw a pattern to unlock");
          } else if (st == unlock) {
                System.out.println("Unlocked");
          }
    }
}

public class InterfaceDemo {
    public static void main(String[] args) {
          Phone ref; // reference of interface Phone
          ref = new Nokia();
          ref.checkStatus(0);
          ref = new Samsung();
          ref.checkStatus(1);

    }
}
```

Output:

```
Phone unlocked
Draw a pattern to unlock
```

In the example above, we have the interface variables *lock* and *unlock* with a value of 1 and 0 respectively, and an abstract method *checkStatus(int)*. There are two classes *Nokia* and *Samsung* implementing the interface *Phone*. Both the classes, give their implementation for the abstract method present in the interface by accessing the interface variables. None of these classes are able to alter the value of these variables as they are final variables implicitly.

SUMMARY

- A package is analogous to a folder which can include related classes and interfaces; also used to resolve name space collisions.
- A package statement must be written in the beginning of every source file using the *package* keyword else the files are put into a default package which does not have any name.
- A hierarchy of packages can be accessed using the dot(.) operator.
- Access to package members can be done via one of the three approaches:
  - Using fully qualified name of the package
  - Importing a single member of the package
  - Importing the entire package
- Compilation and execution of packages can be done by either giving the complete path till the package or setting the *classpath*.
- Private members of a class are visible inside their own class whereas package private members are available inside the entire package. The protected members are visible inside their package and to their immediate subclasses outside the package. And the public members are accessible everywhere.
- An interface acts like a blueprint which can be given any implementation as and when required. They are used to facilitate multiple inheritance in java.
- Interfaces cannot be instantiated.
- Interfaces consist of abstract methods only and all its variables are public, final and static implicitly.
- One interface can extend another interface but cannot implement it.

COMMON ERRORS

- The most frequent mistake a java programmer does is to forget about importing the required package.
- Another mistake can be trying to instantiate an interface, which is not permitted.

- One often forgets to precede the public keyword before an implemented method inside a concrete class. Always remember the methods of an interface are public abstract methods. Therefore, one needs to define the methods as public in their implementing class.
- Reinitializing the value of an interface variable can result into a compile time error as they are public, final and static by default.
- Omitting the implementation for all the abstract methods of the interface in an implementing class can again yield a compile time error.
- Accessing members of a class inside an outside a package incorrectly.

SELF-TEST

1. Discuss how do we create packages in java. Also explain how does packages resolve name space collision in java?
2. Describe the various access protection levels available for packages in java.
3. What is the need for an interface in java when we have abstract classes available? Can interfaces be instantiated?
4. Discuss how to define an interface by giving an example for the same.
5. Differentiate between PATH and CLASSPATH variables in java.

PRACTICAL QUESTIONS

1. What will be the output for the following code:

a)
```
public interface A {
protected void check();

 }
```

b)
```
package pkg1;

class A {
      public void meth() {
              System.out.println("In A");
      }
}

package pkg1;

public class B extends A {
       public void meth() {
              System.out.println("In B");
       }
}
```

```
package pkg2;

import pkg1.A;
import pkg1.B;

public class Main {
    public static void main(String[] args) {
        A a = new B();
        a.meth();

    }
}
```

c)
```
package pkg1;

public class A {
    public static int id = 20;

}

package pkg2;

import pkg1.A;

public class Main {
    public static void main(String[] args) {
        System.out.println(A.id);

    }
}
```

2. Which of the following is a valid statement?

a)
```
public interface A {
public final static id = 3;

}
```

b)
```
public interface A {
int id = 3;

}
```

c)
```
public interface A {
public final static int id;

}
```

9
CHAPTER

Exception Handling

This chapter will enable you to learn the following:

- Learning exception handling fundamentals and the types of exception.
- Implementing exception handling using the *try, catch, throw, throws and finally* keyword.
- Catching multiple exceptions using a single catch block.
- Writing nested try blocks.
- Creating user-defined and chained exceptions.

Till now we have been studying majorly about compile time errors but we do encounter a lot of errors that occur at runtime while programming in java. This chapter focuses on handling mechanisms of such errors. *Exception is basically an abnormal circumstance that occurs at runtime.* Exception handling is the handling of such situations in a graceful manner so that it helps the developer to debug their code easily as well as facilitates the end user in using the product. It also helps in maintaining the normal flow of execution.

9.1 EXCEPTION HANDLING MECHANISM

An exception is a *java object* which is created when an exceptional or abnormal condition occurs in programming. For example, *attempting to divide a number by 0*. This computation is raises an exceptional condition. In such a case, an exception object is created by the method in which this error occurs and *thrown* to the *java runtime system.*

An exception object encompasses the *type of error that occurred* and the *current state of the program* when the error occurred. The java runtime system then tries to search an exception handler which can handle the exception. This search is initially done in the method which created the exception object. If an exception handler is not found here, then it tries to search it in the calling method. If no exception handler is present, java runtime system terminates the program.

Let us now formally define the five keywords that are used in exception handling:

try, catch, throw, throws and finally.

The statements that are susceptible to a runtime error are monitored under a *try* block. A block as we said earlier defines a new scope which starts and ends with a curly brace. When an exception in a method under a *try* block occurs, this method creates a corresponding exception object containing the type of error and the current state of program and throws this object to the java runtime system using the *throw* keyword. The JVM now finds a mechanism to handle this exception for which it tries to find a *matching catch* block. A matching catch block simply means that the type of exception object that was thrown should match with the type of exception defined in the catch block. If the JVM fails to find a matching catch block in the program, it terminates the program. The *throws* keyword is normally used with a method prototype and indicates the type of exceptions that the method might throw to the java runtime system. The *finally* block can be used when we want a set of statements to be executed whether or not an exception is thrown. Figure 9.1 portrays the exception handling mechanism clearly:

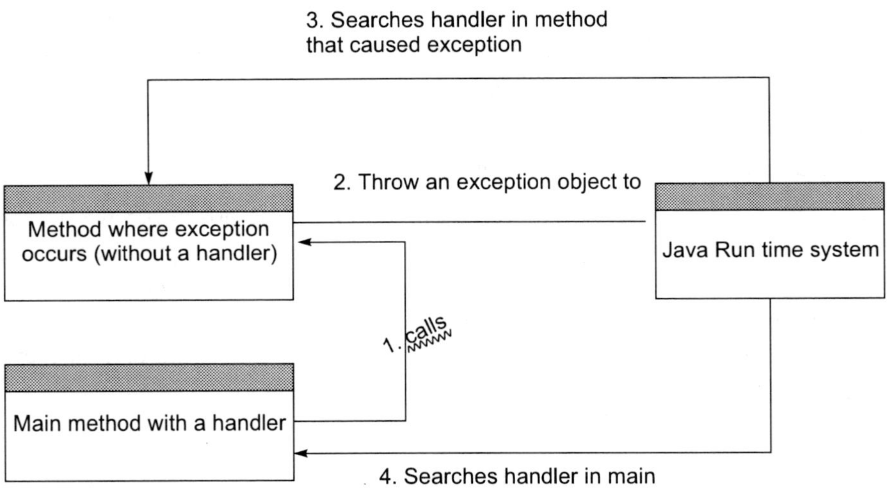

Fig. 9.1 Exception handling mechanism

The above figure shows the flow for handling exceptions. According to the figure, let us assume that the main method calls another method where an exceptional condition occurs. This method then creates an exception object based upon the type of exception that occurred and the current state of program and throws it to the java runtime system (using *throw*). The JVM then searches an exception handler (catch block) in the method that caused the exception. As this method does not contain a handler, the JVM now makes an attempt to find it in its calling method which is the main method, in this case. As the main method has a matching handler (catch block) for the same, exception is caught in here. If the JVM fails to find a catch block throughout the program, it leads to abnormal termination of the program.

Syntax for a simple try catch block:

```
try
{
    //code to be monitored for an exception
throw exception_Object   //throw an exception object to the jvm
}
catch(exception_Object)
{
//exception handler for catching exception_Object
}
finally
{
 //code to be executed in any case
}
```

9.2 LIFE WITHOUT EXCEPTION HANDLING

The above section gives an overview of how to handle abnormal conditions that occur while programming. But before we actually learn how to handle exceptions in detail, let us first have a look at what happens, if we do not handle such conditions in our program.

```
public class UncaughtExceptionDemo {
  public static void main(String args[]) {
        int var1 = 32;
        double result;
        result = var1 / 0; // exception arises
        System.out.println("The result is: " + result);
  }
 }
```

Output:

```
Exception in thread "main" java.lang.ArithmeticException: / by zero
    atUncaughtExceptionDemo.main(UncaughtExceptionDemo.java:5)
```

The above code indicates what happens if we do not incorporate exception handling mechanism in our code. There is an attempt to perform a divide by zero computation at line number 5. As this computation is undefined, an exception arises for which an exception object is created and thrown to the java runtime system by the main method. The next step is for the JVM to find a catch block in the main method. But as there is no catch block available in the main, JVM terminates the program and prints the *stacktrace*. A stacktrace generally shows up when a thrown exception is not caught. It displays the point where the error occurred and also a description about how the program terminated. In our case, an exception of type *ArithmeticException* is thrown. For each type of exception, java provides an Exception class for the same. To handle divide by zero errors, we have a corresponding class *ArithmeticException* available.

The stacktrace contains a description of the following:

- The type of exception that arises along with its package: `java.lang.ArithmeticException`
- The description of the error: `/ by zero`
- The class name in which the error occurs: `UncaughtExceptionDemo`
- The method where exception arises: `main`
- The filename and the line number at which the exception arises: `UncaughtExceptionDemo.java:5`

9.3 TYPES OF EXCEPTIONS

Every exception class in java follows a hierarchy. At the top of the hierarchy is the *Throwable* class. *Throwable*, in turn, inherits from the *Object* class, which is the super class of all the classes in java. Figure 9.2 shows the hierarchy of exception classes.

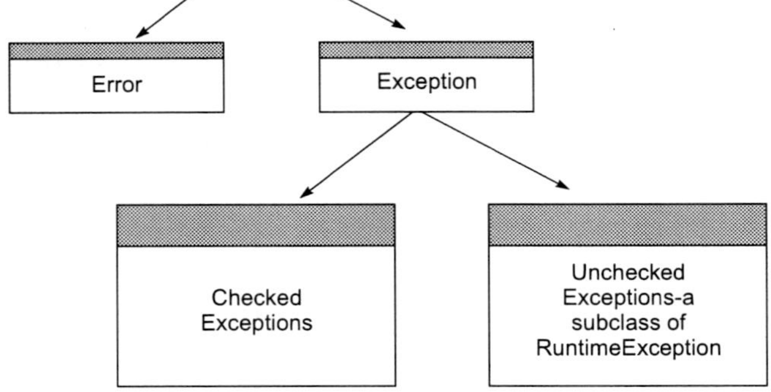

Fig. 9.2 Hierarchy of exception classes

As you can see from Fig. 9.2 the *Object* class stands at the root of hierarchy. *Throwable*, a subclass of Object class, serves as a super class for *Error* and *Exception* classes. The Error class denotes errors that are caused by the java runtime system. Example, errors like *OutOfMemoryError*. Such errors cannot be handled because even if you handle such an error, it will come up again and again till the garbage collector acts and frees up some memory. On the contrary, we have the Exception class which represents exceptions that can be handled using a try catch block. These exceptions generally refer to the errors caused by programmers while development. Exception classes can be further divided into two categories: *Checked* and *Unchecked Exceptions*. A checked exception is a must to handle, failing which the compiler reports an error. Unchecked Exceptions on the other hand, are a subclass of *RuntimeException* class. These exceptions need not be handled as the java runtime system catches the same.

Note: All these classes are present in java.lang package.

9.4 USING A TRY CATCH BLOCK

In the previous section, the program terminated abruptly because we did not handle the arising exceptions. Let us now see how to handle these errors in the below example using a simple try catch block. But before that, let us study some of the rules to using a try catch block:

1. *try* and *catch* are blocks, therefore, all the statements under them will be enclosed within curly braces.
2. The moment an exception arises under a *try* block, the flow of execution jumps to a *matching* catch block and all the statements in between, are bypassed. A *matching* catch block is a block which is capable of catching exceptions of the same type as were thrown using the *throw* keyword. After completing the statements under a catch block, the control never goes back to the try block, it simply continues to execute statements after the catch block.[1]
3. *try* and *catch* blocks are used a single unit.
4. A *catch* block used without a *try* results into a compile time error.
5. In case of multiple *catch* blocks, only one of the *catch* block is executed and the rest are bypassed.
6. A super class object, used as a parameter to a catch block, is capable of catching exceptions of its type and of its subclass type.
7. Multiple exceptions can be caught with a single *catch* block.
8. A *try* block cannot exist independently. It has to accompany either a *catch* or a *finally* block.

---

[1] *Catch* is a block and not a method therefore, the control never goes back to a *try* after an exception is handled.

//An example for a simple try catch block

```
1 public class TryCatchDemo {
2   public static void main(String args[]) {
3           int var1 = 32;
4           double result;
5           try {                       // try block
6                   result = var1 / 0; // exception arises
7                   System.out.println("The result is: " + result);
8           } catch (ArithmeticException e) {    // catch block
9                   System.out.println("Caught exception: " + e);
10          }
11
12  }
13 }
```

Output:

```
Caught exception: java.lang.ArithmeticException: / by zero
```

Notice, an exception arises at line number 6 under the *try* block. As a divide by zero exception arises, therefore, an object of *ArithmeticException* class is created and thrown to the java runtime system. The java runtime system, in turn, searches a matching catch block inside the main method and finds it at line number 8. Line number 7 in this case is bypassed as the control of execution now jumps directly to a catch block. *Remember, if an exception is thrown, the flow of control goes directly to a matching catch block bypassing all the statements in between.*

Observe that the catch block catches an object of type *ArithmeticException* (as the parameter passed is a reference of type *ArithmeticException*). The catch block prints a message *caught exception* along with an object *e* of *ArithmeticException. Note that whenever an object of a class is printed, a toString() method of that class is invoked.* This method will be discussed at length while we are studying string handling in the coming chapters. But for now, a *toString()*, simply prints a description of the exception here.

9.5 MULTIPLE CATCH BLOCKS

There are times when a code inside a method can throw varied types of exceptions. In such a case, one needs to have multiple catch blocks inside a program. The type of exception thrown determines which catch block will be executed. *Also, if one catch block executes, all the others are bypassed for that particular execution.*

The following example demonstrates the flow of execution when there are multiple catch blocks inside a program:

```
public class A {
    void call() {
            System.out.println("Getting called");
    }

  }
```

```
1 public class MultipleCatchDemo {
2    public static void main(String args[]) {
3           int var1 = 32;
4           int var2 = 0;
5           double result;
6           A ob = null; // null reference of class A, not an object
7           try {
8                  ob.call(); // NullPointerException arises
9                  result = var1 / var2; // ArithmeticException arises
10                 System.out.println("The result is: " + result);
11
12          } catch (ArithmeticException e) {
13                 System.out.println("Caught exception: " + e);
14          } catch (NullPointerException e) {
15                 System.out.println("Caught exception: " + e);
16          }
17
18   }
19 }
```

Output:

```
Caught exception: java.lang.NullPointerException
```

Notice that we have two catch blocks in the above program. One of them catches an exception of type *ArithmeticException* and the other of the type *NullPointerException*. The *ArithmeticException* class as we said earlier is capable of handling errors of type divide by zero. *NullPointerException* arises when we attempt to use null references in our program. Null references are references that have been assigned to null. *It is a good practice to assign references to null initially so that they don't point to invalid locations.* A *NullPointerException* arises at line number 8 for which an object of *NullPointerException* is created and thrown to JVM. JVM then executes a matching catch block which it finds at line number 14. This is why, the line numbers from 9-13 are not executed. The catch block for *NullPointerException* prints a description of the exception when printing its object as the *toString()* gets called.

Note: If the JVM fails to find a matching catch block in a program, it leads to abnormal termination of the program.

Multiple catch using subclass and super class reference

A catch block with a super class object is capable of catching all exceptions of its type and of its subclass type. Therefore, make sure whenever you have a multiple catch block which contains a super class and a subclass object, the catch block with the subclass object must appear before the super class object. This will ensure specific description of the exception.

The following example shows the same:

```
public class A {
    void call() {
        System.out.println("Getting called");
    }

}
```

```
1 public class MultipleCatchDemo {
2     public static void main(String args[]) {
3         int var1 = 32;
4         int var2 = 0;
5         double result;
6         try {
7             result = var1 / var2; // ArithmeticException arises
8             System.out.println("The result is: " + result);
9         } catch (Exception e) {
10            System.out.println("Caught exception: " + e);
11        } catch (ArithmeticException e) { // error! Unreachable code
12            System.out.println("Caught exception: " + e);
13        }
14    }
15 }
```

Line number 11 generates a compile time error stating "unreachable code" because we have a super class object up in the hierarchy handling the exception object (Exception class is the super class for all the exception and error classes). Therefore, the next catch block catching an object of *ArithmeticException* will never be executed. To correct this version of the program, simply place the second catch block above the first catch block.

9.6 MULTIPLE EXCEPTIONS USING A SINGLE CATCH BLOCK

Java 7 has introduced a new feature wherein one can catch multiple exceptions using a single catch block. This reduces a lot of duplicity in the code and also eases development effort. Have a look at the following example to see how it works:

```
public class A {
    void call() {
        System.out.println("Getting called");
    }

}
```

```
1 public class MultipleExceptionDemo {
2    public static void main(String args[]) {
3          int var1 = 32;
4          int var2 = 0;
5          double result;
6          Base ob = null; // reference of class A, not an object
7          try {
8                ob.call(); // NullPointerException arises
9                result = var1 / var2; // ArithmeticException arises
10               System.out.println("The result is: " + result);
11
12         } catch (ArithmeticException | NullPointerException e) {
13               System.out.println("Caught exception: " + e);
14
15         }
16
17   }
18 }
```

Output:

```
Caught exception: java.lang.NullPointerException
```

Observe carefully the arguments passed to the above catch block. Multiple exception types can be passed as a parameter to a single catch block separated by a pipe (|). Therefore, line number 12 indicates that this catch block is capable of handling exceptions of type *ArithmeticException* as well as of type *NullPointerException*. The type of exception thrown is inspected and a matching catch block is executed.

9.7 NESTED TRY BLOCK

A nested try block means a try block inside another try block. This can be useful when the inner block throws a different type of exception than the outer block. When the inner block throws an exception, it is checked for a handler. If it fails to provide a handler, the outer block is then inspected for the same. And if there does not exist any handler throughout the program, the java runtime system handles the exception. The subsequent example displays how a nested try block can be used in a program.

```
1 public class NestedTryDemo {
2   public static void main(String[]args) {
3           int var1 = 32;
4           int var2 = 0;
5           double result;
6           int []arr={1,2,3,4};
7           try {
8                   try{ // inner try block
9                           System.out.println("The fourth element of the
                            array  is:"+ arr[4]); // exception arises
10                  } catch (ArrayIndexOutOfBoundsException e) {
11                          System.out.println("Caught exception: " + e);
12                  }
13                  result = var1 / var2; // exception arises
14                  System.out.println("The result is: " + result);
15          } catch (ArithmeticException e) {
16                  System.out.println("Caught exception: " + e);
17          }
18    }
19 }
```

Output:

```
Caught exception: java.lang.ArrayIndexOutOfBoundsException: 4
Caught exception: java.lang.ArithmeticException: / by zero
```

The output shows that the above code handles two types of exceptions using two catch blocks. Let us have a close look at the example. Line number 9 inside the inner try block throws an exception of type *ArrayIndexOutOfBoundsException* for which a catch block is found at line number 10 (inside inner try block). An *ArrayIndexOutOfBoundsException* arises when there is an attempt to access an element of the array which does not exist. In this example the array *arr* comprises 4 elements indexing from 0 to 3. The moment there is an access to *arr[4]*, the method throws an exception of the above type. After handling the exception at line number 10, the flow goes to the next line after inner catch block, i.e., at line number 13. This line further throws an exception of type *ArithmeticException* for which a handler is found at line number 15. This is how the program is able to catch two different types of exceptions.

9.8 THROW

Till now you have learnt how exceptions are generated and thrown *automatically* by a method to the JVM. This section will focus upon how exceptions can be thrown *manually* by a method to the JVM. An exception can be thrown manually using the *throw* keyword. The syntax for the same is given below:

throw instance_Of_Throwable;

Any method can throw an exception but the exception thrown should be an instance of *Throwable*. *Throwable* is a predefined class in java in the *java.lang* package. An instance of *Throwable* is an object of *Throwable* class or any of its subclasses. *Throwable* is said to be the super class of all the errors and exception classes in java. Therefore, classes like *ArithmeticException*, *NullPointerException*, *ArrayIndexOutOfBoundsException* are all subclasses of *Throwable*.

Why throw exceptions manually?

Consider an application where users are required to upload their personal details which includes their name, age, gender, etc. In such a scenario, the developers can make a check if the end user has uploaded a valid age or not. (An example of an invalid age could be 1000 where the user has mistyped his/her age.) If the user has entered an invalid age, the developers can throw/raise an exception manually signifying invalid data.

The following example illustrates throwing exceptions manually

```
class A {
    public void callMe() {
//throw exception using throw
          throw new NullPointerException("Null Pointer Access");
    }
}

public class ThrowDemo {
    public static void main(String[] args) {
          try {
                A o = new A();
                o.callMe();
          } catch (NullPointerException e) {
                System.out.println("Caught exception: " + e);
          }
    }
}
```

Output:

```
Caught exception: java.lang.NullPointerException: Null Pointer Access
```

The program shows a little different version of exception handling from the previous programs. We have a try catch block inside the main method under which the *callMe()* method gets called. The below line creates an object of *NullPointerException* and throws it to the JVM:

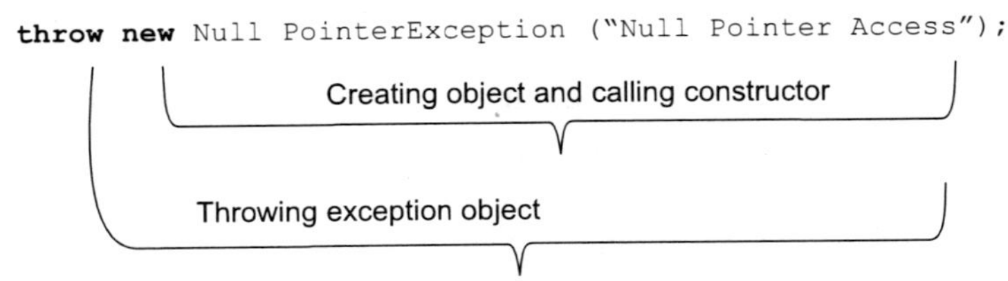

Fig. 9.3

Notice the parentheses in the above statement. The parentheses indicate that a call to the parameterized constructor of the class *NullPointerException* is made upon its object creation. This string parameter denotes the detailed description for the exception thrown. As soon as the exception is thrown, an inspection for the same type of catch block is made (the one, which is capable of handling NulPointerException). The compiler fails to find it in the *callMe()*method therefore, now the search is made its calling method, i.e., the main method. And yes! there exists a matching catch block which catches the exception and ends the program execution.

Re-throwing an exception

Sometimes, we may want to log a specific exception and then forward the exception object in the program. In such a case, we can re-throw an exception which has already been thrown once.

The following example shows how to re-throw an exception object from inside the catch block:

```
class A {
  public void callMe() {
        try {
              throw new NumberFormatException("conversion failed");
        } catch (NumberFormatException e) {
              throw e; // re-throwing exception object
        }
  }
}
```

```
public class RethrowDemo {
  public static void main(String args[]) {
        try {
              A o = new A();
              o.callMe();
        } catch (NumberFormatException e) {
              System.out.println("Caught again " + e);
        }
  }
}
```

Output:

```
Caught again java.lang.NumberFormatException: conversion failed
```

Line number 4 in class *A* throws an exception of type *NumberFormatException*. This type of exception arises when an invalid conversion between a string and a number takes place. Notice, the compiler finds a catch block for the same at line number 5. But this time, inside the catch block, the exception object is re-thrown. When an exception object is re-thrown, a handler (catch block) with the same type is searched initially in the same method. If the compiler is not able to find one, it then tries to find it in its calling method. If it does not find it throughout the hierarchy, then the JVM handles the exception by printing the stacktrace.

9.9 THROWS

The *throws* keyword is different from the *throw* keyword. The *throw* keyword which you studied above is used to throw an exception object explicitly and is used inside a method. The *throws* keyword, on the other hand, is used with a method prototype to warn a programmer that this method might throw exception types as specified in the *throws-list*. A *throws-list* is a list of comma separated exceptions, a method might throw.

Syntax:

```
public void callMe() throws throw-list{
}
```

Relation of throws with checked and unchecked exceptions

As discussed above, a checked exception is mandatory to handle. So if a method throws a checked exception, it must handle the exception either by enclosing its code inside a try catch block or using the *throws* keyword. Using throws with such a method is a way to indicate the compiler that *"this method might throw an exception of the specified type but might not handle it, therefore, do not report an error, instead look for its handler in the calling method."*

On the contrary, it is not compulsory to specify the throws keyword with an unchecked exception type. Unchecked exceptions are not checked at compile time and if not handled, they are handled by the java run time system.

List of checked and unchecked exceptions

Table 9.1 Unchecked exceptions

Exception	Arising situation
ArithmeticException	Arithmetic operation errors like divide by zero
ArrayIndexOutOfBoundsException	Access to an invalid array index

(Contd.)

ArrayStoreException	Assigning an incompatible type element in an array
ClassCastException	Casting an invalid type
IllegalArgumentException	Illegal argument being passed to a method
IllegalMonitorStateException	Illegal monitor operation
IllegalStateException	Indicates an invalid state for an application
IllegalThreadStateException	Inappropriate state for a thread in operation
IndexOutOfBoundsException	Some index is out of bound
NegativeArraySizeException	Array with a negative size
NullPointerException	Using a null reference
NumberFormatException	Invalid conversion between a string and a number
SecurityException	Indicates some sort of security has been violated
StringIndexOutOfBounds	Access to an invalid index of a string
UnsupportedOperationException	Unsupported operation takes place

Table 9.2 Checked exceptions

Exception	Arising situation
ClassNotFoundException	When an attempt to load a class fails
CloneNotSupportedException	Access to an invalid array index
IllegalAccessException	Illegal access to a class has been made
InstantiationException	Attempt to instantiate abstract classes or interfaces
InterruptedException	Occurs when one thread is interrupted by another
NoSuchFieldException	Attempt to access an invalid field
NoSuchMethodException	Attempt to access an invalid method

//An example of checked exception

```
class A {
  public void callMe(){
             //error! checked exception
        throw new IllegalAccessException("access denied");
  }
}
```

```
public class ThrowsDemo {
  public static void main(String args[]) {
```

```
3           try {
4                  A o = new A();
5                  o.callMe();
6           } catch (IllegalAccessException e) {
7           System.out.println("Caught exception" + e);
8           }
9     }
10}
```

Notice Line number 4 in the *callMe()* method throws a checked exception of the type *IllegalAccessException*. As checked exceptions are a mandate to handle and this method does not do so, it results in a compile time error. In such a case, it does not look into its calling method if it has handled the exception or not.

//Corrected version of the above program

```
class A {
    public void callMe() throws IllegalAccessException {
           throw new IllegalAccessException("access denied");
    }
}

public class ThrowsDemo {
    public static void main(String args[]) {
           try {
                  A o = new A();
                  o.callMe();
           } catch (IllegalAccessException e) {
                  System.out.println("Caught exception" + e);
           }
    }
}
```

The throws keyword used above indicates that this method might not handle the thrown exception, therefore, look into its calling method to find its handler. If the calling method is also unable to provide a handler, it results into a compile time error.

//An example of unchecked exception

```
class A {
    public void callMe() {
           throw new ArithmeticException("divide by zero");
    }
}
public class ThrowsDemo {
    public static void main(String args[]) {
           try {
```

```
                A o = new A();
                o.callMe();
            } catch (ArithmeticException e) {
                System.out.println("Caught exception" + e);
            }
        }
    }
```

The *callMe()* method here throws an unchecked exception and does not handle it. But the compiler does not report an error in this case. The next thing a compiler does is to find a handler in its calling method. If the calling method also does not provide a try catch block, the java runtime system handles the exception.

9.10 FINALLY

Consider a method that throws an exception, wherein you have written a code for opening and closing a file inside a try block. There is a possibility that the code for closing the file is bypassed when the exception is thrown. To avoid such situations we can use *finally* and ensure proper opening and closing of files. *Finally keyword is used with a try block.* The code inside the finally block executes once the try block ends.

There can be three types of flows in a program:

1. An exception does not occur.
2. An exception occurs but is not handled.
3. An exception occurs and is handled.

In all these cases, code inside the finally block always execute. This is why it is a good idea to place the code which is extremely important and needs to be executed in every case, inside a finally block. In other words, finally ensures execution of the set of statements falling under it in all the above cases. Let us examine each case with an example:

//finally when no exception occurs

```
class A {
    public void callMe() {
        try {
            return;
        }
        finally {
            System.out.println("finally executes when no exception
            occurs");
        }
    }
}
```

```
public class FinallyDemo {
    public static void main(String args[]) {
          A o = new A();
          o.callMe();
    }
}
```

Output:

```
finally executes when no exception occurs
```

Note that the *callMe()* method doesn't throw any exception instead uses a return statement to return to its caller method inside the try block. But as we know, finally block executes in every case therefore, the code gets executed even before we return to the caller method.

//finally when an exception occurs but is not handled

```
class A {
    public void callMe() {
          try {
                throw new ArithmeticException("divide by zero");
          } finally {
                System.out
                                  .println("finally executes when an unhandled
exception occurs");
          }
    }
}

public class FinallyDemo {
    public static void main(String args[]) {
          A o = new A();
          o.callMe();
    }
}
```

Output:

```
finally executes when an unhandled exception occurs
Exception in thread "main" java.lang.ArithmeticException: divide by zero
    at A.callMe(A.java:4)
    at FinallyDemo.main(FinallyDemo.java:4)
```

The output clearly shows that finally executes even when the exception thrown is not handled by any method. After the execution of finally block, the exception is handled by the JVM as it is an unchecked exception.

//finally when an exception occurs and is handled

```
class A {
    public void callMe() {
        try {
            throw new IllegalAccessException("access denied");
        } catch (IllegalAccessException e) {
            System.out.println("Caught exception " + e);
        } finally {
            System.out
                        .println("finally executes when the thrown
                         exception is handled");
        }
    }
}
public class FinallyDemo {
    public static void main(String args[]) {
        A o = new A();
        o.callMe();
    }
}
```

Output:

```
Caught exception java.lang.IllegalAccessException: access denied
finally executes when the thrown exception is handled
```

In this case, an exception of type *IllegalAccessException* is thrown by the method *callMe()* and caught inside its catch block, executing the finally block thereafter. After the termination of the catch block, the flow returns to its caller method.

9.11 USER-DEFINED EXCEPTION

Although, we have a set of in-built exception classes in java, still there might be situations when one needs to create his/her own exception class. Consider an order management system where we do not want the customer to order below a certain quantity and if he does, an exception should be thrown by that method. *Custom exceptions* or *user defined exceptions* accomplish this need. One can easily create a custom exception class by creating a subclass of the predefined Exception class. In a way, it becomes a subclass of *Throwable* class (as *Throwable* is the superclass for all exception and error classes). Let us now see how a custom exception class can be created.

```
class CustomException extends Exception {
    int qty;

    public CustomException(int qty) {
        this.qty = qty;
    }
```

```
    public String toString() { // overriding toString() from Object class
        return "Order quantity " + qty + " is not sufficient";
    }
}
public class CustomExceptionDemo {
    public static void main(String args[]) {
        checkQuantity(150);
        checkQuantity(240);
    }

    static void checkQuantity(int qty) { // validating the quantity ordered
        try {
            if (qty< 200) {
// throwing a user- defined exception
                throw new CustomException(qty);
            } else
                System.out.println("Order Successful");
        } catch (CustomException e) { // toString() getting invoked
            System.out.println(e);
        }

    }
}
```

The class *CustomException* is defined as a subclass of *Exception* class. The main method above gives a call to the *checkQuantity()* method which checks if the ordered quantity is less than 200 or not. If it is, it throws an object of our user-defined class *CustomException*. *All user-defined exception classes are checked exception classes, therefore, you either need to enclose your code inside a try catch block or use the throws keyword.* Upon creation of an object of the *CustomException* class, its constructor is invoked which initializes the class instance variable *qty*. Thereafter, this object is thrown. The flow then travels to its matching catch block where it prints the object of the class. As you know from earlier topics, whenever we print an object of the class, the *toString()* method of the Object class is invoked hence, here the overridden version of *toString()* is called.

9.12 CHAINED EXCEPTIONS

There are times when one exception in an application can cause another exception. For example, you might encounter a divide by zero exception in your application when an attempt to divide a number by zero is made. But it is possible that the underlying cause for the exception could be some error in input output operations. Therefore, if we do not pass an exception object of IOException, the user would never get to know the cause of the exception. Such kind of exceptions are called *Chained Exceptions*. Following are some of the methods and constructors of class *Throwable* which facilitate us accomplishing the above goal.

Throwable(Throwable instance)
Throwable(String desc, Throwable instance)
Throwable getCause()
Throwable initCause(Throwable instance)

In the first version, we have an object of *Throwable* class which depicts the cause of the underlying exception. The second version of the constructor allows us to give a description of the exception as well as specify the object which caused the exception.

The *getCause()* method returns the cause of the exception as the throwable object. Whereas, the *initCause()*method allows us to set the cause of the current exception.

The following example portrays the use of chained exceptions:

```
import java.io.IOException;

public class ChainedExceptionDemo {
    public static void main(String args[]) {
            try {
                    check(4, 0);
            } catch (ArithmeticException e) {
                    System.out.println("caught " + e);
//getting the underlying cause for exception
                    System.out.println("underlying cause " + e.getCause());
            }

    }

    static void check(int num1, int num2) {
            if (num2 == 0) {
                    ArithmeticException a=new ArithmeticException("divide
                    by zero");
                    // setting the underlying cause for exception
            a.initCause(new IOException());
                    throw a;
            }
    }
}
```

Output:

```
caughtjava.lang.ArithmeticException: divide by zero
underlying cause java.io.IOException
```

The first statement uses an import statement to import the class *IOException* as it is being used in the program. The main method calls another static method *check()* to see if there exists a divide by zero error on dividing two numbers. If it is, an object for *ArithmeticException* class is created and the *initCause()* method is invoked to set the underlying cause for the *ArithmeticException* as *IOException*. This object is then thrown and caught by a catch block in the main method wherein we get the real cause for the exception by calling the *getCause()* method.

SUMMARY

- Exception handling is handling abnormal conditions that occur at runtime by using the five keywords: try, catch, finally, throw and throws.
- The code susceptible to a runtime error is placed inside a *try* block.
- An exception object is created based upon the type of the error and the state of the program.
- A catch block can be used to handle different types of exception.
- *Throwable* stands at the top of the hierarchy of exception classes having subclasses *Exception* and *Error*.
- The *Error* class deals with the errors that are caused by java runtime system whereas the *Exception* class deals with the errors produced by programmers.
- The *Exception* class has two subclasses further, checked and unchecked exceptions.
- Multiple catch blocks can be used to handle varied type of exceptions arising in a single piece of code. If one catch block executes, others are bypassed.
- A nested try block is one *try* block inside another *try* block.
- The throw keyword is used to throw an exception explicitly.
- The throws keyword is used with a method prototype to indicate a list of exceptions a method might throw.
- Checked exceptions are the exception classes for which when an object is thrown and not caught, generates a compile time error. In such a case, these exceptions should either be caught inside a catch block or should use the throws keyword with them. This is not the case with unchecked exceptions.
- The *finally* block is used to ensure the execution of a set of statements in every case whether or not an exception is thrown, when a try block exits.
- An user-defined exception is the one created by the user to handle any custom exceptions.
- A chained exception indicates when one exception in an application is a cause of another exception.

COMMON ERRORS

- Putting an empty catch block. In such a case, you will be able to avoid a compile time error but what exception actually occurred will be unknown.
- Using a superclass exception type to catch a specific exception.
- Forgetting to handle checked exceptions.

- Handling unchecked exceptions. Unchecked exceptions are a mistake of the programmer therefore, instead of handling them, one should try avoiding performing divide by zero errors or using null references.
- Handling exceptions of Error class. They fall into errors caused by java runtime system. Therefore, there is no use handling such errors.

SELF-TEST

1. What are exceptions? Explain how they are handled in java.
2. How can we deal with multiple exceptions in java?
3. Differentiate between throw and throws keyword.
4. Explain the usage of finally keyword.
5. What are custom exceptions in java? How do we create them?
6. Write a short note on chained exceptions.

PRACTICAL QUESTIONS

1. Give the output for the following:

a)
```
public class SelfTest {
public static void main(String[] args) {
     try {
          meth();
     } catch (IllegalAccessException e) {
          System.out.println(e);
     }

}

public static void meth() {
     try {
          throw new IllegalAccessException("access denied");
     } catch (IllegalAccessException e) {
          System.out.println(e);
     }
}
}
```

b)
```
public class SelfTest {
public static void main(String[] args) {
     try {
          meth();
```

```
        } catch (Exception e) {
            System.out.println(e);
        }

    }
    public static void meth() {
        try {
            throw new IllegalAccessException("access denied");
        } catch (IllegalAccessException e) {
            System.out.println(e);
        }
    }
}
```

c)
```
public class SelfTest {
    public static void main(String[] args) {
        try {
            meth();
        } catch (Exception e) {
            System.out.println(e);
        } finally {
            System.out.println("Main finally");
        }
    }

    public static void meth() throws IllegalAccessException {
        try {
            throw new IllegalAccessException("access denied");
        }
        finally {
            System.out.println("Meth finally");
        }
    }
}
```

d)
```
public class Base {
        public void meth() throws IllegalAccessException,
    NoSuchMethodError {
            System.out.println("Base version");
        }
    }

    public class Child extends Base {
        public void meth() throws IllegalAccessException,NoSuchMethod
        Error, ClassNotFoundException {
            System.out.println("Child version");
        }
    }
```

```
public class SelfTest {
   public static void main(String[] args) {
        Base b = new Child();
        try {
              b.meth();
        } catch (Exception e) {
              System.out.println(e);
        }
   }
}
```

10 CHAPTER

Multithreading

This chapter will enable you to learn the following:

- Defining a thread.
- Differentiating between single threaded and multi-threaded model.
- Learning the life cycle of a thread.
- Creating threads using the Thread class and the Runnable interface.
- Creating multiple threads.
- Studying the significance of *isAlive()* and *join()* methods.
- Scheduling threads based on their priority.
- Implementing thread synchronization and interthread communication.

This chapter focuses on introducing concurrency in our applications. Concurrency in an application means, having several parts of the application run simultaneously. Java introduced threads to facilitate this concept. The upcoming sections of the chapter will talk in detail about the creation of threads and the communication between several threads.

10.1 OVERVIEW

Concurrency today has become an important part of our lives which can be defined as performing multiple tasks at the same time. Concurrent Programming consists of two concepts: *multitasking* and *multithreading*.

Multitasking, as you must be well aware, exists between a set of processes. *A process can be treated analogous to a program or an application that is executing currently.* It has its own address space to store instructions. An example of multitasking could be when one is working with text editor, skype and eclipse simultaneously. As two processes will have a different address space therefore there is no possibility of them overlapping, hence no synchronization is needed to access a shared resource. The processes use Inter Process Communication to communicate between two processes.

Multithreading on the other hand, exists between threads. *A thread is said to be a lightweight process as it is a part of an existing process.* Since, a thread is a part of a process, it shares its address space but has its own *stack, program counter* and *local variables.* An example for the same would be a music application which is capable of playing, downloading, and searching music, all at the same time. Java schedules several threads for performing these tasks concurrently. Therefore, *multithreading is executing multiple tasks within the same application whereas multitasking is executing multiple tasks between different processes at the same time.* As two threads within the same application will be sharing the same address space of the application/process, hence synchronization is needed to ensure proper access to a shared resource.

10.2 SINGLE THREADED VS MULTITHREADED MODEL

Imagine a scenario in the above-mentioned music application, where you have to wait to download a music piece till one of them stops playing. It leaves the user with an annoying experience. In a single threaded model, only one thread executes at a particular point in time. And the other one has to wait till the former completes. *Threads can be considered workers which are assigned certain tasks to be performed within the same application.* When a program gets started, the JVM schedules a main thread to start executing the main method. A single threaded model starts with the main thread and the next thread cannot initiate till the main thread completes.

A multithreaded model incorporates multiple threads in action. Here, multiple tasks within the same application can be performed at the same time as different threads are scheduled to do different tasks. The flow of an application starts with the main thread but the main thread can spawn multiple child threads from within itself, in a multithreaded environment.

Multithreading was introduced to increase the degree of responsiveness of an application. Having too many threads in an application will prove to be beneficial only if there are those many tasks to be completed else there will be a lot of time wasted upon *context switching* from one thread to another, putting the task to be performed at cost. Context switching takes place when the CPU has to switch from one thread to another. Example, switching from downloading music to searching music. It seems to the user that the tasks are performed concurrently but the underlying fact is the CPU is switched so rapidly between the threads that the end users do not get to know about it.

10.3 THREAD CLASS AND RUNNABLE INTERFACE

The Thread class and the Runnable interface are one of the most significant entities in multithreading. They both encompass several methods that aids in creation of threads. Below is the list of some of the constructors and methods in Thread class and the Runnable interface used in this book.

Runnable interface

As an interface cannot define any constructors, therefore, the Runnable interface has no constructors available.

- Methods

Table 10.1

Method name	Description
void run()	Capable of defining the task to be performed by a thread.

Thread class

The Thread class implements the Runnable interface, therefore, is responsible for providing definition for *run()* method.

- Constructors

Table 10.2

Constructor	Description
Thread()	Does memory allocation for a new thread object
Thread(Runnable target)	Does allocation for a new thread object to run a target
Thread(Runnable target, String name)	Does allocation for a new thread on a target with a given name
Thread(String name)	Does allocation for a new thread object with a given name

- Methods

Table 10.3

Method name	Description
long getId()	Returns the unique identifier for a thread as a long value.
String getName()	Returns the name of the current thread as a string value.
int getPriority()	Returns the priority of a thread object.

(Contd.)

void join()	Waits for a thread to finish execution.
boolean isAlive()	Checks whether the given thread is alive or not.
void run()	Is invoked when the thread starts its execution.
static Thread currentThread()	Returns a reference to the currently executing thread.
void setName(String name)	Sets the name of a given thread.
void setPriority(int p)	Sets the priority of the given thread.
static void sleep(long millis)	Suspends the execution of the current thread for the given milliseconds.
static void sleep(long millis, int nanos)	Suspends the execution of the current thread for the given milliseconds plus nanoseconds.
void start()	Starts the execution of a particular thread.
static void yield()	Indicator of current thread yielding its use of processor to another thread.
String toString()	Returns a string representation of the thread including its name, priority and group.

10.4 LIFE CYCLE OF A THREAD

A thread, like other processes, undergoes a life cycle beginning from its creation till its termination. Following are the states which a thread passes by during its life cycle:

1. *New*: When a thread is created, it is said to enter into a new state and is not alive at this moment.
2. *Runnable*: When a thread is ready to be assigned a processor but has not been assigned one, it is said to be in a runnable state. A thread enters into runnable state when the *start()* method is invoked and is said to be alive in this state.
3. *Running*: When a thread is allocated a processor, it is said to be in running state. The *run()* method is invoked at this stage which defines the task to be performed by the thread.
4. *Sleeping/waiting/blocked*: *A thread can switch from running state to this given state in case it chooses to sleep,wait or block itself.*

   A thread can move into a sleeping state using the *sleep()* method and wake up after the timer has expired. It can also go into a waiting state and return back to the runnable state once it gets a notification from the other thread. A thread enters a blocking state if the resource it is waiting for, is not available at that time. Remember, no thread can cause another thread to go into a *sleeping /waiting/blocked* state. Also, such threads will once again move from runnable to running state once the scheduler picks them for execution.

5. *Terminated/Dead:* Once the thread completes its *run()*, it is considered to be dead/not alive, i.e., it now cannot be considered a separate thread of execution. Invoking *start()* on this thread would yield a runtime exception.

Note that a thread is said to be alive from runnable to running state. It is neither alive in the new state nor in the dead state.

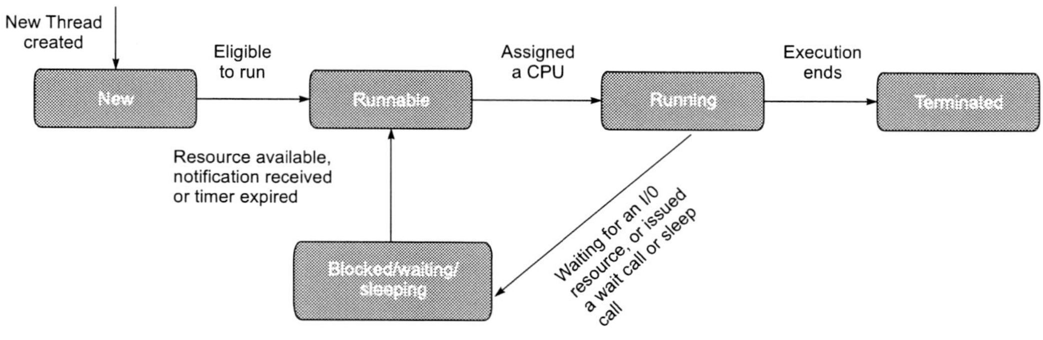

Fig. 10.1

10.5 MAIN THREAD

The first thread to be created and executed inside any program is the *main thread.* Let us see how a main thread works:

```
public class MainThreadDemo {
  public static void main(String[] args) {
        Thread t = Thread.currentThread(); // reference to main thread
        System.out.println("Id:" + t.getId()); //returns unique
                                                //identifier for thread
        System.out.println("Name: " + t.getName()); //returns name of
                                                     //the thread
        System.out.println("Thread object:"+ t); //prints thread object
        t.setName("My Main Thread"); //sets the name of the thread
        System.out.println("Name: " + t.getName());
  }
}
```

Output:

```
Id:1
Name: main
Thread object:Thread[main,5,main]
Name: My Main Thread
```

Let us look at the syntax for all the methods used in the above program:

- **public static** Thread currentThread()

  This method is a static method of Thread class, (hence invoked on the class name) and returns a Thread class instance, which is a reference to the currently executing thread, i.e., the main thread, in the example above.

- **public final void** setName(String name)

  This method sets the name of the thread. In our program it sets the main thread name as *My Main Thread.*

- **public final** String getName()

  This method returns the name of the thread as a string.

- **public long** getID()

  Every thread has an ID to uniquely identify it from other threads. The getID() method returns the ID for a thread which is 1 here.

Now let us examine line number 8

```
System.out.println(t); //prints thread object
```

Whenever an object of a class is printed, it calls the *toString()* method originally residing in Object class. This method used here, prints the string representation of the object as follows:

```
Thread[main,5,main]
```

where the first element specifies the name of the thread which is *main* by default. The next is an indicator of the priority of the main thread which is 5 by default. Every thread has a priority on the basis of which they are executed, ranging from 1 to 10, (1 being the lowest). The last element refers to the group to which the current thread belongs. Threads when created belong to a group so that they can be managed efficiently. In this case, the main thread belongs to its own group as it was the first thread to be created.

10.6 CREATION OF THREADS

A thread can behave as a worker which works upon certain jobs. *A thread always needs a target job to work upon. A job to be performed by a thread can be created using one of the below approaches:*

- Implementing Runnable interface
- Extending Thread class

Let us look at these closely.

```
public class Job1 implements Runnable {
```

```
    public void run() {      // job 1 to be performed
          System.out.println("I  am  a  job  created  by  implementing
          Runnable");
    }
}

public class Job2 extends Thread {
    public void run() {     // job 2 to be performed
          System.out.println("I am a job created by extending Thread
          which implements Runnable. Bad design");
    }
}

public class MainRunner {
    public static void main(String[] args) {
          Job1 job1Instance = new Job1();
          Thread jobRunner = new Thread(job1Instance);// thread working
                                                          //on job 1
          jobRunner.start();
          Job2 job2Instance = new Job2();
          Thread job2Runner = new Thread(job2Instance);// thread working
                                                          //on job 2
          job2Runner.start();
    }
}
```

Output:

```
I am a job created by implementing Runnable
I am a job created by extending Thread which implements Runnable. Bad
design
```

The program above shows three classes namely, *Job1*, *Job2* and *MainRunner*. The *Job1* and *Job2* classes defines the task or the job to be performed by a thread in their *run()* method. The *run()* method is overridden in both the classes as the former implements *Runnable* and the latter extends *Thread* which itself implements *Runnable*. The *MainRunner* class creates two objects of *Thread* class and passes an instance of *Job1* and *Job2* respectively to it. *Instantiating the Thread class creates a thread, however one has to pass a Runnable instance*[1] *(job1Instance and job2Instance, in our case) to the Thread constructor as a thread always needs a task to work upon.* Therefore, we can conclude from our program that threads *jobRunner* and *job2Runner* works upon the jobs *job1Instance* and *job2Instance* respectively. After creating a thread and assigning a job to it, one also has to start a thread by using *start()*. The *start()* method then invokes the *run()* of the class whose job has been assigned to it. Confused?? Alright, take for an example,

```
jobRunner.start();
```

---

[1] A Runnable instance is an instance of a class which implements Runnable interface.

will invoke the *run()* of *Job1* class as *job1Instance* is passed as a parameter to *jobRunner*. Similarly,

```
job2Runner.start();
```

will give a call to *run()* of *Job2* class.

The next example demonstrates a slightly different way of creating threads. Let us have a look upon it.

```
//ChildThread.java
public class ChildThread implements Runnable {
    Thread t; // Thread class reference

    ChildThread() {
          t = new Thread(this, "child thread"); // creating thread to
          // work upon ChildThread instance
          System.out.println("Child" + t);
          t.start(); // starting a thread
    }

    public void run() { // job to be performed
          try {
                for (int i = 1; i< 5; i++) {
                      System.out.println("child running " + i + "
                      time");
                      Thread.sleep(500); // child thread sleeping
                }
          } catch (InterruptedException e) {
                System.out.println(e);
          }
    }
}

//ChildThreadDemo.java
public class ChildThreadDemo {
    public static void main(String[] args) {
          new ChildThread(); // instantiating class ChildThread
          try {
                for (int i = 1; i< 5; i++) {
                      System.out.println("Main running " + i + " time");
                      Thread.sleep(1000); // main thread going to sleep
                }
          } catch (InterruptedException e) {
                System.out.println(e);
          }
    }
}
```

Output:

```
ChildThread[child thread,5,main]
Main running 1 time
child running 1 time
child running 2 time
Main running 2 time
child running 3 time
child running 4 time
Main running 3 time
Main running 4 time
```

The project above uses two classes: *ChildThreadDemo* and *ChildThread.* The JVM starts the main thread initially by invoking the main method. The main method in *ChildThreadDemo* instantiates the class *ChildThread* which calls the constructor for the same. The *ChildThread* constructor further instantiates the Thread class, the constructor of which creates a new thread spawned from the main thread to work upon a task/job. The task here is specified by *this*, which refers to the *ChildThread* instance (a runnable instance).

The *start()*method starts the newly created thread, t, which further invokes *run()*method of the class *ChildThread.* This method also invokes another method *sleep()*, the syntax for which is given below:

```
public static void sleep(long millis) throws InterruptedException
```

The *sleep()*method is a static method in the Thread class, hence invoked on the class name. It is used to suspend or shift a running thread to a sleeping state for a *millis* time period, passed as a parameter to the method. One should always ensure the execution of the main thread to be completed at last as it is the one which performs several shut down operations before getting terminated. The *sleep()* method also throws an *InterruptedException,* in case its normal flow of execution is interrupted.

Now observe the output carefully. We have an intermixed output where the main and the child thread executes in any order. This order depends on the order in which the JVM schedules the threads to be executed from the thread scheduler queue and can vary from one platform to another.

Note: One cannot predict the order in which multiple threads are scheduled in an application, but there are ways to run them in an orderly manner which we will be learning in the coming sections.

//Above example by extending Thread class

//ChildThread.java

```
public class ChildThread extends Thread {
    ChildThread() {
```

```
            super("Child Thread"); //creating a new thread on ChildThread
            //instance
            start();
        }
        public void run() {
            try {
                for (int i = 1; i< 5; i++) {
                    System.out.println("child running " + i + "
                    time");
                    Thread.sleep(500); // child thread sleeping
                }
            } catch (InterruptedException e) {
                System.out.println(e);
            }
        }
    }
```

//ChildThreadDemo.java

```
public class ChildThreadDemo {
    public static void main(String[] args) {
        new ChildThread(); //instantiating class A
        try {
            for (int i = 1; i< 5; i++) {
                System.out.println("Main running " + i + " time");
                Thread.sleep(1000); // main thread going to sleep
            }
        } catch (InterruptedException e) {
            System.out.println(e);
        }
    }
}
```

Output:

```
Main running 1 time
child running 1 time
child running 2 time
Main running 2 time
child running 3 time
child running 4 time
Main running 3 time
Main running 4 time
```

Observe the lines inside the *ChildThread* constructor. It gives a call to *super()* which invokes its super class *Thread* constructor. This constructor basically creates a new thread with the name "*Child Thread*" on the current object, *this*, which refers to the *ChildThread* instance. This instance is also a *Runnable* instance as the *Thread* class itself implements *Runnable*. The *start()* method is inherited inside the *ChildThread* class, therefore, invoked directly.

10.7 CREATING MULTIPLE THREADS

The above section already has dealt with creation of multiple threads working upon different jobs. Now let us examine how they behave when they work upon the same job.

```
public class Job1 implements Runnable {
    public void run() {
            try {
                    System.out.println("[This is child ");
                    Thread.sleep(500); // child thread sleeping
                    System.out.println("running]");

            } catch (InterruptedException e) {
                    System.out.println(e);
            }
    }
}

public class MainRunner {
    public static void main(String[] args) {
            Job1 job1Instance = new Job1(); //creating a job1Instance
            Thread jobRunner1 = new Thread(job1Instance); //thread1 assigned
                                                          //job1Instance
            jobRunner1.start(); //starting the thread
            Thread jobRunner2 = new Thread(job1Instance); //thread2 assigned
                                                          //job1Instance
            jobRunner2.start();
    }
}
```

Output:

```
[This is child
[This is child
running]
running]
```

The program demonstrates creation of two threads working upon the same job, *job1Instance*, an instance of *Job1* class. Here, we have three threads working simultaneously namely, *main*, *jobRunner1* and *jobRunner2*. As they are working upon the same *Runnable* instance *job1Instance*, their order of execution is not synchronized, hence resulting in a garbled output. In such a case, we need to devise a mechanism which synchronizes our execution. This can be done using a synchronized method or a block, which will be discussed in the coming sections.

10.8 ISALIVE() AND JOIN()

The isAlive() and join() methods are defined in java.lang package in the Thread class.

- *isAlive():* The *isAlive()* method is used to check the status of a thread. It returns true if the thread is alive else false. A thread is said to be alive if it has been started and not yet finished its *run()* method. The following code gives an example for the same:

```
public class Job1 implements Runnable {
    public void run() {
          System.out.println(“I am Job1”);
    }
}

public class Job2 implements Runnable {
    public void run() {
          System.out.println(“I am Job2”);
    }
}

public class MainRunner {
  public static void main(String[] args) {
          Job1 job1Instance = new Job1();
          Thread jobRunner = new Thread(job1Instance);
          jobRunner.start();
          System.out.println(“jobRunner status: ” +
             jobRunner.isAlive()); //checks if jobRunner is alive or
                                    //not

          Job2 job2Instance = new Job2();
          Thread job2Runner = new Thread(job2Instance);
          job2Runner.start();
          System.out.println(“job2Runner status: ” +
  job2Runner.isAlive()); //checks if job2Runner is alive or
                              //not
          System.out.println(“jobRunner status: ”+
          jobRunner.isAlive());
    }
  }
```

Output:

```
jobRunner status: true
I am Job1
job2Runner status: true
jobRunner status: false
I am Job2
```

The JVM schedules the threads in the above program in the following manner:

- Starts by creating the main thread
- The main thread creates the *jobRunner* thread, working on *job1Instance* and starts it.
- Ideally after starting this thread, its *run()* should have been called, but the JVM chooses to run the main thread here and checks if the *jobRunner* thread is alive or not. This method returns true as *jobRunner* has started but its *run()* method has not yet been complemented.
- It now schedules the *jobRunner* thread and completes its *run()*.
- The JVM now switches back to the main thread, creates and starts the *job2Runner* thread but doesn't schedule it to run.
- Checks if the *job2Runner* and *jobRunner* is still alive which returns true in the former case and false in the latter case as *jobRunner* has finished its run().
- In the end, JVM schedules the *job2Runner* thread and call its run().

Note that this output can vary from one build to another also as it completely depends on how the thread scheduling is done.

- *join():* The join method joins one thread onto the end of another. It helps in ensuring a specific order of execution for threads. The syntax for the same is given below:

  ```
  public final void join() throws InterruptedException
  ```

  As you can see, the *join()* method is a final method, hence cannot be overridden. Also, the method throws an object of class, *InterruptedException*, which must be handled in the calling code using a try catch block or the throws keyword.

  Let us see this through an example:

```
public class Job1 implements Runnable {
    public void run() {
          System.out.println("I am Job1");
    }
}

public class MainRunner {
    public static void main(String[] args) {
          try {
                Job1 job1Instance = new Job1();
```

```
                Thread jobRunner = new Thread(job1Instance);
                jobRunner.start();
                System.out.println("jobRunner status:" +
                                   jobRunner.isAlive());
                jobRunner.join(); //joins jobRunner to the end of
                                  //main thread
                Job2 job2Instance = new Job2();
                Thread job2Runner = new Thread(job2Instance);
                job2Runner.start();
                job2Runner.join(); //joins jobRunner2 to the end of
                                   //main thread
                System.out.println("job2Runner status: " +
                            job2Runner.isAlive());
                System.out.println("jobRunner status: " +
                                   jobRunner.isAlive());
                System.out.println("Main thread completing");
            } catch (InterruptedException e) {

            }
        }
}
```

Output:

```
jobRunner status: true
I am Job1
I am Job2
job2Runner status: false
jobRunner status: false
Main thread completing
```

The join method used here ensures that the currently executing thread, (*main* in our case), is joined to the end of *jobRunner* and *job2Runner* child threads. The execution starts from the main thread but as soon as the *jobRunner* thread is started, the JVM switches to execute this thread, thereby completing its execution and then returning to the main thread. Similar execution takes place for *job2Runner* thread causing the main thread to terminate in the end.

Note that the join() method is capable of putting threads in an order for execution.

Figure 10.2 describes the flow of program. The figure clearly shows how the flow of execution takes place for the above program. *Remember, every thread will have its own call stack.*

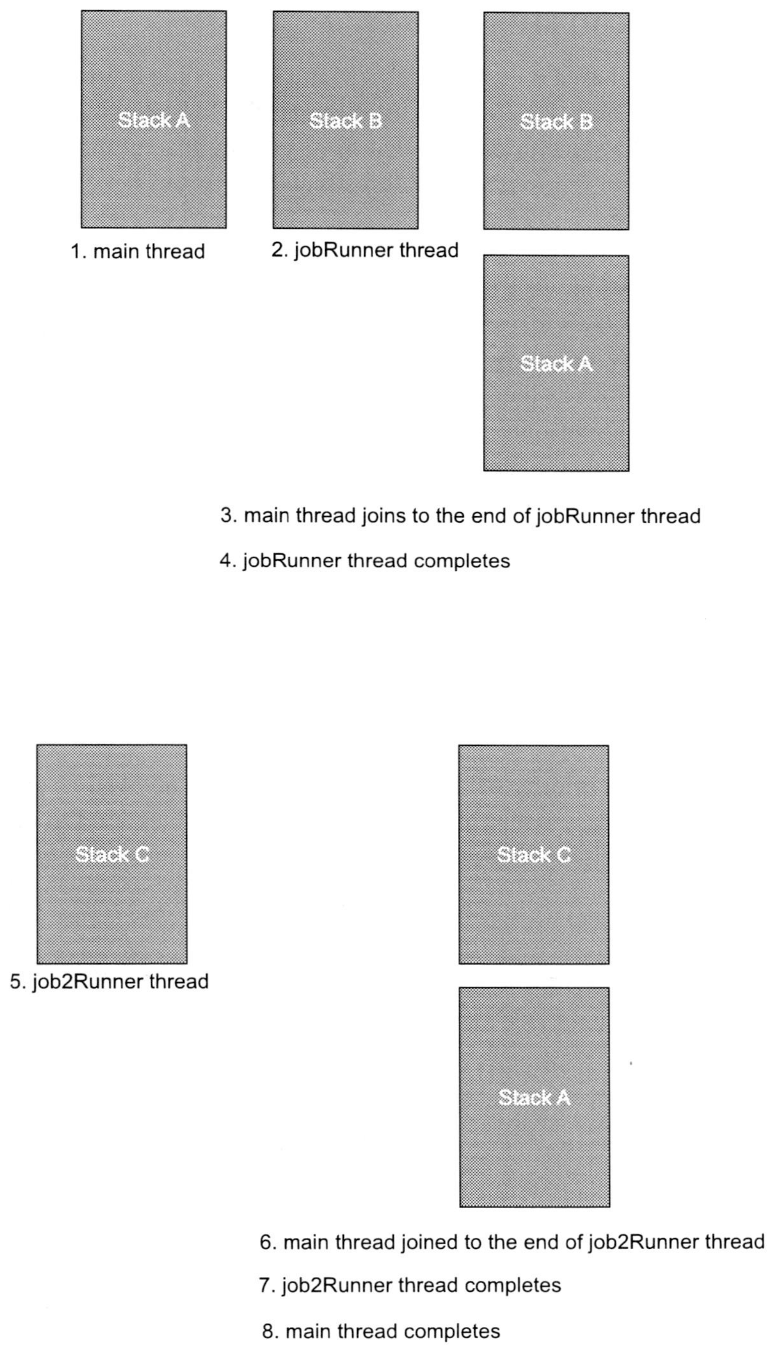
Stack A
Stack B
Stack B
1. main thread
2. jobRunner thread
Stack A
3. main thread joins to the end of jobRunner thread
4. jobRunner thread completes
Stack C
Stack C
5. job2Runner thread
Stack A
6. main thread joined to the end of job2Runner thread
7. job2Runner thread completes
8. main thread completes

Fig. 10.2

10.9 THREAD PRIORITIES

Every thread has a priority based on which the JVM might schedule it for execution. Normally, all threads have a priority on a scale of 1 to 10, 1 being the lowest and 10 being the highest. By default, a thread has the same priority as that of its creating/parent thread. So, in the above example, the *jobRunner* and the *job2Runner* threads will have the same priority as its parent thread, main, by default, i.e., 5.

The JVM may use a priority based scheduling algorithm to schedule the threads. A priority based scheduling of threads follows a preemptive approach which means if the currently running thread is of lower priority than that of any thread in the runnable state, the JVM chooses to pre-empt the lower priority thread by a higher priority thread. Though, one should not rely completely on thread priorities as the JVM might use varying algorithms for thread scheduling.

Note that when all the threads are of equal priority the JVM behaviour is unpredictable as to how the threads will be scheduled.

A thread's priority can also be set up explicitly by using the *setPriority()* method, the syntax for which is given below:

```
public final void setPriority(int newPriority)
```

The parameter *newPriority* specifies the priority as an integer value that you want to set up for that thread.

One can also get the current priority for a thread by using the *getPriority()* method:

```
public final int getPriority()
```

This method displays the priority of the thread on which it is invoked as an integer value.

The Thread class encompasses the following static final variables used to denote minimum, normal, and maximum priority of any thread:

Table 10.4

Static final variables	Value
Thread.MIN_PRIORITY	1
Thread.NORM_PRIORITY	5
Thread.MAX_PRIORITY	10

Let us now examine an example for the same:

```
public class Job1 implements Runnable {
    public void run() {
        System.out.println("I am Job1");
    }
}
```

```
1 public class MainRunner {
2   public static void main(String[] args) {
3
4           Thread mainThread = Thread.currentThread();
5           System.out.println(“The priority of main thread is: "
6                       + mainThread.getPriority()); // gets the default
7                                 //priority of main thread
8
9           Job1 job1Instance = new Job1();
10          Thread jobRunner = new Thread(job1Instance);
11          jobRunner.setPriority(Thread.MIN_PRIORITY); // sets the
12                                          //priority for jobRunner
13          jobRunner.start();
14          System.out.println(“Main thread still working”);
15
16  }
17 }
```

Output:

```
The priority of main thread is: 5
Main thread still working
I am Job1
```

Line 6 gets the priority of main thread which is 5 by default, whereas line number 11 sets the priority of the *jobRunner* thread to minimum priority. In the previous example, we ensured the main thread to complete at the end using the join method. In this example, we can easily see that the *jobRunner* thread is a lower priority thread than the main thread therefore, it is likely for the JVM to schedule the main thread first, for execution. Remember, JVM may or may not schedule threads based on their priority.

yield() method

The *yield()* method is capable of moving a running thread to its runnable state back again. This method is always invoked on the currently executing thread to relinquish its control of CPU to some other higher priority thread. *This is the reason why yield has been marked as a static method of Thread class because a thread can call this method only on itself and not on other threads*. Note that calling yield on a thread does not move it to a waiting/sleeping/blocking state. It just moves it to the runnable state where it waits again to be allocated a CPU. However, this behaviour is not guaranteed.

The syntax for the method is as follows:

```
public static void yield()
```

10.10 SYNCHRONIZATION

Section 10.7 talked about a concurrency problem where multiple threads work upon a single object. Multiple threads when working upon a single shared object at a particular time can create inconsistency in the state of that object. For example, consider a counter variable being incremented by 30 threads at the same time. An increment statement, counter++ can be rewritten as:

counter=counter+1;

which means incrementing the value first and then performing assignment. But as multiple threads might be accessing the shared variable, there might be a case where the first thread increments the value of the counter and just before assignment, the other thread reads the same value of counter resulting in an inconsistent output. So, if the counter value is equal to 0, both the threads might display the same value as 1 after incrementing. This condition is known as a *race condition.* Let us see this through an example:

```
public class B {
     int counter=0; //counter variable

     void incrementCounter() {   //incrementing the counter variable
            counter++;
            System.out.println(counter);
     }
}

public class Job1 implements Runnable {
     B ob; // composition

     Job1(B o) {
            ob = o;
     }

     public void run() {
            ob.incrementCounter();
     }
}

public class MainRunner {
     public static void main(String[] args) {
            B b = new B();
            Thread jobRunner1;
            Job1 job1Instance = new Job1(b); // passing B type object to
                                                //Job1 constructor
            for (int i = 1; i<= 30; i++) {
                   jobRunner1 = new Thread(job1Instance); // threads
                                //accessing the shared object job1Instance
                   jobRunner1.start(); // starting the thread
```

```
            }
        }
}
```

Output:

```
2
3
2
4
5
6
7
8
9
10
12
11
13
14
15
16
17
18
19
20
21
23
22
24
25
30
29
28
27
26
```

The program above uses a class *B* which has a counter variable and a method which increments the value of that counter variable. Another class *Job1* implementing the *Runnable* interface, has a reference variable of type *B* in it[2] and provides a *run()* method which invokes the *incrementCounter()* method of class B. The *MainRunner* class creates 30 threads running on the same instance of *Job1* class and that is where the whole mess up occurs.

[2] A class containing references of other classes as their instance variables is called composition. It depicts a HAS relationship.

Notice the irregularity in the output. If the threads were running in a synchronous manner, the last output would have been 30. But, as you can see, multiple threads are returning the duplicate value for the counter variable because of the race condition problem. To synchronize the output, we can employ the *synchronized* keyword. *The synchronized keyword can be applied to methods as well as blocks.*

- **Synchronized method**

  A method declaration preceded with a synchronized keyword marks a synchronized method. The following example alters the above example to synchronize the output.

```
public class B {
    int counter=0; //counter variable

    synchronized void incrementCounter() { //synchronized method
    counter++;
           System.out.println(counter);
    }
}

public class Job1 implements Runnable {
    B ob; // composition

    Job1(B o) {
           ob = o;
    }

    public void run() {
           ob.incrementCounter();
    }
}

public class MainRunner {
    public static void main(String[] args) {
           B b = new B();
           Thread jobRunner1;
           Job1 job1Instance = new Job1(b); // passing B type object
                                                //to Job1 constructor
           for (int i = 1; i<= 30; i++) {
                  jobRunner1 = new Thread(job1Instance); // threads
                                 //accessing the shared object job1Instance
                  jobRunner1.start(); // starting the thread
           }
    }
}
```

Output:

```
1
2
```

```
3
4
5
6
7
8
9
10
11
12
13
14
15
16
17
18
19
20
21
22
23
24
25
26
27
28
29
30
```

The above output depicts a synchronous behaviour now after the usage of the *synchronized* keyword. This keyword uses the concept of locks. When a thread enters the *incrementCounter()* method, as it is a synchronized method, the thread obtains a lock on the B's object, so that until one of the thread increments and assigns the value back to the counter variable, the other thread doesn't start upon the same object. This assures no thread reads a dirty value (inconsistent value). In other words, when a thread tries to give a call to the synchronized method *incrementCounter()*, it first checks whether some other thread has already obtained a lock on the same object or not. If it has, the former thread waits for the latter thread to complete its task. Once the latter thread has completed its task, it releases its lock on the object so that other threads can obtain them and perform their task.

- **Synchronized block**

  One can also facilitate this synchronous behaviour by using a synchronized block, the example for which is given below:

```
public class B {
    int counter = 0; // counter variable

    void incrementCounter() { // incrementing the counter variable
        counter++;
        System.out.println(counter);
    }
}

public class Job1 implements Runnable {
    B ob; // composition

    Job1(B o) {
        ob = o;
    }

    public void run() {
        synchronized (ob) { //obtaining a lock on ob in
//synchronized block
ob.incrementCounter();
        }
    }
}

public class MainRunner {
    public static void main(String[] args) {
        B b = new B();
        Thread jobRunner1;
        Job1 job1Instance = new Job1(b);
        for (int i = 1; i<= 30; i++) {
            jobRunner1 = new Thread(job1Instance);
            jobRunner1.start();
        }
    }
}
```

The below line shows how to define a synchronized block:

```
synchronized (ob){
}
```

The parameter *ob* signifies the object on which the lock has to be obtained. While one thread is working upon the *incrementCounter()* inside the synchronized block, the other thread waits till the former completes resulting in a synchronous output.

> *A synchronized method limits concurrency as it does not allow two threads to interleave each other. The degree of concurrency is less in using a synchronized block as compared to a synchronized method as one can restrict the number of statements inside a block.*

10.11 INTER THREAD COMMUNICATION

The previous section talked about how one can provide synchronization in cases when multiple threads try to work upon a shared object. This section will provide an extension to it. Here, we see how different threads can talk to each other to facilitate synchronization using the methods below:

```
public final void wait() throws InterruptedException
public final void notify()
public final void notifyAll()
```

All these methods belong to the Object class in the java.lang package.

The *wait()* method is invoked on the currently executing thread. It suspends or pauses the current thread temporarily until some other thread notifies to come back again. A very important thing to note down here is that a waiting thread does not keep polling an object. It simply waits and does not do anything till some other thread notifies it to do so.

The *notify()* method notifies or wakes up the first thread that issued a *wait* call on its object to acquire a lock.

The *notifyAll()* method wakes up all the threads that called *wait* on its object.

The following example states the famous *producer consumer problem.* Herein, we have a producer which produces an item in a variable and a consumer which consumes items from the variable. To ensure synchronization here, one needs to keep a check that the producer should not produce items when the variable has no more storage or is full and the consumer should stop consuming when the variable has no value in it. But checking the status of the variable again and again will waste a lot of CPU cycles. Therefore, there has to be a mechanism in which the producer waits when the variable already has a value and gets notified when there is a space created by the consumer to produce more items. The same thing should be present for the consumer also. The three methods discussed above help us to create such a mechanism. Let us now examine the example:

```
//Queue.java
public class Queue {
    private int var; // shared variable

    synchronized public void produce(int item) {
          if (var> 0) { // check if the variable has a value
                try {
                      System.out.println("I am waiting to produce " +
                                        item);
                      wait(); // current thread waits
                } catch (InterruptedException e) {
                      System.out.println(e);
                }
          }
```

```
            var = item; // produce the item
            System.out.println("Produced " + item);
            notify(); // notify other threads waiting to consume
    }

    synchronized public void consume() {
            if (var == 0) { // check if the variable does not have a
            //value
                    try {
                            System.out.println("I am waiting to consume");
                            wait(); // current thread waits
                    } catch (InterruptedException e) {
                            System.out.println(e);
                    }
            }
            int item = var; // consuming the item
            var = 0; // updating the variable
            System.out.println("The item consumed is " + item);
            notify(); // notifies other threads to produce
    }
}

//Producer.java
public class Producer implements Runnable {
    Queue b;

    public Producer(Queue b) {
            this.b = b;
    }

    public void run() {
                    for (int i = 1; i<= 10; i++) {
                            b.produce(i);
                    }
    }

}

//Consumer.java
public class Consumer implements Runnable {
    Queue b;

    public Consumer(Queue b) {
            this.b = b;
    }

    public void run() {
            for (int i = 1; i<= 10; i++) {
                    b.consume();
```

```
            }
        }
}

//MainRunner.java
public class MainRunner {
    public static void main(String[] args) {
            Queue b = new Queue();
            Producer p = new Producer(b); // passing Queue type object to
                                          // Producer constructor
            Consumer c = new Consumer(b); // passing Queue type object to
                                     // Consumer constructor
            Thread one = new Thread(p);
            one.start(); // thread one starting on Producer
            Thread two = new Thread(c);
            two.start(); // thread two starting on Consumer

    }
}
```

Output:

```
Produced 1
I am waiting to produce 2
The item consumed is 1
I am waiting to consume
Produced 2
I am waiting to produce 3
The item consumed is 2
I am waiting to consume
Produced 3
I am waiting to produce 4
The item consumed is 3
I am waiting to consume
Produced 4
I am waiting to produce 5
The item consumed is 4
I am waiting to consume
Produced 5
I am waiting to produce 6
The item consumed is 5
I am waiting to consume
Produced 6
I am waiting to produce 7
The item consumed is 6
I am waiting to consume
```

```
Produced 7
I am waiting to produce 8
The item consumed is 7
I am waiting to consume
Produced 8
I am waiting to produce 9
The item consumed is 8
I am waiting to consume
Produced 9
I am waiting to produce 10
The item consumed is 9
I am waiting to consume
Produced 10
The item consumed is 10
```

The flow starts from the *MainRunner* class wherein we create two threads working on *Producer* and *Consumer* Runnable objects. The *run()* methods in these classes invoke the *produce()* and *consume()* methods present in the *Queue* class that work upon a shared variable *var*. The producer checks if the variable already has a value(var>0), it will have to issue a *wait()* else it can produce the items.

The consumer checks if the variable has a zero value, the consumer has to *wait()* else it can consume items.

Note that every time a producer produces, it issues a *notify()* to the consumer so that it can consume items. Similarly, the consumer issues a *notify()* to the producer after consuming an item.

SUMMARY

- A thread is a part of a process having its own stack, program counter and local variables.
- A thread can also be treated as a worker which can be assigned jobs or tasks. These tasks are runnable objects.
- A multithreaded application is the one which uses multiple threads to perform several tasks simultaneously.
- A single threaded application employs a single thread to do a job and the other threads block till the former completes its task.
- A thread can be created in two ways: either by implementing the runnable interface or by extending the thread class.
- A thread can exist in multiple states: new, runnable, running, waiting, blocking, and terminated.
- A thread is said to be alive from the time it is started till the time it completes its *run()* method.

- Once a thread has completed its *run()*, one cannot call *start()* again on that thread.
- The *join()* joins one thread to the end of another whereas the *yield()* causes the currently executing thread to release its control of CPU to some other thread.
- Multiple threads working upon the same object can cause inconsistency in the state of an object. The synchronized keyword comes for the saviour in such a case and ensures synchronized access upon a shard object by multiple threads.
- Interthread communication is the communication between two or more threads using methods like *wait()*, *notify()* and *notifyAll()*.

COMMON ERRORS

- Calling the *run()* before starting a thread. In such a case, the compiler calls the *run()* on the current thread.
- Forgetting to pass a Runnable object to the Thread constructor. It calls the empty Thread class constructor which does not do anything.
- Restarting a thread after it has completed its *run()*.

SELF-TEST

1. Discuss how multithreading is different from multitasking?
2. What is a thread? Do they have a separate call stack for each thread? Describe ways to create them.
3. What are the states in which a thread can enter during its life cycle? Explain with examples and diagram.
4. Discuss the is Alive(), join() and yield().
5. Do threads have priorities? How can thread priorities affect the execution of a program?
6. Can multiple threads work upon a single object? If yes, what are the problems one faces in such a situation? Advise solutions for the same.
7. Discuss how interthread communication between threads can take place? Explain the methods used to facilitate this communication.

PRACTICAL QUESTIONS

1. Generate the output for the following:

a)
```
public class SelfTest implements Runnable {
public static void main(String[] args) {
    Thread t = new Thread(new SelfTest());
    t.run();
}
```

```
    public void run() {
        System.out.println(Thread.currentThread());
    }
}
```

b)
```
public class SelfTest implements Runnable {
public static void main(String[] args) {
    Thread t = new Thread(new SelfTest());
    run();

}

public static void run() {
    System.out.println("I am inside run method");
}

}
```

c)
```
public class SelfTest implements Runnable {
public static void main(String[] args) {
    Thread t = new Thread();
    t.start();

}

public void run() {
    System.out.println("I am created from empty Runnable");
}
}
```

d)
```
public class SelfTest implements Runnable {
public static void main(String[] args) {
    Thread t = new Thread(new SelfTest());
    t.start();
    t.start();

}

public void run() {
    System.out.println("I am started twice");
}
}
```

11 CHAPTER

Java Libraries

This chapter will enable you to learn the following:

- Creating immutable and mutable strings using String and StringBuffer class.
- Introducing wrapper classes and implementing the process of boxing and unboxing.
- Learning to read and write from files and console using the concept of streams.
- A brief about the Object class.

11.1 STRING HANDLING

Java identifies String as a class and not as a data type. One can create Strings in java by just instantiating the *String* class present in *java.lang* package. This section focuses upon creation, manipulation and searching of strings.

11.1.1 String Class

The String class provides a set of constructors and methods used for creation, manipulation and searching of strings. Let us examine all of these one by one.

- *String creation*

  Strings can be created by merely instantiating the String class. Following are some of the constructors available in the String class used for String creation which the book will be following:

Table 11.1

Constructor	Description
String()	Creates an empty String object.
String(char[] arr)	Creates a String object with the contents from the character array passed.
String(char[] arr, int offset, int num)	Creates a String object with the contents as that of the subsequence of the array passed.
String(String obj)	Creates a String object with the contents of the String object passed.

The following example shows how to create strings:

```
public class StringDemo {
    public static void main(String[] args) {
          String ob1 = new String(); // empty string
          System.out.println("Empty String " + ob1);
          char arr[] = { 'j', 'a', 'v', 'a' };
          String ob2 = new String(arr); // String from an array
          System.out.println("Contents of ob2 are " + ob2);
          String ob3 = new String(arr, 1, 2); // String from a
                                              // subsequence of an array
          System.out.println("Contents of ob3 are " + ob3);
          String ob4 = new String(ob3); // String from another
                                        // String object

          System.out.println("Contents of ob4 are " + ob4);
    }
}
```

Output:

```
Empty String
Contents of ob2 are java
Contents of ob3 are av
Contents of ob4 are av
```

The output clearly depicts how several stings are being created.

The first String object *ob1* is created with empty contents in it as there is no source from where the contents will be put in. The second object fetches its contents from the character array, *arr*. The third one uses the below constructor:

```
String ob3 = new String(arr, 1, 2);
```

where the first argument to the constructor specifies the array from which the contents will be copied to the String object. The second argument depicts the offset or the position from where the characters have to be copied and the third argument indicates the number of characters to be copied from index 1. Hence, the output: *a v*

The object ob4 fetches its contents from the already created object ob3.

> *String objects are immutable which means their contents cannot be overwritten. Every time, we try to alter the contents of a String object, a new Object is created.*

Another way to create a String object is by using String Literals. Consider the following code snippet:

```
String ob = "Hello I am a new String object";
```

The object *ob* is a String object created by String literal `"Hello I am a new String object"`. Hence, after this statement, the value of the String literal is assigned to the String object *ob*.

- String Manipulation

  The String class in java has several methods for manipulating the contents of a string like changing the case, trimming the contents of a string, fetching characters from a string, etc. Let us examine some of them.

  1. *length()*: This method returns the number of characters present in the string as an integer.

     Syntax:

     ```
     public int length();

     //finding the length of a string
     public class LengthDemo {
             public static void main(String[] args) {
                     String ob = "Hello I am a new String object";
                     System.out.println("The length of the string
                     object is " + ob.length());
             }
     }
     ```

     Output:

     ```
     The length of the string object is 30
     ```

     Note that space is also counted as a character.

  2. *concat()*: This method returns a new concatenated string object built from the given string objects. It can also be used to concatenate a string with a value of any other type. The + operator can also be used for concatenation.

     Syntax:

     ```
     public String concat(String str);

     //concatenating two strings
     public class ConcatDemo {
         public static void main(String[] args) {
             char[] arr = { 'a', 'b', 'c' };
             String ob = new String(arr);
             String ob2 = "def";
     //returns a new string object using concat()
             System.out.println("Concatenated String " +
                                 ob.concat(ob2));
     int age = 15;
     //concatenates using + operator
     ```

```
            System.out.println("I am " + age + "years old");
        }
    }
```

Output:

```
Concatenated String abcdef
I am 15 years old
```

The important thing to note down here is that the *concat()* method does not alter the contents of object *ob*, it simply creates a new string object containing contents of object *ob* concatenated with the object *ob2*.

3. charAt(): This method returns the character at the given index from the string object.

   Syntax:

```
public char charAt(int index)
//using charAt()
public class CharAtDemo {
    public static void main(String[] args) {
            String str = "I am using charAt() method";
            System.out.println(str.charAt(3));
    }
}
```

   Output:

```
m
```

4. *toUpper() and toLower():*The *toUpper()* method returns a string object with all its contents in upper case whereas the toLower() method does the same returning the string object in lower case contents.

   Syntax:

```
public String toUpperCase();
public String toLowerCase();
```

//changing case of string objects

```
public class ChangeCaseDemo {
    public static void main(String[] args) {
            String str = "I am using toUpper() method";
            String str1 = "I am using toLower() method";
            System.out.println(str.toUpperCase()); // converting
                                        //string to upper case
            System.out.println(str1.toLowerCase()); // converting
                                        // string to lower case
    }
}
```

Output:

```
I AM USING TOUPPER() METHOD
i am using tolower() method
```

5. *split():* This method returns a string array by splitting a source string based on some delimiter or a regular expression.

   Syntax:

```
public String[] split(String regex,int limit);
public String[] split(String regex);
```

The former version of the method splits a source string based upon the regular expression *regex* returning limit number of strings.

The latter version splits source string based upon the regular expression regex.

//using split()

```
public class StringSplitDemo {
    public static void main(String[] args) {
          String str = "aa-bb-cc-dd-ee-ff";
          System.out.println("Using split(regex)");
          for (String res : str.split("-"))    // returns all
          //strings delimited by -
                System.out.println(res);
          System.out.println("Using split(regex,limit)");
          for (String res1 : str.split("-", 2)) //returns 2
          //strings delimited by -
                System.out.println(res1);

          }
    }
```

Output:

```
Using split(regex)
aa
bb
cc
dd
ee
ff
Using split(regex,limit)
aa
bb-cc-dd-ee-ff
```

6. *contains():* This method is a boolean method which tests whether the given string contains the specified characters or not.

Syntax:

```
public boolean contains(CharSequence s);
```

where *CharSequence* is an interface.

//using contains()

```
public class ContainsDemo {
    public static void main(String[] args) {
          String str = "Using contains method";
          System.out.println(str.contains("ing")); //matching char
                                                    //sequence "ing" in str
    }
}
```

Output:

```
true
```

7. *replace()*: This method has the following syntax:

```
public String replace(char oldChar, char newChar);
public String replaceAll(String regex, String replacement);
```

The former method replaces all occurrences of *oldChar* with *newChar* whereas the latter one replaces a substring based upon the regular expression passed with a new replacement string.

//using replace methods

```
public class ReplaceDemo {
    public static void main(String[] args) {
          String str = "abcdefff";
          System.out.println(str.replace('f', 'e')); // replaces
                                          //all occurrences of f with e
          String str1 = "Using replaceAll";
          System.out.println(str1.replaceAll("ing","e"));
//replaces occurrence of ing with e

    }
}
```

Output:

```
abcdeeee
Use replaceAll
```

8. *substring():* This method extracts a substring out of the given string.

Syntax:

```
String substring(int beginIndex);
String substring(int beginIndex, int endIndex);
```

The first method extracts a substring beginning at the specified index whereas the second one specifies a substring beginning and ending at the given indices.

//using substring()

```
public class SubStringDemo {
    public static void main(String[] args) {
        String str = "Using substring method";
        System.out.println(str.substring(6));//extracts
        //substring starting at index 6

        System.out.println(str.substring(6,15));//extracts
                            //substring between 6-15 indices

    }
}
```

Output:

```
substring method
substring
```

9. *toString():* This method is used to provide a description of the object as a string.

   Syntax:

   ```
   public String toString();
   ```

   ```
   //using toString()

       public class ToStringDemo {
       public static void main(String[] args) {
           String str = "Hi I am doing string handling";
           System.out.println(str.toString());
           String str1 = "toString() called implicitly";
           System.out.println(str1); //str1.toString()
       }
   }
   ```

   Output:

   ```
   Hi I am doing string handling
   toString() called implicitly
   ```

10. *trim():* This method is used to remove leading and trailing white spaces around a string object.

    Syntax:

    ```
    public String trim();
    ```

    //using trim()

```
public class TrimDemo {
    public static void main(String[] args) {
          String str = "     Hi I am doing string handling    ";
          System.out.println(str.trim());
    }
}
```

Output:

```
Hi I am doing string handling
```

- *String comparison*

  There are several methods in String class which can be used for comparison between string objects. A list of some of them is given below:

  1. *equals()*: This method compares two string objects to check if they are equal or not. The *equals* method checks the contents of two objects to determine their equality. The == operator on the other checks whether two string references are same or not. In other words, if two string objects point to the same memory location or not.

     Syntax:

     ```
     public boolean equals(Object o);
     ```

     //using equals()

     ```
     public class EqualsDemo {
         public static void main(String[] args) {
               char arr[] = { 'a', 'b', 'c' };
               String str = new String(arr);
               String str1 = new String(str);
               System.out.println(str.equals(str1)); //comparing
                                                  //contents of str and str1
               System.out.println(str==str1); //comparing the references
                                                  //of two strings
         }
     }
     ```

     Output:

     ```
     true
     false
     ```

  2. *equalsIgnoreCase()*: This method works exactly like the *equals()* method with a difference of ignoring the case while comparing two string objects for equality.

     Syntax:

     ```
     public boolean equalsIgnoreCase(String anotherString);
     ```

     //using equalsIgnoreCase()

```
public class EqualsIgnoreCaseDemo {
    public static void main(String[] args) {
        char arr[] = { 'a', 'b', 'c' };
        String str = new String(arr);
        String str1 = "ABC";
        System.out.println(str.equalsIgnoreCase(str1)); //ignore
                                            //case while comparison
    }
}
```

Output:

```
true
```

3. *compareTo()*: checks two strings based on their lexicographic order. This method returns 0 if both the strings being compared are equal, a value less than 0 if the first string is less than the second else a value greater than 0.
   Syntax:

```
public int compareTo(String anotherString);
```

//using compareTo()

```
public class CompareToDemo {
    public static void main(String[] args) {
            String str = "John";
            String str1 = "Snow";
            System.out.println(str.compareTo(str1));
    }
}
```

Output:

```
-9
```

This is how the method works. It checks the two strings letter by letter, matching the first letter of the first string with the first letter of the second string.

The moment we get a non-matching character, the difference of the ascii values of the letters is returned.

4. *compareToIgnoreCase()*: This method works exactly the same as the above method with a difference of ignoring the case of two string objects while comparing.
   Syntax:

```
public int compareToIgnoreCase(String str);
```

//using compareToIgnoreCase()

```
public class compareToIgnoreCaseDemo {
    public static void main(String[] args) {
        String str = "John";
        String str1 = "john";
        System.out.println(str.compareToIgnoreCase(str1));
    }
}
```

Output:

```
0
```

5. *startsWith():* This method checks if the given string starts with the given prefix or not. Returns true if it does, else returns false.

   Syntax:

```
public boolean startsWith(String prefix);
public boolean startsWith(String prefix, int toffset);
```

The latter version of the method checks if the given substring, starting at index toffset, begins with the given prefix string.

//using startsWith()

```
public class StartsWithDemo {
    public static void main(String[] args) {
       String str = "Using startsWith method";
       System.out.println(str.startsWith("Us")); //tests if str
       //starts with the string "Us"
       System.out.println(str.startsWith("Us", 2)); //tests if
                                  //string at index 2 starts with "Us"

    }
}
```

Output:

```
true
false
```

6. *endsWith*: This method checks if the given string ends with a given suffix.

   Syntax:

```
public boolean endsWith(String suffix)
```

//using endsWith()

```
public class EndsWithDemo {
    public static void main(String[] args) {
       String str = "Using endsWith method";
       System.out.println(str.endsWith("th")); // tests if str
                              //ends with the string "th"
```

```
    }
}
```

Output:

```
False
```

- *String Searching:* The String class also incorporates methods for searching characters in a string object at specified indices. Some of the methods are discussed below:

  1. *indexOf()*: returns the index representing the first occurrence of a string or a substring.

     Syntax:

     ```
     public int indexOf(int ch);
     public int indexOf(int ch, int fromIndex);
     public int indexOf(String str);
     public int indexOf(String str, int fromIndex);
     ```

     The first version of the method returns the index of the first occurrence of the character passed. The second version returns the index of the first occurrence of the character passed, searching from a starting index. The third version of the method searches the first occurrence of the substring passed in the given string object. And the last one searches the first occurrence of the given substring starting from the specified index.

     ```
     public class IndexOfDemo {
         public static void main(String[] args) {
                 String str = "I am using indexof() method";
                 System.out.println(str.indexOf('i'));
                 System.out.println(str.indexOf('i', 8));
                 System.out.println(str.indexOf("using"));
                 System.out.println(str.indexOf("using", 10));
         }
     }
     ```

     Output:

     ```
     7
     11
     5
     -1
     ```

     Notice the last output returns the index -1, as starting from index 10, the substring *"using"* could not be found. Also note, the indices for a string object start from 0.

  2. *lastIndexOf()*: returns the index representing the last occurrence of a string or a substring.

Syntax:

```
public int lastIndexOf(int ch);
public int lastIndexOf(int ch, int fromIndex);
public int lastIndexOf(String str);
public int lastIndexOf(String str, int fromIndex);
```

The first version of the method returns the index of the last occurrence of the character passed. The second version returns the index of the last occurrence of the character passed, searching backward from the given index. The third version of the method searches the last occurrence of the substring passed in the given string object. And the last one searches the last occurrence of the given substring tracing backward from the specified index.

```
public class LastIndexOfDemo {
    public static void main(String[] args) {
            String str = "Using lastIndexOf() method";
            // returns last occurrence of s in str
            System.out.println(str.lastIndexOf('s'));
            // returns the last occurrence of s in str searching
            // backwards from index 4
            System.out.println(str.lastIndexOf('s', 4));
            // returns the last occurrence of string ing in str
            System.out.println(str.lastIndexOf("ing"));
            // returns last occurrence of ing searching backwards
            //from index 1

            System.out.println(str.lastIndexOf("ing", 1));

    }

}
```

Output:

```
8
1
2
-1
```

The last output is returned as -1 as there does not exist any string *ing*, searching backwards from index 1.

- *String conversion methods*

  The String class provides certain conversion methods which return a string representation for the specified argument, example, the *valueOf()* method.

Syntax:

```
public static String valueOf(boolean b);
public static String valueOf(float f);
public static String valueOf(double d);
public static String valueOf(boolean b);
public static String valueOf(char c);
public static String valueOf(char[] data);
public static String valueOf(int i);
public static String valueOf(long l);
public static String valueOf(char[] data, int offset, int count);
public static String valueOf(Object obj);
```

The various versions of *valueOf()* method return the string representation of the argument passed. For example, the first one returns the string representation for the boolean argument passed whereas the second version returns the string representation for the float value passed.

11.1.2 StringBuffer class

Just like the String class in java, we have its sibling called *StringBuffer*. The major difference between *String* and *StringBuffer* class is that *String creates immutable objects which means once created, cannot be altered.* In other words, when you replace a character using the *replace()* in a string object, it creates a new String object with the replaced character and does not alter in the same string object. Therefore, one can also say, *String class is thread safe* as no two threads will be able to work on the same object.

On the other hand, the *StringBuffer class creates mutable objects, i.e., one can alter the state of the same object again and again.* Hence, two or more threads can work upon the same object at the same time. But still, *StringBuffer* class is thread safe, as all its methods are synchronized. *Another class called StringBuilder has exactly the same methods as that of the StringBuffer with a difference that it is a non-thread safe class.*

Some of its constructor forms are given below:

StringBuffer(): creates a string buffer with no characters and an initial capacity of 16 characters.

*StringBuffer(**int** capacity):* creates a string buffer with no characters and an initial capacity equal to the specified capacity passed as an argument to the method.

StringBuffer(String str): creates a string buffer with contents as that of the string object passed.

Some of its methods under the *StringBuffer* class are discussed below:

1. *length():* This method returns the number of characters in the *StringBuffer* object.

   Syntax:

   ```
   public int length();
   ```

   //using length()

```
public class LengthDemo {
  public static void main(String[] args) {
        StringBuffer sb=new StringBuffer(); //creating
                //StringBuffer object with no characters
        System.out.println(sb.length()); //returns 0
        sb=new StringBuffer("hello world"); //mutable
//StringBuffer object sb with characters
        System.out.println(sb.length()); //returns 11
  }
}
```

Output:

```
0
11
```

2. *capacity():* This method returns the capacity of a *StringBuffer* object as in how many characters it is capable of holding. It is different from the *length()* method as it returns the number of characters in the *StringBuffer* object at present.

Syntax:

```
public int capacity();
```

//using capacity()

```
public class CapacityDemo {
  public static void main(String[] args) {
        //creating StringBuffer object with initial capacity as 16
        StringBuffer sb=new StringBuffer();
        System.out.println(sb.capacity()); //returns 16
        sb=new StringBuffer("hello world"); //initial capacity as
//sum of 16 and 11
        System.out.println(sb.capacity()); //returns 27
        sb=new StringBuffer(34);   //initial capacity 34
        System.out.println(sb.capacity()); //returns 34
  }
}
```

Output:

```
16
27
34
```

Notice the fact that the same reference has been used over and over again to modify the contents of the StringBuffer object and the compiler does not report an error! Also observe the following line:

```
sb=new StringBuffer("hello world");
```

The capacity of this object turns out to be 27 as the initial capacity(16) gets incremented by the number of characters in the object at present which is 11.

3. *ensureCapacity():* This method ensures a *StringBuffer* object to have a minimum capacity passed as an argument to the method.

   Syntax:

```
public void ensureCapacity(int minimumCapacity);
```

//using ensureCapacity()

```
public class ensureCapacityDemo {
  public static void main(String[] args) {
        StringBuffer sb=new StringBuffer();
        sb.ensureCapacity(64); //ensuring a minimum capacity of 64
        System.out.println(sb.capacity());      //returns 64
  }
}
```

4. *append()*: This method appends or attaches at the end, the string representation of the argument passed. Some of the versions of this method are discussed below:

   Syntax:

```
public StringBuffer append(boolean b);
public StringBuffer append(double d);
public StringBuffer append(String str);
public StringBuffer append(char[] str);
```

The first version appends the string representation of the boolean argument passed, at the end of the StringBuffer object whereas the second version appends the double argument. The third version appends the given String object at the end of the StringBuffer object and the last version appends a whole character array.

//using append()

```
public class AppendDemo {
    public static void main(String[] args) {
        StringBuffer sb = new StringBuffer(
                    "The value of the boolean argument is:");
        boolean b = false;
        System.out.println(sb.append(b));//appends a boolean value to
                                         // sb
        sb = new StringBuffer("10 dollars =");
        double d = 685.37;
        System.out.println(sb.append(d)); //appends a double value
        sb = new StringBuffer("I am getting appended to ");
        String str = "a String object";
```

```
            System.out.println(sb.append(str)); //appends a String object
            sb = new StringBuffer("I am being appended to a character
            array: ");
            char arr[] = { 'a', 'b', 'c' };
            System.out.println(sb.append(arr)); //appends a character
            //array
      }
}
```

Output:

```
The value of the boolean argument is:false
10 dollars=685.37
I am getting appended to a String object
I am being appended to a character array: abc
```

5. *charAt()*: This method returns the character at the given index from the StringBuffer object.

   Syntax:

   ```
   public char charAt(int index);
   ```

   //using charAt()

   ```
   public class CharAtDemo {
     public static void main(String[] args) {
           StringBuffer sb = new StringBuffer("I am using charAt()");
           System.out.println(sb.charAt(4)); //returns a space
     }
   }
   ```

   This program outputs a space as the character the fourth index in the above object is a space.

6. *insert()*: This method inserts a given argument at the given index. Some of the versions of the method are discussed below:

   Syntax:

   ```
   public StringBuffer insert(int offset, boolean b);
   public StringBuffer insert(int offset, double d);
   public StringBuffer insert(int offset, String str);
   public StringBuffer insert(int offset, char[] str);
   ```

   The above methods insert a boolean value, a double value, a String object and a character array at the specified index.

   //using insert()

   ```
   public class InsertDemo {
     public static void main(String[] args) {
           StringBuffer sb = new StringBuffer("This is a  value");
   ```

```
        System.out.println(sb.insert(10, true)); //inserts true
                                                  //value at index 10
        sb=new StringBuffer("The radius of the circle can be calculated
        by using pie= value");
        double d=3.14;
        System.out.println(sb.insert(56, d)); //inserts a double
                            //value at index 56
        sb=new StringBuffer("I am an umbrella");
        String str=" using";
        System.out.println(sb.insert(4, str)); //inserts a string
                                                //at index 4
        sb=new StringBuffer(" are the contents of my character array");
        char arr[]={'a','b','c'};
        System.out.println(sb.insert(0, arr)); //inserts an array
                                                //arr at index 0
  }
}
```

Output:

```
This is a true value
The radius of the circle can be calculated by using pie=3.14 value
I am using an umbrella
abc are the contents of my character array
```

7. *deleteCharAt and delete()*: These methods are used to delete a specific character or characters in a range from a StringBuffer object.

   Syntax:

```
public StringBuffer delete(int start, int end);
public StringBuffer deleteCharAt(int index);
```

Note that the first version deletes characters from a starting index till end index-1 whereas the second one only deletes the specific character specified in the argument.

//using delete and deleteCharAt()

```
public class DeleteDemo {
  public static void main(String[] args) {
        StringBuffer sb = new StringBuffer("123456789");
        System.out.println(sb.delete(3, 7)); //deletes characters
                                              //from index 3 to 6
        System.out.println(sb.deleteCharAt(3)); //deletes
                                   //character at index 3
  }
}
```

Output:

```
12389
1239
```

8. *replace()*: This method replaces characters in a StringBuffer object with another string beginning from a start index till end index-1.

Syntax:

```
public StringBuffer replace(int start, int end, String str);
```

//using replace

```
public class ReplaceDemo {
    public static void main(String[] args) {
        StringBuffer sb = new StringBuffer("I am getting replaced by
        another StringBuffer object");
        String str="being";
        System.out.println(sb.replace(5, 12, str));//scans index
                                                    //5 to 11
    }
}
```

Output:

```
I am being replaced by another StringBuffer object
```

9. *reverse()*: This method is used to reverse the contents of a StringBuffer object.

Syntax:

```
public StringBuffer reverse();
```

//using reverse()

```
public class ReverseDemo {
  public static void main(String[] args) {
        StringBuffer sb = new StringBuffer("123456");
        System.out.println(sb.reverse());//reverses the object
  }
}
```

Output:

```
654321
```

10. *substring()*: This method returns a substring or a subsequence of the given StringBuffer object.The method takes as a parameter the starting index and the end index from which the substring has to be extracted. The extraction starts from start index and runs till end index-1.

Syntax:

```
public String substring(int start);
public String substring(int start, int end);
```

//using substring()

```
public class SubStringDemo {
  public static void main(String[] args) {
        StringBuffer sb = new StringBuffer("I am using substring()
        method");
        System.out.println(sb.substring(11));
        System.out.println(sb);//prints the original object
        System.out.println(sb.substring(11, 22));//scans index 11
                                                  //to 21
  }
}
```

Output:

```
substring() method
I am using substring() method
substring()
```

11. *indexOf and lastIndexOf()*:These methods work in a similar fashion as they worked in the String class, just that the objects created are mutable now.

Syntax:

```
public int indexOf(String str)
public int indexOf(String str,int fromIndex)
public int lastIndexOf(String str)
public int lastIndexOf(String str,int fromIndex)
```

//Using the above methods

```
public class Main {
  public static void main(String[] args) {
        StringBuffer sb = new StringBuffer("Buffer in a StringBuffer");
        // returns the first occurrence of the string ff in sb
        System.out.println(sb.indexOf("ff"));
        // returns the first occurrence of the string ff in sb
        //starting from index 10
        System.out.println(sb.indexOf("ff", 10));
        // returns the last occurrence of string ff in sb
        System.out.println(sb.lastIndexOf("ff"));
        // returns last occurrence of ff searching backwards from
           //index 4
        System.out.println(sb.lastIndexOf("ff", 4));
  }
}
```

Output:

```
2
20
20
2
```

11.2 WRAPPER CLASSES

Java introduces a concept of wrappers wherein we have predefined wrapper classes corresponding to each of the primitive types in java. These wrapper classes have the same name as that of the primitive types (written in sentence case) case and are defined in java.lang package. Have a look at Table 11.2 for the various wrapper classes available in java.

Table 11.2

Primitive type	Wrapper class
boolean	Boolean
char	Character
int	Integer
long	Long
short	Short
byte	Byte
float	Float
double	Double

- *Creation of Wrapper objects*

  A wrapper class object can be created by instantiating any of the classes above. Example:

  ```
  Integer i=new Integer(3);
  ```

  This line creates an object of Integer class and its constructor initializes the object state with the primitive value passed.

  Every wrapper class constructor is of two types: 1) which accepts primitive type as its argument, 2) which accepts a string representation of the type as its argument. Example:

  ```
  Integer i=new Integer("3");
  ```

  Note that the Character class contains only the former type of constructor.

  This process wherein we wrap a primitive type value into an object of its type is called *wrapping* an object.

  Another approach to wrap primitive types into objects involves the usage of *valueOf()* method which has the following syntax:

```
1.public static Integer valueOf(int i):
```

returns an Integer object which has the value of the specified integer.

```
2.public static Integer valueOf(String s)throws NumberFormatException;
```

returns an Integer object with the value extracted from the string specified. This method throws an exception of type *NumberFormatException* in case the conversion from string to int fails.

```
3.public static Integer valueOf(String s, int radix)throws
  NumberFormatException;
```

returns an Integer object with the value extracted from the specified string and the given radix. The radix indicates the base of the integer value extracted. *NumberFormatException* is thrown in case conversion from string to int fails.

Let us now examine a simple example wherein we employ both these approaches to wrap objects.

```
public class WrappingDemo {
    public static void main(String[] args) {
        Integer i = new Integer(3); // wraps 3 to object i
        System.out.println(i); // prints string
                          //representation of i
Float f = new Float("3.14");// wraps float value
                          //3.14 from string to f
        System.out.println(f);
// converts 1011001 to binary and assigns to i1
        Integer i1 = Integer.valueOf("1011001", 2);
    System.out.println(i1);

    }
}
```

Output:

```
3
3.14
89
```

The output and the comments in the program clearly show wrapping of objects. When a string value is passed to the constructor of a wrapper class, it is first parsed into the corresponding primitive type and then assigned or wrapped into the wrapper class object. Also while printing an object, the *toString()* method gets called, which prints the string representation of the object. The *valueOf()* method used above first parses the string argument into an integer, converts this value from binary to decimal and then assigns it to object i1.

- *Unwrapping objects*

  The process of extracting back the primitive type value from the wrapper class object is called *unwrapping*. The two important methods to unwrap objects are discussed below:

  1. *xxxValue()*: One of the eight primitive types can replace the *xxx* in the method. Table 11.3 summarizes the methods of this type capable of unwrapping objects.

Table 11.3

xxxValue()	Description
byte byteValue()	Returns the primitive byte value from the Byte object.
short shortValue()	Returns the primitive short value from the Short object.
int intValue()	Returns the primitive int value from the Integer object.
long longValue()	Returns the primitive long value from the Long object.
float floatValue()	Returns the primitive float value from the Float object.
double doubleValue()	Returns the primitive double value from the Double object.

The following example demonstrates unwrapping of objects using some of the methods defined above:

```
public class UnWrappingDemo {
    public static void main(String[] args) {
          Float f=new Float(3.12f); //creates a Float wrapper
          int i=f.intValue(); //converts into integer value
          System.out.println(i);
          byte b=f.byteValue();//converts into byte value
          System.out.println(b);
          double d=f.doubleValue(); //converts into double
                                    //value
          System.out.println(d);
          short s=f.shortValue(); //converts into short value
          System.out.println(s);
    }
}
```

Output:

```
3
3
3.119999885559082
3
```

Note that while converting the float value into int, byte and short, the decimal part is truncated whereas when converting into a double, the precision of the argument increases.

2. parseXxx(): The Xxx in the method can replace one of the primitive types. Table 11.4 gives a brief introduction about the various methods of this type:

Table 11.4

parseXxx	Description
static byte parseByte(String s)	Parses the string object into the primitive byte value. Present in the Byte class.
static short parseShort(String s)	Parses the string object into the primitive short value. Present in the Short class.
static int parseInt(String s)	Parses the string object into the primitive int value. Present in the Integer class.
static long parseLong(String s)	Parses the string object into the primitive long value. Present in the Long class.
static float parseFloat(String s)	Parses the string object into the primitive float value. Present in the Float class.
static double parseDouble(String s)	Parses the string object into the primitive double value. Present in the Double class.

All the above methods are static by nature, hence invoked on their class names.

//using parseXxx()

```
public class ParseXxxDemo {
  public static void main(String[] args) {
        double d = Double.parseDouble("12.32");
        System.out.println("Double primitive type:" + d);
        int i = Integer.parseInt("234");
        System.out.println("Integer primitive type:" + i);
        byte b = Byte.parseByte("2");
        System.out.println("Byte primitive type:" + b);
  }
}
```

11.3 BOXING AND UNBOXING

In the earlier versions of java, to perform an increment operation on an object, we had to first unwrap it and then rewrap after incrementing. Consider the following code to understand this problem statement:

```
public class BoxingUnBoxingDemo {
     public static void main(String[] args) {
          Integer i=new Integer(23); //wrap 23 into i
          int v=i.intValue(); //unwrap i to v
```

```
            v++; //increment v
            i=new Integer(v); //rewrap v into i
        }
}
```

To avoid this fuss, Java 5 introduced the concept of *autoboxing/boxing and auto-unboxing/unboxing*. Boxing and unboxing feature does the unwrapping and rewrapping of the object itself.

The following code explains this concept:

```
public class BoxingUnboxingDemo {
    public static void main(String[] args) {
            Integer i = new Integer(23); // wrap 23 into i
            i++; // unwrap i
                  // rewrap i
            System.out.println(i);
    }
}
```

Output:

```
24
```

The examples discussed in the earlier sections, showed passing strings to the wrapper class constructors. In such a case, the string value passed is first parsed into the primitive type using parseXxx() method.

11.4 STREAMS

A stream is a concept which helps in performing input/output (I/O) operations. They can be used to either input or output some data. This data can be of different types, for example, a byte, character, object, etc. Java provides an input stream to read data from a data source and also an output stream to write data to a destination. The data source can vary from a keyboard (standard input device) to a file and a destination can be anything from console (standard output device) to a file. Therefore, a stream represents some form of data being read from or written to a destination.

Java provides a number of streams for reading and writing varied types of data in the *java.io* package. This book will be focusing upon Byte, Character and Buffered Streams.

- **Byte Streams**

  These streams basically deal with input and output of byte or binary data in the form of 8-bit bytes. *InputStream* and *OutputStream* are the abstract classes which stand at the top of the hierarchy of Byte Stream classes responsible for performing I/O operations. *FileInputStream* and *FileOutputStream* are descendants of the above classes which help perform various file operations.

The following tables give an overview of some of the methods available in *InputStream* and *OutputStream* classes.

Table 11.5 Methods defined in InputStream class

Method	Description
int available()	Returns the number of bytes that can be read from this input stream.
void close()	Closes this input stream. Any further attempt to read using this input stream will result in an IOException.
abstract int read()	Returns as an integer value, the next byte read from the input stream. In case of end of file, -1 is returned.
int read(byte[] b)	Returns as an integer value the next byte read and stores it into a byte array. In case of end of file, -1 is returned.
int read(byte[] b, int off, int len)	Reads and returns up to length number of bytes starting from an offset position and stores the same in a byte array. In case of end of file, -1 is returned.

Table 11.6 Methods defined in OutputStream class

Method	Description
void close()	Closes the output stream associated with the object. Any further attempt to use this stream will result into an IOException.
void flush()	Flushes any buffered output available in this stream and force writes it to the disk.
void write(byte[] b)	Writes the complete byte array to the output stream.
int write(byte[] b, int off, int len)	Writes the byte array starting from the offset position specified, up to length number of bytes.
abstract void write(int b)	Writes the single byte to the output stream.

Table 11.7 Constructors defined in FileInputStream class

Constructor	Description
FileInputStream(File file)	Creates a FileInputStream to a file specified by the File object.
FileInputStream(FileDescriptor fdobj)	Creates a FileInputStream to an existing file specified by the file descriptor.
FileInputStream(String name)	Creates a FileInputStream to a file specified by the path of the file.

Table 11.8 Constructors defined in FileOutputStream class

Constructor	Description
FileOutputStream(File file)	Creates a FileOutputStream to a file specified by the File object.
FileOutputStream(File file, boolean append)	Creates a FileOutputStream to a file specified by the File object. If the append value is true, the file is opened in the append mode.
FileOutputStream(FileDescriptor fdObj)	Creates a FileOutputStream to an existing file specified by the file descriptor.
FileOutputStream(String name)	Creates a FileOutputStream to a file specified by the path of the file.
FileOutputStream(String name, boolean append)	Creates a FileOutputStream to a file specified by the path of the file. If the append value is true, the file is opened in append mode.

Note that the FileInputStream and FileOutputStream constructors throw a FileNotFoundException.

The below program copies text from one file to another using classes FileInputStream and FileOutputStream.

```
package pkg1;

import java.io.FileInputStream;
import java.io.FileNotFoundException;
import java.io.FileOutputStream;
import java.io.IOException;

public class CopyFile {
    public static void main(String[] args) throws FileNotFoundException {
          int i;
          FileInputStream fin = new FileInputStream("C:\\Users\\Surbhi\\
          MyFile.txt");
          FileOutputStream  fout  =  new  FileOutputStream("C:\\Users\\
          Surbhi\\YourFile.txt");
          try {
                do {
                      i = fin.read(); //reading from MyFile.txt
                      if (i != -1)
                            fout.write(i); //writing to
                                              //YourFile.txt
                } while (i != -1); //checking if end of file has
                                    //reached
                //closing the streams
                fin.close();
                fout.close();
```

```
            } catch (IOException e) { //exception thrown by read and
                                       //write methods
                  e.printStackTrace();
            }
    }
    }
```

The *FileInputStream* and *FileOutputStream* constructors throw an exception of type *FileNotFoundException* and the *read*, *write* methods throws *IOException*, therefore, handling the same in the above code is extremely important else the compiler reports an error. The *fin* object (*FileInputStream*) is connected to the file *MyFile.txt* whereas the *fout* object (*FileOutputStream*) is associated with *YourFile.txt*. The do while loop used above reads from *Myfile.txt* which returns an integer value every time and writes it to *YourFile.txt* using *read* and *write* methods till the end of file (eof) has reached. The *read* method returns -1 when the *eof* has been reached. It is imperative to close all the input and output streams using the *close()* method as it automatically flushes the data to the disk.

> *Follow a simple rule: If you need to read or write binary or byte data in a file, create objects of FileInputStream and FileOutputStream. Futher, use read and write methods to perform read and write operations.*

Note that the byte streams perform IO operations at a lower level but still are important to read as all the other stream classes are built on byte stream classes. Also, character streams should be adopted to read and write character data which are discussed in the next section.

- **Character Streams**

  Character streams are the streams which facilitate reading and writing character data. On the top of the hierarchy, we have the abstract classes: *Reader* and *Writer*. To handle character file IO, we use *FileReader* and *FileWriter*. Given below is the description of some of the methods and constructors of these classes.

Table 11.9 Methods defined in Reader class

Method	Description
abstract void close()	Closes the character input stream. Any further attempt to read using this input stream will result in an IOException.
int read()	Returns as an integer value, the next character read from the input stream. In case of end of file, -1 is returned.
int read(char[] cbuff)	Returns as an integer value the next character read and stores it into a character array. In case of end of file, -1 is returned.
int read(char[] cbuff, int off, int len)	Reads and returns up to length number of characters starting from an offset position and stores the same in a character array. In case of end of file, -1 is returned.

Table 11.10 Methods defined in Writer class

Method	Description
abstract void close()	Closes the output stream associated with the object. Any further attempt to use this stream will result into an IOException.
abstract void flush()	Flushes any buffered output available in this stream and force writes it to the disk.
void write(char[] cbuff)	Writes the complete character array to the output stream.
abstract void write(char[] cbuff, int off, int len)	Writes the character array starting from the offset position specified, up to length number of bytes.
void write(int c)	Writes the single character to the output stream.
void write(String str)	Writes the String object to the output stream.
void write(String str, int off, int len)	Writes the length number of characters of the String object starting from the offset position.

All the above methods in the Reader and Writer class throw an exception of type IOException.

Table 11.11 Constructors defined in FileReader class

Constructor	Description
FileReader(File file)	Creates a FileReader to a file specified by the File object.
FileReader(FileDescriptor fd)	Creates a FileReader to an existing file specified by the file descriptor.
FileReader(String fname)	Creates a FileReader to a file specified by the path of the file.

Table 11.12 Constructors defined in FileWriter class

Constructor	Description
FileWriter(File file)	Creates a FileWriter to a file specified by the File object.
FileWriter(File file, boolean append)	Creates a FileWriter to a file specified by the File object. If the append value is true, the file is opened in the append mode.
FileWriter(FileDescriptor fdObj)	Creates a FileWriter to an existing file specified by the file descriptor.
FileWriter(String name)	Creates a FileWriter to a file specified by the path of the file.
FileWriter(String name, boolean append)	Creates a FileWriter to a file specified by the path of the file. If the append value is true, the file is opened in append mode.

The constructors in the *FileReader* class throw an exception of type *FileNotFoundException* whereas ones in the *FileWriter* class throw an exception of type *IOException*.

The following program amends the above program to copy character text from one file to another.

```
package pkg1;

import java.io.FileReader;
import java.io.FileNotFoundException;
import java.io.FileWriter;
import java.io.IOException;

public class CopyFile {
    public static void main(String[] args) throws FileNotFoundException {
            int i;
FileReader fr = new FileReader("C:\\Users\\Surbhi\\MyFile.txt");
            try {
FileWriter fw = new FileWriter("C:\\Users\\Surbhi\\YourFile.txt");

                  do {
                        i = fr.read(); // reading from MyFile.txt
                        if (i != -1)
                              fw.write(i); // writing to YourFile.txt
                  } while (i != -1); // checking if end of file has
                                          //reached
                  fr.close(); // closing the streams
                  fw.close();
            } catch (IOException e) { // exception thrown by read and
                                    //write methods
                  e.printStackTrace();
            }
      }
}
```

- **Buffered Streams**

  Till now the streams we have studied were all unbuffered streams. The unbuffered streams use the operating system to perform read and write operations. Every read and write operation results into a disk access which incurs a cost. On the other hand, we have buffered IO wherein all the data read or written to, is done via a memory area called a buffer. This buffer is written only after it is full, therefore, it reduces the disk access. Java introduces four buffered streams: *BufferedInputStream*, *BufferedOutputStrean* for handling byte data and *BufferedReader*, *BufferedWriter* for handling character data.

  These buffered streams are used by wrapping up the unbuffered streams with them which means passing an object of the unbuffered stream class to the constructor of the buffered stream class.

Table 11.13 Constructors defined in BufferedReader class

Constructor	Description
BufferedReader(Reader in)	Creates a buffered character input stream with a default sized input buffer.
BufferedReader(Reader in, int size)	Creates a buffered character input stream with the specified size of the buffer.

Table 11.14 Constructors defined in BufferedWriter class

Constructor	Description
BufferedWriter(Writer out)	Creates a buffered character output stream with a default sized input buffer.
BufferedWriter(Writer out, int size)	Creates a buffered character output stream with the specified size of the buffer.

Let us take up an example for *BufferedReader* and see how we wrap up unbuffered streams with it.

```
package pkg1;

import java.io.BufferedReader;
import java.io.BufferedWriter;
import java.io.FileReader;
import java.io.FileNotFoundException;
import java.io.FileWriter;
import java.io.IOException;

public class BufferedStreamDemo {
    public static void main(String[] args) throws FileNotFoundException {
            int i;
            FileReader  fr  =  new  FileReader("C:\\Users\\Surbhi\\MyFile.
            txt"); //unbuffered stream
//wrapping of unbuffered stream object fr to br
            BufferedReader br = new BufferedReader(fr);
            try {
            FileWriter  fw  =  new  FileWriter("C:\\Users\\Surbhi\\YourFile.
            txt");
            BufferedWriter bw = new BufferedWriter(fw);
                  do {
                        i = br.read(); // reading from MyFile.txt
                        if (i != -1)
                              bw.write(i); // writing to YourFile.txt
```

```
            } while (i != -1); // checking if end of file has
                                    //reached
            br.close(); // closing the streams
            bw.close();
        } catch (IOException e) { // exception thrown by read and
                                //write methods
            e.printStackTrace();
        }
    }
}
```

Notice we passed an object of *FileReader* to the *BufferedReader* constructor in the above example whereas in Table 11.13, a *Reader* class reference is being passed in the constructor. This is still possible as *FileReader* is a descendent of *Reader* class and the super class reference variable can point to a subclass object.

11.5 SYSTEM.IN AND SYSTEM.OUT

As talked in the initial chapters, *System* is a predefined class in the *java.lang* package. *in*, *out* and *err* are reference variables of class *InputStream* and *PrintStream* defined as a static class member of *System* class. Because of their static nature, they are accessed via their class name, System.

Table 11.15 Fields defined in System class

Fields	Description
static PrintStream err	Refers to standard error stream where the errors will be displayed.
static InputStream in	Refers to standard input stream from where the inputs will be taken, generally, keyboard
static PrintStream out	Refers to standard output stream where the output will be displayed, generally, console.

11.6 READING AND WRITING ON CONSOLE

Reading and writing on console employs methods from the above stream classes.

- *Reading from standard input*

  Java uses *System.in* to read data from standard input.To read buffered character data, a character based buffered stream can be used wrapping up an unbuffered stream object.

  - *Reading characters*

    The *read()* method defined in the *BufferedReader* class can be used to read characters from console.

Syntax:

```
public int read()throws IOException;
```

This method returns the character read from standard input as an integer value. It returns -1 in case end of file is encountered.

```
package pkg1;

import java.io.BufferedReader;
import java.io.IOException;
import java.io.InputStreamReader;

public class ReadCharacterDemo {
public static void main(String[] args){
          int i;
          System.out.println("Enter characters:");
//connected to standard input
          InputStreamReader ir = new
InputStreamReader(System.in);
// buffered stream
          BufferedReader br = new BufferedReader(ir);
          try {
                do {
                      i = br.read(); // reading character by
                                  // character
                      System.out.print((char) i); // writing
                                                  //to console
                } while (i != -1);
                br.close();
          } catch (IOException e) {
                e.printStackTrace();
          }
}
}
```

Output:

```
Enter characters:
abcd123
abcd123
```

The above program reads characters from standard input using an object of *InputStreamReader* class. *InputStreamReader* is a concrete descendent of *Reader* class which converts bytes into characters. The object of this class is wrapped into the constructor of *BufferedReader* class to generate a character based stream connected to standard input. As the *read()* returns characters as an integer value, we need to typecast back into a character to display characters on the console.

- *Reading Strings*

  To read a string from standard input involves usage of the *readLine()* method of *BufferedReader* class.

  Syntax:

```
public String readLine()throws IOException
```

  This method reads and returns a String object.

  //using readLine()

```
package pkg1;

import java.io.BufferedReader;
import java.io.IOException;
import java.io.InputStreamReader;

public class ReadStringDemo {
public static void main(String[] args){
    String str;
    System.out.println("Enter the string:");
//connected to standard input
    InputStreamReader ir = new
InputStreamReader(System.in);
    //buffered stream
    BufferedReader br = new BufferedReader(ir);
    try {
        do {
            str = br.readLine(); // reading strings
            System.out.print(str); // writing to
                                    //console
        } while (!str.equals("quit"));
        br.close();
    } catch (IOException e) {
```

```
                e.printStackTrace();
        }
    }
}
```

Output:

```
Enter the string:
This is not the end, just the beginning
This is not the end, just the beginning
```

- *Writing on standard output*

  To print on the console, methods of the *PrintStream* class like *print(), println() and write()* can be used. The book has been extensively using *print()* and *println()* methods throughout where *println()* method prints a newline after printing the output.

  The *write()* method on the other hand has the below syntax:

```
public void write(int b);
public void write(byte[] buf, int off, int len);
```

  The former version writes the byte value of the argument to the stream specifying the low order 8 bits, whereas, the latter, writes the complete byte array, *buff* of length *len* starting from an offset position. If automatic flushing is enabled, the output is flushed to the console else the flush method needs to be invoked explicitly. Printing a newline also invokes the flush method.

  These methods are used with System.out variable when required to print on the console as the out reference variable is connected to the console.

//using write()

```
import java.io.BufferedReader;
import java.io.IOException;
import java.io.InputStreamReader;

public class WriteDemo {
public static void main(String[] args) {
    byte[] b = { 'a', 'b', 'c', 'd' };
    System.out.write(b, 1, 3); //writing array from index 1
    System.out.write('\n');
  }
}
```

Output:

```
Bcd
```

Reading and Writing on console using Scanner class

Java introduces another class, *Scanner* to read and write on the console. Some of its constructors and methods are discussed below.

Table 11.16 Constructors defined in Scanner class

Constructor	Description
Scanner(File source)	Creates a scanner that takes input from the specified file.
Scanner(Inputstream source)	Creates a scanner that takes input from the specified input stream.
Scanner(String source)	Creates a scanner that takes input from the specified string source.

Table 11.17 Methods defined in Scanner class

Method	Description
int nextInt()	Scans the input as the next integer from the user.
long nextLong()	Scans the input as the next long from the user.
float nextFloat()	Scans the input as the next float from the user.
boolean nextBoolean()	Scans the input as the next boolean from the user.
double nextDouble()	Scans the input as the next double from the user.
void close()	Closes the stream associated with the object.

//using Scanner

```
import java.util.Scanner;

public class ScannerDemo {
    public static void main(String[] args) {
        Scanner sc = new Scanner(System.in); // specifying the
                                              //source
        System.out.println("Enter the first integer");
        int val1 = sc.nextInt();// taking first input
        System.out.println("Enter the second integer");
        int val2 = sc.nextInt();// taking second input
        int sum = val1 + val2;
```

```
            System.out.println("The sum of two numbers is:" + sum);
            sc.close(); //closing the stream
        }
    }
```

Output:

```
Enter the first integer
 3
Enter the second integer
 4
The sum of two numbers is:7
```

11.7 OBJECT CLASS

Object class is a predefined class in *java.lang* package. It is the super class for all the classes available in java. Even the user-defined classes are the subclasses of the Object class directly or indirectly. So, all the classes which we have discussed in this book are also a subclass of Object class.

Object class references are beneficial when we do not know the type of object being pointed to. In other words, *object class reference can point to any class object as super class reference can point to any subclass object.*

```
public class A {
}

public class Main {
    public static void main(String[] args) {
        Object o=new A();
    }
}
```

Table 11.18 discusses some of the methods available in the Object class. These methods are always inherited in all the classes in java as they are public in nature. The non-final methods may also be overridden in any of the subclasses.

Table 11.18 Methods defined in Object class

Method	Description
public final Class getClass()	Returns the information of the class like the class name, its super class as a Class object.
public int hashCode()	Returns as an integer value the hash code of the object. Two objects are said to be equal if their hash codes are equivalent.

public boolean equals(Object obj)	Compares the object being passed with this object.
public String toString()	Returns the string representation of the object as a String object.
public final void notify()	Notifies the first thread that called wait() on an object.
public final void notifyAll()	Notifies all the threads that invoked wait() on an object.
public final void wait(long timeout)throws InterruptedException	Waits on a thread to complete execution for the specified interval of time.
public final void wait(long timeout,int nanos) throws InterruptedException	Waits on a thread to complete execution for the specified interval of time.
public final void wait()throws Interrupted Exception	Waits on a thread to complete execution.
protected void finalize()throws Throwable	Invoked just before the garbage collection takes place. Important code like releasing locks can be written here.

SUMMARY

- String handling can be done in java using *String*, *StringBuffer* and *StringBuilder* classes, available in *java.lang* package.
- *String* class creates immutable objects which when once created, cannot be altered whereas *StringBuffer* class creates mutable objects.
- *StringBuffer* class is said to be thread safe as compared to *StringBuilder* as all its methods are synchronized in nature.
- Wrapper classes lets you wrap a primitive type into an object and unwrap it back to its primitive type value.
- Boxing unboxing feature wraps and unwraps object implicitly.
- A stream is either used to produce some information or consume some information.
- The three streams discussed in the book are:

  (1) *Byte streams* for input and output of byte data

  (2) *Character streams* for input and output of character data

  (3) *Buffered streams* use a buffer/memory area to input output byte and character data.

- System.in, System.out and System.err refer to standard input, standard output and standard error respectively.
- Object class is the super class for all the predefined and user-defined classes in java. Therefore, an object class reference can point to any of the classes in java.

COMMON ERRORS

- Using == for equating two string objects. One should always use the equals() method to compare two string objects as == operator only compares the references and not the contents.
- Forgetting that the String class creates immutable objects.
- Reusing a stream object. A stream object once used cannot be used again. It results into a compile time error.
- Forgetting to close streams can result into a resource leak. A resource leak is a situation where a resource is not being released for a long time.

SELF-TEST

1. Differentiate between mutable and immutable objects. Which classes in java enable us to create them? Discuss them.
2. What are wrapper classes? How can we wrap/unwrap objects? Explain in detail.
3. Write a short note on:
   - Boxing and unboxing
   - Streams
   - Object class
4. Discuss the classes and the methods that can be used to take input from the console.

PRACTICAL QUESTIONS

1. Generate the output for the following:

a)
```
public class SelfTest {
    public static void main(String[] args) {
        String str="String";
        str.concat("Handling");
        System.out.println(str);
    }
}
```

b)
```
public class SelfTest {
    public static void main(String[] args) {
        StringBuffer str="Hello World";
        str.append('s');
        System.out.println(str);
    }
}
```

c)
```
import java.io.FileNotFoundException;
import java.io.FileReader;
import java.io.IOException;

public class SelfTest {
    public static void main(String[] args) throws Exception {
          String fname=null;
          FileReader fr=new FileReader(fname);
          char c=(char)fr.read();
          System.out.println(c);
    }
}
```

d)
```
import java.io.*;
public class SelfTest {
    public static void main(String[] args) throws Exception {
          System.out.println("Enter characters");
          BufferedReader br=new BufferedReader(new
          InputStreamReader(System.in));
          char c=(char)br.read();
          br.close();
          System.out.println(c);
    }
}
```

12 CHAPTER

Applets and AWT

This chapter will enable you to learn the following:

- Defining, creating and running an applet using the applet tag and applet class.
- Studying the life cycle of an applet and various applet display methods.
- Diving into the AWT package, going through classes like, Graphics, Font, Color and Frame.
- Adding and removing AWT controls on a window.
- Understanding layout managers to manage the diverse AWT components.

12.1 INTRODUCTION

This chapter focuses on *graphical user interface programming (GUI)* using applets and AWT. GUI programming employs interaction between the user and the application through a graphical interface. Example, a user clicking on the send mail button, to send an email, to a recipient.

An applet is an application which can be written in java. The code for applets is downloaded from the web server and is embedded in the web page by the web browser. The JVM on the client machine executes the applet code (downloaded at the client side). Hence, these applets can run on any platform.

Java provides an Applet class to implement applets in our code.

AWT stands for Abstract Window Toolkit and is defined as a package in java. It provides several classes and methods to implement GUI programming.

12.2 APPLET CLASS AND ITS METHODS

Before we actually see how to implement applets in java, let us first have a look on the applet class and its methods. Applet is a predefined class in *java.applet* package. Following are some of the constructors and methods defined in this class:

Table 12.1 Constructor defined in Applet class

Constructor	Description
public Applet()	Creates a new applet

Table 12.2 Methods defined in Applet class

Method	Description
public void init()	Indicates that an applet has been loaded into the system. Generally invoked by the browser or the appletviewer only once during the life cycle of the applet.
public void start()	Indicates that the applet has been started by the browser or the appletviewer.
public void paint(Graphics g)	Paints on the applet using a Graphics class reference.
public void stop()	Indicates that the applet has been stopped temporarily. Once the applet resumes, the start() and the paint() methods are invoked once again.
public void destroy()	The call to this method destroys an applet, reclaims the memory and other resources from the applet.
public boolean isActive()	Checks whether the given applet is alive or not. An applet is said to be alive from the time it starts till the time it gets destroyed. The method returns false if the applet has been destroyed.
public void resize(Dimension d) public void resize(int width, int height)	Resizes the given applet according to the specified dimensions.
public void showStatus(String msg)	Displays the specified string message in the status bar of the applet.
public String getParameter(String name)	Returns the value corresponding to the name specified from the HTML tag.

All java applets are created by extending the above *java.applet.Applet* class. The Applet class is a subclass of *Panel* class which is further a descendant of the *Container* class present in the *java.awt* package. These classes will be discussed in the coming sections where we talk about AWT hierarchy.

12.3 THE APPLET TAG

As described above, an applet needs a web browser to run, therefore comes the role of the applet tag. The applet tag basically deploys the applet in the web browser.

This tag has several properties/attributes which describe how the applet has to be displayed on the browser.

Table 12.3 Attributes defined in applet tag

Attribute	Description
CODE	This attribute specifies the compiled applet class (.class file) to execute in the browser. It searches the file in the same directory as that of your applet source file and is mandatory to be specified.
CODEBASE	This attribute specifies the complete directory location where to search the compiled applet class mentioned in the CODE attribute.
WIDTH	Specifies the width of the applet.
HEIGHT	Specifies the height of the applet.
ALT	Specifies the alternate text to be displayed on the browser in case the applet is not loaded.
NAME	Specifies a unique name to the applet.
PARAM NAME AND VALUE	Specifies the argument name and value pairs for the applet which can be accessed using the getParameter() method.

12.4 LIFE CYCLE OF APPLETS

Just as humans have a life cycle starting from birth till death, applets are also characterized by their life cycle. During its life cycle, it undergoes several states which are discussed below:

- *init():* This method is the first method to be invoked and called only once during the life cycle of the applet. All the initialization parameters can be set here.
- *start():* After the init() method, a call to the start() method is made which starts an applet. An applet window appearing on the browser indicates the start of an applet. This method will be called over and over again whenever the applet window appears.
- *paint():* This method is used to draw some output on the applet. It is called each time when an output has to be redrawn. The method takes the *Graphics* class reference variable as an input parameter which can be used to further draw various figures on the applet.
- *stop():* This method temporarily suspends the execution of the applet by hiding the applet window. It is invoked when an applet window is minimized. On maximizing the applet window, the applet is restarted, thereby calling the start() and the paint() methods.

- *destroy():* This method is invoked when we close an applet window. In such a case, all the resources allocated to the applet are reclaimed.

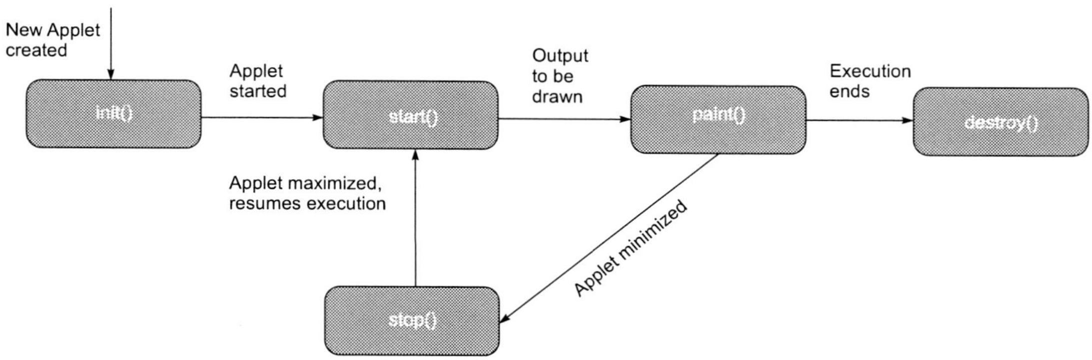

Fig. 12.1

> *In case an applet is run on a browser that is not Java-enabled, it will ignore the applet and the param tags.*

12.5 CREATING AND RUNNING AN APPLET

Now that we have read about the Applet class, applet tag and the applet life cycle, we are ready to dive into the creation of applets. Every applet you create in your program, will be a subclass of the predefined *Applet* class present in *java.applet* package.

Below is a simple program that demonstrates creation of an applet:

```
import java.applet.*;
import java.awt.*;

/*
<applet code="MyApplet.class" width=300 height=200>
</applet>
 */

public class MyApplet extends Applet {

    // overriding applet methods
    public void init() {   // initializing the applet
          System.out.println("Init Called once");
    }

    public void start() {   // starting the applet
```

```
            System.out.println("Start called");
    }

    public void paint(Graphics g)  { // drawing output on the applet
            g.drawString("My First Applet", 20, 30);
    }

    public void destroy() {   // closing the applet
            System.out.println("Destroy called");
    }
}
```

Output:

Applet Window

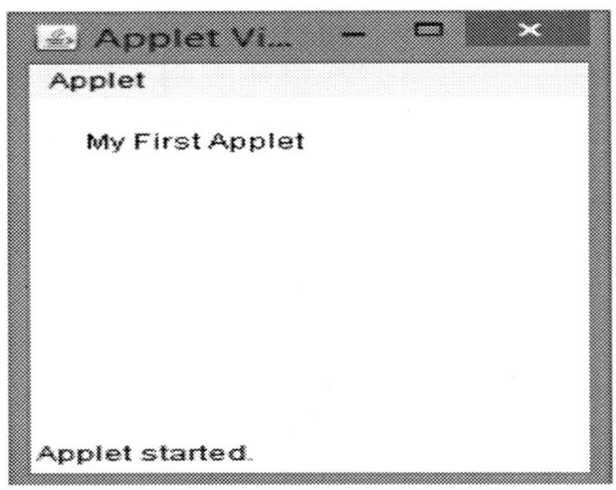

Console Window:

```
Init Called once
Start called
Destroy called
```

Let us first have a look at the code before going for an explanation of the output.

The above class extends the predefined Applet class as every applet is a subclass of the Applet class, therefore importing the *java.applet* package. The program then overrides the applet class methods demonstrating its life cycle. Notice the definition for the *paint()* method:

```
public void paint(Graphics g) { // drawing output on the applet
            g.drawString("My First Applet", 20, 30);
    }
```

The *paint()* method accepts a reference of *Graphics* class as a parameter. This reference is necessary as it can be used to call *Graphics* class methods. The Graphics class exists in *java.awt* package, hence the import statement. The *drawString()* method, in turn, takes a String object as an input parameter to be drawn on the applet, and the x and y coordinates as a location to be drawn upon.

Syntax:

```
public abstract void drawString(String str, int x, int y);
```

Also notice the applet tag in the above program just after the import statements.

As discussed above, the code attribute specifies the name of the .class file to be embedded in the HTML file. The applet tag is required to be specified inside your source file, in case you are developing the file in a text editor like notepad. The width and height attributes set the size of the applet window to be displayed on the screen.

Now let us examine the output for this program.

This program can be either run on an IDE or from command prompt. The command to execute this program from command prompt is as follows:

//compiling MyApplet.java

javac MyApplet.java

//Executing MyApplet.java

appletviewer MyApplet

The program can also be executed from an IDE by running the class as a simple applet.

Upon running the above program, two windows appear; *applet* and *console* windows. The *drawString()* method writes on the applet window whereas *System.out.println()* method writes on the console window.

> *Applets do not have a main method as their execution starts from the init() method.*

12.6 APPLET DISPLAY METHODS

To set the background and the foreground colour of an applet, we have the following methods available inside the Component class defined in *java.awt* package. (The Applet class is a descendant of *Component* class as we will shortly see in the AWT hierarchy of classes.)

Table 12.4

Method	Description
public Color getForeground()	Returns the foreground color of the applet.
public Color getBackground()	Returns the background color of the applet.
public void setForeground(Color c)	Sets the foreground color of the applet to the given color.
public void setBackground(Color c)	Sets the background color of the applet to the given color.

The *setBackground()* and the *setForeground()* methods accepts a *Color* class reference as their parameter. *Color* is another predefined class in the *java.awt* package. This class defines the below static final *Color* constants to represent different colors.

Table 12.5

Fields	Description
static Color black	Represents the color black.
static Color BLACK	Represents the color black.
static Color blue	Represents the color blue.
static Color BLUE	Represents the color blue.
static Color cyan	Represents the color cyan.
static Color CYAN	Represents the color cyan.
static Color DARK_GRAY	Represents the color dark gray.
static Color darkGray	Represents the color dark gray.
static Colorgray	Represents the color gray.
static Color GRAY	Represents the color gray.
static Color green	Represents the color green.
static Color GREEN	Represents the color green.
static Color LIGHT_GRAY	Represents the color light gray.
static Color lightGray	Represents the color light gray.
static Color magenta	Represents the color magenta.
static Color MAGENTA	Represents the color magenta.
static Color orange	Represents the color orange.
static Color ORANGE	Represents the color orange.
static Color pink	Represents the color pink.
static Color PINK	Represents the color pink.
static Color red	Represents the color red.
static Color RED	Represents the color red.
static Color white	Represents the color white.
static Color WHITE	Represents the color white.
static Color yellow	Represents the color yellow.
static Color YELLOW	Represents the color yellow.

All these variables are accessed by their class name, as they are static final variables of the *Color* class, example, Color.BLACK,

The following example sets the background and the foreground color of the applet to blue and white respectively:

```
import java.applet.*;
import java.awt.*;

/*
<applet code="MyApplet.class" width=300 height=200>
</applet>
 */

public class MyApplet extends Applet {
    String str;
          public void init() {   // initializing the applet
          str = "Initializing colors to the applet...";
          setBackground(Color.BLUE); // sets background color of the
                                     //applet

          setForeground(Color.WHITE); // sets foreground color of the
                                      // applet
          }
    public void start() {   // starting the applet
          str += "Starting the applet...";
}
    public void paint(Graphics g) { // drawing output on the applet
          g.drawString(str, 20, 30);
    }
}
```

Output:

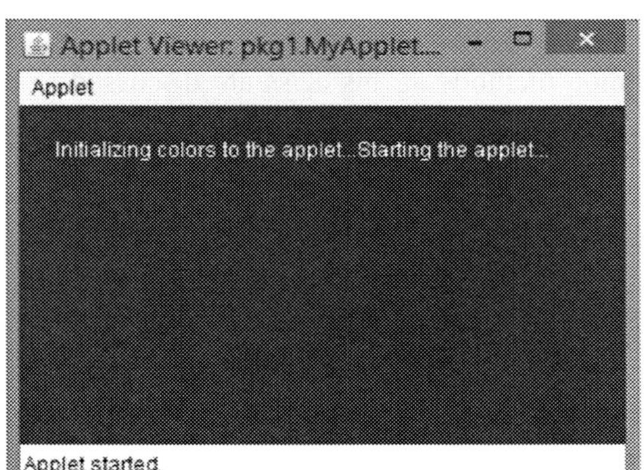

The program prints the appended String object *str* on the applet. The *init()* method invokes the *setBackground*() and *setForeground()* methods directly as the class *MyApplet* extends *Applet* and these methods are available in the *Applet* class(inherited from the *Component* class).

12.7 AWT PACKAGE AND ITS CLASSES

This section focuses upon the various classes available in the AWT package. AWT stands for abstract window toolkit and this package defines all the classes and methods which provide support for graphical user interface programming. Figure 12.2 describes the AWT class hierarchy:

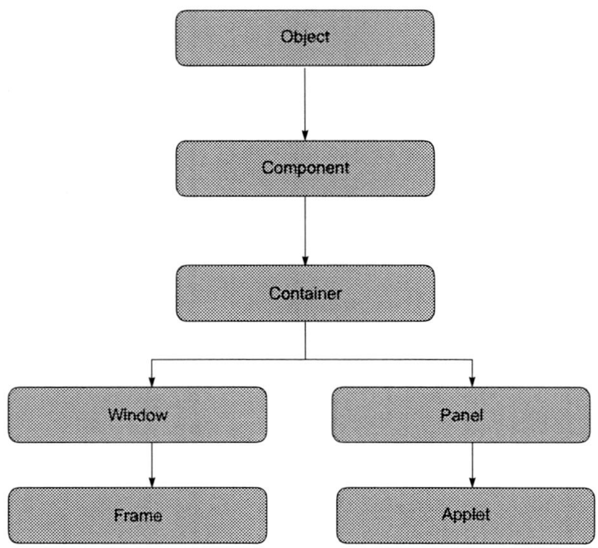

Fig. 12.2 AWT heirarchy

- **Component:** This class stands at the root of the awt hierarchy. It is an abstract class and provides all the components to support GUI programming. The well-known applet class, you read above is also a component. The Component class defines several methods for handling events, changing font, color and drawing components.

  Some of the common methods of this class are discussed below:

  `public void setBackground(Color c):` sets the background color of the component.

  `public void setForeground(Color c):` sets the foreground color of the component.

  `public void add(Component c):` adds the specified component on this component.

  `public void setSize(int width, int height):` sets the size of the component to the specified width and height.

  `public void setSize(Dimension d):` sets the size of the component to the specified dimension object.

`public Dimension getSize():` returns the size of the component as a Dimension object.

`public void setLayout(LayoutManager m):` sets the layout of the component to the specified layout manager type. This method will be discussed at length in the coming sections.

`public void setVisible(boolean status):` sets the visibility of the component to either true or false.

- **Container:** A container is a component that holds other components like Button, TextField, Label or even another container. It is a subclass of Component class, therefore contains methods inherited from it.
- **Window:** is a subclass of Container that does not contain any borders or a menu bar. To create a window with a border or a menu bar, one must use its subclass, Frame.
- **Frame:** is a window with a title, border and a menu bar. It can contain other components like Button, TextField, Label, etc. We will shortly see working with frame windows.
- **Panel:** is a container with no title bar, menu bar or borders. Applets are a subclass of Panel class and it is on the Panel's surface that the applet's output are drawn.

12.8 WORKING WITH FRAME WINDOWS

A frame as we discussed above, is a window that has a title bar, menu bar and a border. There are two ways to create a frame:

- Instantiating Frame class
- Extending Frame class

But before we go on to create a frame, let us have a look on some of the constructors and methods of the Frame class:

Constructors:

Frame():creates a new frame without any title.
Frame(String title):creates a new frame with the specified title.

Methods:

`public void setTitle(String title):` sets the title of the frame to the specified title.
`public String getTitle():` gets the title of the frame.

Now let us examine both the approaches to create a frame one by one.

- **Instantiating Frame class**

  The first approach describes the creation of a frame by instantiating the frame.

```
import java.awt.*;
```

```
public class FrameDemo {
    public static void main(String[] args) {
        Frame f = new Frame(); //creates a frame
        f.setSize(300, 400);// sets the size of the frame
        f.setTitle("My new frame"); // sets the title of the
                                    // frame
        f.setBackground(Color.blue); //sets the background of the
                                    // frame
        f.setVisible(true); // sets the visibility of the frame
                                    // to true
    }
}
```

Output:

The program clearly shows the creation of frames using different methods of the *Frame* class and the inherited methods from the *Component* class. The above code creates a frame using the default constrictor of the Frame class and sets the title using its *setTitle()* method.

Note that the *setBackground()*, *setSize()* method belong to the *Component* class and are inherited into the *Frame* class. These methods set the background color and the size of the frame to the specified arguments. You will also notice that this frame does not close on pressing the close button. To close frames we need to use event handling for closing frames which will be discussed in the next chapter.

- **Extending Frame class**

  A frame can also be created by extending the Frame class.

//Modifying the above program to extend the Frame class

```
public class FrameDemo extends Frame {
    public FrameDemo()
    {
        //call to super();
        setTitle("My new frame");
        setBackground(Color.BLUE);
        setSize(300,400);
        setVisible(true);
    }
}
public class Main {
    public static void main(String[] args) {
        FrameDemo f=new FrameDemo();
    }
}
```

The constructor of the *FrameDemo* class gives an implicit call to the super class constructor of the *Frame* class and *it is actually inside the Frame class constructor that a new frame is created.*

12.9 WORKING WITH GRAPHICS, COLOR AND FONT CLASS

This section deals with Graphics, Color, Font classes and its associated methods. All these classes are members of the *java.awt* package.

- **Graphics class**

  This class provides some of the significant methods to draw various figures on a container. The container can be either an applet or a frame.

  Table 12.6 defines some of the methods defined in Graphics class.

Table 12.6

Methods	Description
public abstract void drawString(String str,int x, int y)	Draws or writes the given string at the specified x and y coordinates.
public abstract void drawLine(int x1, int y1, int x2, int y2)	Draws a line with the current colour at the specified start and end points. x1, y1, x2, y2 represent the coordinates of the line to be created.
public void drawRect(int x, int y, int width, int height)	Draws a rectangle at the specified coordinates with the mentioned width and height where x and y denote the top left coordinates of the rectangle.

(Contd.)

public abstract void fillRect(int x, int y, int width, int height)	Fills the rectangle with a default colour at the specified coordinates with the given width and height.
public abstract void drawOval(int x, int y, int width, int height)	Draws an oval that fits inside the rectangle of the given width and height where x and y represent the top left coordinates of the rectangle.
public abstract void fillOval(int x, int y, int width, int height)	Fills an oval with a default colour that fits inside the rectangle with the given width and height where x and y represent the top left coordinates of the rectangle.
public abstract void drawArc(int x, int y, int width, int height, int startAngle, int arcAngle)	Draws an arc at the specified x and y coordinates with the given width and height. The arc starts at the mentioned startAngle and sweeps by the given arcAngle.
public abstract void fillArc(int x, int y, int width, int height, int startAngle, int arcAngle)	Fills an arc at the given coordinates with the given width and height. The arc starts at the mentioned startAngle and sweeps by the given arcAngle.
public abstract void setColor(Color c)	Sets the current graphics context colour to the specified colour. All the subsequent graphics operations will use this colour.
public abstract Color getColor()	Gets the current graphics context colour.

Let us now see a program for the same.

```
import java.applet.*;
import java.awt.*;

/*
<applet code="MyApplet.class" width=300 height=200>
</applet>
 */
public class MyApplet extends Applet {

    public void paint(Graphics g) {
          g.drawString("Using Graphics Methods", 20, 30);
          g.drawLine(150, 200, 240, 400); // draws a line
          g.drawRect(200, 300, 100, 200); // draws an unfilled
                                          // rectangle
          g.fillRect(100, 200, 40, 50); // draws a filled rectangle
          g.drawOval(20, 70, 300, 100); // draws an unfilled oval
          g.fillOval(300, 200, 30, 50); // draws a filled oval
          g.drawArc(150, 300, 300, 200, 0, 120); // draws an unfilled
                                                 // arc
          g.fillArc(340, 165, 200, 100, 45, 170); // draws a filled
                                                  // arc
    }

}
```

Output:

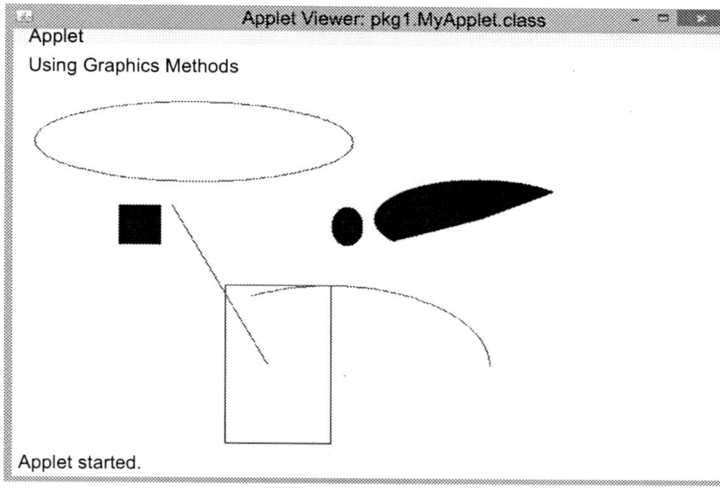

- ***Color class***

  Color class provides methods and constructors to create colours using RGB (Red, green and blue) values. These colours can be used by a graphics class object to set or get the context of a graphics object. Some of the constructors defined in the Color class is as follows:

  Color(int red, int blue, int green): creates a colour object with the specified RGB values as integers in the range 0-255.

  Color(float red, float blue, float green): creates a colour object with the specified RGB values as floats in the range 0.0-1.0.

  As discussed in Table 12.5, the Color class also defines some static final reference variables of type Color to represent different colors.

//A Simple program demonstrating the use of Color class

```
import java.applet.*;
import java.awt.*;

/*
<applet code="MyApplet.class" width=300 height=200>
</applet>
 */
public class MyApplet extends Applet {

    public void paint(Graphics g) {
        Color c=new Color(255, 45, 34); //represents Red color
        g.setColor(c); //sets graphics context to Red color
        g.drawLine(30, 40, 100, 100); //draws a line with Red color
```

```
            g.fillRect(150, 200, 140, 100); //draws a filled rectangle
                                            //with Red color
        }
}
```

Output:

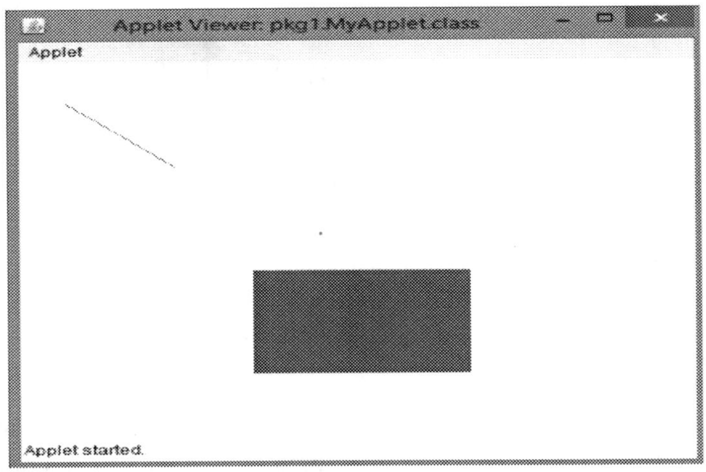

> *Note that setColor() and getColor() methods belong to the Graphics class and not to the Color class.*

- ***Font class***

  The Font class provides ways to create fonts which can render text in a specific font style and size. The Font of a text determines how a particular text is visible which can be described majorly by three parameters:

  Font name: There are numerous fonts available which can change the way a text looks like. Example, Times New Roman, Arial, Courier, etc.

  Font Size: This is the size in which we want our text to appear.

  Font Style: This describes the style in which the text has to be rendered. Example, Plain, Italic or Bold.

  This constructor for the Font class initializes a font object with a specific font name, style and size.

  Font(String name, int style, int size)

  The style is described as static final variables inside the Font class, some of which are given below:

  Font.PLAIN, Font.ITALIC, Font.BOLD

  which formats the text as plain, italic and bold.

The below program sets the font name as Times New Roman, style as Italic and the size as 24 for all the text operations on the applet using the *setFont()* method, the syntax of which is given below:

```
public void setFont(Font f);
```

This method accepts a Font class object as a parameter and sets the font as specified for subsequent text operations.The *setFont()* method originally resides in the *Component* class and gets inherited in the *MyApplet* class as it is a subclass of *Applet*.

```
import java.applet.*;
import java.awt.*;

/*1.
<applet code=”MyApplet.class” width=300 height=200>
</applet>
 */
public class MyApplet extends Applet {
public void init() {
        Font font = new Font(“Times New Roman”, Font.ITALIC, 24);
        setFont(font);
    }

    public void paint(Graphics g) {
        g.drawString(“Using Font class”, 500, 200);
    }
}
```

Output:

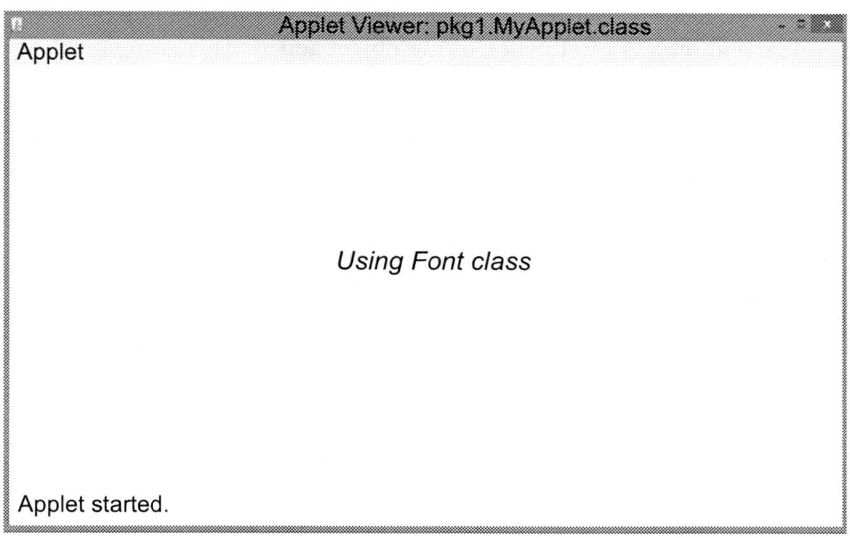

12.10 AWT CONTROLS

A control is a component which lets us interact with an application. For example, you interacting with the *End Call* Button of the dialler application in your mobile phones. Like a button, there are several other controls defined in the *awt* package to interact with a GUI. Moreover, controls can be easily added and removed from a window using different methods defined in the AWT hierarchy.

Following is the list of controls we are going to study in this chapter:

- Label
- Push Buttons
- Checkbox
- CheckboxGroup
- Choice
- Lists
- Scroll Bar
- Text Box and Text Area
- Canvas

The *java.awt* package provides classes to interact with each of the above controls which are a subclass of the *Component* class.

Adding and Removing controls

To add or remove the AWT controls, one has to first create an instance of the control to be added or removed and then use the subsequent methods defined by the *Container* class:

`public Component add(Component comp)`: adds the component object passed as a parameter on the window and returns a reference of the object added. This component object can be any of the AWT control as all AWT controls are a subclass of Component.

`public void remove(Component comp)`: removes the component object passed as a parameter from the current window.

Let us now examine each of the AWT control in detail.

1. **Label**

   A label looks somewhat like a button but is not clickable, i.e., nothing happens upon clicking a label. It is used to show a fixed text for providing information. The *Label* class in java.awt package provides constructors and methods to create or manipulate a label.

Table 12.7 Constructors defined in label class

Constructor	Description
public Label()	Creates a label with no text on it.
public Label(String text)	Creates a label with the specified text on it.
public Label(String text,int alignment)	Creates a label with the specified text and alignment.The alignment of a label can be specified by using one of the following integer constants in the Label class: Label.LEFT, Label.RIGHT, Label.CENTER

Table 12.8 Methods defined in label class

Methods	Description
public void setText(String str)	Sets the text on this label as the specified text.
public String getText()	Gets the text as a string object specified on this label.
public int getAlignment()	Gets the alignment of this label as an integer value.

//Adding a label on an applet

```
import java.applet.*;
import java.awt.*;

/*1.
<applet code="MyApplet.class" width=300 height=200>
</applet>
 */
public class MyApplet extends Applet {
    Label l1, l2;

    public void init() {
          l1 = new Label("Enter your name:    ");
          l2 = new Label("Enter password:");
          //adding labels on the applet window
          add(l1);
          add(l2);
    }
}
```

Output:

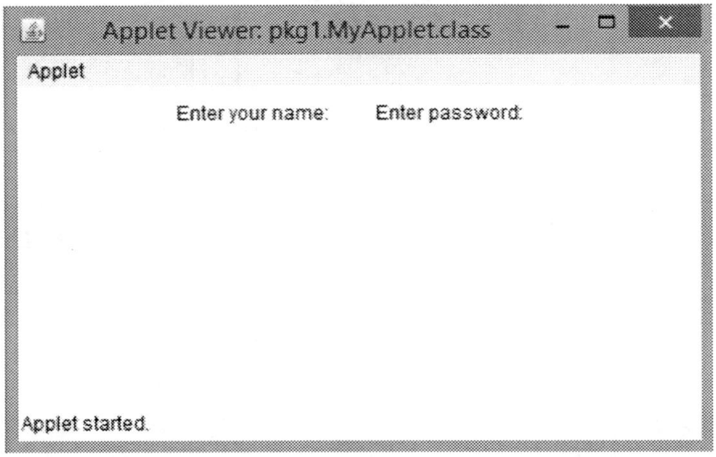

2. Push Buttons

A push button is a simple button which is clickable, i.e., something happens upon clicking that button.

Table 12.9 Constructors defined in Button class

Constructor	Description
public Button()	Creates a button with no text on it.
public Button(String text)	Creates a button with the specified text on it.

Table 12.10 Methods defined in Button class

Methods	Description
public void setLabel(String str)	Sets the label on this button as the specified text.
public String getLabel()	Gets the label as a string object specified on this button.

//Adding a button on a frame

```
import java.awt.*;

public class ButtonDemo {
    public static void main(String[] args) {
        Frame f = new Frame();
        Button b1 = new Button("Login");
```

```
            f.add(b1);
            f.setVisible(true);
        }
}
```

3. Checkbox

A checkbox is a control which can be either checked or unchecked. It consists of two parts: a *text* that describes the checkbox and the *state* that determines whether the checkbox is checked or not. By default, the state of a checkbox is unchecked. It enables the user to check multiple items.

Table 12.11 Constructors defined in Checkbox class

Constructor	Description
public Checkbox()	Creates a checkbox with no specified label.
public Checkbox(String label)	Creates a checkbox with the specified label.
public Checkbox(String text, boolean state)	Creates a checkbox with the specified label and initial state of boolean type. By default, the state is false.
public Checkbox(String label, boolean state, CheckboxGroup cbg)	Creates a checkbox with the specified label and the checkbox state belonging to the CheckboxGroup cbg.
public Checkbox(String label, CheckboxGroup cbg, boolean state)	Creates a checkbox with the given label belonging to the specified CheckboxGroup and the mentioned state.

Table 12.12 Methods defined in Checkbox class

Method	Description
public void setLabel(String label)	Sets the label of the checkbox to the specified parameter.
public String getLabel()	Gets the label of this checkbox as a String object.
public void setState(boolean state)	Sets the state of this checkbox to the specified argument.
public boolean getState()	Gets the state of this checkbox as a boolean value.

//Adding a checkbox on an applet

```
import java.applet.*;
import java.awt.*;

/*1.
<applet code="MyApplet.class" width=300 height=200>
```

```
</applet>
 */
public class MyApplet extends Applet {
    Checkbox cb1, cb2, cb3;

    public void init() {
            cb1 = new Checkbox("Limitless", true);
            cb2 = new Checkbox("BlindSpot");
            cb3 = new Checkbox("Flash");
            // adding checkbox on the applet window
            add(cb1);
            add(cb2);
            add(cb3);
    }
}
```

Output:

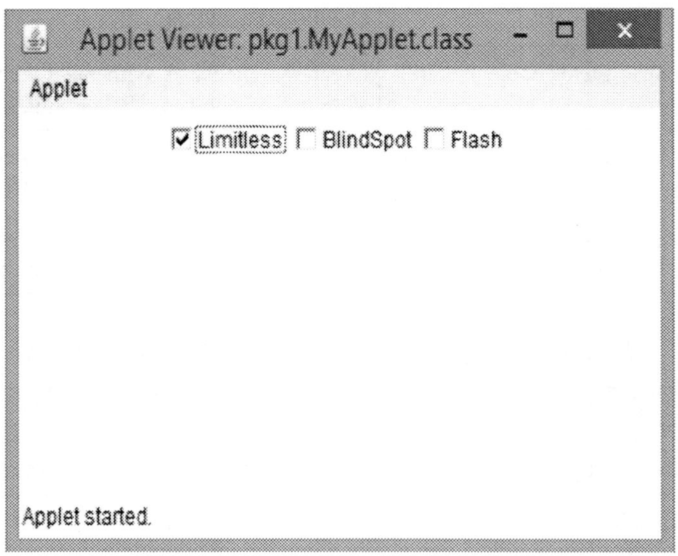

4. **CheckboxGroup**

A CheckboxGroup acts like a radiobutton or an option button. A number of checkboxes can belong to a single CheckboxGroup wherein only one of them can be checked at a time. Hence, it does not support the multi-select option.

Constructors defined in CheckboxGroup class:

public CheckboxGroup(): creates a checkboxgroup.

Methods defined in CheckboxGroup

public Checkbox getSelectedCheckbox(): Gets the current checkbox which is selected.

public void setSelectedCheckbox(Checkbox box): Sets the specified checkbox as selected.

//Adding a CheckboxGroup on an applet

```
import java.applet.*;
import java.awt.*;

/*1.
<applet code="MyApplet.class" width=300 height=200>
</applet>
 */
public class MyApplet extends Applet {
    CheckboxGroup cbg;
    Checkbox cb1, cb2, cb3;

    public void init() {
        cbg = new CheckboxGroup();
        cb1 = new Checkbox("Limitless", cbg, true);
        cb2 = new Checkbox("BlindSpot", cbg, true);
        cb3 = new Checkbox("Flash", cbg, false);
        // adding checkbox on the applet window
        add(cb1);
        add(cb2);
        add(cb3);
    }
}
```

Output:

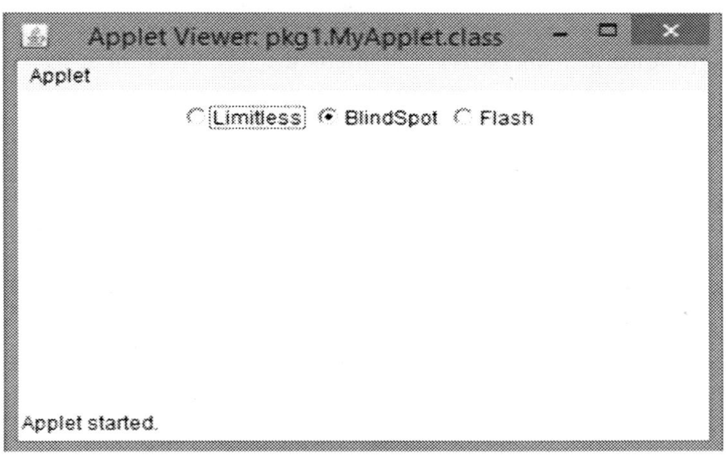

The above code shows how to group several checkboxes in a checkboxgroup. As said above, a checkboxgroup acts like a radiobutton wherein you can select only one option at a time. The code below creates two checkboxes cb1, cb2, group them under the checkboxgroupcbg and marks their default state as checked. But being a checkboxgroup, only one option gets selected at a time which is checked later.

```
cb1 = new Checkbox("Limitless", cbg, true);
cb2 = new Checkbox("BlindSpot", cbg, true);
```

5. **Choice**

A Choice is a type of drop down list where the user can select only one option at a time by a mouse click. It is also called a combo box.

Constructors defined in Choice class

Choice(): creates a choice list with no items in it.

Table 12.13 Methods defined in choice class

Method	Description
public void add(String item)	Adds the specified item to the choice list.
public String getItem(int index)	Gets the item at the specified index as a string object.
public int getItemCount()	Gets the count of the items present in the choice list as an integer value.
public int getSelectedIndex()	Gets the index of the item that is currently selected as an integer value.
public String getSelectedItem()	Gets the item that is currently selected as a string object.
public void insert(String item, int index)	Inserts the specified item at the specified index of the choice list.
public void remove(int position)	Removes the item from the choice list from the specified index.
public void remove(String item)	Removes the specified item from the choice list.
public void removeAll()	Removes all the items from the choice list.
public void select(int pos)	Selects the item at the given index of the choice list.
public void select(String str)	Selects the specified item from the choice list.

To add a choice list on an applet or a frame involves a three step procedure:

(i) Create a blank choice list using the constructor of the Choice class.

(ii) Add items in this list using the *add()* method of this class.

(iii) Now add the choice list with the added items onto the applet window/frame window using the *add()* method of the *Container* class.

//Adding a Choice list on an applet

```
import java.applet.*;
import java.awt.*;

/*1.
<applet code="MyApplet.class" width=300 height=200>
</applet>
 */
public class MyApplet extends Applet {
     Choice c;

     public void init() {
            c = new Choice(); // creating a choice list
            // adding items in the choice list
            c.add("Select one option from the list");
            c.add("Limitless");
            c.add("Blindspot");
            c.add("Flash");
            add(c); // adding choice list on the applet
            c.insert("Suits", 3); // inserting an item at index 3
     }
}
```

Output:

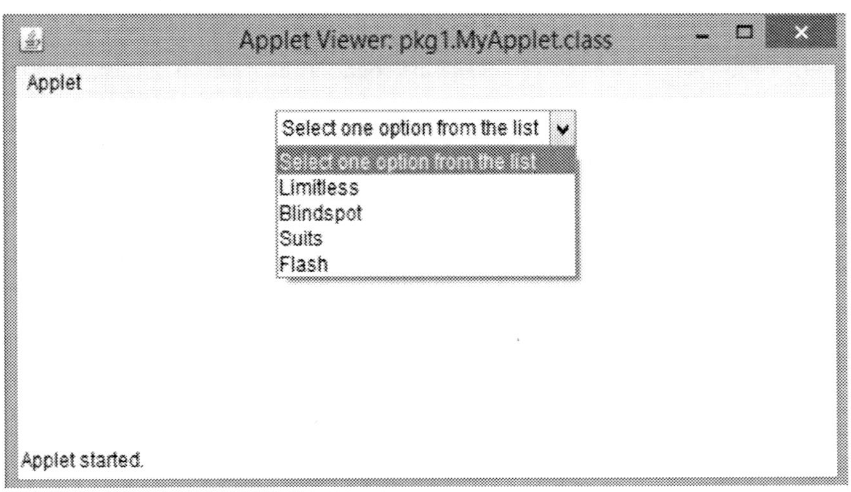

The indexes in a list start from 0 and the default selected item is at index 0. Inserting an item onto an index does not remove the existing item at that index, rather moves the existing item one index down.

6. **List**

A list is similar to a choice list where you can select multiple items at a time. The List class is used for creating a list which provides the following constructors and methods:

Table 12.14 Constructors defined in list class

Constructor	Description
public List()	Creates an empty list with no items in it. By default, multiple selections is not allowed in a list.
public List(int numRows)	Creates a list with the specified number of rows.
public List(int numRows, boolean multiSelect)	Creates a list with the specified number of rows and multiple selections on.

Table 12.15 Methods defined in list class

Method	Description
public void add(String item)	Adds the specified item to the end of list.
public void add(String item, int index)	Adds the specified item at the specified index in the list.
public void deselect(int index)	Deselects the item at the specified index.
public String getItem(int index)	Gets the item at the specified index as a string object.
public int getItemCount()	Gets the count of the items in the list as an integer value.
public int getSelectedIndex()	Gets the index of the selected item as an integer value.
public String getSelectedItem()	Gets the selected item as a string object.
public String[] getSelectedItems()	Gets multiple selected items in the list as a string array.
public void remove(int position)	Removes item at the specified position.
public void remove(String item)	Removes item as specified in the argument.
public void removeAll()	Removes all the items from the list.
public void select(int index)	Selects the item present at the specified index.

//Adding List on an applet

```
import java.applet.*;
import java.awt.*;
```

```
/*1.
<applet code="MyApplet.class" width=300 height=200>
</applet>
 */
public class MyApplet extends Applet {
    List l;
    public void init() {
          l = new List(4, true); // creating a list
          // adding items in the list
          l.add("Limitless");
          l.add("Blindspot");
          l.add("Flash");
          l.add("Suits");
          // selecting items at index 1 and 2
          l.select(1);
          l.select(2);
          // adding list to the applet window
          add(l);
    }
}
```

Output:

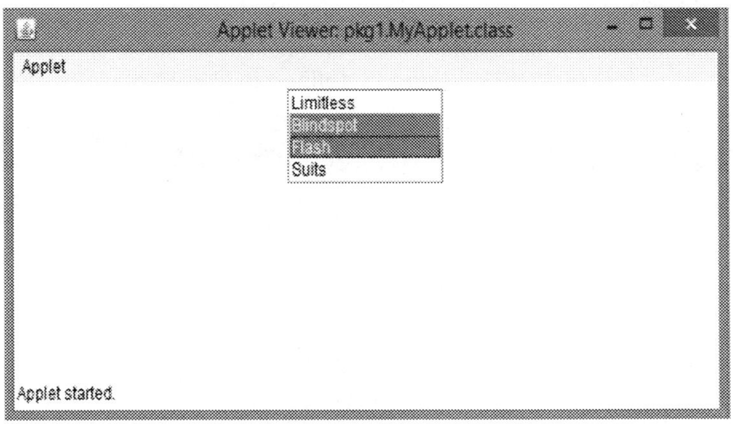

Note that the *select()* method in the List class selects an item by default when the list opens up.

7. **Scrollbar**

Pages with large sized texts are not visible on one screen. To view such pages, we have scrollbars as a control that can help view a full page from top to bottom or left to right. A scrollbar is characterized by the following parameters:

- *Orientation:* is the way a scrollbar is organized. It can be either horizontal or vertical. The default value for orientation is vertical. The orientation has been described as static final integer variables in the class Scrollbar which can take up the values: Scrollbar. HORIZONTAL and Scrollbar. VERTICAL.

- *Initial Value:* The initial value of the scrollbar.
- *Visible Amount:* The amount of the scrollbar that is visible.
- *Minimum value:* The minimum value to which a scrollbar can be scrolled.
- *Maximum value:* The maximum value to which a scrollbar can be scrolled.

The default values of *initial value, visible amount, minimum and maximum* were 0 in Java 1.0. But, Java 1.1 has a default value of 10 for visible amount, 100 for maximum and 0 for all the others.

Following are the constructors defined in the Scrollbar class to create a scrollbar:

Table 12.16 Constructors defined in Scrollbar class

Constructor	Description
public Scrollbar()	Creates a vertical scrollbar with the default values.
public Scrollbar(int orientation)	Creates a scrollbar with the specified orientation.
public Scrollbar(int orientation, int value, int visible, int min, int max)	Creates a scrollbar with the specified arguments.

Table 12.17 Methods defined in Scrollbar class

Method	Description
public int getMaximum()	Returns the current maximum value of the scrollbar as an integer value.
public int getMinimum()	Returns the current minimum value of the scrollbar as an integer value.
public int getOrientation()	Returns the current orientation of the scrollbar as an integer.
public int getValue()	Returns the current value of the scrollbar as an integer value.
public int getVisibleAmount()	Returns the current visible amount of the scrollbar as an integer value.
public void setMaximum(int newMaximum)	Sets the maximum value of the scrollbar to the specified value.
public void setMinimum(int newMinimum)	Sets the minimum value of the scrollbar to the specified value.

public void setOrientation(int orientation)	Sets the orientation of the scrollbar to the specified value.
public void setValue(int newValue)	Sets the initial value of the scrollbar as specified in the arguments.
public void setValues(int value, int visible, int minimum, int maximum)	Sets the value for initial value, visible amount, minimum and maximum to the specified value.
public void setVisible Amount (int new Amount)	Sets the value for the visible amount of the scrollbar as specified in the arguments.

//Adding scrollbar on an applet

```
import java.applet.*;
import java.awt.*;

/*1.
<applet code="MyApplet.class" width=300 height=200>
</applet>
 */
public class MyApplet extends Applet {
    Scrollbar sch, scv;

    public void init() {
          sch = new Scrollbar(Scrollbar.HORIZONTAL, 0, 20, 30,  100);
          //horizontal scrollbar
          scv = new Scrollbar(); //vertical scrollbar
          //adding scrollbars on applet window
          add(sch);
          add(scv);
    }
}
```

Output:

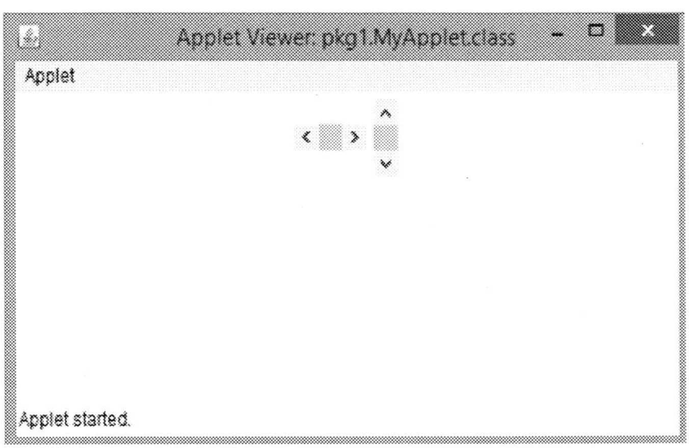

8. TextField and TextArea

To work with textual data, AWT provides the below controls:

- TextField: A TextField accepts a single line of text.

Table 12.18 Constructors defined in TextField class

Constructor	Description
public TextField()	Creates a textfield with no initial text
public TextField(String text)	Creates a textfield with the initial text as specified in the parameters.
public TextField(int n)	Creates a textfield with no initial text and specified number of columns.
public TextField(String text, int n)	Creates a textfield with initial text and number of columns as specified in the argumnets.

Some of the methods available in *TextField* class are as below:

public void setText(String t): Sets the text of the textbox as specified in the arguments.

public String getText(): Gets the text from the textfield as a string object. This method is an inherited method from the class TextComponent.

//Adding a Textfield on an applet

```
import java.applet.*;
import java.awt.*;

/*
<applet code="MyApplet.class" width=300 height=200>
</applet>
 */
public class MyApplet extends Applet {
    TextField tf1;

    public void init() {
          tf1 = new TextField("Enter your name here"); // textfield
                                                       // with initial text
          add(tf1); //adding textfield on applet
          System.out.println(tf1.getText()); //prints the initial
                                             //text on console


    }
}
```

Output:

Applet Window:

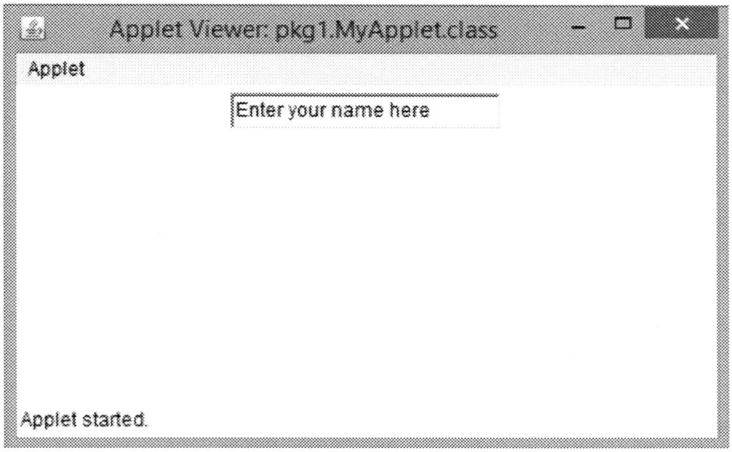

Console Window:

```
Enter your name here
```

- TextArea

  A TextArea is similar to a textfield but can support multiple lines of text.

Table 12.19 Constructors defined in TextArea class

Constructor	Description
public TextArea()	Creates a textarea with no initial text.
public TextArea(String text)	Creates a textarea with the initial text as specified in the parameters.
public TextArea(int rows, int cols)	Creates a textarea with no initial text and specified number of rows and columns.

Table 12.20 Methods defined in TextArea class

Method	Description
public void append(String str)	Appends the specified text at the end of the initial text in the textarea.
public int getColumns()	Returns the number of columns in the textarea as an integer value.
public int getRows()	Returns the number of rows as an integer value.

(Contd.)

public void insert(String str, int pos)	Inserts the specified string at the specified position in the textarea.
public void setColumns(int columns)	Sets the number of columns in the textarea to the specified number of columns.
public void setRows(int rows)	Sets the number of rows in the textarea to the specified number of rows.

//Adding TextArea on the applet

```
import java.applet.*;
import java.awt.*;

/*1.
<applet code="MyApplet.class" width=300 height=200>
</applet>
 */
public class MyApplet extends Applet {
    TextArea ta;

    public void init() {
          ta = new TextArea(
                         "A textarea is an AWT control."
                                     + " Java provides the class TextArea
                          present in the awt package."
                                     + "\nIt can support multiple lines
                                     of text.");
          add(ta);
    }
}
```

Output:

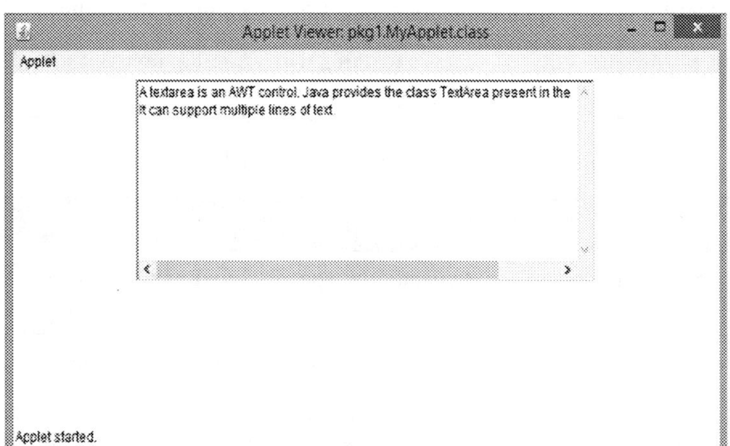

9. Canvas

A canvas is a blank rectangular area on a container which can be used for drawing or painting. A canvas does not have any borders by default.

Its constructor has the below form:

Canvas(): creates a blank canvas.

//Using Canvas

```
import java.applet.*;
import java.awt.*;

/*
<applet code="MyApplet.class" width=300 height=200>
</applet>
 */
public class MyApplet extends Applet {
    Canvas c;

    public void init() {
        c = new Canvas(); // creating a canvas
        c.setBounds(20, 30, 500, 300); // setting the bounds of a
                                       // canvas
        c.setBackground(Color.BLUE); // setting the background of
                                     // the canvas
        setBackground(Color.RED); // setting the background of
                                  //the applet
        add(c); // adding canvas to the applet

    }
}
```

Output:

Note that by default, no borders of a canvas are visible.

12.11 LAYOUT MANAGERS

Now that we have learnt how to put AWT controls on a window, let us now see how to arrange these controls so that we have a better user interface (UI) for our application. The user interface of an application determines how user friendly the application is. It is extremely important for an application to have a good UI in order to increase the number of users for that application.

Java provides four layout manager classes to arrange AWT controls on a window.

Using a Layout Manager class involves three steps:

- Instantiating a Layout Manager class.
- Setting the layout of the container to the above created layout.
- Adding controls on this container.

Let us walk through the various layout managers available.

1. **FlowLayout**

   This class provides a layout where the controls are arranged from upper left corner, left to right and top to bottom. After adding controls in one line, the subsequent controls are moved in the next line. The default layout for any container is *FlowLayout.*

   Following are some of the constructors of the class:

Table 12.21 Constructors defined in FlowLayout class

Constructor	Description
public FlowLayout()	Creates a default FlowLayout for the container.
public FlowLayout(int align)	Creates a FlowLayout with the specified alignment. The alignment can be described by one of three static final variables defined in the class: FlowLayout.LEFT, FlowLayout.CENTER, FlowLayout.RIGHT
public FlowLayout(int align, int horz, int vert)	Creates a FlowLayout with the specified alignment and horizontal, vertical space between the components.

//Using FlowLayout

```
import java.applet.*;
import java.awt.*;

/*1.
<applet code="MyApplet.class" width=300 height=200>
</applet>
 */
```

```
public class MyApplet extends Applet {
    Label l;
    TextField tf;

    public void init() {
//creating a flowlayout at the center
        FlowLayout fl = new FlowLayout(FlowLayout.CENTER);
        setLayout(fl); //setting the layout of the applet
        l = new Label("Enter your name"); //creating a named
                                            //label
        tf = new TextField(20); //creating a textfield of size 20
        //adding label and textfield on the applet
        add(l);
        add(tf);
    }
}
```

Output:

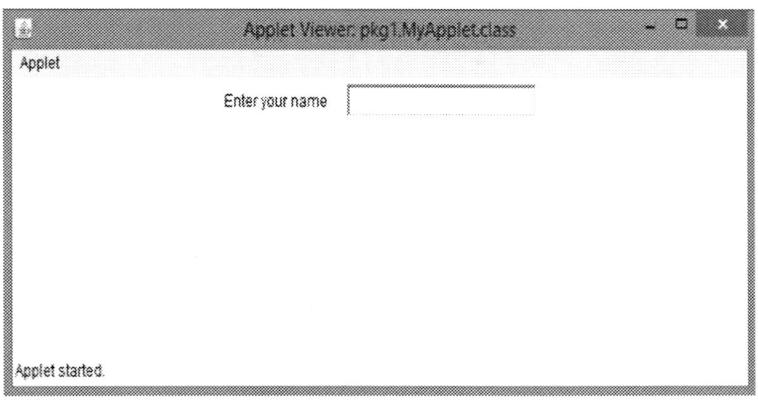

2. **GridLayout**

A*GridLayout* arranges the components on a container in the form of a grid. A grid is divided into rows and columns. Some of its constructors are discussed in Table 12.22.

Table 12.22 Constructors defined in GridLayout class

Constructor	Description
public GridLayout()	Creates a default GridLayout with a single column.
public GridLayout(int rows, int cols)	Creates a GridLayout with the specified number of rows and columns.
public GridLayout(int rows, int cols, int horz, int vert)	Creates a GridLayout with the specified number of rows, columns and horizontal, vertical space between the components.

//Using GridLayout

```
import java.applet.*;
import java.awt.*;

/*1.
<applet code="MyApplet.class" width=300 height=200>
</applet>
 */
public class MyApplet extends Applet {
     Label l,l1;
     TextField tf,tf1;

     public void init() {
            GridLayout gl = new GridLayout(2,2); //creating a grid of
                                                          //2X2
            setLayout(gl); //setting the layout of the applet
            l  = new Label("Introduce yourself:"); //creating a label
            tf = new TextField(); //creating a textfield
            l1 = new Label("Your hobbies/interests");
            tf1= new TextField();
            //adding label and textfield on the applet
            add(l);
            add(tf);
            add(l1);
            add(tf1);
     }
}
```

Output:

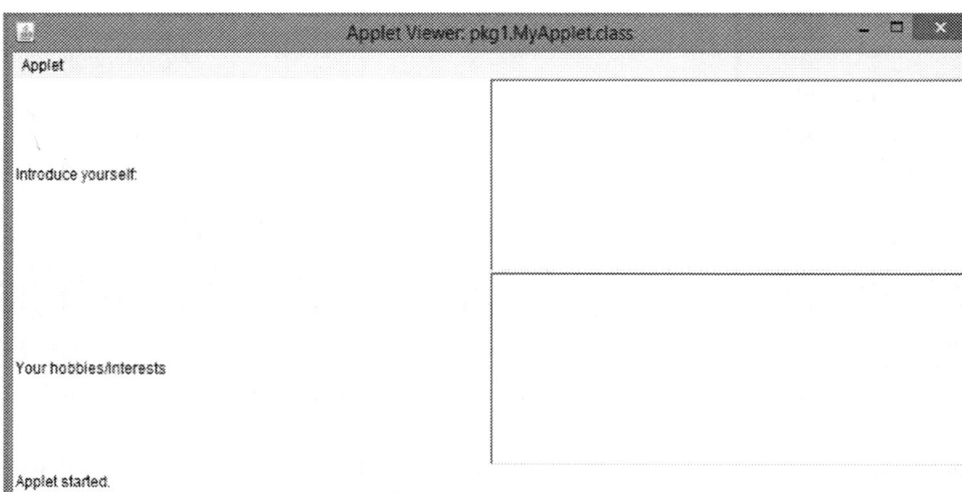

3. **BorderLayout**

The *BorderLayout* class is capable of arranging components across the borders of the container. The border regions where the components can be arranged are defined as static final variables inside the *BorderLayout* class:

BorderLayout.NORTH
BorderLayout.SOUTH
BorderLayout.EAST
BorderLayout.WEST
BorderLayout.CENTER

Some of its constructors are given below:

Table 12.23 Constructors defined in BorderLayout class

Constructor	Description
public BorderLayout()	Creates a default BorderLayout.
public BorderLayout(int horz, int vert)	Creates a BorderLayout with the specified horizontal and vertical space between the components.

The *add()* method in the Container class has an overloaded version which uses an alignment parameter of the *BorderLayout* class.

```
public void add(Component comp, Object constraints);
```

This version adds the specified component to the container where the constraints refer to the alignment of the components to be followed as a *BorderLayout* class constant.

Let us see how to set the layout of a container using *BorderLayout* class:

```
import java.applet.*;
import java.awt.*;

/*
<applet code="MyApplet.class" width=300 height=200>
</applet>
 */
public class MyApplet extends Applet {
    Button east, west, north, south;
    TextArea center;

    public void init() {
          BorderLayoutbl = new BorderLayout(); //creating a
                                                 // borderlayout
          east = new Button("EAST");
```

```
        west = new Button("WEST");
        north = new Button("NORTH");
        south = new Button("SOUTH");
        center = new TextArea();
        //setting the text of the textarea
        center.setText("This applet shows an example of
                    BorderLayout Manager class.");
        setLayout(bl); //setting the layout of the applet
        //adding components across various regions of the applet
        add(east,BorderLayout.EAST);
        add(west,BorderLayout.WEST);
        add(north,BorderLayout.NORTH);
        add(south,BorderLayout.SOUTH);
        add(center,BorderLayout.CENTER);
    }
}
```

Output:

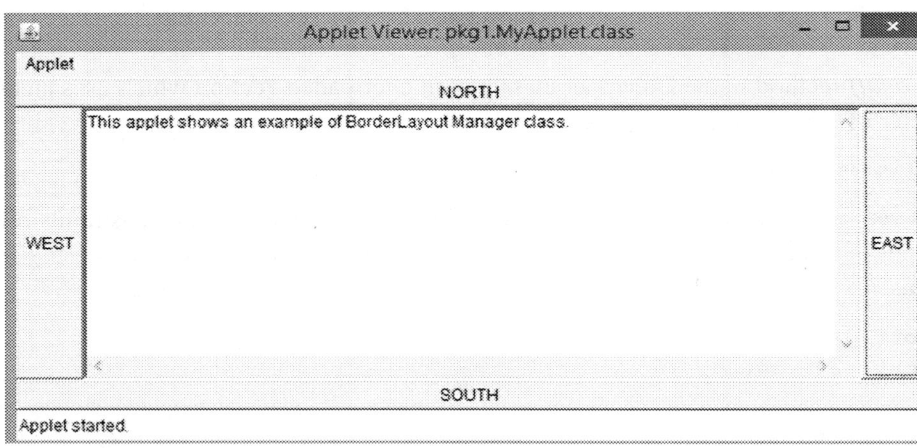

The version of add() method used above, adds the buttons and the textarea to different regions of the applet. The method takes as a parameter a component to be added (buttons and textarea in our case), and the region where it has to be added. This region is one of the static final variables defined above which symbolizes North, South, East, West and Center regions of the container.

4. **CardLayout**

   The CardLayout manager class supports a layout where components can be added as a deck of cards. In other words, one component is added behind the other component with a property of only one being visible at a time.

Following are the constructors of CardLayout class.

Table 12.24 Constructors defined in CardLayout class

Constructor	Description
public CardLayout()	Creates a default CardLayout.
public CardLayout(int horz, int vert)	Creates a CardLayout with the specified horizontal and vertical space.

The cards added can be flipped using diverse methods of the CardLayout class.

Table 12.25 Methods defined in CardLayout class

Method	Description
public void first(Container parent)	Shows the components on the first card in the deck of cards.
public void last(Container parent)	Shows the components on the last card in the deck of cards.
public void next(Container parent)	Shows the components on the next card in the deck of cards.
public void previous(Container parent)	Shows the components on the previous card in the deck of cards.

All these methods takes a Container class reference. This refers to the container on which the deck of cards appears.

//Using CardLayout

```
import java.applet.*;
import java.awt.*;

/*
<applet code="MyApplet.class" width=300 height=200>
</applet>
 */
public class MyApplet extends Applet {
    Panel panelCard1,panelCard2;
    Button b1,b2,b3;
    public void init() {
        final Applet parent = this;
        CardLayout cl=new CardLayout();
        setLayout(cl);
        panelCard1=new Panel();//creating a panel panelCard1
```

```
            b1=new Button("Button on card1"); //creating a button
            panelCard1.add(b1); //adding button on panelCard1
            b2=new Button("Button on card2");
            panelCard2=new Panel();
            panelCard2.add(b2); //adding button on panelCard2
            add(panelCard1); //adding panelCard1 to applet
            add(panelCard2); //adding panelCard2 behind panelCard1
            cl.next(parent); //shows panelCard2
    }
}
```

Output:

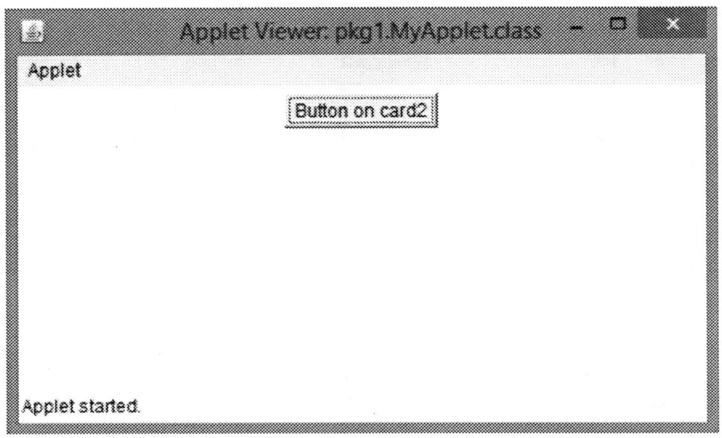

Let us have a look how this program works:

The code creates two panels namely: *panelCard1* and *panelCard2*. Each of the panels adds a button on them. These panels are then added onto the parent container, i.e., the applet, *MyApplet*. As the applet is following a layout of type CardLayout, the second panel to be added on the applet is added behind the first panel. Therefore, only *panelCard1* is visible in the beginning (only one card visible at a time). To see the next card in the deck of panels, we use the *next()* method which shows up the *panelCard2*.

The *next()* method uses *this* as a parameter, as it refers to the container being used, which is our applet *MyApplet* in this case.

SUMMARY

- Applets are small java applications which are executed on the client side. The applet tag helps to embed the code of a java applet in a web browser.
- Every user-defined applet is a subclass of the Applet class defined in the java.applet package.

- Applets follow a life cycle and its execution flows from the init()->start()->paint()->stop()->destroy() methods.
- The init() method is only called once during the life cycle of the applet whereas start() and paint() is invoked every time an applet is reloaded.
- The stop() method is invoked when we minimize our current applet and go off to another applet.
- AWT is a package in java which stands for abstract window toolkit and supports graphical user interface programming.
- AWT package introduces diverse AWT controls with which a user can interact in an application like Button, Label, Scrollbar, etc. Each of these controls have a java class defined for them in the awt package.
- The AWT controls can be added and removed from a container using *add()* and *remove()* methods where a container can be a panel, window, frame or an applet.
- To arrange the AWT components on a container, java introduced layout manager classes namely, FlowLayout, GridLayout, BorderLayout and CardLayout.
- The FlowLayout class arranges components from the upper left corner, left to right and top to bottom.
- The GridLayout class arranges components in the form of a grid on the container.
- The BorderLayout class organizes components across the borders of the container.
- And the CardLayout positions the components as a deck of cards on a parent container.

COMMON ERRORS

- An error stating "plugin missing" is encountered while running an applet, in case JRE is not installed on the client machine.
- One of the mistakes a naive programmer does is assuming the flow of execution of an applet starts from the main method rather init() method.
- Another error can be specifying a .java file in the code attribute of the applet tag. The code attribute of the applet tag takes up only a .class file.
- Often one forgets the order in which the CardLayout arranges cards on a container. The CardLayout organizes a new incoming card or a component behind the older one.

SELF-TEST

1. What are applets in java? Discuss the life cycle of an applet.
2. What is the significance of the applet tag? Describe some of the attributes of the applet tag.
3. Elucidate the significant classes which make up the AWT hierarchy.

4. Illuminate the diverse AWT controls available in java. How can we add a scrollbar and a list on a container?
5. Explain the importance of layout managers in java. How does a FlowLayout manager class differ from BorderLayout class?
6. What does *row* and *col* specify in the constructor of a GridLayout class? What type of a grid is formed by the default constructor of the GridLayout class?
7. The CardLayout manager class places a newer card behind the older one. Explain the statement with an example.

PRACTICAL QUESTIONS

1. What happens on running the following classes as an Applet?

a)
```
import java.applet.*;
import java.awt.*;

/*
<applet code="MyApplet.class" width=300 height=200>
</applet>
*/
public class MyApplet extends Applet {

    public static void main(String[] args) {
            Canvas c=new Canvas();
            c.setBackground(Color.blue);

    }
}
```

b)
```
import java.applet.*;
import java.awt.*;

/*
<applet code="MyApplet.class" width=300 height=200>
</applet>
*/
public class MyApplet extends Applet {
    Button b;

    public void init() {
            b=new Button("Click Me");
            setLayout(new BorderLayout());
            add(b);

    }
}
```

c)
```
import java.applet.*;
import java.awt.*;
/*
<applet code="MyApplet.class" width=300 height=200>
</applet>
*/
public class MyApplet extends Applet {
   Button b;
   public void init() {
         b=new Button("Click Me");
         GridLayout gl=new GridLayout();
         setLayout(gl);
         System.out.println(gl.getColumns());
         System.out.println(gl.getRows());

   }
}
```

13 CHAPTER

Event Handling

This chapter will enable you to learn the following:

- Handling events generated by the controls that we studied in the previous chapter.
- Implementing event handling using Adapter and Inner classes.
- Creation of menu bars.
- Introduction of swings, and a brief comparison of swings with AWT

This chapter emphasize on AWT controls and the methodology of adding them onto containers. These controls also generate events such as events on clicking the mouse, button, scrolling a scroll bar, changing the value of a text field, etc.

13.1 EVENT DELEGATION MODEL

An event is something that causes a change in the state of an object and is always generated by a source. Consider an example of facebook, where the clicking of a login button logs you inside your account. The event that occurs here is, *clicking the login button* and the source of the event is the *login button*. Java provides predefined classes which represents the source of events and their corresponding event classes. *When an event occurs, its corresponding event class is also generated. The information about the source of the event is captured in the state of event class object.* The event classes are defined in *java.awt.event* package and are a subclass of *EventObject*.

Table 13.1 and 13.2 describe the classes available in java which denotes the various event classes and their source of events.

Table 13.1

Event classes	Description
ActionEvent	Is generated when a button, a list or a menu item is interacted with.
AdjustmentEvent	Is generated when a scrollbar is interacted with.
ComponentEvent	Is generated when a component is resized, hidden, shown or moved.
ContainerEvent	Is generated when a component is added or removed from a container.
ItemEvent	Is generated when a checkbox, a choice list or a checkable menu item is interacted with.
KeyEvent	Is generated when an input from a keyboard is received.
MouseEvent	Is generated when the mouse is interacted with.
MouseWheelEvent	Is generated when the mouse wheel is moved.
TextEvent	Is generated when a textfield or a textarea is interacted with.
WindowEvent	Is generated when a window is opened, closed, etc.

Table 13.2

Source of Event	Description
Button	Generates an action event when a button is interacted with.
Checkbox	Generates item event when a checkbox is checked or unchecked.
Choice	Generates item events when the choice list is interacted with.
List	Generates an action event when the list is interacted with.
Menu Item	Generates an action event when a menu item is selected, and an item event when a checkable item is checked or unchecked.
Scrollbar	Generates an adjustment event when a scrollbar is scrolled.
Text Components	Generates text events when a textfield or a textarea is interacted with.
Window	Generates window events when a window opens, closes, etc.

Event handling is the handling of such events generated by a source. In other words, a handler determines what needs to be done on the click of a button or any other control. The handling of events in java is done using the concept of *listeners*.

A Listener listens on a particular source and waits for an event to occur. On occurrence of an event, the listener provides a handler for the same. Listeners are implemented as interfaces in java. Every control capable of generating an event has its corresponding listener interface. These interfaces encompass methods which are capable of handling events.

The event delegation model in java helps delegate events to listeners. It involves a four-step procedure:

1. Adding controls on a container as the source of events.
2. Registering this source with a listener interface, such that the associated listener can handle the events generated by the registered source. On occurrence of an event from this source, the corresponding event class is generated which holds the information about the source in its object.
3. Forwarding the generated event to the appropriate listener interface.
4. Overriding the listener interface methods to handle the events generated.

Table 13.3 gives a brief introduction about the Listener interfaces available. All the listener interfaces inherit the superclass *EventListener*.

Table 13.3

Listener interfaces	Description
ActionListener	Handles action events generated by a button, list or a menu item.
AdjustmentListener	Handles adjustment events generated by a scrollbar.
ComponentListener	Handles component events generated by a component.
ContainerListener	Handles container events generated by a container.
ItemListener	Handles item events generated by a checkbox, checkable menu item or a choice list.
KeyListener	Handles key events generated by a keyboard.
MouseListener	Handles mouse events when a mouse is clicked, pressed or a released.
MouseMotionListener	Handles mouse events when a mouse is dragged or moved.
MouseWheelListener	Handles mouse events when a mouse wheel is moved.
TextListener	Handles text events when the value of a textfield or a textarea is changed.
WindowListener	Handles window events when a window is opened, closed, etc.

Let us now examine these listener interfaces separately.

1. **ActionListener:** handles the events generated by a button, list or a menu item. On interacting with these controls, the *ActionEvent* class is generated.

   The method available in the interface which handles action events is given below:

   `public void actionPerformed(ActionEvent ae): Invoked when a button, a list or a menu item is clicked.`

2. **AdjustmentListener:** handles events generated by a scrollbar. *AdjustmentEvent* class is generated on interacting with a scrollbar. The methods present in the interface which handles adjustment events are:

public void `adjustmentValueChanged(AdjustmentEvent e): Invoked when a vertical or a horizontal scrollbar is scrolled.`

3. **ComponentListener:** handles events generated by a component. A *ComponentEvent* class is generated when the component is moved, shown, hidden or resized. The methods present in the *ComponentListener* are:

   public void `componentHidden(ComponentEvent e): Invoked when a component is hidden.`

   public void `componentMoved(ComponentEvent e): Invoked when a component is moved.`

   public void `componentResized(ComponentEvent e): Invoked when a component is resized.`

   public void `componentShown(ComponentEvent e): Invoked when a component is shown.`

4. **ContainerListener:** handles events generated by a container. A *ContainerEvent* class is generated when a component is added or removed from a container. The methods present in this interface are:

   public void `componentAdded(ContainerEvent e): Invoked when a component is added on a container.`

   public void `componentRemoved(ContainerEvent e): Invoked when a component is removed from a container.`

5. **ItemListener:** handles events generated by a checkbox, a choice list or a checkable menu item. *ItemEvent* class is generated when one of these controls are interacted with. The methods available in this interface are:

   public void `itemStateChanged(ItemEvent e): Invoked when a checkbox, a checkable menu item or a choice list item is selected.`

6. **KeyListener:** handles events generated by a keyboard. A *KeyEvent* class is generated when a key from a keyboard is pressed, released or typed. The methods available in here are:

   public void `keyPressed(KeyEvent e): Invoked when a key which results in a non-printable character is pressed from a keyboard. Example, shift, ctrl keys.`

   public void `keyReleased(KeyEvent e): Invoked when any key from the keyboard is released.`

   public void `keyTyped(KeyEvent e): Invoked when a key which results in a printable character is pressed. Example, A,b,r etc.`

7. **MouseListener:** handles events generated by a mouse. *MouseEvent* class is generated when the mouse is clicked, pressed, released, entered or exited from a container. The methods present here are:

public void `mouseClicked(MouseEvent e): Invoked when the mouse is clicked.`

public void `mouseEntered(MouseEvent e): Invoked when the mouse enters a particular area of a container.`

public void `mouseExited(MouseEvent e): Invoked when the mouse exits from a specific area of a container.`

public void `mousePressed(MouseEvent e): Invoked when the mouse is pressed.`

public void `mouseReleased(MouseEvent e): Invoked when the mouse is released.`

8. **MouseMotionListener:** handles events generated by a mouse. *MouseMotionEvent* class is generated when the mouse is moved or dragged. Following are the methods available in this interface:

   public void `mouseDragged(MouseEvent e): Invoked when the mouse is dragged.`

   public void `mouseMoved(MouseEvent e): Invoked when the mouse is simply moved.`

9. **MouseWheelListener:** handles events generated by a mouse. *MouseWheelEvent* class is generated when the mouse wheel is moved. The interface comprises the below methods:

   public void `mouseWheelMoved(MouseWheelEvent e): Invoked when the mouse wheel is moved.`

10. **TextListener:** handles events generated by a TextField or a TextArea. *TextEvent* class is generated when an interaction with these controls is made. The following method is invoked when a textarea or a textfield is clicked upon:

    public void `textValueChanged(TextEvent e);`

11. **WindowListener:** handles events generated by a window. A *WindowEvent* class is generated when a window is activated, closed, opened etc. Some of the methods in this interface are:

    public void `windowActivated(WindowEvent we): invoked when a window is activated.`

    public void `windowClosed(WindowEvent we): invoked when a window is closed.`

    public void `windowClosing(WindowEvent we): invoked when a window is getting closed.`

    public void `windowDeactivated(WindowEvent we): invoked when a window is deactivated.`

    publicvoid `windowDeiconified(WindowEvent we): invoked when a window is deiconified.`

public void windowIconified(WindowEvent we): invoked when a window is iconified.

public void windowOpened(WindowEvent we): invoked when a window is opened.

13.2 USING EVENT DELEGATION MODEL

Now that we know how the event delegation model works, let us have some fun using event handling in managing various events generated from diverse sources.

1. **Handling Action Events**

   The below example shows how to handle action events generated by a button:

```
import java.applet.*;
import java.awt.*;
import java.awt.event.*;
/*
<applet code="MyApplet.class" width=300 height=200>
</applet>
 */
public class MyApplet extends Applet implements ActionListener {
 Button b,b1;
 public void init() {
        b = new Button("Change Background");
        b1=new Button("No Change");
        //adding buttons on the applet
        add(b);
        add(b1);
        //registering source with listener
        b.addActionListener(this);
        b1.addActionListener(this);
 }
 public void actionPerformed(ActionEvent ae) { //handling action
                                                //events
        if (ae.getSource() == b) { //checking the source of the
                                   //event
              setBackground(Color.BLUE);
        }
    }
 }
```

Output:

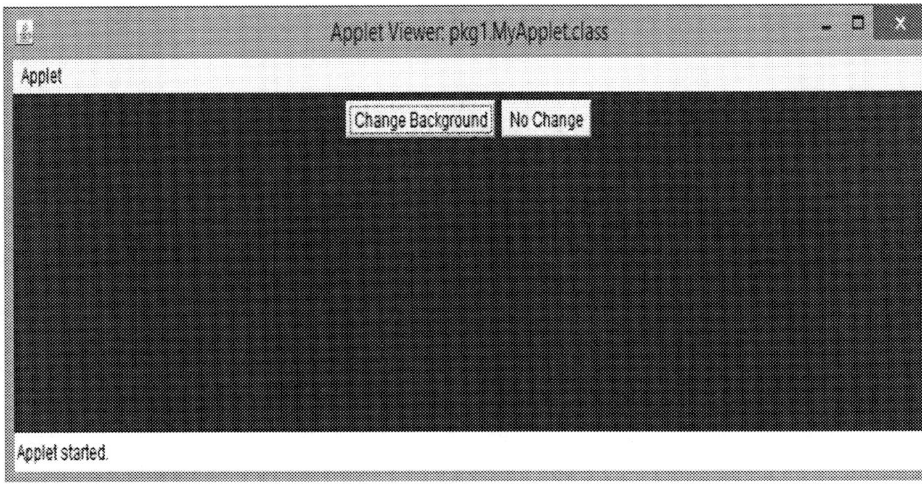

The above program creates an applet class called *MyApplet*. This class implements the *ActionListener* interface as this interface comprises all the methods required to handle action events. The *init()* method of *MyApplet* creates two buttons and adds them on the applet. The next step in the event delegation model is to associate event handling with these buttons. Therefore, we register the *ActionListener* with these buttons using the below method:

```
public void addTypeListener(TypeListener e)
```

The Type used in this method can take several forms depending on the source of the event and the listener interface associated with it.

Example:

```
public void addActionListener(ActionListener l)
public void addItemListener(ItemListener l)
public void addKeyListener(KeyListener l)
```

All these methods takes as a parameter, the corresponding listener with which we want to register our source with. Once a source is registered with a listener, it receives all the notifications regarding the events generated by that registered source. Observe, the program above passes *this* as a parameter to the *addActionListener()* method which refers to the current object of the class, i.e., the *MyApplet* class. The MyApplet class in turn inherits the Applet class and implements the ActionListener, therefore, providing a listener to the *addActionListener()* method.

After registering the source of the event with an appropriate listener, the succeeding step is to override the methods of this interface to handle the events generated by the source which is done in this program using the following method:

```
public void actionPerformed(ActionEvent ae)
```

This method is an abstract method present in the ActionListener interface and takes as a parameter, a reference of the ActionEvent class (The ActionEvent class is generated when the button b is clicked). Further, it uses a getSource() method that checks the source of the event(which button was clicked).

```
public Object getSource();
```

The method belongs to the *EventObject* class which returns the source of the event as an object of Object class.

Note: All the event classes and the listener interfaces are defined in the java.awt.event package, hence the import statement.

2. Handling Scrollbar Events

To handle scrollbar events, one needs to implement the *AdjustmentListener* interface by overriding the *adjustValueChanged*() method. This method is invoked on the scroll of a scrollbar. Every time a user interacts with a scrollbar, the *AdjustmentEvent* class is generated whose reference is passed to the *adjustmentValueChanged*() method.

The below program shows changes the background color of the applet to blue on the click of a scroll bar.

```
import java.applet.*;
import java.awt.*;
import java.awt.event.*;
/*
<applet code="MyApplet.class" width=300 height=200>
</applet>
 */
public class MyApplet extends Applet implements AdjustmentListener {
 Scrollbar sc;
 public void init() {
        sc = new Scrollbar(Scrollbar.VERTICAL, 0, 250, 0, 600);
        sc.addAdjustmentListener(this);// registering source
                                          // with the listener.
 add(sc);
 }
 public void adjustmentValueChanged(AdjustmentEvent a) {
        if (a.getSource() == sc) {// gets the source of the event
setBackground(Color.blue);
```

```
            }
    }
}
```

Output:

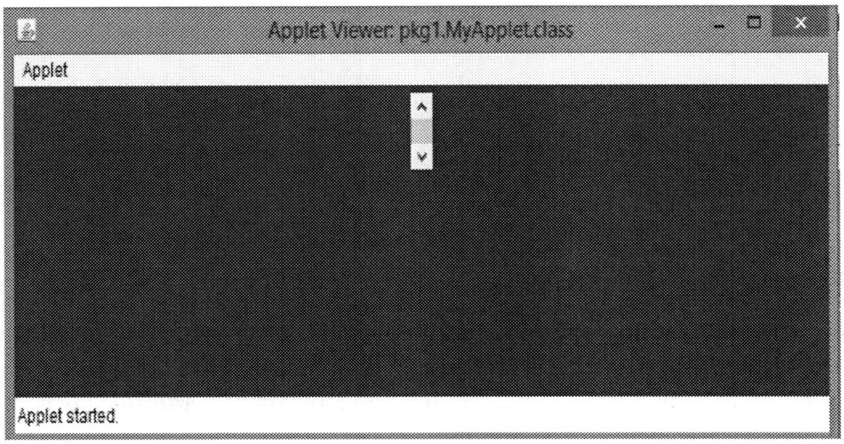

3. **Handling Item Events**

ItemEvent class is generated on selecting or deselecting a checkbox, a choice list or a checkable menu item. One needs to implement *ItemListener* interface by overriding the *itemStateChanged()* method to handle item events.

The below program adds a choice list onto the applet and registers an *ItemListener* with the same to handle item events. On selecting an item from the choice list, the *itemStateChanged()* method is fired. It further calls the *repaint()* method which belongs to the Component class and invokes the *paint()* of this component. The syntax for the repaint() method is as below:

```
public void repaint();
```

In case, the repaint() method is unable to call the paint() method, it invokes the update() method with the following syntax:

```
public void update(Graphics g);
```

//Handling choice list events

```
import java.applet.*;
import java.awt.*;
import java.awt.event.*;

/*
<applet code="MyApplet.class" width=300 height=200>
</applet>
 */
```

```
public class MyApplet extends Applet implements ItemListener {
  String str;
  Choice c;

  public void init() {
        c = new Choice();
        c.add("TV Series");
        c.add("Blindspot");
        c.add("Flash");
        c.add("Suits");
        c.addItemListener(this); //registers itemlistener with
                                   //the choice list
        c.select(2); //selects the item at index 2
        add(c);
  }

  public void itemStateChanged(ItemEvent ie) {
        repaint(); //calls paint() of this component

  }

  public void paint(Graphics g) {

        str = "You selected " + c.getSelectedItem(); //gets the
                                                      //selected item

        g.drawString(str, 200, 300); //writes the selected item
                                      //on the applet

  }
}
```

Output:

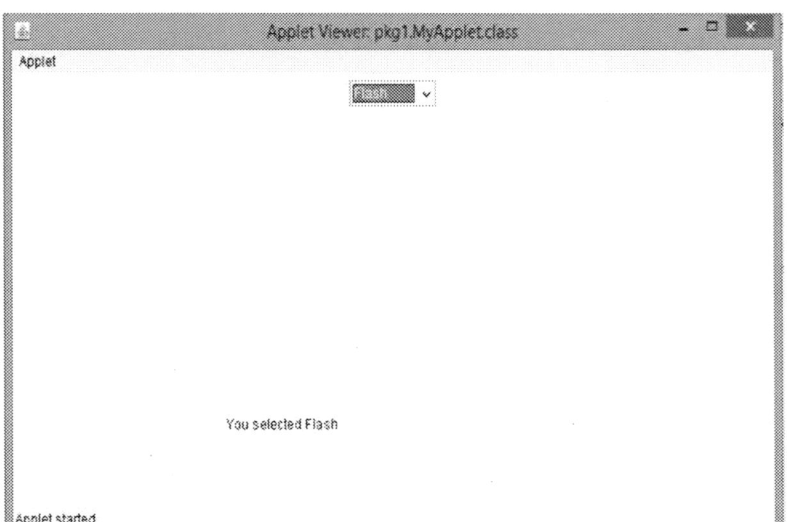

The next program shows handling checkbox events using the ItemListener and itemStateChanged() method. The getLabel() method gets the label of the selected checkbox and displays a string on the status bar of the applet using the subsequent method:

```
public void showStatus(String msg);
```

This method displays the string passed on the status bar of the applet.

//Handling checkbox events

```
import java.applet.*;
import java.awt.*;
import java.awt.event.*;

/*
<applet code="MyApplet.class" width=300 height=200>
</applet>
 */
public class MyApplet extends Applet implements ItemListener {
  String str;
  Checkbox cb, cb1, cb2;

  public void init() {
         cb  = new Checkbox("Biscuits");
         cb1 = new Checkbox("Juice");
         cb2 = new Checkbox("Chips");
         // registering ItemListener to the checkboxes
         cb.addItemListener(this);
         cb1.addItemListener(this);
         cb2.addItemListener(this);
         add(cb);
         add(cb1);
         add(cb2);
  }

  public void itemStateChanged(ItemEvent ie) {
         if (ie.getSource() == cb) {
               str = "You selected " + cb.getLabel(); // getting
                                                   // the label of checkbox

         } else if (ie.getSource() == cb1) {
               str = "You selected " + cb1.getLabel();
         } else
               str = "You selected " + cb2.getLabel();

         showStatus(str); // displays on the status bar
  }
}
```

Output:

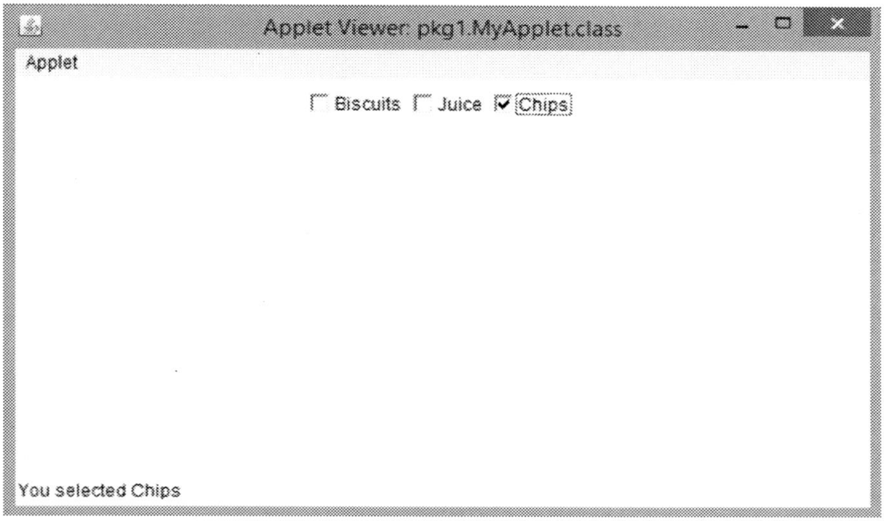

4. Handling KeyEvents

A KeyEvent class is generated when we interact with the keys of a keyboard which involves pressing, releasing or typing a key on the keyboard. To handle key events, one needs to implement the following methods of the KeyListener interface:

```
void keyPressed(KeyEvent e)
void keyReleased(KeyEvent e)
void keyTyped(KeyEvent e)
```

The following program registers a keyboard with its corresponding listener, KeyListener to handle key events. It also uses setFocusable() and requestFocus() to set the focus of the component (applet in our case) to true and request input focus from the keyboard respectively. It then uses showStatus() to display a message in the status bar of the applet on pressing, releasing or typing a key from the keyboard. Another important method this program uses has the below syntax:

public char `getKeyChar(): This method gets the character associated when a key from the keyboard is typed.`

//Handling keyboard events

```
import java.applet.*;
import java.awt.*;
import java.awt.event.*;

/*
<applet code="MyApplet.class" width=300 height=200>
</applet>
```

```
 */
public class MyApplet extends Applet implements KeyListener {
  char c;

  public void init() {
         addKeyListener(this); // registers keyboard with
                                //KeyListener
         setFocusable(true); // sets focusable state of this
                              //component to true
         requestFocus(); // requests input focus for this component
  }

  public void keyPressed(KeyEvent e) { // invoked on pressing a
                                        // key
         showStatus("key pressed"); // shows the output on the
                                    // status bar of an applet

  }

  public void keyReleased(KeyEvent e) { // invoked on releasing a
                                         // key
         showStatus("key released");

  }

  public void keyTyped(KeyEvent e) { // invoked on typing a key
         c = e.getKeyChar(); // gets the key typed
         showStatus(c + " key typed");

  }
}
```

Output:

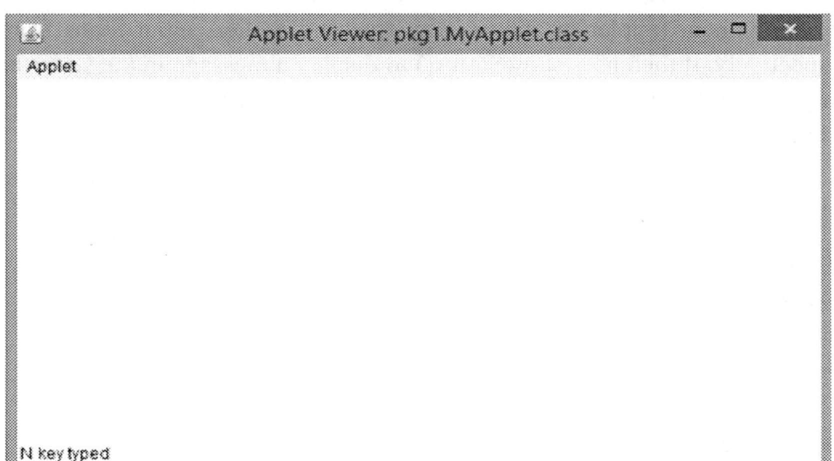

5. Handling MouseEvents

MouseEvents are generated by a mouse. The following methods of MouseListener interface needs to be overridden to handle mouse events:

```
public void    mouseClicked(MouseEvent e)
public void    mouseEntered(MouseEvent e)
public void    mouseExited(MouseEvent e)
public void    mousePressed(MouseEvent e)
public void    mouseReleased(MouseEvent e)
```

The next program uses a *MouseListener* to handle these mouse events. The *getX()* and *getY()* methods are used to get the x and y coordinates where the mouse is currently present on the container. The *showStatus()* method displays the coordinates where mouse is getting clicked currently.

```
import java.applet.*;
import java.awt.*;
import java.awt.event.*;

/*
<applet code="MyApplet.class" width=300 height=200>
</applet>
 */
public class MyApplet extends Applet implements MouseListener {
  int xcoord, ycoord;

  public void init() {
        addMouseListener(this); // registers mouse with
                                   //MouseListener
  }

  public void mouseClicked(MouseEvent me) {
        xcoord = me.getX(); //gets the x coordinate where
        //mouse is present
        ycoord = me.getY(); //gets the y coordinate where
        //mouse is present
        showStatus("Mouse clicking at " + xcoord + "," + ycoord);
  }

  public void mouseEntered(MouseEvent me) {
        showStatus("Mouse Entered");

  }

  public void mouseExited(MouseEvent me) {
        showStatus("Mouse Exited");

  }
```

```
    public void mousePressed(MouseEvent me) {
            showStatus("Mouse Pressed");

    }

    public void mouseReleased(MouseEvent me) {
            showStatus("Mouse Released");

    }

}
```

Output:

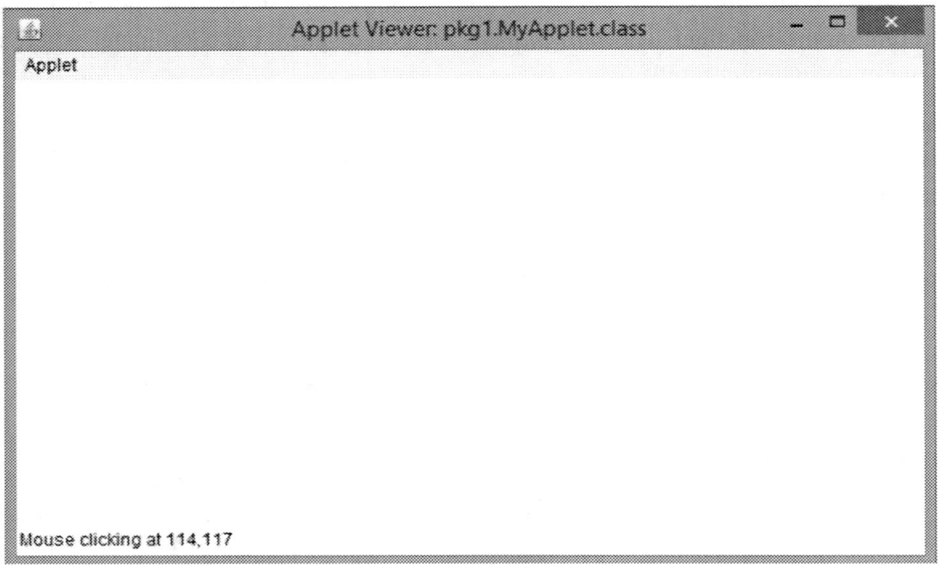

6. **Handling MouseMotionEvent**

   MouseMotionEvent is generated when the mouse is moved or dragged. It is necessary to implement *MouseMotionListener* to handle these events. The methods we need to override to handle *MouseMotionEvent* are:

```
public void   mouseDragged(MouseEvent e)
public void   mouseMoved(MouseEvent e)
```

```
import java.applet.*;
import java.awt.*;
import java.awt.event.*;

/*
<applet code="MyApplet.class" width=300 height=200>
</applet>
 */
```

```
public class MyApplet extends Applet implements MouseMotionListener {
  int xcoord, ycoord;

  public void init() {
        addMouseMotionListener(this); // registers mouse with
                                      // MouseMotionListener
  }

  public void mouseDragged(MouseEvent me) { // invoked when mouse
                                            // is dragged
        showStatus("Mouse Dragged at " + me.getX() + "," + me.getY());
  }

  public void mouseMoved(MouseEvent me) { // invoked when mouse
                                          // is moved
        showStatus("Mouse moved at " + me.getX() + "," + me.getY());
  }

}
```

Output:

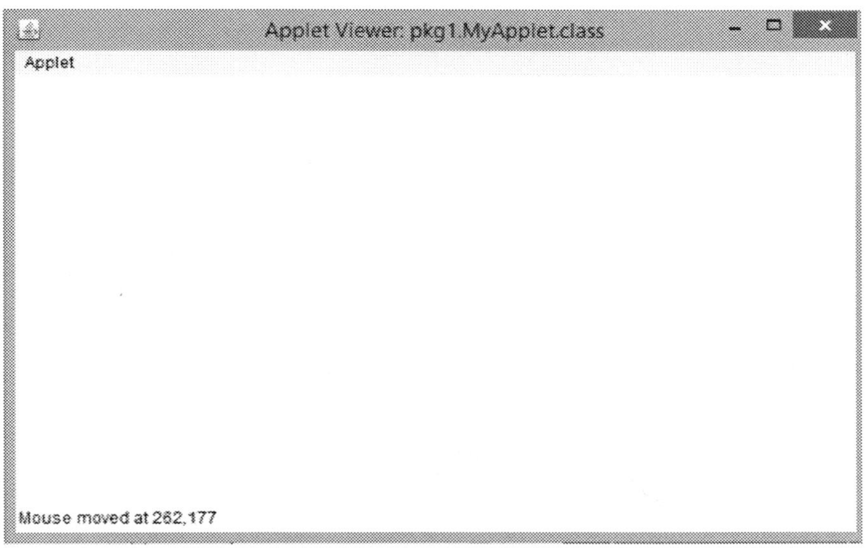

7. Handling TextEvent

A *TextEvent* class is generated on interaction with a *TextField* or a *TextArea*. The *TextListener* interface needs to be implemented by overriding the *textValueChanged()* method, which takes as a parameter a reference of *TextEvent* class, to handle text events.

The below program changes the background of the applet to blue on changing the text value of the textfield.

```
import java.applet.*;
import java.awt.*;
import java.awt.event.*;

/*
<applet code="MyApplet.class" width=300 height=200>
</applet>
 */
public class MyApplet extends Applet implements TextListener {
 TextField tf;

 public void init() {
        tf = new TextField(20);
        tf.addTextListener(this); // registers textfield with
                                  // TextListener
        add(tf);
 }

 public void textValueChanged(TextEvent te) { // invoked on
                        // changing the value of textfield

 if (te.getSource() == tf) {
               setBackground(Color.BLUE);
        }

 }

}
```

Output:

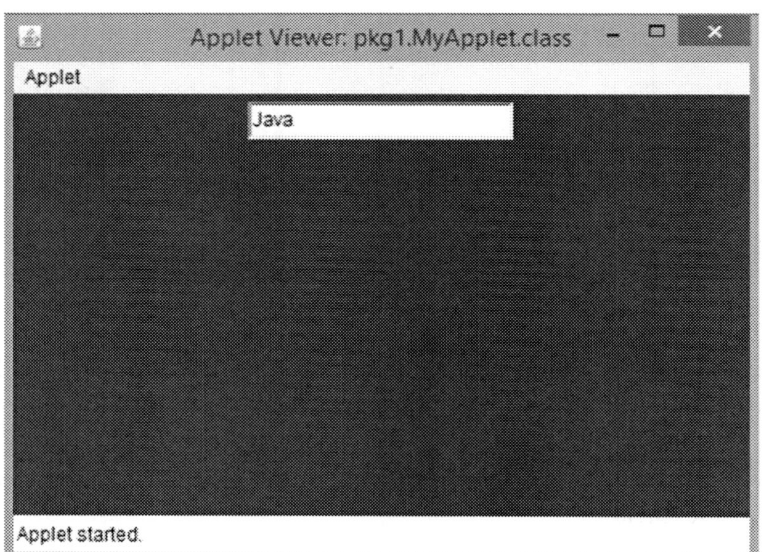

8. Handling WindowEvent

WindowEvent is generated when interacting with a window, like opening or closing a window. To handle window events, the WindowListener interface needs to be implemented by overriding the methods:

```
public void windowActivated(WindowEvent we)
public void windowClosed(WindowEvent we)
public void windowClosing(WindowEvent we)
public void windowDeactivated(WindowEvent we)
public void windowDeiconified(WindowEvent we)
public void windowIconified(WindowEvent we)
public void windowOpened(WindowEvent we)
```

The earlier examples of frames were not capable of closing frame windows. But the below example, uses the *windowClosing()* method, to set the visibility of the frame to false upon closing the frame.

```
import java.awt.*;
import java.awt.event.*;

public class FrameDemo extends Frame implements WindowListener {

  public FrameDemo(String title) {
        super(title); //calling Frame class constructor
        addWindowListener(this); // registers the frame FrameDemo
                                  //with WindowListener
  }

  public void windowActivated(WindowEvent we) {

  }

  public void windowClosed(WindowEvent we) {

  }

  public void windowClosing(WindowEvent we) {
        setVisible(false); // closes the frame window

  }

  public void windowDeactivated(WindowEvent we) {

  }

  public void windowDeiconified(WindowEvent we) {

  }

  public void windowIconified(WindowEvent we) {

  }
```

```
    public void windowOpened(WindowEvent we) {
        setVisible(true); // opens the frame window

    }
}

import java.awt.*;
import java.net.*;

public class Main {
    public static void main(String[] args) {
        Frame f = new FrameDemo("Showcasing window closing");
        f.setVisible(true);

    }
}
```

Observe the main method, the *Frame* class reference is capable of referring to a *FrameDemo* object as a *super class reference variable can point to a subclass object.*

13.3 ADAPTER CLASS

As we all know, one of the drawbacks of the interfaces is that we need to override all the methods present in that interface whether we need it or not. On the contrary, in case of extended classes, only required methods can be inherited and overridden in the subclass. Therefore, the concept of adapter classes emerged. Adapter classes are predefined classes available in *java.awt.event* package. These classes further implement the listener interfaces and provide empty definitions of all the methods present in them.

Take for an example, the MouseListener interface. Any class implementing this interface, will have to implement all the methods of this interface. On the other hand, we have a MouseAdapter class which implements the MouseListener interface and provides empty definitions for all the methods present in it. Hence, any class extending this adapter class has a choice of overriding the methods in it.

There exists an adapter class for each of the listener interfaces. Table 13.4 lists the various adapter class:

Table 13.4

Adapter classes	Listener interfaces
KeyAdapter	KeyListener
MouseAdapter	MouseListener
MouseMotionAdapter	MouseMotionListener
ContainerAdapter	ContainerListener
ComponentAdapter	ComponentListener
FocusAdapter	FocusListener

Let us see a sample definition of the *MouseAdapter* class to get more clarity on adapter classes.

```
public class MouseAdapter implements MouseListener {
    public void mouseClicked(MouseEvent me) {

    }

    public void mouseEntered(MouseEvent me) {

    }

    public void mouseExited(MouseEvent me) {

    }

    public void mousePressed(MouseEvent me) {

    }

    public void mouseReleased(MouseEvent me) {

    }
}
```

The next example shows how the KeyAdapter class can be worked with.

```
import java.awt.event.*;

public class KeyDemo extends KeyAdapter {
    char c;
    MyApplet m1; //reference of MyApplet

    public KeyDemo(MyApplet m) {
          m1 = m;
    }

    public void keyTyped(KeyEvent e) {
          c = e.getKeyChar();
          m1.showStatus(c + " key typed"); //m1 needed to invoke
                                            //showStatus()
    }
}

import java.applet.*;
import java.awt.*;
import java.awt.event.*;

/*
<applet code="MyApplet.class" width=300 height=200>
</applet>
 */
public class MyApplet extends Applet {
```

```
    public void init() {
        KeyDemo key = new KeyDemo(this); //this referring to
                                         //instance of MyApplet
        addKeyListener(key);
        setFocusable(true);
        requestFocus();
    }
}
```

This program uses the KeyAdapter class and overrides only the keyTyped() for handling key events. The addKeyListener() method gets its listener this time from the KeyDemo class as this class extends the KeyAdapter class which, in turn, implements the KeyListener interface. The constructor of the KeyDemo class accepts a reference of MyApplet as the KeyDemo class needs to invoke the showStatus() method, which is a member of the Applet class.

13.4 NESTED CLASSES

A Nested class is a class declared inside an existing outer class. The main advantage of using a nested class is that the enclosed or the nested class can access all the outer class members including the private ones which results in a cleaner and maintainable code.

Nested class are of two types:

1. **Non-Static Nested class/Inner class**

   Non-static nested classes are also called Inner classes. Inner classes can be further divided into three categories. Let us discuss each of them in detail.

   - *Member Inner class*

     A *member inner* class is an inner class which is a member of an outer class but defined outside a method. This class has access to all the members of its outer or enclosing class. A member class is instantiated in the following way:

     OuterClassName.InnerClassNameinnerClassObject=outerClassObject.newInnerClassName();

     //Example for Member Inner class

```
class OuterClass {
    private int var = 4;

    class MemberInnerClass { //member inner class
        void meth() {
            System.out.println(var); //accessing private
                                     //data
        }
    }
}
```

```
public class Main {
    public static void main(String[] args) {
            OuterClass oc = new OuterClass();
            OuterClass.MemberInnerClass mi = oc.new
MemberInnerClass (); // instantiating inner class
            mi.meth(); // accessing inner class method
    }
}
```

Output:

```
4
```

- *Anonymous Inner class*

  These classes are inner classes without a name. Anonymous classes can be used for overriding abstract class or interface methods. The below example explains the same:

```
public interface Inf {
    void meth();

}

public class AnonymousClassDemo {
    public static void main(String[] args) {
            Inf f = new Inf() { // instantiating anonymous
                                //class
                  public void meth() {
                        System.out.println("Implementing meth");
                  }
            };
            f.meth();
    }
}
```

Output:

```
Implementing meth
```

Have a look at the code below:

```
Inf f = new Inf() {// instantiating anonymous
                   //class
    public void meth() {
            System.out.println("Implementing meth");
    }
};
```

The highlighted brace marks the beginning of an anonymous class which is internally named by the compiler referred to by the reference f of type *Inf*.

Note that the Inf interface is not being instantiated here.

- *Local method inner class*

  A Local inner class is an inner class inside a method.

```
class OuterClass {
    void disp() {
        class LocalInnerClass { // local inner class
            void meth() {
                System.out.println("In meth");
            }
        }
// instantiating innerclass
        LocalInnerClass mi = new LocalInnerClass();
        mi.meth(); // invoking inner class method
    }
}

public class Main {
    public static void main(String[] args) {
        // instantiating outerclass
        OuterClass oc = new OuterClass();
        oc.disp();
    }
}
```

The main method here, starts the execution of the program by instantiating the outer class and invoking the method *disp()*.

The outer class method *disp(),* defines an inner class *LocalInnerClass* comprising of the method *meth()*. At the end of inner class, the method *disp()* instantiates the inner class and invokes method *meth()*.

2. **Static Nested class**

A static nested class is a static class defined inside another class. Such a class can only access static members of the outer class including private data members. Note that java does not provide top level(outer class) static classes. A static inner class is instantiated with the help of outer class.

Let us see an example for the same:

```
class OuterClass {
    static int var = 60; //static variable
    int i = 90; //non-static variable

    static class InnerClass { // static inner class
        void meth() {
```

```
                    System.out.println(var); // valid
                    System.out.println(i); // error
                }
            }
        }
public class Main {
    public static void main(String[] args) {
            //instantiating static inner class
            OuterClass.InnerClass oc = new OuterClass.InnerClass();
            oc.meth();
    }
}
```

13.5 MENU BAR

A menu bar is a window capable of incorporating menu choices on it. The *awt* package of java defines three classes for creating menu frames, namely, *MenuBar*, *Menu* and *MenuItem*. Let us discuss each of these classes along with their constructors:

1. **MenuBar**

   Constructor

   - MenuBar(): This constructor creates an empty menu bar with no menus on it, to be put on a container like a frame.

2. **Menu**

   Constructors

   - Menu(): creates empty menu choices to be put on a menu bar.
   - Menu (String menu): creates menu choices with the name specified as a parameter to the constructor like File, Edit, View etc to be put on a menu bar.
   - Menu (String menu, boolean removable): creates menu choices with the name specified as a parameter to the constructor. The boolean removable parameter if true, allows the menu to be removed and float free from the menu bar.

3. **MenuItem**

   Constructors

   - MenuItem(): creates an empty menu item to be put under a menu.
   - MenuItem(String name): creates a menu item with the name as specified in the parameter to the constructor. Example, Open, Save, Save as menu items under a File menu.
   - MenuItem (String name, MenuShortcut ms): creates a menu item named as the given parameter with the specified keyboard shortcut to the menu item.

To create a checkable menu item, the *awt* package provides the *CheckboxMenuItem* class which provides the following constructors:

- CheckboxMenuItem(): creates an empty checkable menu item to be put under a menu.
- CheckboxMenuItem(String itemName): creates a checkable menu item as specified in the parameter to the constructor. By default the menu item is unchecked.
- CheckboxMenuItem(String itemName, boolean on): creates a checkable menu item as specified in the parameter to the constructor. The boolean on parameter if true, marks the checkable menu item as checked initially.

Steps to create and add a menu bar on a frame

1. Create an empty menu bar by instantiating the *MenuBar* class.
2. Use the *setMenuBar()* method to set the above created menu bar on a container.

   ```
   public void setMenuBar(MenuBar mb)
   ```

   This method takes a *MenuBar* object as a parameter which you want to set on the container.
3. Now instantiate the Menu class using the parameterized constructor of the same.
   Menu(String menu)
   This will create named menus to be put on the menu bar.
4. Next instantiate the *MenuItem* class to create menu items under a specific menu.
5. Add the menu item objects onto the menus created above using the below *add()* method.

   ```
   public MenuItem add(MenuItem mi);
   ```

6. Now add this menu along with its menu items onto the menu bar using the following version of add() method.

```
public Menu add(Menu m);
```

//Creating a menu bar

```
import java.awt.*;
import java.awt.event.*;

public class FrameDemo extends Frame implements WindowListener{

 public FrameDemo(String title) {
        super(title);
        addWindowListener(this); // registers the frame FrameDemo with
                                                   // WindowListener
        MenuBar mb = new MenuBar(); //creates empty menu bar
        setMenuBar(mb); //set the menu bar on the frame

        //creating menu File
```

```
        Menu m1 = new Menu("File");
        //creating menu items
        MenuItem mi1 = new MenuItem("New");
        MenuItem mi2 = new MenuItem("Close");
        MenuItem mi3 = new MenuItem("Close All");
        MenuItem mi4 = new MenuItem("Save");
        MenuItem mi5 = new MenuItem("Save As");
        //adding menu items onto menu File
        m1.add(mi1);
        m1.add(mi2);
        m1.add(mi3);
        m1.add(mi4);
        m1.add(mi5);
        //adding menu File onto menu bar mb
        mb.add(m1);
    }
    public void windowActivated(WindowEvent we) {
    }
    public void windowClosed(WindowEvent we) {
    }
    public void windowClosing(WindowEvent we) {
        setVisible(false); // closes the frame window
    }
    public void windowDeactivated(WindowEvent we) {
    }
    public void windowDeiconified(WindowEvent we) {
    }
    public void windowIconified(WindowEvent we) {
    }
    public void windowOpened(WindowEvent we) {
        setVisible(true); // opens the frame window
    }
}
public class Main {
    public static void main(String[] args) {
```

```
FrameDemo f=new FrameDemo("My Menu Frame");
f.setVisible(true);
  }
}
```

Output:

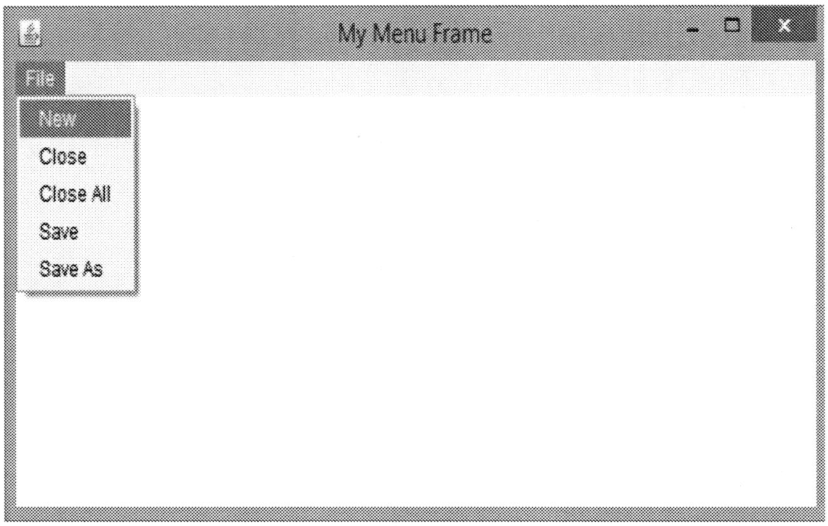

13.6 SWING AND ITS CONTROLS

The Java Foundation Classes (JFC) is used to create window applications and comprises graphical user interface components. The Swing hierarchy of components is built over AWT hierarchy and is part of JFC.

Swing components are lightweight, platform independent and written in java as compared to AWT. It provides an extension of components from AWT like tabbed panes, tables and trees. The package *javax.swing* comprises all the swing components.

Table 13.5 lists some of the classes in this package.

Table 13.5

Class	Description
JButton	Provides swing version of Button.
AbstractButton	Superclass of JButton class.
JApplet	Provides swing version of Applet.

JCheckbox	Provides swing version of Checkbox.
JLabel	Provides swing version of Label.
JScrollPane	Provides a container in form of a scrollable window.
JTabbedPane	Provides an option for the user to select from several tabs.
JTextFeild	Provides swing version of a TextField.
JTree	Provides a means to portray hierarchical data.
JComboBox	Provides a button or an editable textfeild along with a drop down list.
JRadioButton	Provides swing version of CheckboxGroup.

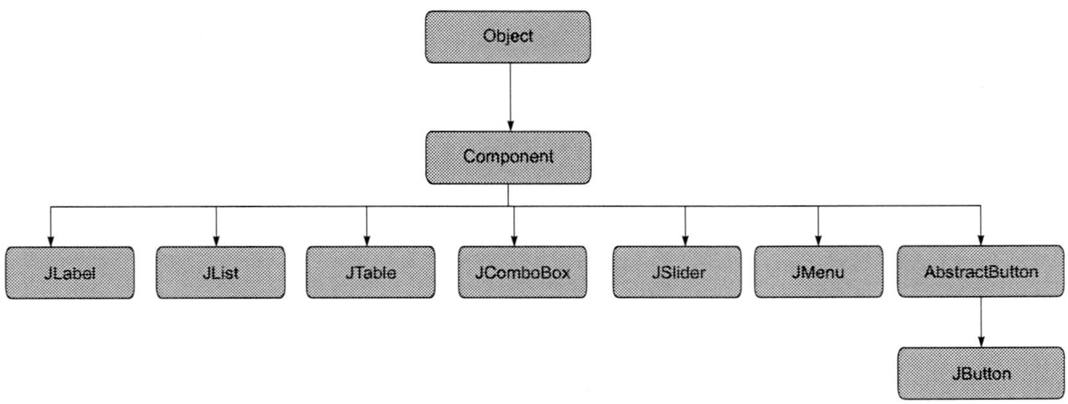

Fig. 13.1 Swing hierarchy

Swing provides classes for each of its component which can be embedded on a container pane. The container pane can be obtained by using the below method:

```
public Container getContentPane();
```

This method returns a Container class reference on which the components can be entrenched.

Let us take up an example to put a JTextField onto a JApplet. JTextFiled and JApplet are swing components showcasing a swing textfield and a swing applet.

```
import java.awt.*;

import javax.swing.*;

public class SwingDemo extends JApplet {

    public void init() {
        setLayout(new FlowLayout()); // set the layout of the container
```

```
            Container pane = getContentPane();// get the content pane
               // creating a swing textfield
            JTextField jtf = new JTextField("Swing textfield....");
            pane.add(jtf); //adding the jtextfield to the container
      }
}
```

Output:

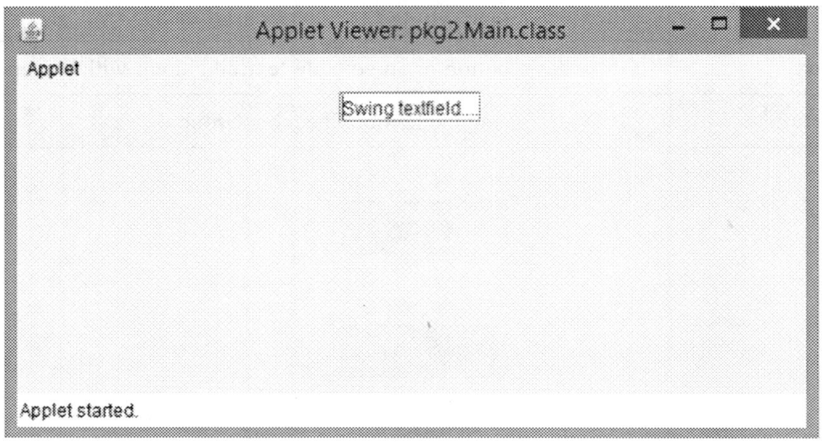

13.7 COMPARING SWINGS WITH AWT

Table 13.6 gives a brief comparison between Swings and AWT components.

Table 13.6

	AWT	Swings
Abbreviation	AWT stands for Abstract Window Toolkit.	Swings are also named Java Foundation classes (JFC).
Package	AWT components exist in java.awt package.	Swings components exist in javax.swing package.
Component Type	AWT components are called heavy-weight components as they rely on native operating system calls to draw GUI components.	Swing components are light weight components as they do not delegate the task of drawing GUI components to the OS.
Platform Independence	AWT components are platform dependent.	Swing components are platform independent as they are written purely in java.
Variety of components	AWT provides limited components and features.	Swing provides a variety of components like tabbed panes, scroll pane, trees, etc.

SUMMARY

- An event is something that happens which results in the change of state of an object.
- Event handling is the handling of such events, generated from a source.
- A source of an event is the one that generates an event.
- Listeners are interfaces in java that are used to handle diverse events.
- When an event occurs, its corresponding event class is also generated which contains the information about the source of the event.
- Adapter classes are useful when we want to handle only a few of the events from a listener interface as these classes provide empty definitions for all the methods present in the listener interfaces.
- A nested class/inner class is a class defined inside another class. It can be either static or non-static. Top level classes cannot be made static classes.
- Anonymous inner classes are inner classes which do not have a name.
- Menu Bar can be used to incorporate menus on a container like frame. Java defines three classes for the same: MenuBar, Menu and MenuItem. These classes provide constructors and methods to create a menu and menu items to be put under a menu bar.
- Swing components (Java Foundation classes) are termed lightweight components as compared to AWT components as they have an inbuilt feature to draw GUI components and they do not rely on the operating system for the same.

COMMON ERRORS

- One of the most common mistakes a java programmer does, is forgetting to register the appropriate source with a listener interface. Till the time a source is not registered with its listener, the listener methods will never be invoked or handle the generated events!
- Extending two adapter classes to handle diverse events will result into a compile time error as multiple inheritance is not supported in java.
- Accessing non-static members of an outer class from a static nested class results into a compile time error.
- Creating a menu bar on an applet. Applets cannot incorporate a menu on them.

SELF-TEST

1. Explain the event delegation model in java. How does the source of an event and a listener interface interact with each other? Discuss.
2. Write a program to show event handling for:
   (a) Lists
   (b) Menu bar

(c) CheckboxGroup

3. What are adapter classes? How did they come into existence? Explain with a program.
4. Write short notes on:
   (a) Non-static nested classes
   (b) Static nested classes
   (c) Anonymous classes
5. Explain the steps to create a menu bar and put it on a container. Include two menus and 4 menu items under each menu.
6. Give a brief comparison between AWT and Swing components.

PRACTICAL QUESTIONS

1. Generate the output for the following:

a)
```
class A {
    public void meth() {
            System.out.println("Method in A");

    }
}

public class B extends A {
A o = new A() {
        public void meth() {
            System.out.println("Method in anonymous class");
        }
};

public void call() {
        o.meth();
        }

}

public class Main {
        public static void main(String[] args) {
            B b=new B();
            b.call();
        }
}
```

b)
```
class A {
        class Inner {
            private int num=6;
            public void meth() {
```

```
                    System.out.println(num);

            }
        }
    }

    public class Main {
        public static void main(String[] args) {
            A.Inner ai = new A.Inner();
    ai.meth();
        }
    }
```

c)
```
    import java.awt.event.*;
    public class A extends MouseAdapter {
        MyApplet m;

        A(MyApplet m) {
            this.m = m;
        }
        public void mouseClicked(MouseEvent me) {
            m.showStatus("mouse clicked");
        }
    }
    import java.applet.*;
        import java.awt.*;

        /*
        <applet code="MyApplet.class" width=300 height=200>
        </applet>
        */
        public class MyApplet extends Applet {

        public void init() {
            A o=new A(this);
    addMouseListener(this);
        }
        public void paint(Graphics g)
        {
            g.drawString("paint method invoked", 300, 40);
        }
    }
```

14
CHAPTER

Networking

This chapter will enable you to learn the following:

- Handling communication over networks by focusing upon the two significant protocols: TCP and UDP.
- Connecting to a database using the JDBC API.
- Introduction about servlets, its life cycle, creation and deployment.

14.1 NETWORKING BASICS

A network refers to a collection of nodes/elements connected in some way so that they can exchange information. Example, a social media network is a network of people connected through a social media website wherein they can exchange their ideas and information with each other.

Java programs are written on Application layer using application layer protocols such as HTTP. However, the application layer protocols run over transport layer protocols such as TCP or UDP. Therefore, to clearly understand how computers communicate over a network, let us visit TCP and UDP protocols.

TCP: *TCP* stands for *Transmission Control Protocol*. This protocol is used when we want to have a reliable communication between two computers. This means data sent from one computer reaches the other computer, *in time and in the order it was sent.* TCP establishes a connection before transmitting any data packet to the other party. Hence, it is also known as a *connection oriented protocol.*

Consider an example of a telephonic conversation. A telephonic conversation requires a dedicated and reliable connection between the sender and receiver over which they can talk. Communication is then done using this dedicated link only. If this link is not reliable, the receiver might not get the complete message disseminated by the sender.

Some of the examples of the application layer protocols using TCP protocol are *HTTP*, *FTP* and *Telnet*.

UDP: *UDP* stands for *User Datagram Protocol* and is named after the concept of mail service. Just as there is no guarantee that a letter sent from the mail service will reach the receiver in time or in the order in which it was sent, UDP also sends datagrams from one computer to another and has no reliability for an in-order delivery of the message. UDP is said to be a *connection-less* protocol.

Consider an example of a multiplayer game like Counter strike which uses UDP. In such a case, a reliable connection is not that critical between the player and the server. Also the order in which the data packets are received from the server is not that acute as the player can still play the game on his console or restart the game.

Understanding Ports

The next set of things significant for us to learn in this context are *ports* and *sockets*.

Contemplate a situation wherein you send a letter to an address on it which is not bearing a name. Such a scenario might raise some confusion regarding the recipient of the letter.

The computers connected on a network follow a similar approach for communication. Each computer on a network has a unique 32-bit or a 128-bit IP Address which is used to distinguish it from other set of computers. It is represented in a dotted decimal form, example, 198.168.0.41. While communicating to another computer on a network, the sender computer specifies the IP address and a port number of the recipient computer. The IP address determines which computer on the network to connect to, and the port number indicates the specific application to connect to on that computer. It is analogous to a letter being sent at a particular address with a named recipient on it. The address denotes the IP address of the computer whom we want to get connected whereas the name of recipient represents the port number of that computer.

14.2 NETWORKING CLASSES

The *java.net* package provides a range of classes to initiate networking between two or more computers on a network. Some of the networking classes available in this package are discussed below:

14.2.1 InetAddress class:

The *InetAddress* class denotes an *Internet Protocol (IP) address*. Its instance mainly comprises of two things: *IP address and the host name*. As IP addresses are difficult to memorize by normal users, we have a concept of host names which are names allotted to a specific machine. These names are mapped by a domain name server to their corresponding IP address of a machine so that a machine can be located on a network.

However, to locate a specific machine on a network you also require a domain name. A domain name is used to signify the network to which a computer belongs. For example, if you have a machine with a name (host name), myPC, on the network (domain name), myNetwork, the following path will be used to identify this machine:

www.myPC.myNetwork.com.

Note that the combination of host name and domain name must be unique for identification.

The *InetAddress* class constitutes the following set of methods but does not have any visible constructors:

- **public static** `InetAddress getLocalHost()` **throws** `UnknownHostException`

  This method gets the host name and the IP address of the local host machine in an *InetAddress* instance. Local host signifies the local computer on which a program is running. Example, if we search from our own browser, our machine is treated as a local host in the network of computers.

  This method throws an *UnknownHostException*, if the local host name could not be resolved to an IP address.

- **public static** `InetAddress getByName(String host)` **throws** `UnknownHostException`

  This method returns the IP address of a host in an *InetAddress* instance, given the host name. It also throws an exception of type *UnknownHostException* in case no IP address is resolved to the given host name.

- **public** `String getHostName()`

  This method gets the host name as a String object for this IP address.

- **public** `String getHostAddress()`

  This method returns the IP address as a String object.

  The next program demonstrates the use of the above methods:

```
import java.net.*;

public class Main {
  public static void main(String[] args) throws UnknownHostException {
        InetAddress localHost = InetAddress.getLocalHost();
        System.out.println("The local host for this computer is: " +
        localHost);
        InetAddress ipAddress = InetAddress.getByName("java.sun.com");
        System.out.println(ipAddress);
        System.out.println(ipAddress.getHostName());
        System.out.println(ipAddress.getHostAddress());
   }
}
```

Output:

```
The local host for this computer is: myPC/192.168.3.123
```

```
java.sun.com/156.151.59.19
Host name:java.sun.com
IP Address:156.151.59.19
```

14.2.2 URL class

Another class, java.net package provides is the URL class. URL is an abbreviation for *Uniform Resource Locator*. It is used to locate resources over the web. It essentially includes of two parts:

- The protocol used to access the resource.
- The absolute or the relative path to reach that resource. The absolute path lists the complete path to a given resource whereas the relative path defines the path from the current directory to the specified resource. The path to a resource can further be categorized into the following parts:
    - Host Name: specifies the machine on which the resource resides.
    - File Name: mentions the file to be accessed on this host.
    - Port Number (optional): refers to the specific program/application to connect to on this host.
    - Reference (optional): denotes a particular location within a file to be opened.

  Amongst all of them, only the host name and the file name is mandatory to be mentioned.

  An example of a URL is http://www.MySite.com/Myfile.txt

  In this URL, the protocol used is *HTTP*. Other protocols include *FTP*, *SMTP*, etc. The host name to connect is *MySite.com* and the file to be located is *MyFile.txt*. (Notice the colon and double forward slashes separating the protocol and the host name).

Constructing and Querying a URL

To construct a URL, one needs to create an object of the URL class. This class consists of the following constructors which initializes a URL object with its components.

Table 14.1 Constructors in URL class

Constructor	Description
URL(String url)	Creates a URL object from the given string.
URL(String protocol, String host, int port, String file)	Constructs a URL object from the given protocol, host name, port number and the file name.
URL(String protocol, String host, String file)	Builds a URL object given the protocol, host name and the file name.
URL(URL url, String res)	Creates a URL object using a base URL object and a relative resource.

Some of the methods belonging to the class which help us query a URL object are discussed below:

Table 14.2 Methods in URL class

Method	Description
public String getHost()	Gets the host name for this URL as a String object.
public String getPath()	Gets the path for this URL as a String object.
public int getPort()	Gets the port number for this URL as an integer. If the port is not mentioned, it defaults to -1.
public String getProtocol()	Gets the protocol used to access this URL as a String object.
public String getFile()	Gets the file name from this URL as a String object.

Note that the constructors for the URL class throws a MalformedURLException. Therefore, this exception needs to be handled by either using a try catch block or a throws keyword in the calling code.

Let us now examine the URL class methods and constructors using an example.

```
import java.net.*;

public class Main {
    public static void main(String[] args) throws MalformedURLException {
// URL object
            URL url = new URL("http://ipu.ac.in/exam_datesheet.php");
            System.out.println(url.getHost()); // gets the host name
            System.out.println(url.getPath()); // gets the path
            System.out.println(url.getPort()); // gets the port
            System.out.println(url.getProtocol());//gets the protocol
            System.out.println(url.getFile()); // gets the file name
    }
}
```

Output:

```
ipu.ac.in
/exam_datesheet.php
-1
http
/exam_datesheet.php
```

The important thing to note here is that `"http://ipu.ac.in/exam_datesheet.php"` is simply a String object as it is enclosed between a double quotes. It becomes a URL object only when passed to a constructor of the URL class. This object then can be used to query the URL regarding its protocol, host name, path, file name, etc., using the methods present in this class. Also, as the port number has not been mentioned in the URL, it defaults to -1.

14.2.3 URLConnection class

After an URL object has been constructed, one can also connect to this URL to read, write or inspect the resource specified in the URL. The *openConnection()* method allows us to establish a connection with the given URL. This method is present in the *URL* class and returns *URLConnection* instance. Its syntax is given below:

```
public URLConnection openConnection()throws IOException
```

Some of the methods available in *URLConnection* class are listed below:

Table 14.3

Method	Description
public long getLastModified()	Gets the value of the last modified date header field. Specifies the date time when the URL was last modified.
public long getExpiration()	Gets the value of expires field. Specifies the date time when the URL is going to get expired.
public String getContentType()	Gets the value of content type header field. Specifies the type of content present in the URL, example, text/html.
public int getContentLength()	Gets the value of content length header field. Specifies the length of the content present in the URL.
public long getDate()	Gets the value of the date header field. Indicates the date of the URL document.

The next program uses the above methods to inspect the given URL.

```
import java.io.IOException;
import java.net.*;
import java.util.Date;

public class Main {
    public static void main(String[] args) throws IOException {
//URL object
         URL url = new URL("https://en.wikipedia.org/wiki/Java_
(programming_language)");
URLConnection conn = url.openConnection(); // connection to URL
         long d1 = conn.getLastModified(); //gets the last modified
                                            //date
//parsing into a Date object
         System.out.println("Last modified on:" + new Date(d1));
         long d2 = conn.getExpiration(); //gets the expiration date
```

```
            System.out.println("Expiration Date:" + new Date(d2));
            System.out.println("Content Type:" + conn.getContentType());
            //gets the content type
            System.out.println("Content Length:" + conn.getContentLength());
            //gets the content length
            long d3=conn.getDate(); //gets the date of the URL
            System.out.println(new Date(d3));
    }
}
```

Output:

```
Last modified on:Tue May 03 22:37:27 IST 2016
Expiration Date:Thu Jan 01 05:30:00 IST 1970
Content Type:text/html; charset=UTF-8
Content Length:-1
Wed May 04 15:49:46 IST 2016
```

Notice the below line:

```
System.out.println("Last modified on:" + new Date(d1))
```

The *getLastModified()* method returns a long value which needs to be parsed into a Date Time format which can be done using the Date class parameterized constructor that converts this long value into a Date Time format.

14.3 SOCKETS

Till now we learnt networking using the classes *URL* and *URLConnection*. These classes are said to implement high level networking as the lower level details of how one machine gets connected to the other is abstracted from the developer. The developer has to just write the code to connect to a URL and use the various methods of these classes to read, write or inspect the URL.

But internally, this mechanism uses the concept of sockets. The best example to learn sockets is via a client server architecture wherein a client sends a request to a server and the server responds back with the requested resource. A client and a server are both programs running on a specific machine. Prior to establishing communication between a client and a server, the server program must be always running and available to which a client can connect. The server has a socket which is a combination of the IP address of the machine on which it is running and its port number. *A socket is an endpoint of a communication link between two machines.*

The server listens and waits for a client to connect on this socket. The client on the other side, knows the IP address and the port number of the server machine it wants to connect to. But, it also needs to generate its own identification to the server, for which, it binds itself to a local port number assigned by the system.

On receiving a client connection, the server creates a new socket and accepts the incoming connection. It uses the formal socket to accept other incoming client connections..

The client and server can now communicate using these sockets by sending or receiving data.

Java provides *Socket* and *ServerSocket* classes present in the *java.net* package, for creating client and server sockets respectively.

Following are some of the constructors of the *Socket* class that will be used in the book:

```
public Socket(InetAddress address, int port)throws IOException
```

This constructor establishes a connection of the client with the server machine using the given IP address and the port number. The constructor throws an IOException, in case an input output error comes up while creating a socket.

```
public Socket(String hostName, int port)throws UnknowHostException,
IOException
```

The above constructor creates a socket which connects this machine to the machine with the given host name and port number and throws an exception of type UnknownHostException if it fails to connect to the given host and an IOException in case of an input output error.

Next we have some of the constructors of the *ServerSocket* class discussed below:

```
public ServerSocket(int port)throws IOException
```

This constructor creates a server socket on the given port number. The server should always be available and listening on this port number for a client to establish a connection with it. This port number should be the same as that of the port number, the client uses to connect to this server. It also throws an exception of type IOException.

```
public ServerSocket(int port, int maxQueue)
```

This constructor creates a socket for the server using the given port number and the maximum queue length. If a connection arrives and the maximum queue length is reached, the connection is rejected.

Reading and Writing using Sockets

The service these sockets provide is purely bidirectional, wherein both the client and the server can send or receive data. Such kind of sockets are also called *TCP/IP sockets (Transmission Control Protocol, Internet Protocol).* TCP/IP sockets provide a reliable communication between two machines and ensures an in-order delivery of messages which means *transmitting messages to the receiver in the order they were sent.*

Once a socket has been created, a client can read from or write to a server easily by using its input and output streams.

The next program depicts an *Echo client and server*. Echo client and server are two programs running on machines wherein any message that the client transmits to the server is echoed back to the client.

This example has two programs namely, *Client.java* and *Server.java. While running these programs, Server.java should be executed first so that the server is available for an incoming client. Thereafter, Client.java should be executed.*

Let us start discovering Client.java to see how a client program creates a socket and gets connected to server.

//Client.java

```
import java.io.*;
import java.net.*;

public class Client {
    public static void main(String[] args) throws UnknownHostException,
            IOException {
          String str;
          // 1. Creating and connecting a socket to the local host
          Socket s = new Socket(InetAddress.getLocalHost(), 10007);
          System.out.println("client running");
          // 2. Opening an output stream connected to socket
          PrintWriter out = new PrintWriter(s.getOutputStream(), true);
          // 3. Opening an input stream connected to the socket
          BufferedReader brIn = new BufferedReader(new InputStreamReader(
                    s.getInputStream()));
          // 4. Opening an input stream connected to standard input
          BufferedReader br = new BufferedReader(new
          InputStreamReader(System.in));
          // 5. Reading from standard input
          while ((str = br.readLine()) != null) {
                // 6. Writing onto output stream of socket
                out.println(str);
                // 7. Reading from input stream of socket
                System.out.println(brIn.readLine());
          }
// 8. Closing the streams
          brIn.close();
          br.close();
          out.close();
          s.close();
    }
}
```

The program can be understood through the following steps:

Step 1: A Socket class object is created with the given IP address and the port number of a server machine.

```
Socket s = new Socket(InetAddress.getLocalHost(), 10007);
```

The getLocalHost() method connects our computer with the local host, thereby, ensuring the client and the server are running on the same machine.

Step 2: Once the connection has been established, the client, may now like to write some data or receive data from the server. Therefore, the next step is to get the output stream connected to the socket and opening a *PrintWriter* object onto it.

```
PrintWriter out = new PrintWriter(s.getOutputStream(), true);
```

The output stream can now be accessed using this PrintWriter object, *out*.

The *getOutputStream()* method, present in the Socket class, can be used to get the output stream for a socket which has the following syntax:

```
public OutputStream getOutputStream()throws IOException
```

The PrintWriter constructor used in the program has the below syntax:

```
public PrintWriter(OutputStream out, boolean autoFlush)
```

This constructor creates a *PrintWriter* to write data from an already existing output stream. The boolean parameter if true, indicates that auto flushing is enabled.

Step 3: Opening an input stream, *brIn* connected to this socket, using the *BufferedReader* constructor.

```
BufferedReader brIn = new BufferedReader(new InputStreamReader(
                        s.getInputStream()));
```

The *getInputStream()* method returns an input stream to read from the socket which has the below syntax:

```
public InputStream getInputStream()throws IOException
```

Step 4: Opening an input stream connected to the standard input, *br*. This stream enables the user to read from the standard input which is normally, the keyboard.

```
BufferedReader br = new BufferedReader(new InputStreamReader(System.in));
```

Step 5, 6: The next step is to read from the standard input and write this data to the output stream of the socket.

```
while ((str = br.readLine()) != null)
    out.println(str);
```

After writing to the server, the client waits for a reply from the server. At this point in time, the server program is already running and replies with an echoed data.

Note: The code for the Server.java will be discussed after this program.

Step 7: The client machine can now read the data sent by the server, from its socket input stream using the *brIn* input stream.

```
System.out.println(brIn.readLine());
```

Step 8: Closing all the stream objects associated with the socket and finally closing the socket.

```
brIn.close();
br.close();
out.close();
s.close();
```

The next program describes how the server communicates with the client. The server program has to be started first, as a server should always be up and running so that a client can send a request to it.

//Server.java

```
import java.io.*;
import java.net.*;

public class Server {
    public static void main(String[] args) throws IOException {
            String str;
            // 1. Server connected to a socket and listening on a port
            ServerSocket s = new ServerSocket(10007);
            System.out.println("server running");
            // 2. Server accepting an incoming client connection
            Socket newSocket = s.accept();
            // 3. Opening the output stream on this socket
            PrintWriter out = new PrintWriter(newSocket.getOutputStream(),
            true);
            // 4. Opening the input stream on this socket
            BufferedReader brIn = new BufferedReader(new InputStreamReader(
                        newSocket.getInputStream()));
            // 5. Reading from the input stream and writing back on the
            // output stream
            while ((str = brIn.readLine()) != null) {
                  out.println("Server echoing " + str);

            }
            // 6. Closing the streams
            brIn.close();
            out.close();
            newSocket.close();
            s.close();

    }
}
```

Following are the steps to create a communication link from the server to the client:

Step 1: Server creates a server socket named *s* listening on the given port number.

```
ServerSocket s = new ServerSocket(10007);
```

Step 2: The moment a client comes up with an incoming connection, the server creates a new socket, *newSocket*.

```
Socket newSocket = s.accept();
```

using the *accept()* method call:

```
public Socket accept()throws IOException
```

This socket is then used as a communication link between the client and the server.

Note that, the server continues to listen on the former socket s, for other client connections.

Step 3: The next step is to get the output stream using the *getOutputStream()* method and open a PrintWriter *out*, on the *newSocket*. This socket can be used by the server to write back to the client.

```
PrintWriter out = new PrintWriter(newSocket.getOutputStream(), true);
```

Step 4: Using the *getInputStream()* method to get the input stream for the socket and connecting it to the *BufferedReader* object *brIn* which can now be used to read data from the client.

```
BufferedReader brIn = new BufferedReader(new InputStreamReader(
                        newSocket.getInputStream()));
```

Step 5: Reading from the input stream *brIn* and writing back the echoed data to the client using the output stream *out*.

```
while ((str = brIn.readLine()) != null) {
       out.println("Server echoing " + str);
}
```

Step 6: Closing all the streams connected to the socket and finally closing the socket.

```
brIn.close();
out.close();
newSocket.close();
s.close();
```

14.4 DATAGRAMS

The TCP/IP protocol that we learnt in the last section provided a reliable means of communication guaranteeing the delivery of messages in the order they were sent.

UDP protocol on the other hand, establishes communication between hosts by sending datagrams over the network, but does not guarantee the delivery of these messages to the receiver. In addition to this, UDP does not ensure an in-order delivery of the messages either.

A Datagram is an independent packet of data to be transmitted over the network using the UDP protocol whose delivery, timely delivery or an in-order delivery is not guaranteed.

Java provides two predefined classes *DatagramPacket* and *DatagramSocket* to create datagrams and send them over a socket respectively. Both these classes are available to you in the *java.net* package.

The constructors below are used to create a *DatagramSocket* over which datagrams can be sent or received.

```
public DatagramSocket()throws SocketException
```

This constructor creates a datagram socket and binds it to any available port number and a random IP address chosen by the kernel. It throws a *SocketException* if the socket could not be created.

```
public DatagramSocket(int port)throws SocketException
```

This constructor creates a datagram socket and binds it to the given port number and a random IP address chosen by the kernel. Also throws a *SocketException* if the socket could not be created or bound to the given port number.

Following constructors of the *DatagramPacket* class can be used to create datagrams:

```
public DatagramPacket(byte[] buf, int length, InetAddress address, int
port)
```

This constructor creates a datagram packet to be sent to the machine with the given IP address and port number with contents as that of the byte array *buff* of length *l*.

```
public DatagramPacket(byte[] buf, int length)
```

This constructor creates a datagram packet to be received by a machine whose contents are stored in the byte array *buff* of length *l*.

Let us now go through an example showing the client and server sending and receiving datagrams.

//Client.java

```
import java.net.*;

public class Client {
    public static void main(String[] args) throws Exception {
            String str = "Received Datagram"; //Message to be sent

            //1. Creating a DatagramSocket
            DatagramSocket ds = new DatagramSocket();
            //2. Creating a DatagramPacket to be sent to the server
            DatagramPacket dp = new DatagramPacket(str.getBytes(), str.
            length(),InetAddress.getLocalHost(), 2304);
            //3. Sending the DatagramPacket to the server
            ds.send(dp);
            //4. Closing the DatagramSocket stream
```

```
            ds.close();
        }
}
```

The client program described above follows the following steps to send datagrams to the server:

1. Create a datagram socket,*ds*, over which the datagram will be sent using the below *DatagramSocket* constructor:

   ```
   DatagramSocket ds = new DatagramSocket();
   ```

2. Create datagram packet to be sent to the server using the given constructor:

   ```
   DatagramPacket dp = new DatagramPacket(str.getBytes(),
   str.length(),InetAddress.getLocalHost(), 2304);
   ```

   The *getBytes()* method is used to convert the contents of the String object *str* into a sequence of bytes, storing the result in a byte array. Its length is calculated using the *length()* method.

   The datagram packet *dp*, created gets its contents from the byte array of the given length and is destined to be delivered to the local host machine with the port number 2304.

3. The next step is to send the prepared datagram to the server machine using the *send()* method having the below syntax:

   ```
   public void send(DatagramPacket p)throws IOException
   ```

   This method sends the given datagram packet over this socket. The method also throws an IOException in case an IO error comes up.

4. The last step is to close the datagram socket, *ds*, so that no more datagrams can be sent via this datagram socket.

   ```
   ds.close();
   ```

   //Server.java

   ```
   import java.net.*;

   public class Server {
     public static void main(String[] args) throws Exception {
           //1. Creating a DatagramSocket
           DatagramSocket ds = new DatagramSocket(2304);
           byte arr[]=new byte[1024];
           //2. Creating a DatagramPacket in which data will be received
           DatagramPacket dp = new DatagramPacket(arr,1024);
           //3. Receiving data into the DatagramPacket
           ds.receive(dp);
   ```

```
            //4. Extracting the contents of the received DatagramPacket
            String str = new String(dp.getData(),0,dp.getLength());
            //5. Displaying contents on console
            System.out.println(str);
            //6. Closing DatagramSocket stream
            ds.close();
    }
    }
```

The above program can be explained using the subsequent steps:

1. Create a datagram socket for the server listening on the port number 2304 by using the constructor:

   ```
   public DatagramSocket(int port)throws SocketException
   ```

   This port number should also be used by the client while sending the datagram packet to the server. The method throws a *SocketException* if the socket could not be created.
2. The next step is to create a datagram packet of the given length, into which the received data will be stored.

   ```
   DatagramPacket dp = new DatagramPacket(arr,1024);
   ```

   This statement creates a datagram packet *dp*, of length 1024 whose contents are stored into the byte array *arr*.
3. The third step is to receive the data from the given datagram socket and the port number. The data received is stored into the byte array *arr*. The *receive()* method is used to receive a datagram over a datagram socket:

   ```
   public void receive(DatagramPacket p)throws IOException
   ```

   The method throws an IOException if an IO error is generated.
4. The last step is to close the datagram socket so that no more datagram packets can be received over this socket.

   ```
   ds.close();
   ```

14.5 JDBC

14.5.1 JDBC API and Architecture

JDBC (Java Database Connectivity) is an API, (application programming interface), used to connect a java application to a wide variety of databases. This API has certain methods and interfaces available in the *java.sql and javax.sql* package, which helps the developer to do the following:

- Establish connection with a database.
- Create and execute sql statements.

- View and alter the database results.
- Insert entries into a database.

A JDBC Driver on the other hand, is a program which lets us connect to various heterogeneous databases. It basically gives an implementation for all the methods defined in the JDBC API.

Following are the classes and the interfaces available in the JDBC API defined in the java. sql package:

1. ***DriverManager***: is a class which maintains a registered list of JDBC drivers. On an incoming request of a connection, the *DriverManager* class matches the appropriate driver to specific databases for a successful connectivity of a java application with a database.
2. **Driver**: is an interface which every jdbc driver needs to implement to connect to a data source. The *DriverManager* class uses the *Driver* interface, in turn, to load a specific driver for connecting to a database.
3. **Connection**: is an interface required to be implemented to establish a connection with the database. The Connection object contains the connection string for a specific database or a data source.
4. **Statement**: is defined as an interface in java. Its method enables one to execute or submit SQL statements to the database server.
5. **ResultSet**: is an interface whose objects are capable of holding results from a database. These results are derived from executing a SQL query using the methods of *Statement* interface. The results in this object are stored in form of rows and columns.
6. **PreparedStatement**: is an interface extending the Statement interface. It is used to hold precompiled and parameterized sql queries.
7. **SQL Exception**: is a class that handles all the exceptions that occur while accessing a database.

JDBC Architecture

The JDBC architecture in general has two components:

- *JDBC API:* The java application talks directly to the JDBC API. The JDBC API, in turn, gets in touch with the JDBC Driver Manager.
- *JDBC Driver Manager:* The Driver Manager is responsible for loading the various JDBC drivers. These drivers, in turn, interact with heterogeneous databases like Oracle, MySql, SQL Server, etc., and process the queries being sent. The results are then submitted back to the java application.

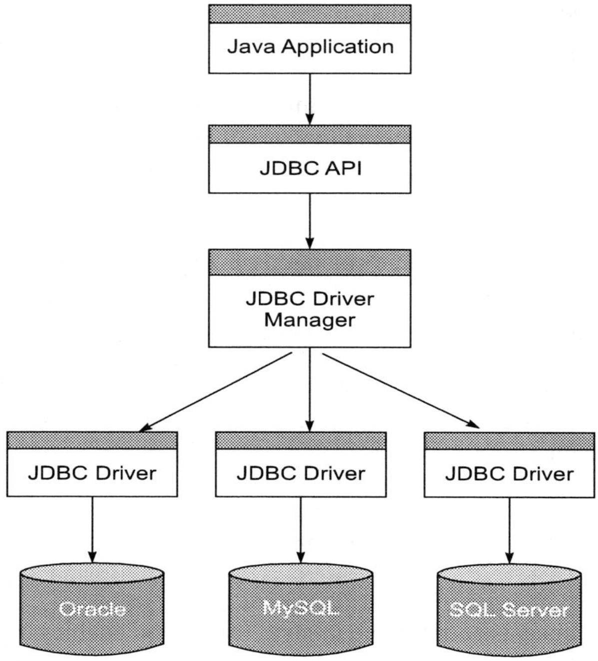

Fig. 14.1 JDBC architecture

JDBC architecture can be designed by two approaches:

- *Two-tier architecture:* Herein, the java application directly interacts with a data source/ database using a JDBC Driver. The database can be available on the same machine or on a remote machine. The machine on which the java application runs is treated as a client machine whereas the machine on which the database resides is called the server machine. The client and the server send and receive data using this two-tier architecture.

  Normally, the database server contains data in the form of relational tables.

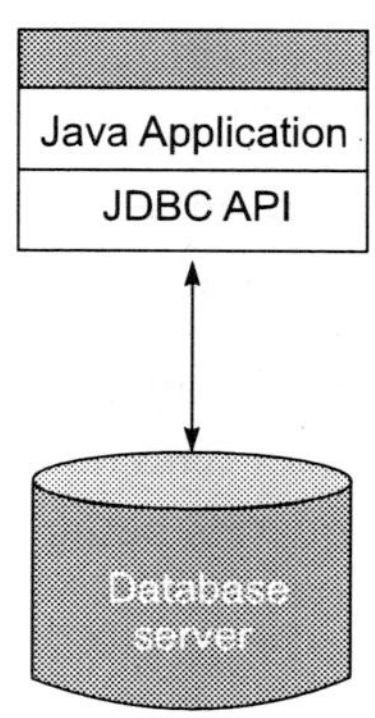

Fig. 14.2 Two-tier JDBC architecture

- *Three-tier architecture:* The java application here, interacts with the database server via a middle-tier layer. The client application submits its queries to the middle tier layer. This layer further talks to the database server, processes the query and sends back the result to the middle-tier. The middle-tier then sends the result to the client.

  Using a middle-tier layer in between a client and server increases the response time of the server but also results in better maintainability and scalability.

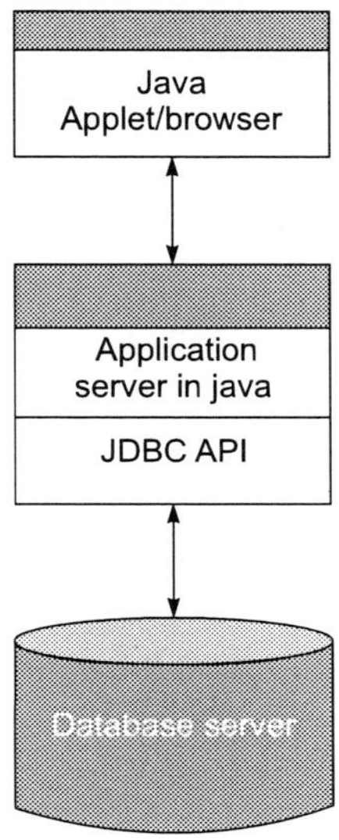

Fig. 14.3 Three-tier JDBC architecture

14.5.2 JDBC Drivers

As discussed above, a JDBC driver is a program that can be used to access heterogeneous databases. JDBC drivers are basically third party programs which implement the interfaces of JDBC API. All these third party drivers have to essentially implement the *java.sql.Driver* interface for successful connectivity between the java application and the databases.

JDBC drivers can be categorized into four types:

- **Type 1 Driver/JDBC-ODBC Bridge**

  This type of driver uses a JDBC-ODBC bridge to connect to the database. As this driver was one of the first JDBC drivers to be implemented, it used the existing ODBC connectivity. ODBC stands for open database connectivity and was used to connect to any database. The JDBC calls from the java application were converted to ODBC calls and ODBC, in turn, connected with the database to perform query operations. This driver is generally used for experimental purposes now.

Advantages

1. As the ODBC drivers were already existing, it incurred less cost.
2. The ODBC driver could connect to any database as it provided open database connectivity.

Disadvantages

1. The usage of this driver involved a performance issue because of the ODBC Bridge in between. There was no direct interaction of the java application with the database.
2. As the ODBC driver was not written in java, it was not portable.
3. It required installing the ODBC driver on the client machine.
4. This driver was not suitable for web applications.

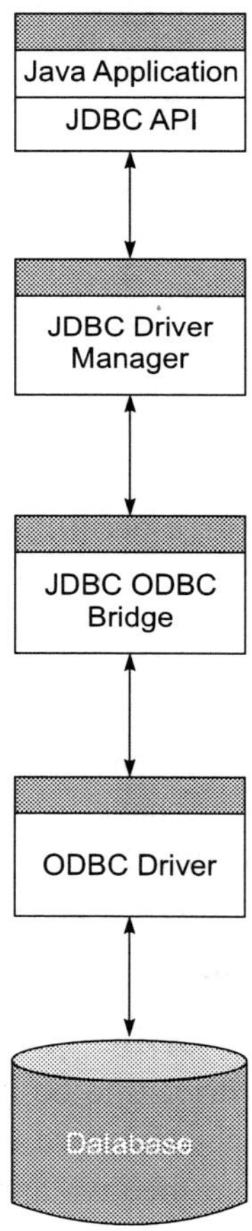

Fig. 14.4 Type 1 driver

- **Type 2 Driver/Native API driver**

  This type of driver converts the JDBC calls from a java application into native API calls written in C/C++. These native API calls are database specific. Using a Type 2 Driver, requires the native API's to be installed on the client machine. This means, to connect to an Oracle database, the oracle native API driver must be installed on the client machine.

  Advantages

  1. The performance issue faced in Type 1 Driver because of JDBC-ODBC Bridge was taken care of, in this driver.

  Disadvantages

  1. Type 2 drivers were partly written in java, hence no portability.
  2. Connecting to different databases, required native API's to be installed on the client machine first.
  3. In case of a change in a database, the native API's also had to be changed.

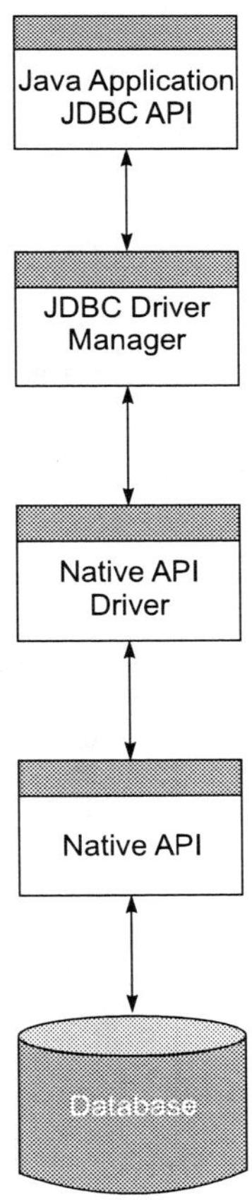

Fig. 14.5 Type 2 driver

- **Type 3 Driver/Network Protocol Driver**

  Here, the java application accesses the database by using a three-tier architecture. The JDBC calls are first sent to the middle level application server using socket communication. The application server then submits these calls as per the specific database. The middle level application server can, in turn, use Type 1, 2 or 4 drivers. The biggest advantage of using this driver is it can connect to multiple databases.

  Advantages

  1. Individual installation of any type is not required on the client machine.
  2. As the driver is completely written in java, portability is not an issue.
  3. The middle-tier application server also provides features like caching to improve the performance.
  4. A single driver is able to provide connectivity to multiple databases.
  5. Suitable for web applications.

  Disadvantages

  1. It requires installation and maintenance of an application server.

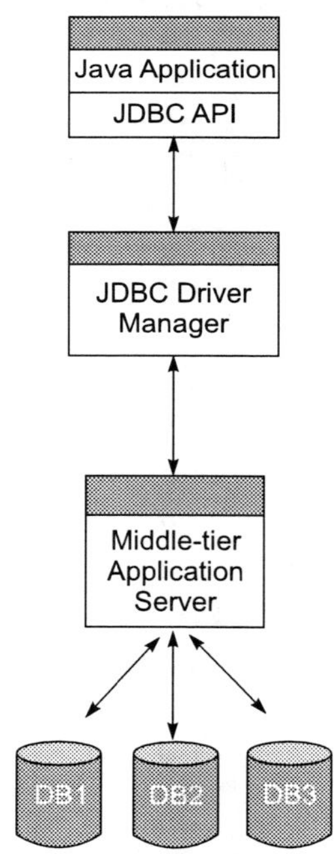

Fig. 14.6 Type 3 driver

- **Type 4 Driver/Database Protocol Driver**

  This type of driver aids the java application to directly interact with the database. It does not use any intermediate layer in between for the interaction.

Advantages

1. Purely written in java, therefore portable and platform independent.
2. Suitable for web applications.
3. Additional installation of any type on the client machine not required.

Disadvantages

1. Separate drivers are needed to connect to different databases.

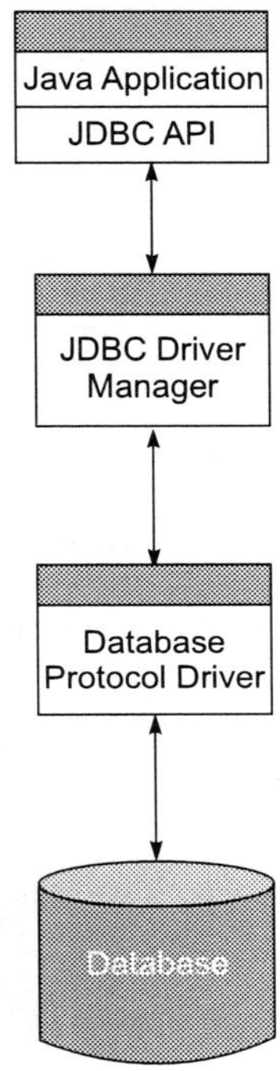

Fig. 14.7 Type 4 driver

14.5.3 Installing MySql

A java application can connect to a variety of databases such as Oracle, MySql, Sql Server, etc., to retrieve or post data to the server. SQL, structured query language, is used to query these databases. The data in a relational table is in the form of rows and columns. Relational tables can be created and manipulated using the CREATE, SELECT, INSERT, UPDATE AND DELETE statements.

This section focuses on installing the MySql database and using it as a back end to connect to a java application.

Following are the steps to install MySql service on a Windows 8 machine:

1. Check the configuration of your machine as to, if it is a 32-bit or 64-bit machine by right clicking on *This PC*. Go to properties and then check *System type* under the *System* section.

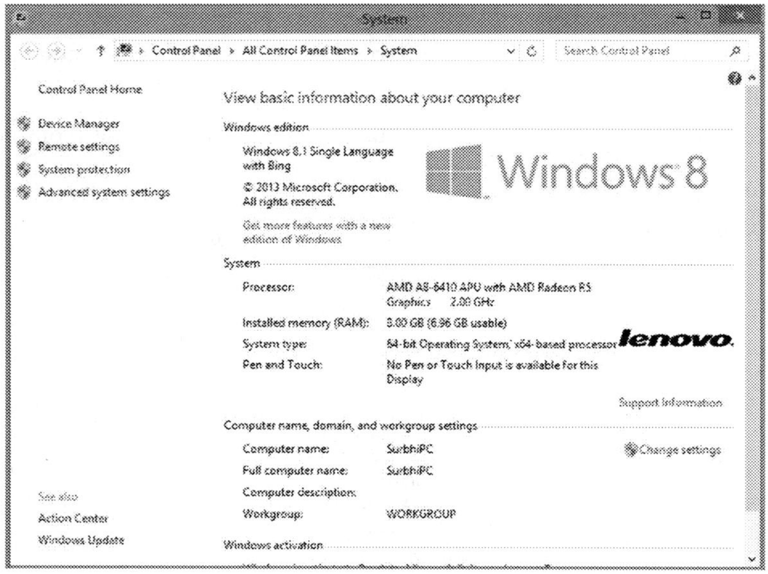

Fig. 14.8

2. Click on the link, http://dev.mysql.com/downloads/mysql/, to install MySql for your system type. Your system type can be x86 32 bit or x86 64 bit which denotes a 32-bit operating system and a 64-bit operating system respectively. According to the system type, download the corresponding version of MySql.

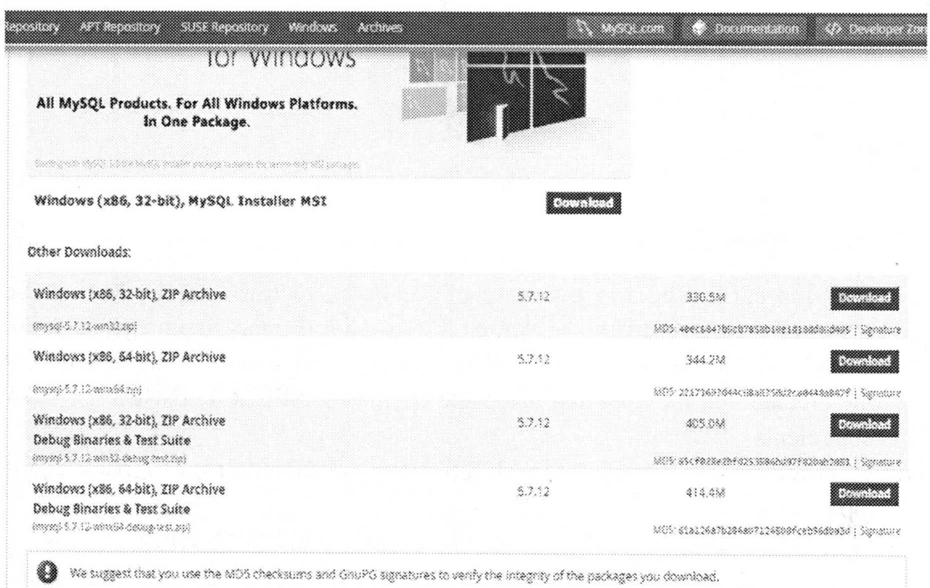

Fig. 14.9

3. Next step is to set the path for MySql. Right click on *This PC* and go to properties. Now move to Advanced system settings->Environment variables. Under this, edit the already set Path variable and append the MySql path till bin, to the value field. Don't forget to end the path variable value with a semicolon.

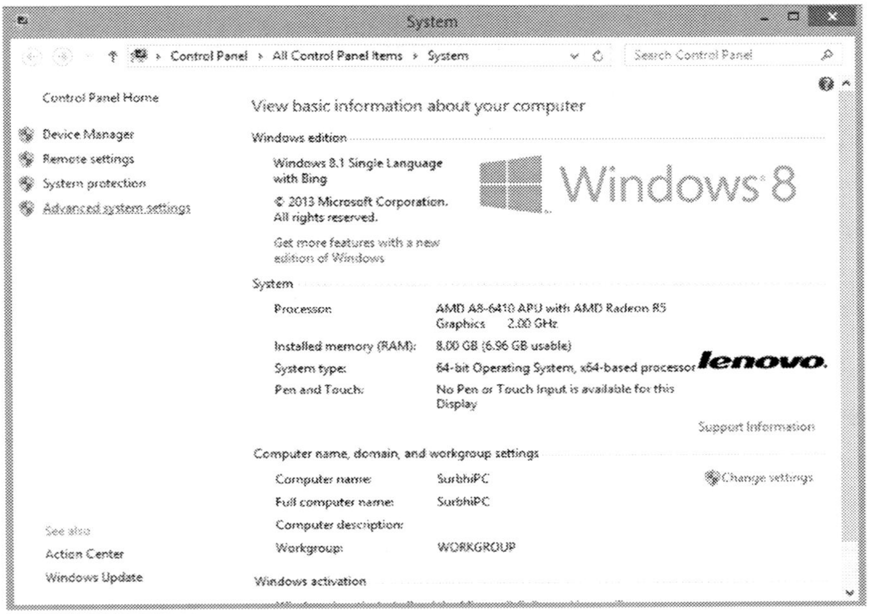

Fig. 14.10

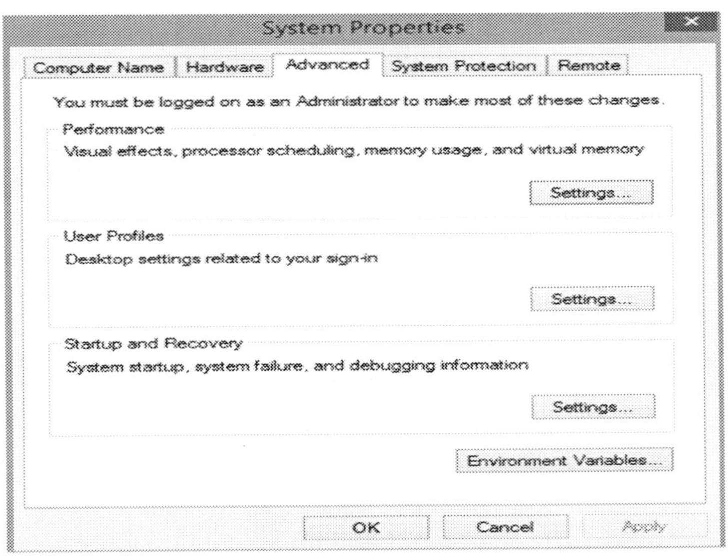

Fig. 14.11

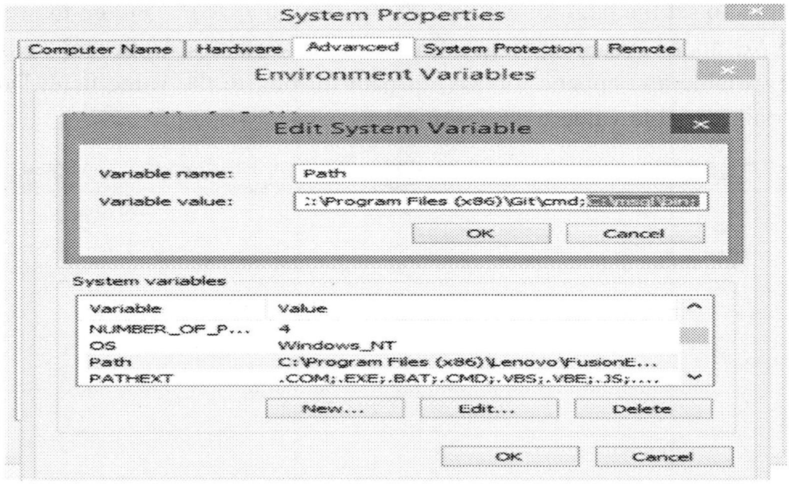

Fig 14.12

4. Now open your terminal and execute the following command:

   mysqld --install

   This will install the Mysql service on your machine.
5. Next, go to services.msc and start the MySql service.

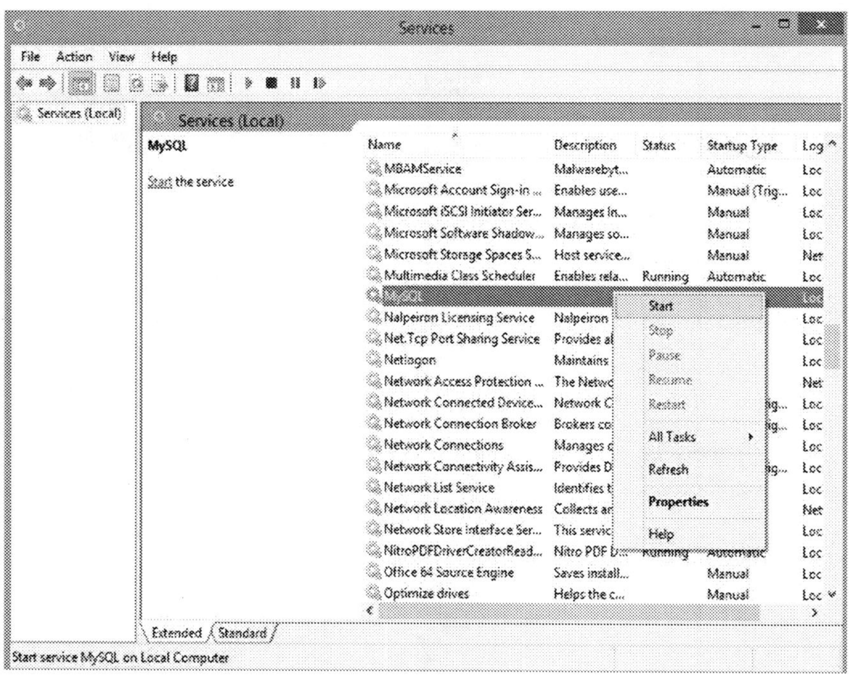

Fig. 14.13

6. Issue the following command on the terminal:

   mysql -u root –p

   This command lets you enter the password for using the MySql service. You can also set your own password by using the following command:

   mysqladmin –u root newpassword

7. Now, the service is ready to be used. SQL statements can be used on the terminal to create a database or a table. Also statements like INSERT, DELETE and UPDATE can be used to manipulate the entries of a table.

14.5.4 Database Connectivity

Now that you have a clear idea about a java application and a database, let us learn how to connect the two of them. Most of the applications today, involve an interface interacting with databases to fetch or post some data. Take for example, the login page for facebook. It asks you your username and password and you submit your response. On submitting the response, a call to the database server is being made wherein an authentication check is done against the username and password entered, to the username and password stored in the database. If there is a valid match, login is successful else login fails.

This section will teach you about connecting a java application with the MySql database.

Following are the steps to connect a java application with a database:

1. *Register the appropriate driver to connect to the database.*

   As we all are aware, JDBC drivers are required to connect a java application with a database, the first step in establishing this connection is to load and register the JDBC driver compatible with the database. This is done by using the *forName()* method belonging to the class *Class*.

   ```
   public static Class<?> forName(String className) throws
   ClassNotFoundException
   ```

   There exist classes for each of the drivers that are to be registered with a java application. This method takes as a parameter the Driver class/interface name as a string object. It also throws a *ClassNotFoundException* in case the application fails to load or register the given driver.

2. *Create a connection with the database.*

   The next step is to create a connection to the desired database for which the *getConnection()* method in the *DriverManager* interface can be used:

   ```
   public static Connection getConnection(String url)throws SQLException
   ```

   This static method creates a connection with the given url of the database and returns a Connection object.

```
public static Connection getConnection(String url,String name,String
password)  throws SQLException
```

This static method establishes a connection with the given url of the database using the mentioned username and password returning a Connection object.

MySql uses the latter version of the method as it requires a username and password to connect to the database. As the method is marked as static, hence invoked upon the class name. This method throws *SQLException* in case the connection is not established.

3. *Create a statement*

   A Statement needs to be created to submit SQL queries to the database server. This can be done using the *createStatement()* method present in the Connection interface:

   ```
   public Statement createStatement()
   ```

   The method returns a Statement object which can be used to submit sql queries for this database.

4. *Execute SQL statements*

   The subsequent step is executing the sql queries to interact with the database. It requires using the following methods from the Statement class.

   ```
   ResultSet executeQuery(String sql)
   ```

   This version of the method is used to execute only SELECT queries which helps retrieving data from the database. It returns a ResultSet object which contains data in form of rows and columns.

   ```
   int executeUpdate(String sql)
   ```

   This version is capable of executing INSERT, UPDATE and DELETE statements which helps in updating or modifying a database. It returns an integer value indicating the number of rows affected after the sql operation.

   ```
   boolean execute(String sql)
   ```

   This method can be used to execute any type of sql statements. A true value from the method signifies that a *ResultSet* object was returned from the query whereas a false value indicates an integer value was returned, depicting the number of rows affected after the sql query operation.

   All these methods throw an exception of type *SQLException* in case a database error comes up while establishing a connection with the database.

5. *Traversing the ResultSet*

   Once we have the results in a ResultSet object, we can traverse these values using the *next()* method of the ResultSet interface:

```
boolean next() throws SQLException
```

The *getString()* method is used to get the data out from this *ResultSet* object.

```
String getString(int columnIndex)
```

Returns the column with the given index from the current row in this ResultSet object.

```
String getString(String columnLabel)
```

Returns the column with the given label from the current row in this ResultSet object.

6. *Close the connection.*

   The last step is to close the connection so that no more interactions can be done with the database using this connection.

   The next program uses the database *mydb* and table *emp* to demonstrate database connectivity.

```
import java.sql.*;

public class ConnectivityDemo {

  public static void main(String[] args) throws Exception {
        //1. Registering the MySql Driver
        Class.forName("com.mysql.jdbc.Driver");
        //2. Establishing Connection
        Connection conn = DriverManager.getConnection(
        "jdbc:mysql://localhost:3306/mydb", "root", "root");
        //3. Creating Statement
        Statement stat = conn.createStatement();
        //4. Executing Query
        ResultSet rs = stat.executeQuery("Select * from emp");
        //5. Traversing through ResultSet
        while (rs.next()) {
               System.out.println("Id:" + rs.getString("Id") + " " +
               "Name:"+ rs.getString("Name"));
        }
//6. Closing the connection
        conn.close();
     }

}
```

Output:

```
Id:1 Name:Jane Doe
Id:2 Name: Kurt Weller
```

Notice the string in the *forName()* method:

```
Class.forName("com.mysql.jdbc.Driver");
```

The method loads and registers the driver for MySql which is present in com.mysql.jdbc. Driver class.

The *getConnection()* method accepts the url to the database *mydb* (present on the local computer) with the username and password as *root*.

The *createStatement()* method prepares a *Statement* object *stat*, with the help of which you will be able to execute and submit sql queries to the database server.

The *executeQuery()* method executes the given query and stores the result in the form of rows and columns in the *ResultSet* object.

Using a while loop, this *ResultSet* object *rs,* can be traversed through, employing the *next()* method of the ResultSet class.

The *getString()* method returns the value stored in the database, corresponding to the string name passed.

Note: To establish database connectivity with MySql, mysql connector jar should also be put on the class path before execution.

Using PreparedStatement

PreparedStatement is an interface that inherits the Statement interface. Its object is used to hold sql queries that are precompiled and can be executed multiple times. The *prepareStatement()* method in the *Connection* interface is used to construct parameterized sql queries which are stored in a *PreparedStatement* object. The parameter values sent to the query are depicted by a ? and each parameter index starts from 1. The *setXXX()* method binds the parameter names with the values.

Following is an example showing the use of *PreparedStatement* interface.

```
import java.sql.*;

public class ConnectivityDemo {

    public static void main(String[] args) throws Exception {
        // 1. Registering the Sql Driver
        Class.forName("com.mysql.jdbc.Driver");
        // 2. Establishing Connection
        Connection conn = DriverManager.getConnection(
            "jdbc:mysql://localhost:3306/mydb", "root","root");
        // 3. Creating PreparedStatement for executing parameterized
        //queries
        PreparedStatement stat = conn.prepareStatement("update emp set
        id=? Where name=?");
        // 4. Supplying values to query parameters
        stat.setInt(1, 3);
        stat.setString(2, "Jane Doe");
        // 5. Executing Query
        stat.executeUpdate();
```

```
            // 6. Closing the connection
            conn.close();
      }
}
```

The above example updates the table *emp* and sets the id of *Jane Doe* to *3*. The ? in the sql query depicts that the value to the parameters *id* and *name* will be bound by the *setXXX()* method. The *setXXX()* method takes up two parameters where the former indicates the parameter index and the latter specifies the value to be bound to this parameter. The *setInt()* method binds the value 3 to the first parameter of the given sql query, *id*. And the *setString()* method binds the value *Jane Doe* to the second parameter, *name*. Hence, the sql query takes up the following form:

```
update emp set id=3 Where name=Jane Doe
```

The *executeUpdate()* method executes the query held in the *stat* object and updates the table *emp*.

Statement vs PreparedStatement

Table 14.4

Statement	PreparedStatement
Can execute static sql statements.	Can execute sql statements at runtime as well.
Cannot accept parameters to a sql query at run time.	Can accept parameters to a query at runtime.
Sql queries executed using Statement object are slower as compared to PreparedStatement.	Sql queries executed using PreparedStatement object are faster as compared to Statement.
Appropriate for executing DDL commands like CREATE, DROP, ALTER.	Appropriate for executing DML commands like SELECT, INSERT, DELETE statements.
Sql statements build using Statement are less readable.	Sql statements build using PreparedStatement are more readable.

14.6 SERVLETS

14.6.1 Introduction

A web application is an application that runs on the web. It is launched from a browser which acts as a client that gives a request to the server. The server, on the other hand, makes a provision to process this request and send back the response to the client.

Servers are of two kinds: *Application Server* and *Web Server.*

An *Application Server* is a server that can handle both static and dynamic content. It uses a variety of protocols including HTTP. Some of the examples of an application server is *JBoss, WebLogic, GlassFish*, etc.

A *Web Server*, on the other hand, can handle only static content and delegates the processing of dynamic data to other *helper applications*. It is limited to use only the HTTP protocol. Example, *Tomcat server*.

When a *request* goes from a client to the web server, the server first checks, if it can handle the request or not. If it can, it generates the corresponding response in form of a HTML document and sends it to the client.

If the web server cannot handle the incoming request, it looks for other *helper applications* to handle the arriving requests. One of the examples of such helper applications is Servlets. A Servlet is a java application which executes inside the address space of the server. Web container or a Servlet container, (a component of the web server) is actually responsible for locating the requested servlet.

14.6.2 Servlets vs CGI

Prior to servlets, we had the CGI technology, Common Gateway Interface, to establish communication between a client and a server. Traditionally, servers forwarded the incoming requests from clients to other applications like CGI, capable of handling dynamic data. Herein, CGI created a new process for each request. The disadvantages of using CGI technology are:

1. The response time from the server increases with the increasing number of requests.
2. Creating a new process for each request takes up lot of address space and is expensive.
3. It is platform dependent as the service is written in C, C++ languages.

On the contrary, using the servlet technology yields a better performance. When the web server forwards the arriving requests to the servlet, it creates a new thread for handling each request in the address space of the server. Also, the servlet technology is written in java, hence it is platform independent.

14.6.3 Types of Requests

HTTP, Hyper Text Transfer Protocol, is a protocol used to initiate communication between a client and a server. Such communications are held using a request response structure as we discussed earlier. The requests from a client can be of two types:

- **GET:** A GET request is mainly issued to retrieve or get some information from the server. Example, getting all the employees working in department "Finance". Such information parameters are appended as a query string in the URL. These kind of requests can be cached and bookmarked. The parameters passed remain in the browsing history.

- **POST:** A POST request on the other hand, is used to post or submit a form data to the server. Example, you submitting your login details to the server is also a POST request.

These type of requests are neither cached nor bookmarked. The data submitted does not remain in the browsing history.

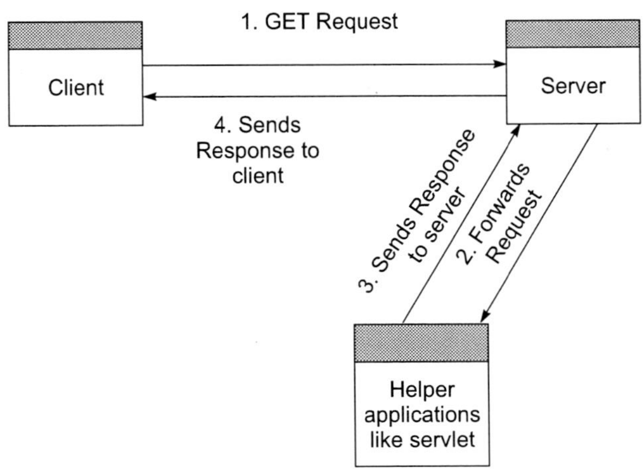

Fig. 14.14 GET request

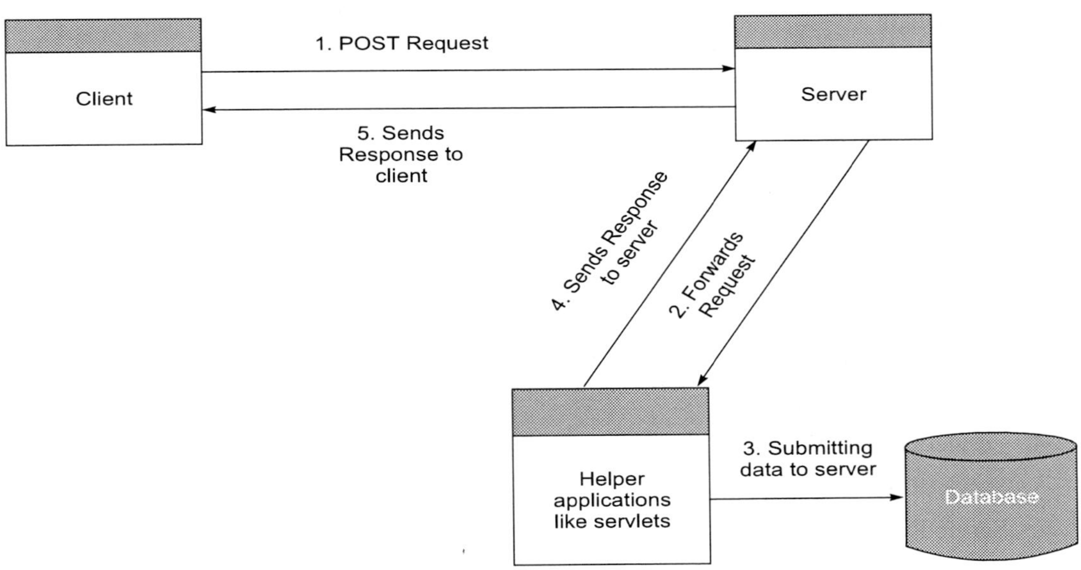

Fig. 14.15 POST request

The HTML form tag has an attribute *method*. If the method attribute's value is POST, it signifies a POST request else it is a GET request. *By default every request is a GET request.*

14.6.4 Life Cycle of Servlets

To begin with the servlet life cycle, let us first have a look at the packages, the Servlet API provides us. Two most important packages the Servlet API comprises are *javax.servlet* and *javax.servlet.http.*

Classes and interfaces under these packages are listed below:

Interfaces in the javax.servlet package

1. Servlet
2. ServletRequest
3. ServletResponse
4. RequestDispatcher
5. ServletConfig
6. ServletContext
7. SingleThreadModel
8. Filter
9. FilterConfig
10. FilterChain
11. ServletRequestListener
12. ServletRequestAttributeListener
13. ServletContextListener
14. ServletContextAttributeListener

Classes in javax.servlet package

1. GenericServlet
2. ServletInputStream
3. ServletOutputStream
4. ServletRequestWrapper
5. ServletResponseWrapper
6. ServletRequestEvent
7. ServletContextEvent
8. ServletRequestAttributeEvent
9. ServletContextAttributeEvent
10. ServletException
11. UnavailableException

Interfaces in javax.servlet.http package

1. HttpServletRequest
2. HttpServletResponse
3. HttpSession
4. HttpSessionListener
5. HttpSessionAttributeListener
6. HttpSessionBindingListener
7. HttpSessionActivationListener

Classes in javax.servlet.http package

1. HttpServlet
2. Cookie
3. HttpServletRequestWrapper
4. HttpServletResponseWrapper
5. HttpSessionEvent
6. HttpSessionBindingEvent

The classes and interfaces the chapter will be focusing upon are: *Servlet, GenericServlet, HttpServlet, HttpServletRequest, HttpServletResponse, ServletException*.

Every servlet class you create has to subclass the *HttpServlet* class. The interfaces and classes that come in the hierarchy of servlet creation are given below:

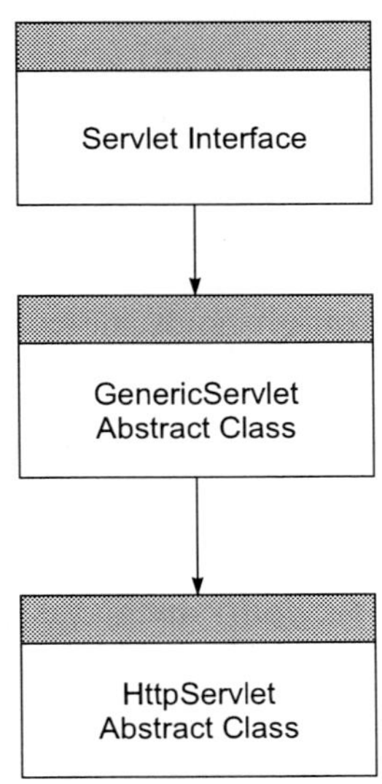

Fig. 14.16

1. *Servlet Interface*: One of the ways to create a servlet is by implementing the Servlet interface. The servlet interface has the following methods:

Table 14.5

Method	Description
public void init(ServletConfig config)	Initializes the servlet. Called by the servlet container only once.
public void service (ServletRequest request, ServletResponse response)	Services or processes the request given the client.
public void destroy()	Destroys the servlet and reclaim its memory.
public ServletConfig getServletConfig()	Gets the startup configuration of the servlet.
public String getServletInfo()	Gets the basic information of the servlet such as author, version and copyright details.

Developers who want to write their own container, implement the Servlet interface wherein they have to implement all the abstract methods of the interface.

2. *GenericServlet*: Another way to create a servlet is to extend the *GenericServlet* abstract class. This class implements all the methods of the Servlet Interface except the *service()* method. It is open to any protocol like *HTTP, FTP, SMTP etc.*
3. *HttpServlet*: This abstract class was designed to support specifically the *HTTP* protocol. The class implements all the methods of the *GenericServlet* class including the *service()* method, therefore, it is best to extend your servlet class by *HttpServlet*. The *service()* method here, can also be replaced by *doGet()* and *doPost()*, method called in case of GET and POST request respectively.

Servlets go through a life cycle that starts from its initialization and ends at its termination. Following are the life cycle methods of a servlet:

1. *init()*: The web server actually gives a call to the servlet container which further locates and loads the corresponding servlet by instantiating the servlet. Thereafter, the container invokes the *init()* method of the servlet. This method initializes a given servlet and is called only once during the life cycle of a servlet. It takes as a parameter a *ServletConfig* object and throws an exception of type *ServletException* in case the container fails to load the servlet. The *ServletConfig* object holds the configuration parameters for the servlet which the *init()* method requires to perform its initialization.

```
public void init(ServletConfig config) throws ServletException
```

The servlet is said to be in its *new state* right now.

2. *service()*: After the *init()* method, the *service()* method is invoked for each of the requests given by the client. Note that the *init()* method is invoked for the servlet, hence called only once during the life time whereas the *service()* method is called every time with an incoming request. The *service()* method accepts as a parameter *ServletRequest* and *ServletResponse* objects. The request object contains the type of request and the parameters sent by the client to the server. The response object can be used to write the response back to the client. This method throws an exception of type *ServletException* and *IOException* in case the container fails to invoke the *service()* method or write the response back to the client.

```
public void service(ServletRequest req, ServletResponse res)
     throws ServletException, IOException
```

The servlet right now is in the *alive or ready state*, running currently.

The *service()* method further invokes *doGet()* and *doPost()* method depending upon the type of request received.

```
protected void doGet(HttpServletRequest req, HttpServletResponse resp)
throws ServletException, IOException

protected void doPost(HttpServletRequest req, HttpServletResponse resp)
throws ServletException, IOException
```

Both the methods accept the *HttpServletRequest* and *HttpServletResponse* objects. *HttpRequest* object contains the information regarding the request received whereas anything that needs to be sent back to the client can be written over the *HttpResponse* object.

3. *destroy():* This method is called when the servlet is to be removed from the address space of the server, therefore, invoked only once during its life cycle.

```
public void destroy();
```

The servlet is in the *dead state* now.

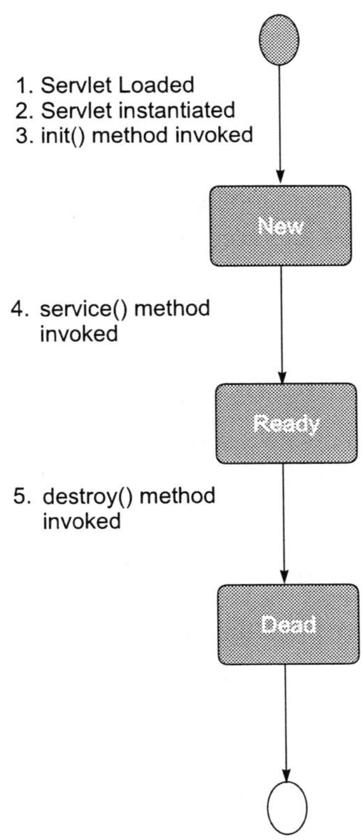

Fig. 14.17 Servlet life cycle

14.6.5 Deployment Descriptor

As we know, when a dynamic request comes to a web server, it forwards the request to a web container. The web container then locates the appropriate servlet by looking into an xml file called *web.xml*. This *web.xml* file is also called the *Deployment Descriptor* as it comprises elements that help in deploying a web application over the web. It is put under the *WEB-INF* folder. Some of its key elements are given below:

```
<web-app>
<servlet>
    <servlet-name>DemoServlet</servlet-name>
<servlet-class>pkg.DemoServlet</servlet-class>
</servlet>
<servlet-mapping>
    <servlet-name>DemoServlet</servlet-name>
    <url-pattern>/DemoPage</url-pattern>
</servlet-mapping>
</web-app>
```

Let us see the description of the above xml elements:

<web-app>: describes that the web.xml file is for the whole web application.

<servlet>: a sub-tag under the <web-app> tag which represents a specific servlet.

<servlet-name>: sub tag of <servlet> which signifies the name of the servlet.

<servlet-class>: sub tag of <servlet> which characterizes the package and the class this servlet belongs to.

<servlet-mapping>: represents the mapping of a servlet. It is required to map the external name of the servlet(visible to the end user) to the internal name used by the web application.

<url-pattern>: a sub tag of <servlet-mapping> which specifies the external name of the servlet visible to the end user.

14.6.6 Creating and Running of a Simple Servlet

This section will teach you how to create a servlet using the eclipse IDE and run it on a servlet container. We will be using the *Tomcat Server* as the container for executing servlets. So before we actually see how to create a servlet, let us first add the Tomcat Server in our list of servers.

Downloading, installing and configuring the Tomcat Server.

1. Download the Tomcat Server from the link https://tomcat.apache.org/download-60.cgi.
2. Add this server to list of servers in the Eclipse IDE. Go to Window tab->Show View->Servers. The Servers window appears. In the blank area of the Server tab, right click and go to New->Server. Now select the *Apache Tomcat v7.0 Server*. Press Next and go to the browse button to browse the Tomcat Installation Directory path to the root folder of Apache Tomcat, one step before bin. Click Finish. Tomcat server is now configured for your eclipse IDE.

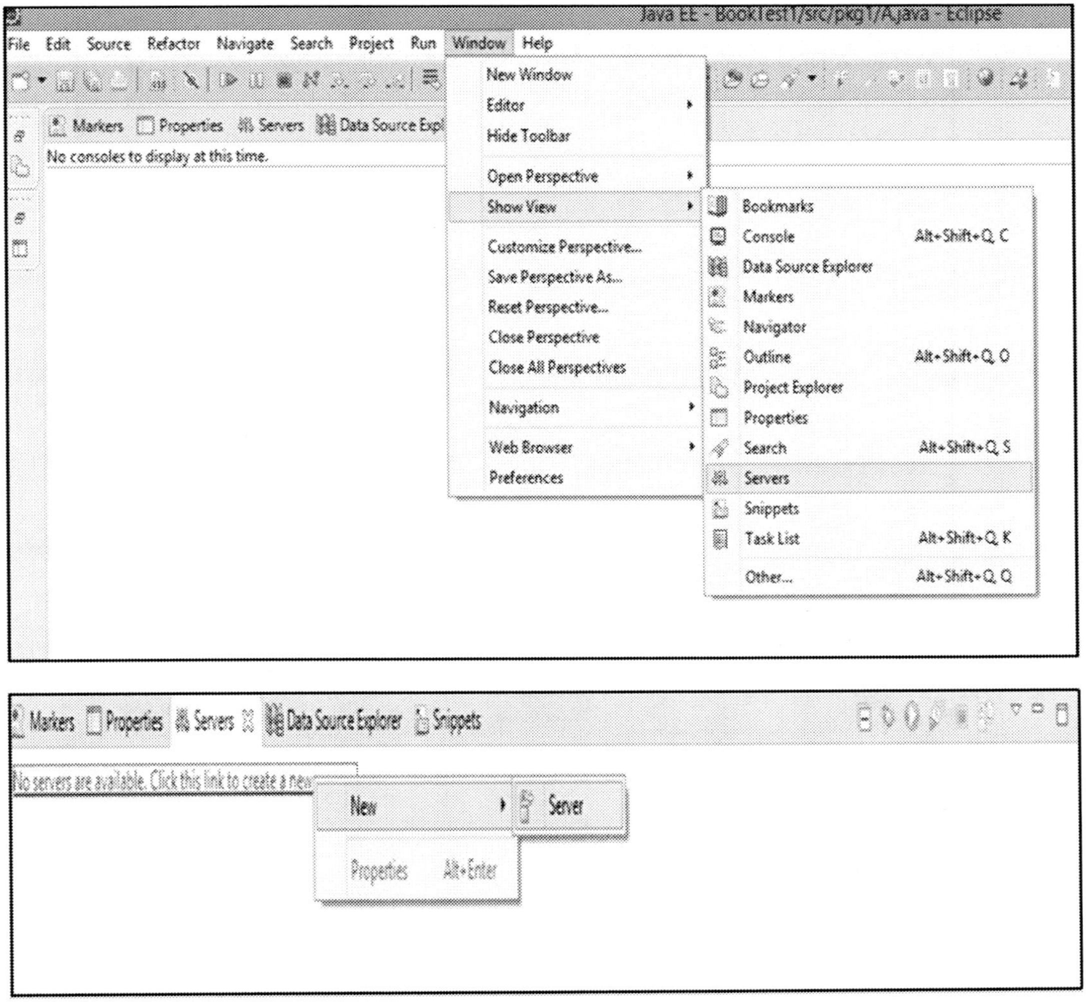
Java EE - BookTest1/src/pkg1/A.java - Eclipse
File Edit Source Refactor Navigate Search Project Run Window Help
Markers Properties Servers Data Source Expl
No consoles to display at this time.
New Window
Editor
Hide Toolbar
Open Perspective
Show View
Customize Perspective...
Save Perspective As...
Reset Perspective...
Close Perspective
Close All Perspectives
Navigation
Web Browser
Preferences
Bookmarks
Console Alt+Shift+Q, C
Data Source Explorer
Markers
Navigator
Outline Alt+Shift+Q, O
Project Explorer
Properties
Search Alt+Shift+Q, S
Servers
Snippets
Task List Alt+Shift+Q, K
Other... Alt+Shift+Q, Q
Markers Properties Servers Data Source Explorer Snippets
No servers are available. Click this link to create a new
New
Server
Properties Alt+Enter

Fig. 14.18

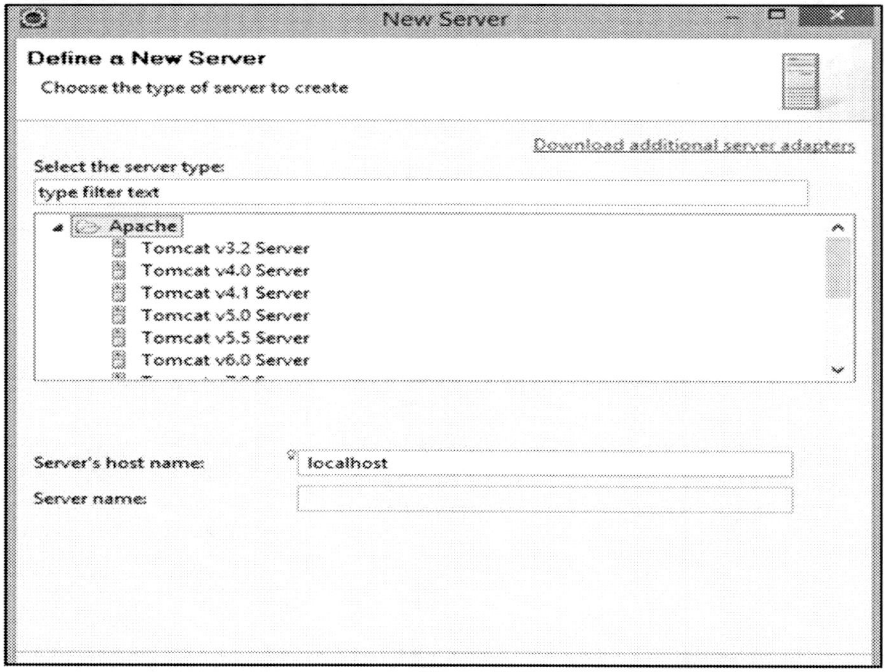
New Server
Define a New Server
Choose the type of server to create
Download additional server adapters
Select the server type:
type filter text
Apache
Tomcat v3.2 Server
Tomcat v4.0 Server
Tomcat v4.1 Server
Tomcat v5.0 Server
Tomcat v5.5 Server
Tomcat v6.0 Server
Server's host name:
localhost
Server name:

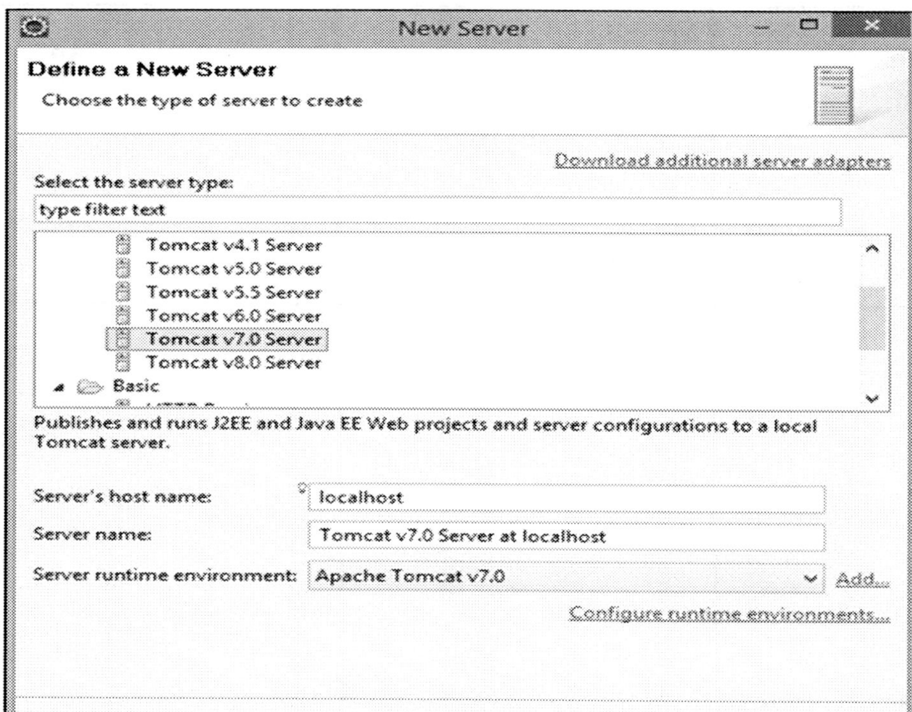
New Server
Define a New Server
Choose the type of server to create
Download additional server adapters
Select the server type:
type filter text
Tomcat v4.1 Server
Tomcat v5.0 Server
Tomcat v5.5 Server
Tomcat v6.0 Server
Tomcat v7.0 Server
Tomcat v8.0 Server
Basic
Publishes and runs J2EE and Java EE Web projects and server configurations to a local Tomcat server.
Server's host name:
localhost
Server name:
Tomcat v7.0 Server at localhost
Server runtime environment:
Apache Tomcat v7.0
Add...
Configure runtime environments...

Fig. 14.19

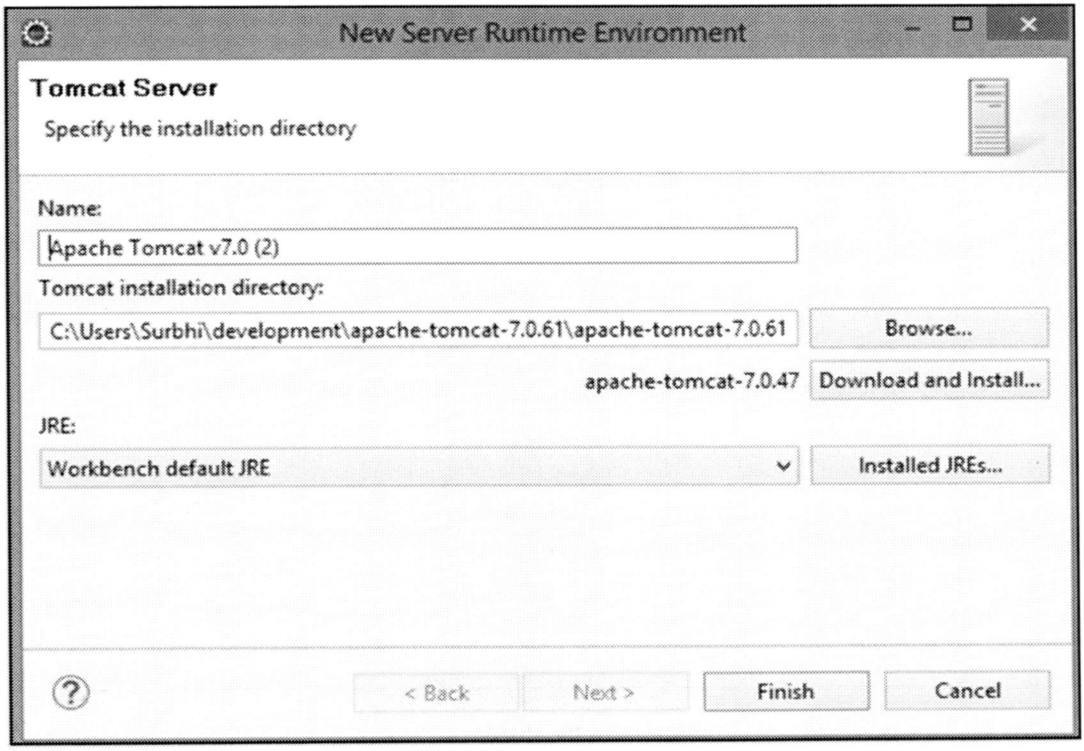

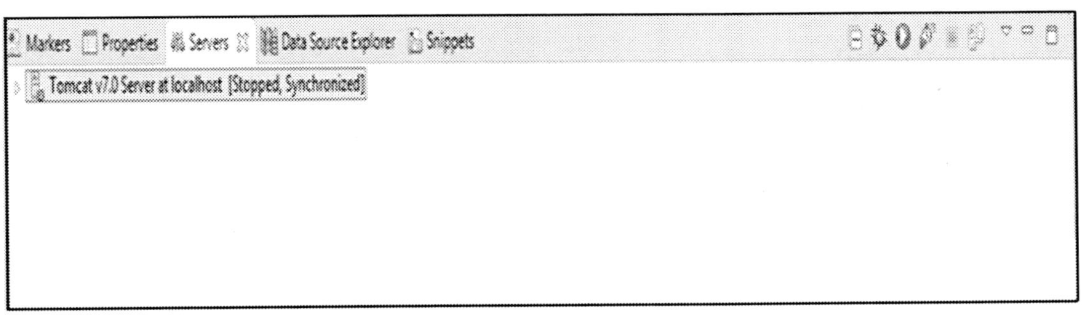

Fig. 14.20

Right click and start the Tomcat Server and your server is up and running.

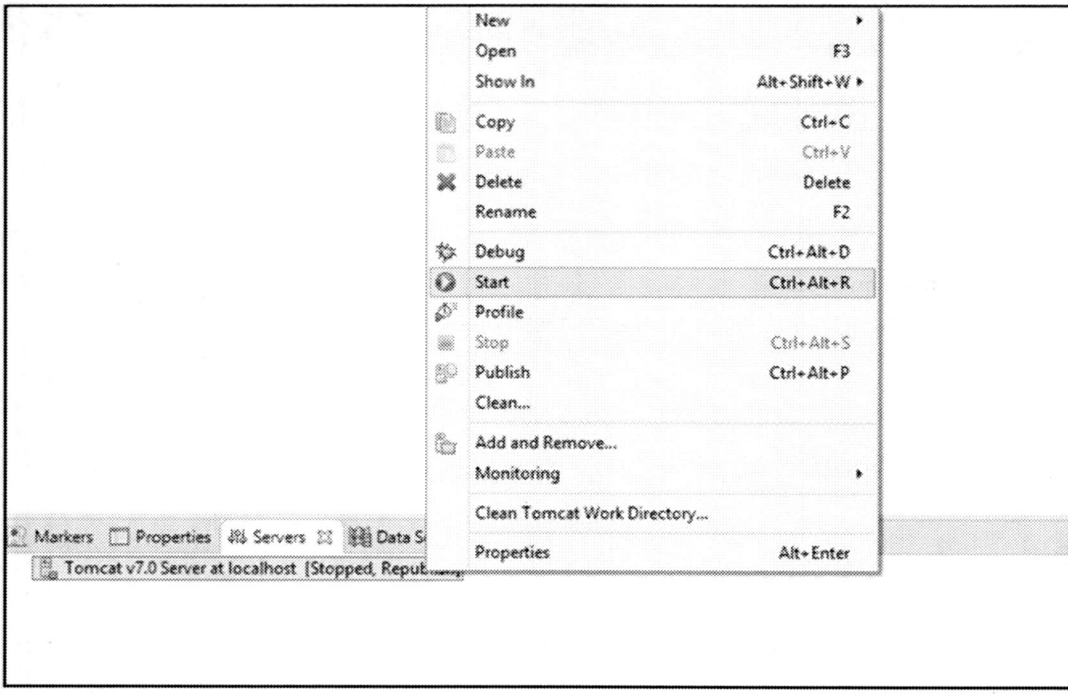

Fig. 14.21

Configuring Tomcat Server is a one-time process and it needs to be started to execute any servlets requested by the client.

Creating a Servlet

1. To create a servlet open the Eclipse IDE. Go to File->New->Dynamic Web Project. Enter the Project name, (DemoProject, in our case) and click Finish.
2. Now go to the Project Explorer and open up the project you just created. Go under Java Resources->src folder. Right click->New->Servlet.
3. A new window appears. Enter the Java Package name (optional). If you do not specify the package name, the servlet you are going to create will be put in the default package. Also specify the servlet name (DemoServlet here).

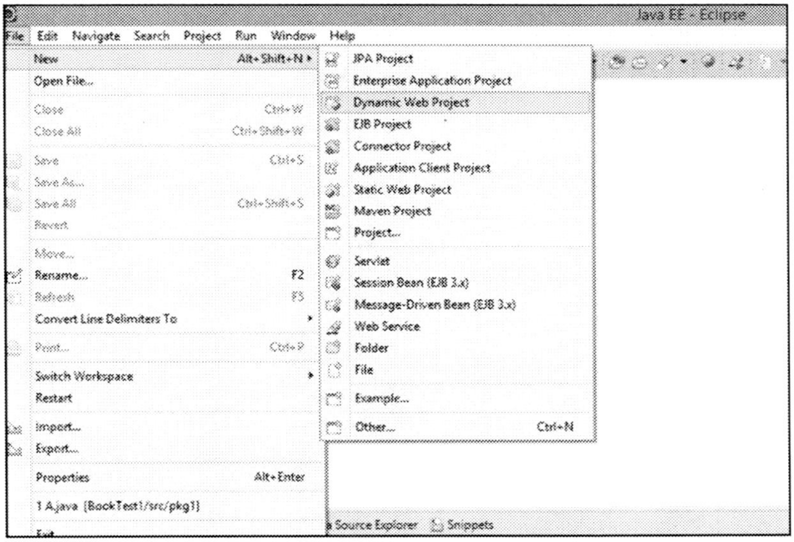
Java EE - Eclipse
File
Edit
Navigate
Search
Project
Run
Window
Help
New
Alt+Shift+N
Open File...
Close
Ctrl+W
Close All
Ctrl+Shift+W
Save
Ctrl+S
Save As...
Save All
Ctrl+Shift+S
Revert
Move...
Rename...
F2
Refresh
F5
Convert Line Delimiters To
Print...
Ctrl+P
Switch Workspace
Restart
Import...
Export...
Properties
Alt+Enter
1 A.java [BookTest1/src/pkg1]
JPA Project
Enterprise Application Project
Dynamic Web Project
EJB Project
Connector Project
Application Client Project
Static Web Project
Maven Project
Project...
Servlet
Session Bean (EJB 3.x)
Message-Driven Bean (EJB 3.x)
Web Service
Folder
File
Example...
Other...
Ctrl+N
Source Explorer
Snippets

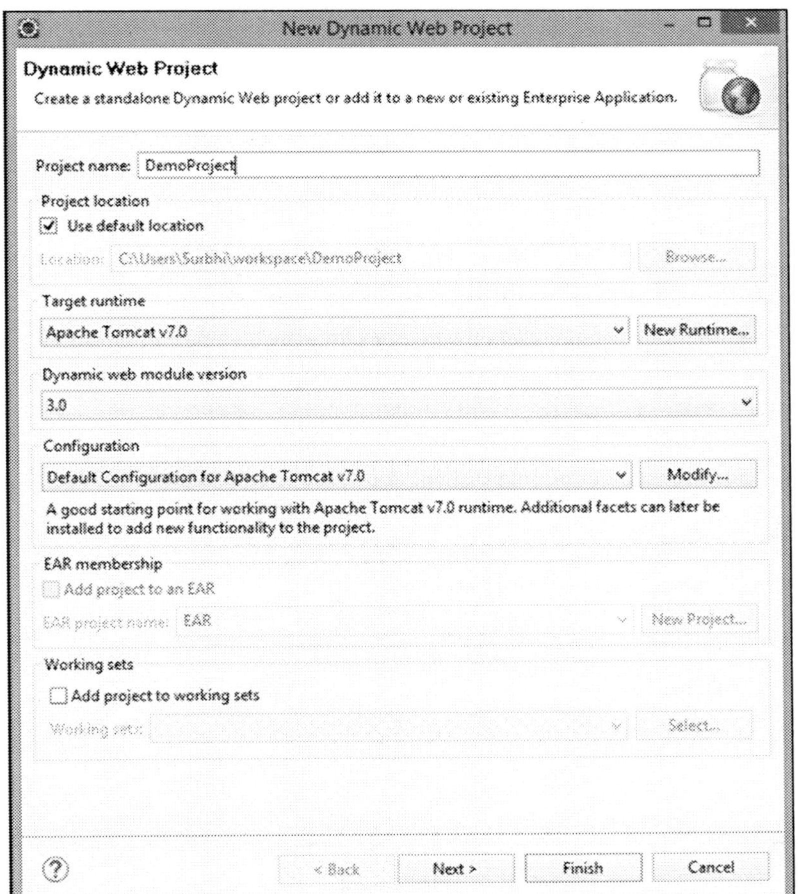
New Dynamic Web Project
Dynamic Web Project
Create a standalone Dynamic Web project or add it to a new or existing Enterprise Application.
Project name:
DemoProject
Project location
Use default location
Location:
C:\Users\Surbhi\workspace\DemoProject
Browse...
Target runtime
Apache Tomcat v7.0
New Runtime...
Dynamic web module version
3.0
Configuration
Default Configuration for Apache Tomcat v7.0
Modify...
A good starting point for working with Apache Tomcat v7.0 runtime. Additional facets can later be installed to add new functionality to the project.
EAR membership
Add project to an EAR
EAR project name:
EAR
New Project...
Working sets
Add project to working sets
Working sets:
Select...
< Back
Next >
Finish
Cancel

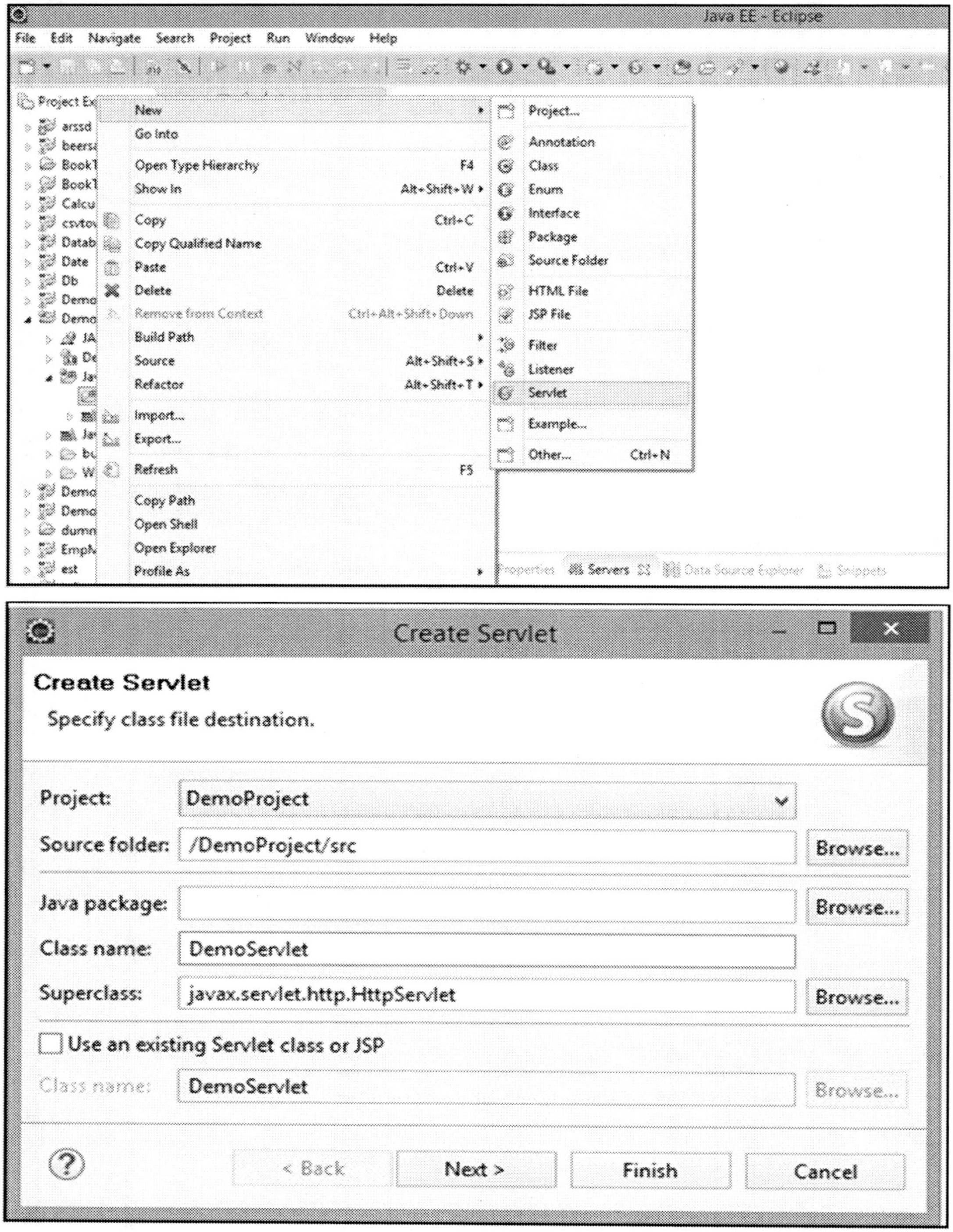
Java EE - Eclipse
File Edit Navigate Search Project Run Window Help
New
Go Into
Open Type Hierarchy F4
Show In Alt+Shift+W
Copy Ctrl+C
Copy Qualified Name
Paste Ctrl+V
Delete Delete
Remove from Context Ctrl+Alt+Shift+Down
Build Path
Source Alt+Shift+S
Refactor Alt+Shift+T
Import...
Export...
Refresh F5
Copy Path
Open Shell
Open Explorer
Profile As
Project...
Annotation
Class
Enum
Interface
Package
Source Folder
HTML File
JSP File
Filter
Listener
Servlet
Example...
Other... Ctrl+N
Create Servlet
Create Servlet
Specify class file destination.
Project: DemoProject
Source folder: /DemoProject/src Browse...
Java package: Browse...
Class name: DemoServlet
Superclass: javax.servlet.http.HttpServlet Browse...
Use an existing Servlet class or JSP
Class name: DemoServlet Browse...
< Back Next > Finish Cancel

Fig. 14.22

4. Your servlet *DemoServlet* has now been created. The next step is to download the servlet api jar and put in on the class path of the project. The packages in the servlet API packages does not come along with Java Development Kit, therefore, we need to download its jar, java archive file. This is a compressed file which contains all the packages in the servlet api needed to create servlets. Download this from the link http://mvnrepository.com/artifact/javax.servlet/javax.servlet-api/3.0.1.

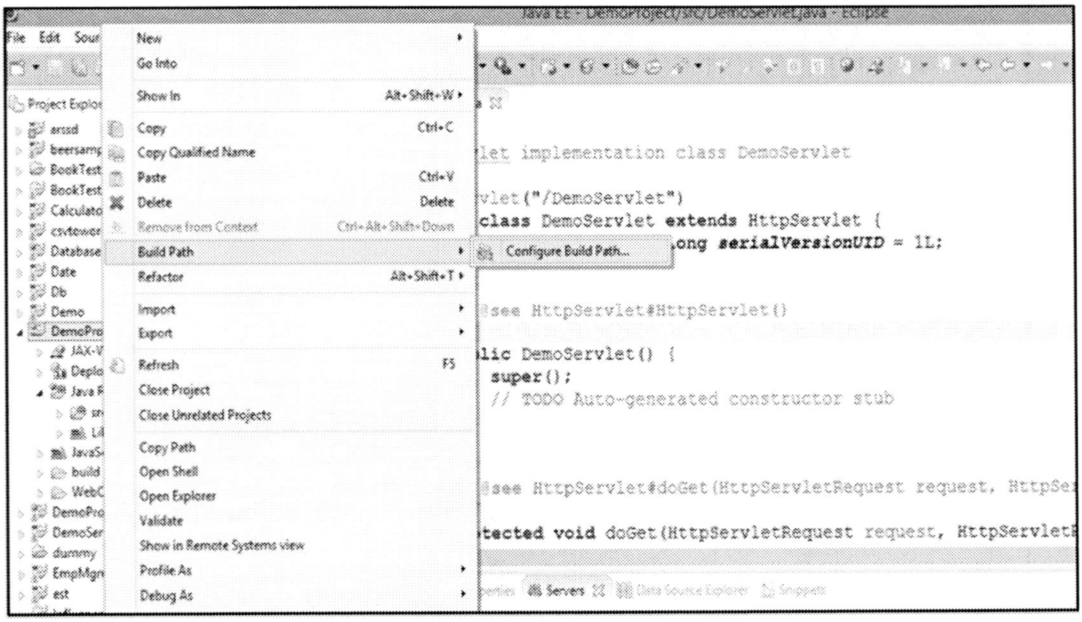

Fig. 14.23

5. This jar needs to be put on the class path now. So, right click your project, *DemoProject* and go to Build Path->Configure Build Path.
6. Now go under the Libraries head->Add External JARs. Browse the path to the downloaded servlet api and click OK. Your servlet api jar will now appear in the Project Explorer-> Libraries section.

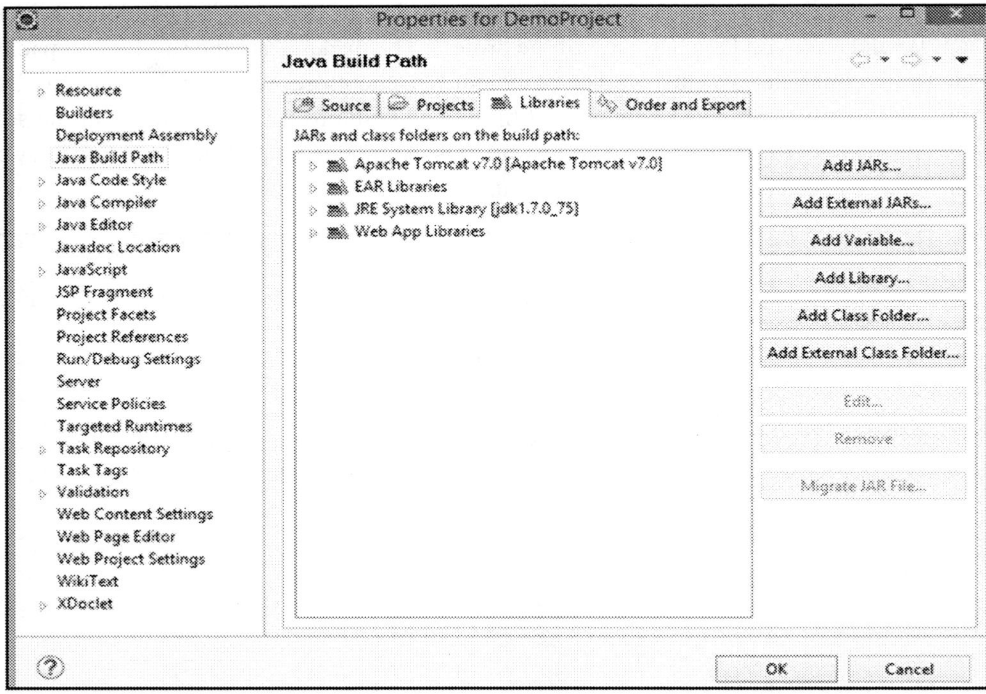
Properties for DemoProject
Java Build Path
Resource
Builders
Deployment Assembly
Java Build Path
Java Code Style
Java Compiler
Java Editor
Javadoc Location
JavaScript
JSP Fragment
Project Facets
Project References
Run/Debug Settings
Server
Service Policies
Targeted Runtimes
Task Repository
Task Tags
Validation
Web Content Settings
Web Page Editor
Web Project Settings
WikiText
XDoclet
Source
Projects
Libraries
Order and Export
JARs and class folders on the build path:
Apache Tomcat v7.0 [Apache Tomcat v7.0]
EAR Libraries
JRE System Library [jdk1.7.0_75]
Web App Libraries
Add JARs...
Add External JARs...
Add Variable...
Add Library...
Add Class Folder...
Add External Class Folder...
Edit...
Remove
Migrate JAR File...
OK
Cancel

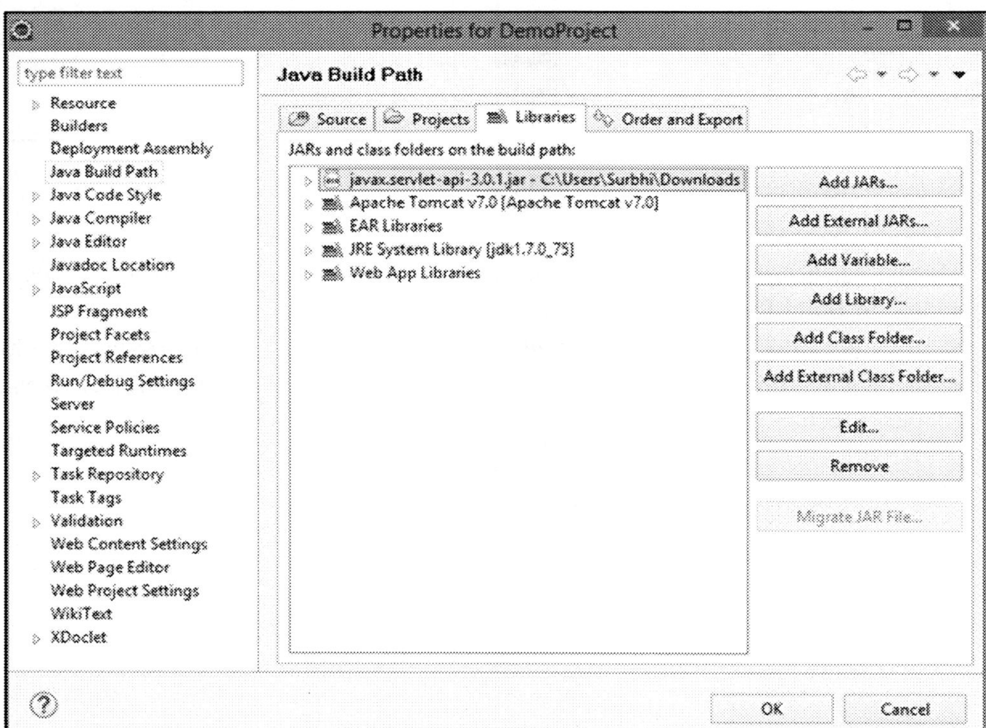
Properties for DemoProject
type filter text
Java Build Path
Resource
Builders
Deployment Assembly
Java Build Path
Java Code Style
Java Compiler
Java Editor
Javadoc Location
JavaScript
JSP Fragment
Project Facets
Project References
Run/Debug Settings
Server
Service Policies
Targeted Runtimes
Task Repository
Task Tags
Validation
Web Content Settings
Web Page Editor
Web Project Settings
WikiText
XDoclet
Source
Projects
Libraries
Order and Export
JARs and class folders on the build path:
javax.servlet-api-3.0.1.jar - C:\Users\Surbhi\Downloads
Apache Tomcat v7.0 [Apache Tomcat v7.0]
EAR Libraries
JRE System Library [jdk1.7.0_75]
Web App Libraries
Add JARs...
Add External JARs...
Add Variable...
Add Library...
Add Class Folder...
Add External Class Folder...
Edit...
Remove
Migrate JAR File...
OK
Cancel

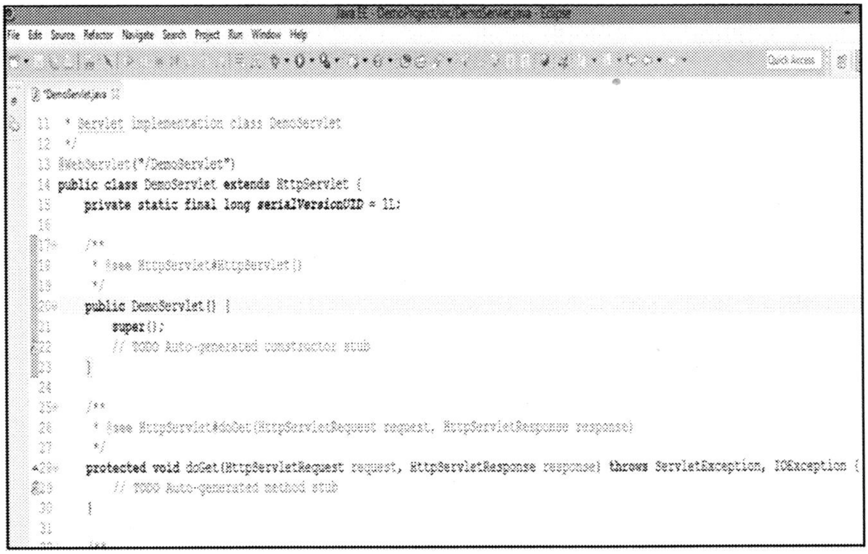

Fig. 14.24

7. Write the deployment descriptor for this servlet in the web.xml file.Note that by default, the web.xml file does not exists under the WEB-INF folder. You can generate one by right clicking the Project->Java EE Tools->Generate Deployment Descriptor.
8. As our Tomcat Server is already up and running, the next step is to deploy this created servlet, *DemoServlet* onto the Tomcat Server to start running it.
9. Right click on your project name, *DemoProject* and go to Run As->Run on Server. Go to choose an existing server and select Tomcat v7.0 Server at localhost and click Finish. This deploys your servlet to the Tomcat server.

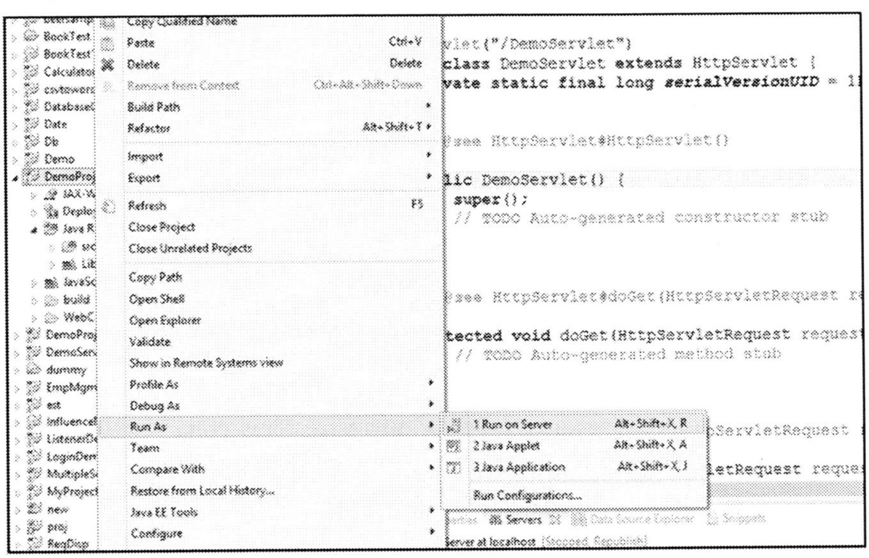

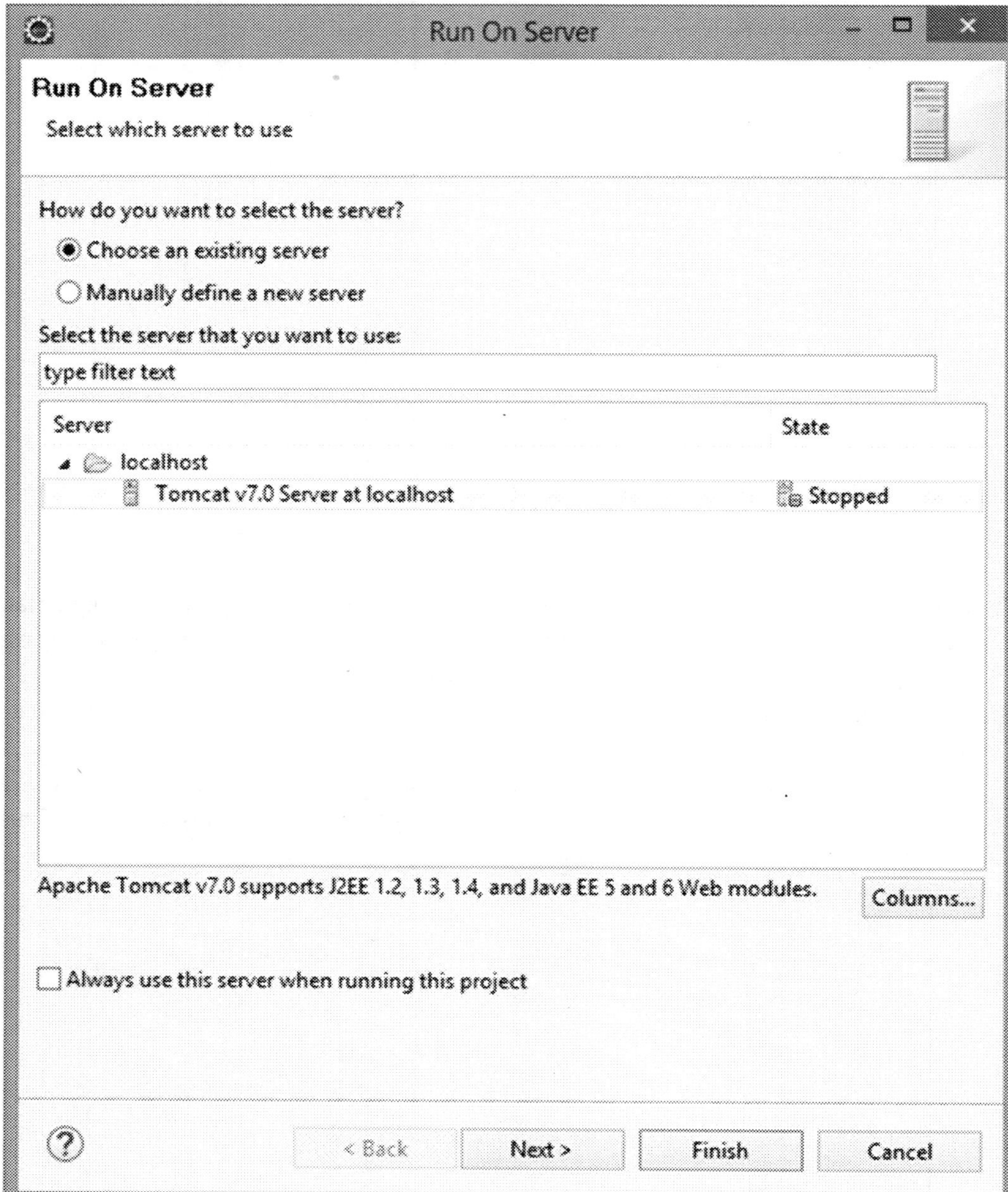

Fig 14.25

10. Deploying the servlet brings us the below 404 error. This comes up when the requested servlet has not been located. Observe the path visible in the window. The path has been given till *DemoProject* but to locate the *DemoServlet* servlet, we need to give the complete path till the servlet name.

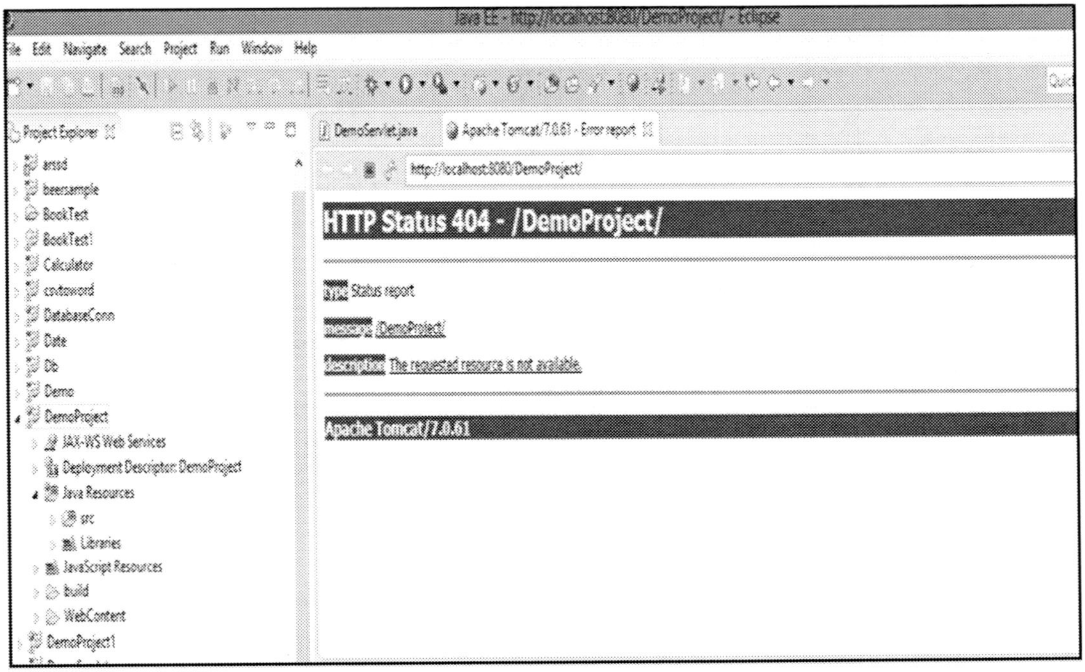

Fig. 14.26

11. Therefore, giving in the complete path in the browser deploys our servlet on the web.

Writing the first Servlet

```
import java.io.IOException;
import java.io.PrintWriter;

import javax.servlet.ServletException;
import javax.servlet.annotation.WebServlet;
import javax.servlet.http.HttpServlet;
import javax.servlet.http.HttpServletRequest;
import javax.servlet.http.HttpServletResponse;

/**
 * Servlet implementation class DemoServlet
 */
@WebServlet("/DemoServlet")
public class DemoServlet extends HttpServlet {
    private static final long serialVersionUID = 1L;

    /**
     * @see HttpServlet#HttpServlet()
     */
```

```
    public DemoServlet() {
           super();
           // TODO Auto-generated constructor stub
    }

    /**
     *    @see    HttpServlet#doGet(HttpServletRequest   request,
     HttpServletResponse
     *       response)
     */
     protected void doGet(HttpServletRequest request,
                HttpServletResponse response) throws ServletException,
    IOException {
           // TODO Auto-generated method stub
           PrintWriter out = response.getWriter(); // getting the writer
           out.println("My Demo Servlet"); // writing response on writer
           out.close(); // closing the writer
     }

    /**
     *    @see    HttpServlet#doPost(HttpServletRequest   request,
     HttpServletResponse
     *       response)
     */
    protected void doPost(HttpServletRequest request,
                HttpServletResponse response) throws ServletException,
    IOException {
           // TODO Auto-generated method stub
    }

}
```

Output:

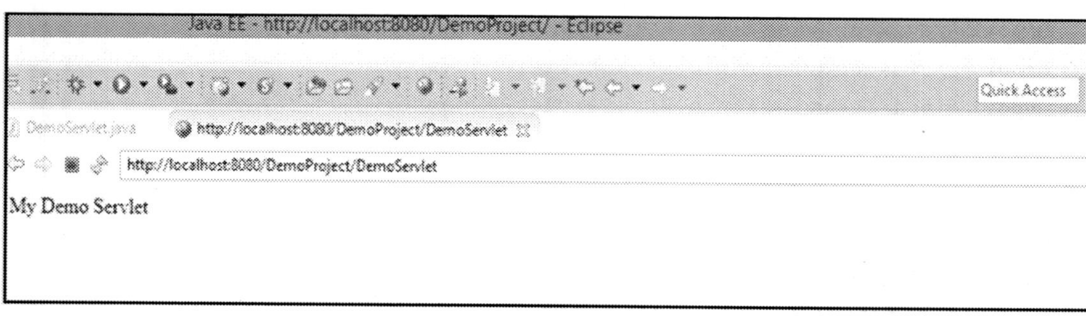

Now that we have learnt how to create a simple servlet, let us learn how to write responses to the client machine using the output stream of *PrintWriter*.

The following code

```
protected void doGet(HttpServletRequest request,
            HttpServletResponse response) throws ServletException,
            IOException {
        // TODO Auto-generated method stub
        PrintWriter out = response.getWriter(); // getting the writer
        out.println("My Demo Servlet"); // writing response on writer
        out.close(); // closing the writer
    }
```

is invoked when a GET request is issued from a client to the server. Remember all the requests from a client by default are GET requests. The *getWriter()* method returns an object, *out*, of *PrintStream* class which can be used to write data as a response, back to the client. Therefore, the *println()* method, here, writes data to the output stream of the client as a response.

SUMMARY

- Networking in java is establishing connections between computers to enable communications between them.
- Each machine on a network has a unique IP address and a port number.
- IP address is either a 32-bit or 128-bit dotted decimal address.
- The IP address of a machine indicates the address of a machine where a message has to be delivered whereas the port number specifies the program to which the message is to be communicated on that machine.
- InetAddress, a predefined class in java provides some of the methods to examine the host names or IP addresses of machines involved in a client server communication.
- URL and URLConnection classes offer methods to construct and connect to a specific URL and inspect its contents.
- A socket is an endpoint of a communication link and is identified by a combination of IP address and port number.
- Reading and Writing from these sockets can be done by using TCP/IP sockets. TCP/IP sockets are bidirectional and guarantee the delivery of messages in the order they were sent from the client.
- Datagram Sockets on the other hand, are an example of unreliable communication between a client and a server where the reception of a message is not guaranteed by the server to the client.
- JDBC, Java Database connectivity, is an API comprising various classes and interfaces that are used to connect a java application with the diverse databases using JDBC Drivers.

- A JDBC Driver is a software component that enables the java application to connect to a database and are of four types: Type 1, Type 2, Type 3 and Type 4.
- JDBC architecture can be of two types: two tier or three tier. A two tier architecture is the one where the java application directly interacts with the database whereas a three tier is the one which uses a middle tier to interact with a database.
- Servlets are simple java classes used to build a web application. Servlet API comprises various packages necessary for the creation of servlets.
- Servlets require a web container for their execution. One of the examples of a web container is the Tomcat Server.
- The life cycle of a servlet starts involves the *init()->service()->destroy()*methods.
- The *service()* method can be substituted by *doGet()* and*doPost()* methods invoked in case of GET and POST requests respectively.

COMMON ERRORS

- One of the mistakes a java developer might make while executing the echo client server program is starting the client first and waiting for the message to be sent to the server. Always remember, you need a server running which can receive your messages before the client sends any message to the server.
- Another common error while connecting to a database is specifying the wrong connection string including the database name to be connected with.
- Common errors like 404 error results because of specifying an incorrect URL to locate a specific servlet.

SELF-TEST

1. Write short notes on:
   (a) TCP
   (b) UDP
   (c) IP Address
   (d) Port number
2. Discuss the InetAddress, URL and URLConnection classes along with their methods.
3. What are sockets? Differentiate between TCP/IP and Datagram sockets.
4. Discuss the need of JDBC drivers in java. List and explain the various drivers available.
5. Describe the steps to connect a java application with the MySql database.
6. What is a servlet? What is the role of a web container in creation of servlets? Discuss the steps to create a simple servlet.

PRACTICAL QUESTIONS

1. Write a client server program where the client displays the current date sent from the server.
2. Write the code to establish database connectivity for adding a record into the table emp in the database db.
3. Create a servlet which shows your personal information.

Index

D

E

F

G

H

I

J

L